The Chronicles of the

ROYAL THAMES

YACHT CLUB

The Chronicles of the
ROYAL THAMES
YACHT CLUB

Compiled by
Captain A.R. Ward CBE, RN.

Foreword by
H. R. H. The Duke of Edinburgh

Copyright © Bob Ward 1999

First published in 1999 by:
Fernhurst Books,
Duke's Path, High Street,
Arundel, West Sussex,
BN18 9AJ.
Tel: 01903 882277   email: sales@fernhurstbooks.co.uk
Fax: 01903 882715   web: www.fernhurstbooks.co.uk

British Library Cataloguing in Publication Data:
A catalogue record for this book is available from the British Library

ISBN 1 898660 62 X

Printed in Hong Kong through World Print

Designed by Creative Byte, Poole, Dorset

Cover design by Simon Balley

Photography by Chris Davies and Clive Woodley

Foreword

by H.R.H. The Duke of Edinburgh

Yachting and yacht racing are both immensely popular sports, but how and when did they start? The first well-recorded yacht race took place on the Thames between King Charles II and his brother, the Duke of York in 1662. The course was from Greenwich to Gravesend and back for a wager of £100. It was to be over 100 years before some enthusiasts introduced competitive sailing matches on an organised basis on the Thames in 1775.

This very carefully researched book traces the ensuing development of the sport, the beginnings of the Royal Thames Yacht Club in 1823 and its significant influence on the sport right through to the present day. The author provides a fascinating insight into the internal affairs of the Club, its personalities and the many dramas and incidents they had to face in the long process of achieving a successful international sport. His account is also embellished by a selection of anecdotes, which graphically illustrate the ever-changing behaviour and social attitudes of the major participants.

Many things in yachting have changed in the last 225 years, but there is one thread that runs throughout. It is the sheer enthusiasm of the captains and crews for their sport that ties the whole book together. I caught the bug while I was at school on the Moray Firth and it has given me great pleasure and satisfaction ever since.

All yachtsmen of this, and future generations, owe Captain Ward and the Royal Thames Yacht Club a great debt of gratitude for this important contribution to the history of yachts and yachting.

Acknowledgements

The author would like to express his gratitude to John Vernon and Brigadier John Constant for their encouragement and advice, which ensured that these Chronicles would be compiled. Thanks are also due to David Arnold who made available his considerable library of photographs taken at Royal Thames regattas and rallies as well as major championships run by the Royal Thames Race Committee. Lastly the author is grateful for the typing undertaken by the secretaries - Vicky, April and Nikki - who valiantly transcribed his manuscript and, not least, to Ruth, who cheerfully handled the complex editing process.

Contents

The Provenance of the Royal Thames Yacht Club

When searching for the origins of the Royal Thames Yacht club it is prudent to remind oneself of the purpose of the Club. Today its purpose, as defined in the Club Rules, starts with the words 'encouragement of yacht sailing and racing' while in the context of the more limited horizons of the 19th Century the words used were 'the encouragement of yacht building and sailing on the River Thames'. Today's form of words was not introduced until 1914. It is perhaps surprising that the word 'racing' did not appear until that date since, above all, the Royal Thames Yacht Club can, with justification, claim to have its origins in the body of men who first introduced competitive sailing matches on an organised and regular basis in the United Kingdom, starting with the race held on the River Thames on 13 July 1775 and continuing through to the second quarter of the nineteenth century when regattas became more generally popular and when many yacht clubs were established.

While the sailing of small boats for pleasure was not unknown in the 16th Century, it was in the middle of the 17th Century that King Charles II popularised the sailing of yachts. The term yacht, derived from the Dutch 'yaghten', was common in this country by 1661, by which time yachts of 20 Tons were being sailed on the Thames. King Charles' enthusiasm for the sport is illustrated by what many consider to be the first recorded yacht race. This took place on 6 September, 1662 from Greenwich to Gravesend and back for a £100 stake by boats owned by King Charles II and his brother, The Duke of York, the former being victorious.

Yachts of the Cork Water Club (1720) - Sketch by R T Pritchett.

The next significant year in the origins of sailing is 1720 when the gentlemen of the Water Club of the Harbour of Cork established the practice of manoeuvring sailing boats in their spacious harbour. After completing their manoeuvres under the direction of their Admiral, these gentlemen repaired ashore for a convivial dinner. The Club appears to have become moribund by 1856 and for a further 50 years, by which time the present Royal Cork Yacht Club was established.

The next landmark in yacht racing arose once again from royal patronage. In 1749, King George III presented a cup that was competed for by 12 sailing vessels over a course from Greenwich to the Nore and back, the cup being won by the *PRINCESS AUGUSTA* owned by George Bellas, Esq.

The event that gives what is probably the earliest clue to the origins of the Royal Thames is referred to in the 1 June 1775 edition of the Public Advertiser which said that 'Several very respectable gentlemen, proprietors of sailing vessels and pleasure boats on the river (Thames) held their annual meeting at Battersea and resolved that on the day of the (rowing) regatta they would draw their boats up in a line opposite Ranelagh Gardens so as not to be in the way of the competing boats'. The regatta (a description taken from the style of Venetian Regattas) took place on 23 June and provided a great spectacle for the multitudes gathered in boats and on the shore.

A pamphlet issued on 29 March, 1926 with a preface by Rear Commodore J S Highfield, gives a description 'of the First Regatta held in England on 23 June 1775 under the flag of the Cumberland Fleet'. While the Duke of Cumberland was undoubtedly in attendance at this regatta it is also clear from the earlier paragraph that the sailing vessels present were not competing but were there to view the rowing regatta taking place from Ranelagh Gardens. It is therefore, less easy to substantiate that this regatta was organised under the flag of the Cumberland Fleet even though Francis Swain's painting of the regatta (now hanging in the Edinburgh Room) shows the sailing vessels ahead of the rowing boats. On the other hand this regatta of 23 June must surely have been the event that inspired the Duke of Cumberland, younger brother of King George III, to present a silver cup which, as reported in the Public Advertiser on 6 July 1775, 'was to be sailed for on 11 July from Westminster Bridge to Putney Bridge and back by Pleasure Sailing Boats from 2 to 5 Tons burthen, and constantly lying above

**Thomas Taylor,
Commodore (1780 - 1816)**

London Bridge'. The weather caused the race to be postponed until 13 July when it was won by *AURORA* owned by Mr. Parkes, late of Ludgate Hill, with *FLY* second.

While this race is the source of the title Cumberland Fleet or Cumberland Sailing Society, the gentlemen, whose annual meeting in Battersea on 1 June is mentioned above, were almost certainly the only body of owners of pleasure sailing boats on the Thames and must have comprised the bulk of the 18 or 20 owners who competed on 13 July in aquatic uniforms (the Morning Post of 10 July tells us). It does seem probable therefore, that the gentlemen, who first comprised the membership of the Cumberland Fleet, had been gathering, on at least on annual basis, for some years prior to 1775.

The Duke of Cumberland gave a 20 guinea silver cup each year from 1775 until 1782 except for 1781 when he gave a 50 guinea silver gilt cup - it being the seventh successive cup. It seems that a septennial anniversary is an occasion for special celebration - elsewhere it is described as a jubilee year. It is not clear why the Duke gave no more Cups after 1782, especially as he continued as patron of the Club until his death in 1790 at the age of 45. The most probable reason is that towards the end of his life he lived abroad and his financial situation was precarious.

The ceremonial associated with these early races was on a grand scale. The Duke of Cumberland attended in a state barge with the royal standard hoisted at the bow. In another barge would be a band to play martial airs. The owners of each vessel were styled 'Captain' and were required to steer their own vessel. Their position at the start was determined by lot and, as in later years in the Thames Yacht Club, each vessel was anchored with furled sails until the starting gun fired. The competitors could readily be identified as each carried at the gaff a white flag with a red St. George's Cross and with one or more blue balls according to their starting position (examples of these flags are displayed in the entrance hall of the present clubhouse). Once the Duke's barge arrived at the start, the Captains, who had been waiting in nearby wherries, were ordered by signal to board their vessels to await the starting gun. At the end of the race the winning Captain was taken on board the Commodore's barge and presented to the Duke of Cumberland. Meanwhile the Duke's butler would fill the cup with claret, hand it to the Duke who drank to the health of the winning Captain before presenting him with the cup. In his turn the winner drank to the Duke and Duchess and called for three cheers; throughout this ceremony the band would have been playing, there would be salvoes of artillery and cheers from the crowds on the river and ashore. The fleet would then proceed up river to Smith's Tea Gardens, on the Surrey side of Vauxhall Bridge, to dine together. Later in the evening the festivities would continue in the adjacent Vauxhall Gardens.

The first Commodore of the Fleet was Mr. Smith who, it is believed, was the owner of Smith's Tea Gardens (later called the Royal Cumberland Gardens). He remained in office until 1779 by which year the Club was dining at the Royal Oak, Vauxhall and Mr. Thomas Taylor became Commodore, an office he was to hold until he retired from yachting thirty six years later in 1816. All commentators credit Thomas Taylor with being the practical founder of yacht racing on the Thames. In 1770 he had had built by Adam and Doe of Bull Stairs, Blackfriars, the yacht *KING'S FISHER*, a sturdy clinker built vessel of 20 feet length and 7 feet beam with a cutter rig and a running bowsprit. In 1776 *KING'S FISHER* won the Cumberland Cup. In 1780 he had had built his first yacht named *CUMBERLAND* and this was no more than 22 feet in length. Thomas Taylor owned four yachts named *CUMBERLAND*, the last one having five centreboards while the *COLUMBUS* built for him in 1795 had three. Models of *KING'S FISHER* and the five centreboard *CUMBERLAND IV* are on display in today's Clubhouse as are plans of *CUMBERLAND II* and *CUMBERLAND IV*.

Members of the Cumberland Fleet flew the white Ensign (without the St. George's Cross in the fly) and their burgee was also white with an 'equal armed' red cross i.e. the cross did not extend to the point of the flag. It also seems that the Club had some form of Admiralty Warrant. An advertisement in the Public Advertiser on 7 June 1788 requested members to meet at the Crown and Anchor Tavern in the Strand and added 'The gentlemen who enter their boats to attend at the same time to draw lots for situation at starting; and are hereby informed that they are expected either to produce their licence from the Admiralty, or other proofs of being owners of the vessels they intend to sail'.

After the first Cumberland Cup race in 1775 the course was altered and started from Blackfriars Bridge, thence to Putney and back to Smiths' Tea Gardens. Commodore Taylor in addition to winning the Cup in 1776 was successful with *CUMBERLAND* in 1880 and 1881, his first two years in office. As already mentioned 1881 was a septennial year and the Cup presented by the Duke of Cumberland was to be sailed for by the boats that had won the former prizes but the notice advertising the race in the Morning Chronicle of 5 May 1781 said 'The members of the Society do hereby, with the permission of His Royal Highness, challenge and invite all gentlemen, proprietors of pleasure sailing boats, within the British dominions, to join with them in the contention'. This first ever 'open' match attracted much interest and drew large crowds to the river when, after weather caused a postponement on 25 June, it was sailed on 9 July. The 1782 and last of the Cumberland Cups was sailed for on 23 July and won by *CAROLINE* owned and steered by Captain Coffin. A print depicting this race with Cumberland Fleet passing St. Paul's Cathedral is today hanging on the Quarterdeck.

The complete list of yachts that won the Cumberland Cups is as follows:

1775	**AURORA**
1776	**KING'S FISHER**
1777	**EAGLE**
1778	**TARTAR**
1779	**SEA HORSE**
1780	**CUMBERLAND**
1781	**CUMBERLAND**
1782	**CAROLINE**

This 1782 Cup appears to have been found in a pawnshop in San Francisco in 1886 from which it was bought and raced for by the members of an American Yacht Club. The Cup eventually came to light in the possession of one John H. Hughes of Marion, Massachusetts in 1982. On his death, it was learned that there was a bequest in his will which gave the Cup to the Royal Thames Yacht Club.

While the original cup of 1775 was destroyed by fire (as reported in the 23 June 1781 edition of the Morning Herald) those of 1776, 1777, 1780 and the 50 guineas, silver gilt cup of 1781 are together with the 1782 cup located in the display cabinets in the current clubhouse. 1782 also saw the Cumberland Fleet run its first below bridge sailing match on 10 August. This match was between *CAROLINE* (Captain Coffin) and the *EAGLE* (Captain Grubb) and was sailed from Cuckolds Point to the Lower Hope and back for a wager of forty pounds which was won easily by the former.

The activities of the Cumberland Fleet were not confined to the river nor to racing alone. Like the gentlemen at Cork they performed controlled naval-type manoeuvres as in 1776 'in honour of His Majesty's birthday and went up the river with colours flying and music playing'. A print of an engraving by Pouncy, after Kitchingman, at present hanging in the landing outside the Edinburgh Room of the current clubhouse, shows the Cumberland Fleet manoeuvring off Sheerness at the mouth of the River Medway on 1 June 1778 and where the Duke of Cumberland held a review of the Fleet. In 1793 a set of signals, produced to standardise manoeuvring procedures, were printed (they too are on display in the clubhouse). That they did not confine their sailing to the Thames is evident from a newspaper report in 1777 stating that 'the *HAWKE* had been cruising about the Channel and had been chased into Calais by an American privateer'. On 21 August 1784 Commodore Taylor's *CUMBERLAND* went badly ashore on the rocks off Margate (but was recovered), while in 1791 the Commodore, with a party of friends, set off to Bordeaux.

There is no record of Cumberland Fleet races being held in the years 1783-85, but 1786 brought a new era to the Fleet. In that year Jonathan Tyers took over proprietorship of the Vauxhall Gardens. To celebrate the 50th anniversary of the opening of the gardens together with the arrival of the new management he gave an annual silver cup and cover to be sailed for by the Cumberland Fleet. This first Vauxhall Cup was won by the *PRINCE OF WALES*. A curious feature of this race is that in a pre-race advertisement the yacht was offered for sale; the paragraph added that it will no doubt have the best chance of winning the jubilee silver cup on the 17th inst. - prophetic indeed. The Morning Chronicle of 19 July 1786 reporting the race records that 'there was an attempt of foul play against the *PRINCE OF WALES* by other boats getting in her way, but she got all clear by liberal use of

Yacht of the Cumberland Fleet (1781) - Sketch by R T Pritchett

handspikes' - action that may well have been influenced by the way 'ante post wagers' had been placed! The Vauxhall Cup for 1787 was sailed for on 3 August and won by *NANCY* owned by Captain Dore but the report on the race notes that *BLUE DRAGON* was disqualified for booming out her jib.

It was Captain Astley with *MERCURY* who won the 1791 Cup but, as he was passing the winning post, tragedy struck. The cannon, with which his victory was acknowledged, burst on being fired, killing two persons. This was also the year when the Club awarded a prize to the yacht finishing second, the prize being a silver goblet. By 1793 Captain Astley owned the *ECLIPSE* with which on 27 July, he competed against Commodore Taylor's *CUMBERLAND*, the stake being a turtle which the Commodore won and provided a turtle feast for the members of the Club.

Unusual incidents would seem to be accepted without protest in these closing years of the 18th Century. The Times newspaper of 23 July 1795 throws light on one such incident when reporting the race held for the Vauxhall Cup of that year. The report tells us that 'the *MERCURY*, which was the leading boat, somehow got foul of the *VIXEN*; where upon the Captain of the *VIXEN* cut away the rigging of the *MERCURY* with a cutlass and fairly well dismantled her;

another boat, the *MERMAID*, winning the Cup!'

In 1796 the Cumberland Fleet not only raced for the Vauxhall Cup but also for a cup presented by the proprietor of the Cumberland Gardens (formerly Smith's Tea Gardens), while the 15 August 1797 issue of The Star tells us that a sailing match for a 40 guinea wager took place on 11 August between the *MERCURY* and the *PROVIDENCE* over a course from the Gun Wharf at Blackwall out to and round the Nore Light and back. The *MERCURY* won easily in 12 hours 5 minutes and by a distance of 20 miles!

The year 1800 completed 14 years of Vauxhall Cups and was therefore marked as a septennial jubilee, the Cup being won by*CUMBERLAND* now owned by Captain Byrne while the 1801 cup was won by *ATALANTA* owned by Mr. E. Smith who, in the same year, himself presented a cup won by the redoubtable *MERCURY*, Captain Astley. Predictably, 1807 was a third septennial year and the successful owner that year was Captain Farebrother, owner of *BELLISSIMA*. It is of particular interest to note that in the same year the contractors for the State Lottery gave a cup to be competed for on the River Thames - all the owners of the boats entered belonged to the Cumberland Fleet.

The year 1809 saw the opening of a new public garden called 'The Minor Vauxhall'. It's proprietor, one Mr. Sheppard presented a silver cup, to mark the opening, to be sailed for on the Thames. The following year Mr. Sheppard changed the name of his gardens to 'The New Ranelagh' and again presented a silver cup which was won by *SALLY* owned by Captain Hammond. Further cups were given in 1811 and 1812 and although the Cumberland Fleet was not mentioned in connection with the races for these cups only members of the Fleet entered. 1810 was also the year in which the last Vauxhall Cup was donated. This was won by *ST. GEORGE* owned by Captain James Gunston (who, it is suggested in the Chronicles of the Royal Thames Yacht Club, may have been the first Commodore of the newly formed Thames Yacht Club in 1823). The Club still has in its collection of silver trophies the Vauxhall Cups of 1792, 1794, 1802 and 1806. In 1812, in addition to the cup given by Mr. Sheppard, the Cumberland Fleet gave two cups (by subscription) which were won by *MERCURY* and *VIXEN*.

During the years 1813-1822 inclusive, racing on the Thames is recorded in all but the three years 1814, 1821 and 1822, but details are sparse as is mention of the Cumberland Fleet. What is known is that Commodore Thomas Taylor retired in 1816 and it is believed that Mr. Edward Nettlefold was elected in his place. There is however, an element of confusion covering the years 1817-1822, although there is a record of an account book showing the payment to the Secretary of the Cumberland Fleet of the subscription of one guinea. The confusion arises from a newspaper report in 1817 that Edward Nettlefold was Commodore of the 'London Yacht Club' and in a later issue that he was Commodore of the 'New Cumberland Fleet'. As is recorded in the chronicles of the Club, Edward Nettlefold was undoubtedly Commodore in 1823 when there are references to the 'Old Cumberland Fleet'. In spite of these conflicting references there is no doubt about the continuing existence of the Cumberland Fleet. In the absence of detailed records it is possible to do no more than speculate on what took place during the years 1817-22 but the scant evidence available does suggest the possibility that differences of opinion led to some split among members of the Cumberland Fleet and ultimately to the split which was to lead to the formation of the Thames Yacht Club in 1823.

In completing this brief summary of the Provenance of the Royal Thames Yacht Club it is perhaps, appropriate to end with a few remarks about the first patron of the Club, The Duke of Cumberland, Henry Frederick was the grandson of H.M. King George II and a younger brother of H.M. King George III. A hand written note on Buckingham Palace crested notepaper held in the Club's archives tells us that he assumed the title Duke of Cumberland in 1765 from the previous holder of that title who was the victor at the Battle of Culloden which ended the Jacobite Rebellion. The note also says that he was Ranger of Windsor Great Park. Two further notes give an insight into his character by describing him as 'a loose fish' and 'although coarse and brutal he was fond of music!' John Brooke's biography of George III contains paragraphs which give greater detail without amending the style of the young Duke. Brooke describes him as the black sheep of the family who, as a young man chased after women - and sometimes caught them! He adds that he shocked the aristocracy by riding in his carriage in Hyde Park accompanied by his mistress; 'the first member of the Royal Family that ever carried their mistress in a royal equipage'. It seems he was especially attracted to married women and this characteristic of his early days led to him being named in an action in 1770 (at the age of 25) for 'criminal conversation' (an 18th Century term for adultery). It was only a year later that he informed the King that he intended to marry the 27 year old widow, Ann Horton (nee Lutterell) daughter of Lord Irnham, a member of an old Irish family. For a member of the Royal Family to enter marriage to someone outside royalty was not only unthinkable (to King George III) but also unacceptable as shown by his remark 'I now wash my hands of the whole affair and shall have no further intercourse with him'.

The King ensured that such a marriage (especially when it was taken in conjunction with the marriage of the Duke of Cumberland's brother, the Duke of Gloucester to Lady Waldegrave) should never happen again. The Royal Marriage Act of 1772 made it illegal for any member of the Royal Family to marry without the previous consent of the Crown. It also declared that future marriages contracted without such consent would be deemed null and void and imposed penalties upon all who assisted at such marriages.

The Duke of Cumberland's marriage may have distanced him from the King's affections but Ann Horton proved to be a good wife and the Duke a reformed character who 'never looked at another woman after his marriage'.

The Duke spent the last years of his all too short life, financially embarrassed and spent much of those years abroad. When he died in 1790 his nephew, the Duke of Clarence (later King William IV and patron of the Royal Thames Yacht Club) wrote of him to the Prince of Wales (later, Prince Regent and King George IV): 'Poor fellow, he certainly had the best heart in the world. I am glad to hear by Frederick (Duke of York) that the King was so much hurt. But, my dear brother, the Duchess is to be pitied. Her conduct by all accounts was exemplary; indeed her goodness has been manifested on all occasions'. The Duke left nothing but debts and while the widow continued to live at Cumberland Lodge, Windsor Great Park until her death in 1803, the King offered her what the Prince of Wales described as 'a shabby proposal' - a pension of £4,000 a year.

Why did the Duke of Cumberland, brother of the reigning monarch choose to patronise a group of citizens in London who enjoyed sailing on the River Thames? One can do no more than hazard a guess. Certainly the rowing regatta in June 1775 may have provided the ultimate stimulus but these earlier Hanovenians were not interested in sailing as the Stuarts had been even though the Duke of Cumberland held the rank of Admiral. Possibly it was a show of independence and a means of identifying with people outside the Royal Family in whose eyes he was an outcast. Whatever the reason, the sport of yacht racing has much to thank him for since his patronage provided the inspiration to those gentlemen who formed the Cumberland Fleet and whose activities led to the formation of the modern Royal Thames Yacht Club and to the emergence of one of the most popular sports in this country.

This brief account of the origins of the Royal Thames Yacht Club and its activities over the years 1775-1822 has been written to provide a foundation on which to build the Chronicles of the Club which follow. It has been compiled mainly from the Yachting Section of the Badminton Library, the Memorials of the Royal Yacht Squadron and Douglas Phillips Birt's book 'The Cumberland Fleet'.

The Chronicles
of the
ROYAL THAMES YACHT CLUB

Volume I

1823-1867

Introduction

To mark the Bicentenary of the inauguration of the Cumberland Fleet in 1775, Douglas Phillips-Birt wrote an excellent history of that Fleet and the Club which evolved from it - The Royal Thames Yacht Club. The book was published in 1978 (after the death of Phillips-Birt). By virtue of its considerable scope, the author had no choice but to be selective in the details he included. For all that he painted a vivid picture of the evolution of both the Club and Yacht Racing over 200 years.

This book, written in three volumes, is intended to enlarge on Phillips-Birt's history and show in detail how the evolution took place. Each volume will also explain how the activities of the Club expanded and will relate and analyse the problems that accompanied that expansion. For completeness some repetition of paragraphs from the earlier work has been included.

Special attention is given to those individual members, as well as to the Flag Officers, who gave so much to the Club over many years. A section is also devoted to aspects of the Club's treasures, especially the paintings and the silver.

The period selected for this first volume may at first seem arbitrary. It was selected because it encompassed the years between two of the major conflicts which beset the Club. In 1823 the 'Thames Yacht Club' was created out of the Cumberland Fleet or Sailing Society via, briefly, the Coronation Sailing Society. 1867 saw the establishment of the 'New Thames Yacht Club' founded by members of the RTYC who resigned their membership because they found themselves opposed to the direction in which the Royal Thames was moving.

Much that occurred during the years 1823-67 is entirely relevant today. The conflicts that arose and the problems the Club faced have been met again and resolved, hopefully, using the lessons learned. Above all there runs through this period a message for success for the RTYC: good management, combined with a careful balance between member's special interests be they yacht racing, cruising or social pleasure is essential if the Club is to be kept on an even keel, financially sound and at the leading edge of yachting, both nationally and internationally.

The principal source of information for this volume has been the Club's minute books. Sadly these go back only to 1839; that there were formal minutes prior to that date is certain since not only are they referred to in the minutes of the meeting held on 7 March 1839 but also they are identified in the minutes of a general committee meeting held on 7 June 1894. At that meeting the Secretary reported the receipt of a letter from Mr C Wheeler 'presenting the first two Minute Books of the Thames Yacht Club'. Mr C Wheeler would seem to be John Cornelius Wheeler who was elected to the Club in December 1893 and who could well have been the grandson of Captain Cornelius Wheeler, the Club Treasurer until 1856. Sadly, these important books are not among those now held in the Club archives. It would also seem that they were not available when the first list of Flag Officers was included in the Rule Book in 1912 since it records that there are no records available prior to 1839. Fortunately there are a small number of books containing information about early yachting history which, together with newspapers and periodicals, provide the background for the period 1823-39. This volume then, brings together all available information relating to the Club over the years 1823-67.

I

The Thames Yacht Club

In the year 1823, the British people were still very conscious of the successful revolution that had beset France over 30 years earlier; in Great Britain itself the country was in the midst of the Industrial Revolution; around the country Radicals were pressing for Free Trade, Parliamentary Reform, repeal of the Corn Laws, Catholic Emancipation. Against this backdrop, the 'revolution' in the Cumberland Sailing Society may seem insignificant but, nevertheless, it is a matter of vital importance to the Royal Thames Yacht Club and to the lead the Club gave to yachting as a whole and on the River Thames in particular.

The circumstances which led to the formation of The Thames Yacht Club have been well chronicled by Douglas Phillips-Birt in his bicentenary history of the Club. As elsewhere in these accounts of the Club's activities, some repetition (and expansion) of the records is included for completeness.

When, in 1816, Thomas Taylor retired as Commodore of the Cumberland Fleet after 36 years in office, he was succeeded by Mr Edward Nettlefold. The activities of the Fleet over the next six years are vague, while references to a *'London Yacht Club'* and the *'New Cumberland Fleet'* are difficult to understand or substantiate. What is far better documented in at least two newspapers are the events in 1823 which culminated with the formation of the Thames Yacht Club by members of the Cumberland Fleet.

The sequence of events started on Thursday 17 July 1823 when a sailing match in honour of the Coronation of King George IV took place, starting from Blackwall and proceeding to Coal House Point and back. The winner was 'Captain' George Keen. On Saturday 19th July there appeared in the *PUBLIC LEDGER* and *DAILY ADVERTISER* a notice (shown in Appendix 1) inviting subscribers and members of the 'Old Cumberland Fleet': *'to dine that day in honour of the Coronation of King George IV; to present the silver cup to Captain George Keen and to arrange the Articles (Sailing Instructions) for a sailing match on the 30th July'.*

To place these events in their correct historic context it should be noted that George IV, who succeeded George III in February 1820 and who had been Prince Regent since 1812, celebrated his coronation on the 19th July 1821. Thus, these celebrations were held to mark the second anniversary of the coronation, not the actual coronation.

On 27 July *BELL'S LIFE IN LONDON* also gave notice of the sailing match on 30 July for *'new subscribers and members of the Old Cumberland Fleet'* and mentioned

that it was arranged by the Coronation Sailing Society and under the patronage of the proprietors of Vauxhall Gardens. This notice confirms that the title, Coronation Sailing Society, had been established at an earlier date. Douglas Phillips-Birt thought it may have been agreed at the dinner held on 19 July 1823 but other sources including Phillips-Birt's 'History of Yachting' show the Coronation Sailing Society as having originated in 1821. Logic would support 1821, the year of George IV's Coronation, but the difficulty is that all sources tie the change to the title Coronation Sailing Society and the foundation of the Thames Yacht Club to the same year whereas it is known for certain that the Thames Yacht Club was founded in 1823.

A further notice, in the *PUBLIC LEDGER* of 29 July, advertised a Superb Gala in the Royal Gardens, Vauxhall on 30 July and listed the twelve vessels and owners taking part in the sailing match on that day (see Appendix 1).

The next edition of the (weekly) *BELL'S LIFE* reported on 3 August some of the details of the 30 July sailing match. It is clear that *ST. GEORGE* and *SPITFIRE* dominated throughout the race and that *ST. GEORGE* reached the finish at Cumberland Gardens only a few yards in the lead from *SPITFIRE*. It also comments that *'ST. GEORGE exhibited some of the finest manoeuvring and tact ever witnessed on the River'*. It further reported that SWIFT, Captain Field, had carried too great a press of canvas and consequently capsized off Temple Stairs, the crew being rescued by a following boat.

Although not reported by *BELL'S LIFE* it is known that Captain Bettsworth, *SPITFIRE*, protested that between Blackfriars and Waterloo bridges, *ST. GEORGE* had been steered by two different people, contrary to the terms of the Articles. The protest prevented the presentation of the silver cup at Vauxhall Gardens. At a meeting on 6 August of either the Sailing Committee or perhaps of the Club as a whole, to consider the protest, there was a majority decision that the match be re-sailed on Monday 11 August. While Captain Bettsworth attended the meeting and produced witnesses to support his claim, Captain Brocklebank, the owner of *ST GEORGE*, was absent. The issue was clearly very divisive among Club members. Supporters of Captain Brocklebank demanded a further meeting with the latter present to reaffirm or rescind the decision to re-sail the match. The following day, 7 August, eight of the owners who had competed on 30 July, addressed a note to the Commodore protesting vehemently against *'any other measure being adopted contrary to the resolutions passed on August 6th, at which time the merits of the question*

Notice of Race for Sailing Match (1823)

attributed in great measure to a want of unanimity which ought to prevail among all parties - do form itself into a club, to be called the 'Thames Yacht Club' to which the owners of the various pleasure boats on the Thames be invited to belong'.

Douglas Phillips-Birt names the eight 'battling Captains' who led the breakaway from the Coronation Fleet as Thomas Bettsworth; Thomas Groves, Robert Williams, Edward Jones, Charles Clementson, James Tomkins, William Field and Robert Wilkes. It is interesting to note that while the first six gentlemen named entered Thames Yacht Club matches at later dates the latter two did not; on the contrary William Field certainly entered Coronation Fleet matches. Equally surprising, bearing in mind the strength of feelings that caused the split, it is of note that Captains Williams, White and Bettsworth (of all people) entered the Coronation Fleet match held on 16 August 1824.

The Coronation Fleet under their Commodore, Edward Nettlefold continued their business untroubled by the loss of many members to the newly formed Thames Yacht Club and held a 'Second Grand Sailing Match' on 27 August 1823 - a match won by SWIFT (Captain Troughton) - who, according to BELL'S LIFE was a gentleman, advanced in years. That report also recounts that 'it was noted that SAINT GEORGE and SPITFIRE did not dispute the prize'. Whether the pun was intended is not clear but it does suggest that the anger that arose following the protest at the result of the match held on 30 July was still very much alive. The Coronation Fleet continued to promote sailing matches over the next few years but gradually disappeared without trace by the end of the decade. There is a hint as to the possible circumstances that led to the demise of the Coronation Fleet from a report in BELL'S LIFE dated 20 June 1830. This refers to a meeting of the Coronation Fleet held on 16 June at Wood's Hotel, Furnival's Inn. At that meeting the following officers were elected:

Lord Henry Choldmondeley	- Commodore
Henry Chitty Esq	- Captain
John Frost Esq	- President
Thomas Alexander Roberts Esq	- Treasurer
Herbert Coates Trampline	- Secretary

It is of note that both Lord Choldmondeley (AERIEL 8 Tons) and Henry Chitty (VENUS, 13 Tons) entered the Thames Yacht Club racing match on 9 August 1830 and T.A. Roberts had joined the TYC on 1 September 1823. The report also mentions a letter received from the Patron of the Fleet expressing regret at being unable to attend the sailing match to be held on 23 July to celebrate the anniversary of HM King George's IV's coronation. The Patron was, coincidentally, the Duke of Cumberland, brother of George IV and William IV and, therefore, cousin of the founder of the Cumberland Fleet. The report continues saying that due to the flourishing state of the Society the earlier practice of permitting entry to sailing matches by non members, in order to raise money, would be discontinued and entry for this match would be confined to members only. The strange thing is that there is no report of this match having taken place.

In view of the positive evidence of the continuing activities of the Coronation Fleet and its reported healthy financial state it might seem strange that it should 'disappear without trace'.

were fully and fairly discussed'. They stated, further, that 'should the decision be rescinded they would never enter for any Cup presented by the Coronation Fleet'.
The Committee, however, strongly supported Captain Brocklebank and the SUNDAY TIMES reported that when they met on 9 August, they investigated and rejected Captain Bettsworth's protest. Captain Brocklebank immediately gave a supper (presumably for the committee) and it is noted that the cup, which held three quarts, was regularly filled and emptied of port. The notice in the PUBLIC LEDGER on 11 August (see Appendix 1) provides further evidence of the decision taken on the 9th and it is clear that no re-sail took place. Instead the Coronation Fleet proceeded to the Nore and the River Medway to celebrate Captain Brocklebank's victory.

Just three days later on Thursday 14 August 1823 a meeting of the dissenters was held at the White House Tavern, Friday Street, Cheapside. A resolution was passed which founded the Thames Yacht Club and stated:

'That a meeting, considering that the manly and healthy exercise of river sailing, which affords a great deal of amusement to many persons and considerable benefit to the watermen and occupiers of premises on the banks of the Thames, has of late years fallen off - which may be

The explanation may well have been related to the death of HM George IV at Windsor on 26 June 1830. The, apparently moribund, Cumberland Fleet was transformed into the Coronation Fleet in 1823 to commemorate HM George IV's coronation; a celebration which was continued over the years and may well have been seen as the sole 'raison d'etre' of the Coronation Fleet (Society). They undoubtedly cancelled the match on 23 July (other clubs cancelled their matches at that time) and with the death of George IV, the Society may have felt it should end its activities.

The Thames Yacht Club had given notice of their first sailing match to be held on the 9 September 1823 from Blackfriars Bridge to Wandsworth Meadows and back to Cumberland Gardens. Of the ten entries, six had sailed in the disputed match on 30 July while one, Captain B.P. Copper, had sailed in the Coronation Fleet match on 28 August. The report of this match in the 14 September issue of BELL'S LIFE states that 12 boats had started from Blackfriars Bridge at a time too near to high water, with the consequence that even before they were able to reach the turning mark near Putney Bridge the Commodore of the day gave orders to give up the contest. The decision to re-sail the match the following day was much criticised by BELL'S LIFE since few people (especially supporters) would learn of this decision - not least because nearly all newspapers (including the PUB-LIC LEDGER) had mistakenly reported that the race had been competed on the 9th and the prize won by SPITFIRE (which was in the lead when the race was abandoned). In fact SPITFIRE did win the prize, but on the 10 September, the day of the re-sail.

Before ending the account of the founding and early days of the Thames Yacht Club it is enlightening to record the sailing achievements of Thomas Bettsworth and his vessel SPITFIRE, not least because he was all too often the centre of controversy. He has already been identified as the protester in the historically important Coronation Fleet match on 30 July 1823 and as a signatory of the equally important letter of the 7 August which included the statement that he would never enter for any cup presented by the Coronation Fleet. Nevertheless, he did so in 1824 after having won the first TYC match in 1823. In a TYC match in August 1825 he was accused of dumping ballast but this was not supported by the sailing committee. In August 1829 SPITFIRE entered a Clarence Yacht Club match in which she became involved in a protest and counter protest situation based on accusations of handing off another boat while rounding the turning mark of the course. SPITFIRE was declared the winner of the silver cup amidst fierce dispute and threats of mass resignations from the Club. Thomas Bettsworth was undoubtedly a competitive yachtsman.

The Thames Yacht Club was now established and in 1824 held matches above and below bridge for prizes of Silver Cups. Additionally many 'match races' were held which attracted both considerable wagers and proof that DON GIOVANNI (7 Tons) owned by Captain J. M. Davey (who joined the TYC 9 September 1823) was the most successful vessel on the river that year.

There are several interesting matters that appear in the reports in BELL'S LIFE of activities on the Thames in 1824. In the report of the match held on the 16 August it is noted that 'The Silver Cup was given by what is termed the King's Coronation Fleet, an association formed last year in opposition to the Thames Yacht Club'. This is an extraordinary statement since it was the reports in BELL'S LIFE in 1823 that made it clear that the term 'Coronation Fleet' was current before the founding of the Thames Yacht Club. Two other matters included in the report of the TYC match held on 26 August are that some 100 members of the TYC attended the supper held in Cumberland Gardens after the sailing match - a clear indication of the rapid growth of the Club in just one year. On a rather less serious note mention is also made that 'the silversmith who made the Silver Cup and Cover was allowed to carry it in the Commodore's six oared Cutter and he displayed his workmanship to the populace with apparently no little satisfaction!' Mention of the Commodore is, of itself, especially interesting since it confirms that a member of the TYC held the office at that time. Whilst it is known that Edward Nettlefold stayed with the Coronation Fleet as its Commodore, the identity of the Commodore of the Thames Yacht Club is less certain and is examined in depth in the later section dealing with 'Officers of the Club'.

The accession to the throne by the Club's Patron, the Duke of Clarence, as King William IV was the occasion for the assumption of the title 'Royal' by the Thames Yacht Club. This change is noted in the BELL'S LIFE report of the match held on 28 August 1830 but re-sailed after a protest on 28 September. It is also interesting to note the other yacht clubs that were sailing on the Thames at that time. These include the Loyal YC which met at the York Hotel in Waterloo Road, the British Yacht Club, the Sailing Society, the Royal Union YC which met at the Royal Oak, Wapping and the Clarence Yacht Club. The latter, which was founded in 1828 by members of the TYC who wished to encourage small vessels to compete in sailing matches, met at Oliver's Coffee House - the 'ClubHouse' of the Thames Yacht Club. Mention has already been made of the redoubtable Thomas Bettsworth competing in a Clarence YC match in 1829; Thomas Groves was also an entrant in that match. In 1831 it is noted that the treasurer of the Clarence YC was Charles Wheeler Junior who, after joining the RTYC in 1840, was to become an active and successful yacht racing member of the Club. In 1832 it is noted that R C Buckwall Esq was Commodore of the Clarence YC - he had joined the Thames YC in April 1830.

The 'old' Cumberland Fleet and in turn the Thames Yacht Club was clearly the source from which yachting on the Thames sprang; not only among the wealthy but among all aspects of society in the 1820s. The Royal Thames Yacht Club was a solidly established society by 1830 as the foregoing has illustrated. The following sections record the many facets of Club life over the years to 1867 and include details of the Club's Officers; its sailing matches; its financial status as the Club evolved and the manner in which the club managed its affairs.

II
Officers of the Club

The identity of club officers prior to 1839 is in part clouded due to the absence of Minute Books for the period 1823-38. Fortunately other sources including archival papers and contemporary newspapers do provide clues which help to identify club officers - but not with the absolute certainty that the Club's own records would have provided. This section examines the evidence available and attempts to draw conclusions about the succession of office holders in the early years.

The Office of **COMMODORE** during the 45 years covered by this review of Club History was held by just two members, William Horatio Harrison and Lord Alfred Paget. Certainly this is what is recorded in Douglas Phillips-Birt's book 'The Cumberland Fleet' and it is also shown in the list of past Flag Officers included in the current Members Handbook. There is no doubt that Lord Alfred Paget was elected to the Office of Commodore in 1846 and remained in Office until succeeded by HRH The Prince of Wales in 1874. As regards William Harrison, current research gives considerable doubt that the records which show him serving as Commodore 1823-1845 are correct. That he resigned from Office early in 1846 is not in doubt but the date on which he assumed the Office of Commodore is almost certainly not 1823. The documentary evidence which supports the doubt expressed above is:

The minutes of the meeting of the Club on 3 April 1846 record that Lord Alfred Paget, Vice Commodore, was in the chair and *'had a most painful duty to discharge'* in announcing William Harrison's resignation. A motion was put down *'That the cordial and hearty thanks of this Club are eminently due and hereby tendered to W.H. Harrison Esq for his valuable and zealous services as Commodore of this Club during a period of 15 years'* - from which it can be deduced that William Harrison was elected Commodore in 1831.

After the death of William Harrison in 1847 the Club erected a memorial over his remains. The inscription on the memorial read *'This monument is erected by the Royal Thames Yacht Club to commemorate services rendered by the late William Horatio Harrison Esq during a period of 14 years when he held the distinguished Office of Commodore and in testimony of the high honour and strict impartiality with which he discharged its onerous duties'*. A smaller inscription under a Club Ensign read *'Sacred to the memory of W.H. Harrison Esq Died March 17th 1847 in his 49th year'*. The text of these inscriptions is taken from a drawing of the monument by the sculptor, G Lander of Kensal Green.

Lastly, the List of Flag Officers was first included in the 1913

Rule Book and List of Members. This list starts in 1839 *'since there was no prior records'*. (The currently held minute books also start in 1839). By 1915 the list is from 1831 and stated that there were no records prior to 1831 but shows William Harrison as Commodore 1831-1845. That this coincides with the statement (in the Minute Book) dated 3 April 1846 cannot be ignored. It can also be inferred that an earlier Minute Book dating back to 1831 was discovered in 1914 or thereabouts.

If William Harrison was not Commodore between 1823 and 1831 - and the above makes it virtually certain that he was not - then who was the Commodore during that period? Two sources give a partial answer to that question.

Firstly, a letter to the Club Secretary, dated 25 September 1957, from Mr R. L. Freeman-Taylor of Kings Lynn enclosed three letters referring to the Cumberland Fleet. From one of these there is a statement as follows:

Thames Yacht Club 1823   **Chairman:** **Mr J Gunston**
                                   Treasurer: **Robert Williams**
                                   Secretary: **Mr Tomkins**

Whilst the office of Commodore is not mentioned it must be probable that when the Thames Yacht Club was founded, the first action taken by the (forty) members was to elect the above officers to set up the running of the Club. Whether John Gunston was subsequently appointed Commodore cannot be substantiated. What is certain is his date of election to the TYC, which was 1 September 1823. It is also certain that all the three mentioned above entered the first TYC sailing match on 9 September 1823 and that Robert Williams and James Tomkins were also founder members of the TYC.

Secondly, *BELL'S LIFE IN LONDON,* which contains reports of nearly all Thames YC sailing matches, is found to be strong on references to 'The Commodore' but weak on disclosing his name. For all that there is a reference to *'The Commodore of the day'* in the report of that first TYC sailing match held on 9 September 1823 and thus John Gunston might have been the first Commodore. In the weekly issue of the paper dated 26 June 1825, which reports the TYC sailing match held on 23 June, there is an unequivocal reference: The Commodore, Captain Groves of the *VENUS*. This undoubtedly refers to Thomas Groves who was elected on 14 August 1823 and who did own the vessel *VENUS* and who entered the TYC matches on 9 September 1823 and 19 June 1824 - by 1825 the *VENUS* belonged to George Keen (who won the Coronation Fleet match on 17th July 1823). It is an interesting coincidence that

Thomas Groves (senior) was still a member in 1867 but left to become a founder member of the New Thames YC in December 1867 - as did his son Thomas Groves (junior).

The next reference is not until a report in the 14 June 1829 issue of *BELL'S LIFE*, which identifies *'The Commodore, Mr Lyon'*. A year later there is a similar reference in the issue dated 20th June 1830. Mr Lyon cannot be identified absolutely, but it is probable he is the same Mr Anthony Lyon Esq, owner of the vessel *ALERT* (16 Tons) and entered an RTYC match on 23rd June 1832. It is of note that William Lyon (possibly his son) joined the RTYC on 1 November 1832 and entered club sailing matches 1836-38 with the vessel *ALERT* (16 Tons). What is quite certain from the reports in *BELL'S LIFE* is that on 15 September 1831 the Commodore was William Harrison. There are, therefore, three members who, in all probability, held the office prior to William Harrison - but there may have been others. A possible sequence of holders of the office of Commodore from 1823 could be:

1823-24	**J Gunston**
1825-28	**T Groves (Snr)**
1829-31	**A Lyon**
1831-46	**W H Harrison**
1846-74	**Lord Alfred Paget**

Douglas Phillips-Birt, rightly describes Lord Alfred Paget as *'an outstanding figure in the Club story'* while William Harrison is seen as *'the more shadowy figure who forms the long link between what may be regarded as the Club's ancient history and modern'*. There is no doubt that Lord Alfred Paget was a person of far greater stature than William Harrison in terms of both the club history and in the nation's affairs. For all that the Club might not have become pre-eminent in yachting had there not been a sound base for Lord Alfred Paget to build on. William Harrison gave much to the Club; he rarely missed a club meeting, sailing match or social function. The membership grew from around 200 to over 300 in 1845 (and they owned some 140 yachts) - it is interesting to compare these figures with those of 1866 when there were 900 members but only 240 yacht owners; a reflection on the changing balance of interests among the members.

A true expression of William Harrison's achievements as Commodore came from the members. In 1840 they had subscribed one guinea each towards a presentation of a service of silver plate and later commissioned a painting of him (currently hanging in the Britannia Bar) and finally they erected the monument over his remains.

The identity of the holders of the Office of **CAPTAIN OF THE CLUB** prior to 1839 is, to say the least, somewhat speculative. It was only from the time of the publication of the 1965 List of Flag Officers that Robert Williams is included as Captain (as well as Treasurer) from 1823 - with no date for his ending his period of office.

It seems unlikely that Robert Williams would have been both Treasurer (which he undoubtedly was) and Captain of the Club at the same time. *BELL'S LIFE* makes two references to the Captain. In the 18 September 1831 issue it refers to a Mr Brown as Captain and on 5 August 1832 there is mention of a Mr Mansfield, Captain. The latter could be Robert J. Mansfield Esq who entered the TYC match on 15 June 1830 and owned *WILL O' THE WISP* (16 Tons), formerly owned by William Harrison, the Commodore from 1831. What can be substantiated is that at a Club meeting on 7 March 1839

British Coffee House - Meeting house for RTYC 1839 - 1845

Mr William Covington was elected Captain. At that same meeting *'Mr Everitt having expressed his wish to the meeting of retiring from office on account of ill health, it was resolved 'that a Vote of Thanks be given to Mr Everitt, the late Captain'*. Sadly it does not record how many years he had been in office, though it is known that G. Everitt Esq was a member in 1834.

Robert Williams was Treasurer until 1830 and if, in fact, he was also Captain for the period 1823-30, it is possible that Mr Brown was Captain in 1831 and R. Mansfield and Mr Everitt shared the period 1832-38 before William Covington assumed office, but it is all somewhat speculative in the absence of Club minutes for that period.

Mr Covington's term of office was brief indeed for by the time of the 1840 meeting to re-elect Club Officers on 5 March he had resigned and was succeeded by Mr William Egan. At an earlier meeting held on 3 October 1839 it was announced by the Treasurer *'that the Secretary had resigned and gave notice that the club would proceed to elect a Gentleman to succeed Mr Covington at the next meeting'.* Whether William Covington was both Secretary and Captain is not clear. In his turn William Egan held office for only two years after which period he went to live abroad. His successor was Mr Thomas Meeson who was elected to office on 7 April 1842 and was able to hold the office for three years, but on 29 May 1845 he had to write *'with deepest feelings of regret and sorrow I am compelled by a sudden calamity to resign my office'.* The exchange of letters which followed showed him to have been an efficient, popular and generous Captain. Indeed he must also have been a busy Captain for in several sailing matches he not only superintended the arrangements for the start, including the placing of moorings, but was also an active competitor.

When the Club next met on 5 June 1845 Lord Alfred Paget was elected to succeed Thomas Meeson and it had already been agreed that the title of the Office would be changed from Captain to **VICE COMMODORE**. Thus started for Lord Alfred a period of 43 years during which he was to hold the Office of Vice Commodore or Commodore. What could not have been foreseen at that meeting was that the Commodore, William Harrison, would find it necessary to stand down only nine months later, whereupon the Club elected Lord Alfred Paget as Commodore and Captain Thomas Smith Barwell as Vice Commodore on 8 April 1846. Barwell was able to remain in office a little longer than his predecessors but on 16 December 1849 he wrote to the Secretary saying 'the present state of my affairs render such a determination (to resign) inevitable as I have now neither money nor time to spend upon yachting'.

This unfortunate situation was much regretted but accepted by the Officers and members who met on 7 February 1850 and elected Mr Richard Green to the Office of Vice Commodore. The courtesies of the day were then enacted and *'a deputation consisting of Lord Clarence Paget, Mr Craigie and Mr Charles R. Tatham was then appointed to wait on Mr Green and request his acceptance of the Vice Commodoreship'.* Richard Green's long and distinguished period of office ended with his death which was announced at a meeting on 26 January 1863. The vacancy which his death created was the first incident in a series which created great turbulence in the Club over the next five months. Sir Gilbert East briefly held office from 15 April until 6 May and then on the 25 June Lord de Ros accepted election to be Vice Commodore.

The Office of **TREASURER** was, for 40 years, the third of the three administrative offices in the Club together with the Commodore and Captain/Vice Commodore. It is also the only one of these three for which the office holder can be substantiated from 1823. The first Treasurer, Robert Williams was, as mentioned earlier, one of the members of the Cumberland Fleet who seceded to the Thames Yacht Club in 1823. He held office until 1831. A portrait of him hangs on the quarterdeck of the present clubhouse and has more than once been the subject of scrutiny by art experts since it had been attributed to J.W.T. Turner, but this illustrious connection has never been accepted by them. (See Oil Paintings of Club Officers in Section VII).

The second Treasurer was Captain Cornelius Wheeler who took over the Office in 1831. His careful stewardship of Club funds strengthened the Club's financial position significantly as the Club grew in numbers and increased its financial commitments - but he had resigned office before the first comprehensive Clubhouse was acquired on lease. That he was highly respected is more than apparent. In 1842 it was decided *'That a Piece of Plate be presented by members of the Club to Cornelius Wheeler Esq, their efficient and very worthy Treasurer, as a testimonial of their esteem for him and the high opinion they entertain of his valuable attention to the prosperity of the Club'.* At the meeting of the Club on 5 March 1856, the meeting each year when officers had to be re-elected, Cornelius Wheeler rose, after he had been re-elected Treasurer, *'and begged to tender his resignation, a trust which he had held for 24 years'.* At the next meeting in April a Resolution was carried *'That the Club in accepting Captain Wheeler's resignation, begs to express their thanks for the manner in which he has managed and improved its financial condition, and the members hope that though released from the trouble which he has so kindly undertaken during a period of 25 years they may still be cheered with the pleasure of his company at their Matches and Meetings'.* The Resolution was subsequently written on vellum, signed by the Officers of the Club, framed and glazed and presented to Captain Wheeler.

Whether it was pure coincidence is not clear but immediately after Captain Wheeler's resignation had been tendered, Mr R. S. Wilkinson proposed that the Club should open a bank account. Prior to this time it appears that the Treasurer quite literally held the Club funds. Suffice it to say that a solid bank balance at Coutts in the Strand was what Captain Wheeler's successor, Mr James Hutchons inherited when he was elected on 2 April 1856.

The seven years during which James Hutchons was Treasurer of the Club included periods of great tension as far as the finances were concerned. He held office during the years when the Club's annual expenditure was increasing rapidly due to the acquisition of a succession of improved clubhouses. There were also signs that he and the Secretary, Captain Grant, who came into office early in 1854 were not always in accord on financial matters.

At the March 1859 meeting of the Club to elect officers both Mr Hutchons and another member were proposed for the Office of Treasurer, while the latter withdrew, it is apparent that all was not well because later in the meeting it is recorded that *'after some discussion, both the Treasurer and the Secretary resigned and, with regret, their resignations were accepted'.* When the Club next met in April, however, they resolved *'that the request contained in the letter of Captain Grant be accepted and that he be permitted to withdraw his resignation'.* The Sailing and General Purposes Committee were then instructed to appoint a Sub Committee to undertake the duties of Treasurer until the vacancy could be filled. In May a proposal to abolish the Office of Treasurer and appoint a Finance Committee was defeated and James Hutchons offered to continue in office 'Pro Tem'. At the Club meeting on 31 May the Commodore *'announced his having arranged a reconciliation between the Treasurer and the Secretary'* - the first sign of discord between these two. Mr Hutchons was then re-elected to the Office of Treasurer. He had been elected a member in 1841 and in his early years of membership he had served on the Sailing Committee; by 1863 he had lifted the finances of the Club to almost their peak in the period under review, but he was not to know that he would be deeply involved in the problems that arose that year when the time came for the re-election of Officers. The details of those problems is contained in the lengthy account that follows.

When the General Committee met in January 1863 and learned of the death of the Vice Commodore, Richard Green, few present can have foreseen that this, together with other matters that would soon arise, would lead to such bitter argument over the next few months. The second contribution to the debate occurred at the General Committee meeting in February when the committee stated that they would not support the re-election of the Secretary, Captain Grant, at the March Quarterly General Meeting of the Club at which election of Officers took place. At that meeting Lord Alfred Paget and Mr James Hutchons were respectively re-elected Commodore and Treasurer but there was a protracted and probably heated debate over the election of a new Vice Commodore which ended with Mr R. S. Wilkinson proposing the election of Mr John D. Lee. This proposal was defeated and preference given to a deferment of the election until a Special Meeting, to be called on 1 April. Mr Julius H. Thompson then proposed the re-election of Captain Grant as Secretary but this met much critical opposition from the hundred members present and it was decided to defer all other elections.

Over 200 members attended the Special Meeting held on 1 April 1863. The Commodore had given notice that the re-election (or otherwise) of Captain Grant as Secretary should be decided by ballot. In view of all the earlier opposition it must have come as a considerable surprise when the ballot result showed a majority of 34 in favour of re-election. What followed was less surprising. The members of the General Committee felt unable to offer themselves for re-election, Mr James Hutchons, the Treasurer, tendered his resignation from that office and Lord Alfred Paget, feeling that he had lost their support, expressed his desire to resign the office of Commodore. The meeting was adjourned for two weeks.

When the Club re-assembled on 15 April, Lord William Lennox was unanimously voted into the chair to conduct the election of Officers. Lord Alfred Paget was unanimously re-elected to the Office of Commodore by acclamation but there was a lengthy discussion before it could be agreed that the meeting should proceed to elect a Vice Commodore. Three candidates were proposed and seconded: Messrs John D. Lee, Henry Green and Sir G.E. Gilbert East, Bart. A show of hands was in favour of Sir Gilbert East who accepted his election. The meeting then proceeded to elect Mr Stephen Cave as Treasurer and to re-elect the Cup Bearer and 3 Auditors. Finally on the proposal of Mr Julius H. Thompson, seconded by The Rev E.H. Newenham a new General Committee of 21 members were appointed - only 6 of whom had been members of the 1862 General Committee.

It was only five days later that the new General Committee met, with Sir Gilbert East in the Chair and learned that the 'Articles of Partnership' prevented Mr Stephen Cave from accepting the Office of Treasurer. Accordingly a further Special Meeting of the Club was called for the 6 May in order to elect a Treasurer. The Vice Commodore also appointed a completely new House Sub Committee which included none of the 1862 Committee. A week afterwards the General Committee met again and heard the Vice Commodore read a letter from Lord Alfred Paget declining to accept the Office of Commodore (see Appendix 2). The Committee replied expressing their regret. They also learned that Mr W.O. Marshall had become the first member to decline his appointment to the new General Committee; by the time of their next meeting on 4 May Messrs A.J. Otway and H.H. Kennard had also declined. In the meantime a private approach had been made to the Earl of Orkney as to whether he would accept the Office of Commodore if elected.

Lord Alfred Paget's courteous and eloquent but hard hitting letter made it very clear why he withheld from his re-election as Commodore. He must have felt very badly let down by the Club or more particularly by the election to Vice Commodore of Sir Gilbert East who had become a member of the Club as recently as 1 October 1862. When Sir Gilbert East then chaired meetings which appointed virtually new General and House Committees, the die was cast and Lord Alfred Paget's resignation became inevitable.

The adjourned Special General Meeting resumed on 6 May, ostensibly to elect a new Treasurer. This did not happen; instead it was moved *that the minutes of adjourned meeting on the 15th April relating to the appointment of the Vice Commodore should be expunged, the gentleman so elected being ineligible by resolution of the Club as carried on the 4th March'*. That resolution required that *'any member who wishes to propose a candidate for the Office (of Vice Commodore) shall give notice a fortnight before the meeting and that the names of the candidate be set up in the Club'*. The minutes are not explicit in stating the reason for Sir Gilbert East's ineligibility for Office but it seems most probable that either notice was given too late or it was not posted in the Club. When the Club divided on the motion it was carried by a majority of 25 among the 125 members present. Sir George Gilbert East then resigned as Vice Commodore.

The next phase of the adjourned meeting took place on 19 May under the chairmanship of Lord William Lennox. A proposal by Mr Julius H. Thompson that the Earl of Orkney be elected Commodore was overridden by a decision to defer the election to a further meeting. Colonel Josiah Wilkinson then proposed the appointment of 5 members as a Provisional Committee to superintend the Sailing Matches until a Commodore and Vice Commodore were appointed. Although this proposal was carried, it was followed immediately by a written protest from Colonel G.P. Evelyn, a member of the General Committee, that such an appointment was contrary to the fundamental rules of the Club. A further protest was signed by 16 members of the Club. A week later at a meeting of the General Committee chaired by Colonel Evelyn, a report was drawn up for submission to the still adjourned Special Meeting of the Club later the same evening which said that the committee was of the opinion that the Resolution appointing a Provisional Committee was contrary to the Club Rules and Sailing Regulations and was therefore null and void; that it was not competent for the Club to appoint a committee to execute the Office of Commodore or Vice Commodore and that the Sailing Regulations authorise the General Committee to appoint a member to be President of any sailing match in the absence of the Commodore or Vice Commodore.

The member nominated to be President of the first Sailing Match of the season was Mr Alfred Cox - one of the five members appointed to the controversial Provisional Committee. When the Special Meeting eventually convened, Mr Alfred Cox was chairman! Once the report was presented, Colonel Josiah Wilkinson proposed that a Special Committee of 11 members be appointed *'to consider the present position of the Club'* and to report to the Special Meeting. The General Committee agreed to call this meeting, which would receive the report and appoint a Commodore and Vice Commodore, on 25 June. At last the Club had taken the action necessary to put its affairs in order. At the meeting on 25 June Lord de Ros

Yachts of the RTYC in the Solent (1844) - Painting by N M Condy

was asked to take the chair and the report of the Special Committee was read (it is recorded in full in Appendix 3 together with a letter from Lord Alfred Paget). The Club then voted unanimously to elect Lord Alfred Paget and Lord de Ros to the Offices of Commodore and Vice Commodore respectively in the sure knowledge this time that they would accept election. The other recommendations of the report were also carried unanimously except that it had become known that the Bank of England allowed only 4 Trustees and not the 5 recommended in the report. In the event only 3 Trustees were appointed: Lord Alfred Paget, Mr James Hutchons and Colonel Josiah Wilkinson (Lord de Ros having declined the appointment).

The first recorded holder of the Office of **CUP BEARER** is Mr Robert Cooke. He is shown as holding office from 1839-65; however, the re-election of Officers in March 1839 shows that he was being re-elected not elected. He became a member of the Club in 1835 so he could have held office only for a short period prior to 1839. Further research may show when the office was established. It has not always been the responsibility of the Cup Bearer to present trophies to winning owners and certainly in the 1840s it was the Commodore who carried out the presentation of trophies at the conclusion of a sailing match. The Cup Bearer's particular duty was to hold and look after those trophies that were not to be retained by the winner. Robert Cooke's long period in office ended with his death in October 1865. He was succeeded by Mr George Powell in January 1866 but his tenure of office was brief as he too died two years later in January 1868.

It was the practice during the period that committee minute books were available (1839-67) for **AUDITORS** to be elected each year to monitor the control of the Club's finances. During this period of 29 years only 9 members served as Auditor even though 2 (or later) 3 auditors were elected

each year. Mr John Ford was an auditor for 19 of the 29 years and his services were recognised in January 1862 by his being made an Honorary Member. Messrs Jonathan White, Francis McGedy and William Hooper all served as auditors for 10 years or more while Mr Hutchons had served 5 years when he was elected to the Office of Treasurer.

The only other Club Officer who had to re re-elected each year was the **SECRETARY**. Two gentlemen dominated the period 1823-67 - Captain Frederick Durand (1839-53) and Captain P.C. Stuart Grant (1854-71).

It is recorded earlier in the paragraphs concerning the Commodores that at the time of the formation of the Thames Yacht Club in 1823 the Secretary was a member of the Club named James Tomkins. It has also been noted in the section about the Captain of the Club that Captain Durand succeeded Mr Covington. What is less clear is who was Secretary between Messrs Tomkin and Covington.

What is known from a report in *BELL'S LIFE* is that the Secretary, unnamed, resigned in 1830, while a copy of a notice of race for 1831 is signed by William Norris, Secretary. Additionally, *BELL'S LIFE* of 8 July 1838 reported that Mr Murray, who for long had been Secretary, had resigned and been replaced by Mr J. Covington, son of an old and much respected member (this is probably Mr William Covington who joined the Club in 1828 and was Captain of the Club in 1839). It seems therefore that the possible sequence of Secretaries prior to Captain Durand was Messrs Tomkins, Norris, Murray and Covington but the dates of Mr Norris's tenure of office are uncertain.

Captain Durand saw the Club move from the British Coffee House to the Piazza Hotel and then to the Bedford Hotel. Throughout the 14 years in office he appears to have been quietly efficient and to have maintained a good relationship with the Officers of the Club. When he resigned in March 1853 he was *'paid a compliment, during the pleasure of the Club, of £25 per annum'*. The advertisement seeking a successor to Captain Durand was placed in the Times, The Naval Gazette and Bell's Life in London and read *'The Sailing Committee wish to receive applications from Gentlemen desirous to fill the Office of Secretary. All other qualifications being equal, the Committee feel that the Club will give a preference to Officers of the Royal Navy'*. In the event Paymaster James C. Aldridge R.N. was selected and appointed on 4 April 1853. He had barely established himself in his Office than he was obliged to write to the Commodore on Christmas Day 1853 *'I have the honour to inform you that I have this day received Orders from The Lord Commissioners of the Admiralty to take my Commission appointing me to H M Frigate 'Diamond' at Spithead and to repair there instantly to join her'*. The next advertisement omitted any reference to preference being given to Naval Officers although many were included among the list of 42 applicants from which Captain P.C. Stuart Grant, Late Captain 68th Light Infantry, was selected.

Captain Grant's 17 years in office, which started in the Bedford Hotel and ended in 7 Albemarle Street, were in stark contrast to those of Captain Durand. His apparent conflicts with Officers of the Club have been recounted in the paragraphs about the Treasurers and in particular those concerning Mr James Hutchons. For all that, he was able to retain the (majority) support of the membership and survived all the machinations that beset the Club in the 1860s.

When Captain Durand took office as Secretary he was paid a salary of £50 per annum which was increased to £60 in 1845. Additionally he was allowed to retain one shilling from every subscription he collected, which in 1839 amounted to about £11pa. In 1845 this was increased to one shilling from every guinea collected which by then was worth £33pa. His income prospered further in 1851 when it was agreed by the Club that he should receive half a guinea from each member who registered a yacht for sale through the Secretary for vessels up to 25 Tons and a guinea for those over 25 Tons. He also was entitled to 1% of the purchase money when he was the agent for the sale. By the time Captain Grant became Secretary the salary had risen to £70pa and the poundage for collection of subscriptions and entrance fees to 5%, say £50pa. In 1857 there were further increases, the salary to £100 and the yacht sale commission to 2%. In 1863 the Special Committee appointed to resolve the Club's problems with the election of officers in that year recommended the abolition of the Office of Treasurer and required the Secretary in future to pay all monies received directly into the Club's bank account. He was no longer entitled to poundage and consequently his salary was increased to £280pa. It was also decided that he need no longer be re-elected annually since the post of Secretary was a permanent appointment. The General Committee, as distinct from the Club in General Meeting, were by then the body authorised to appoint and dismiss the Secretary.

TRUSTEES of the Club were first appointed at a Club Meeting on 16 December 1863 following the recommendations of the Special Committee set up to resolve the Club's problems with election of Officers in that year. The first members appointed as Trustees were the Commodore, Lord Alfred Paget, the Treasurer, Mr James Hutchons and Colonel Josiah Wilkinson (the Vice Commodore, Lord de Ros having declined the appointment). When Mr Hutchons resigned office in 1865 he

was replaced as Trustee by Mr Henry W. Birch. In the years immediately after their appointment the Trustees were much involved in the problems of the Clubhouse lease and the Club's dwindling finances. This in turn led to differences about the respective responsibilities of the Trustees, the Flag Officers and the General Committee.

NOTABLE MEMBERS

While the foregoing tells of those members who were elected to Office and contributed much towards the development of the Club there were many other members who either did not seek or perhaps simply were not considered for Office but who, nevertheless, made significant contributions. Up to and including the year 1867 records of committee members are available for the Sailing Committee (27 years), the House Committee (20 years) and the General Committee (8 years).

These records show the commitment of certain members to the Club. People such as Charles Stokes, who not only competed regularly and successfully in sailing matches but also served on the Sailing Committee for 24 years and on the General Committee for four years. Charles Smart who does not appear to have been a yacht owner but served for a total of 44 years on the three committees while C.R. Tatham, Alfred Cox, R.S. Wilkinson and Henry W. Birch each served for a total of 20 years and Arthur O Wilkinson served for nearly that many years. Several of these members were Committee Chairmen but, sadly, when the split came in 1867 Messrs Stokes, Tatham, A.O. Wilkinson and R.S. Wilkinson left to join to the New Thames Yacht Club as did John D. Lee (sailmaker to the Club and who served for 12 years on the Sailing Committee) who became the first Commodore of the New Thames Yacht Club with R.S. Wilkinson as Honorary Secretary and Treasurer and William N. Rudge (who served on the RTYC General Committee) becoming Vice Commodore.

When identifying members who made a special contribution to the Club, mention must be made of Lt. Col. Josiah Wilkinson who was a member of the 1863 Special Committee whose report resolved the Flag Officer election crisis and who was in the chair at the critical meetings of 1867 and, unsuccessfully alas, did everything in his power to hold the Club together when dissension was in the air. Mention should also be made of Colonel James Thompson who served for many years on both the General and the House Committees and was at times chairman of both. He fought hard to acquire for the Club a Clubhouse of a style that he deemed to be appropriate for a prestigious Club.

From 1844 there were three members with the surname Wilkinson, 'R.S, A.O. and Colonel J'. Whether they were related is not known, but R.S. and A.O. both joined the Club in 1842. A.O. - Arthur - was a successful racing yachtsman and in the 1860s was regularly chairman of the General Committee when the problems of the Clubhouse lease were relevant. He, primarily, negotiated the new lease for 7 Albemarle Street in 1865. These then, were the members who most influenced the development of the Club during the years 1823-1867 and without whose loyalty and dedication the Club could all too easily have slipped into insignificance instead of growing in prestige as a leading authority in yacht racing. That some of these gentlemen felt compelled to leave the Club in 1867 underlined perhaps their exuberant support of yachting rather than any wish to undermine the future of the Royal Thames Yacht Club.

CLUB PATRONAGE

The earliest Patronage of the Club was given by its founder
The Duke of Cumberland but it is less than clear whether
patronage continued after his death and before the assumption
of the position of Patron in 1827 by The Duke of Clarence -
who on accession to the throne in 1830 as King William IV,
caused the Club's assumption of the title 'Royal'. On the death
of King William in 1837, H.M. Queen Victoria became Patron
for the remainder of her life. Although not strictly a Patron
of the Club, the proprietor of the Royal Gardens, Vauxhall
offered much patronage to the Club in the form of silver cups
and the use of the Gardens which were a notable centre for
London social life in the latter part of the Georgian era.

The Office of Vice Patron appears to have existed for only
a limited period and was held by the Admiral who was
appointed as Governor of the Royal Hospital Greenwich.

The first recorded Vice Patron was Admiral Sir Richard Keats
who was followed in 1835 by Admiral Sir Thomas Hardy
(Nelson's Flag Captain at the Battle of Trafalgar). From 1854
the appointment appears to have lapsed. During the active
years of the Vice Patron they acted as the link between the
Club and the Patron to carry messages of thanks, congratula-
tions or condolence. Two of the attempts made on the life of
Queen Victoria were occasions for such messages. During the
first sailing match of the 1840 season, held on 25 June, a
Special Meeting of the Club was held on board the Steam
Packet 'Royal Sovereign' at which it was agreed *'that an
address be presented to the Queen ..... on her Majesty's
providential escape from the hands of an assassin'.*
Two years ater at a Meeting of the Club on 2 June 1842
a similar address was agreed *'..... congratulating Her Majesty
upon her escape from the late traitorous attack upon her
life'.* A list of Patrons and Vice Patrons is contained in
Appendix 4.

III
Club Sailing Matches

In less than four weeks after its foundation, the Thames Yacht Club had held its first sailing match as has been recounted in the section about that foundation. This section and its associated appendix give some details of the matches organised by the Club over 45 years and explains the expansion of those matches from small river events to genuine offshore racing. It also considers the never-ending attempts to create level racing, the changes in sailing regulations and recounts some of the contentious issues that arose.

For much of the period under review the procedure at the start of each match was that the competing vessels drew lots for their station at the start line. Each vessel was moored to a buoy laid by the Captain of the Club and no sail was set until the starting signal was fired. In the relatively confined waters of the Thames and with the fickle nature of the wind combined with the tide, it is not surprising that collisions and damage to spars and sails were common in the opening minutes of a match. A typical incident is described in the match for second and fourth class vessels held on 7 June 1862 and for which there were 13 starters assembled at Erith. The match started at 1152 with the wind *blowing with considerable force from W.S.W. WASP and QUIVER fouling at the start, the former's bowsprit entangled on the latter's boom, causing QUIVER to lose considerably at the start. PHANTOM got her topping-lift foul of one of the other yachts in Rands Reach and carried away her bowsprit'*. Other hazards faced by the competitors were sandbanks, large numbers of moored craft and craft proceeding to London docks - as was noted at the start of the match held on 11 June 1863 when *'there was a great number of merchant vessels, barges etc going down (the river) which hampered the yachts very much'*. It is not surprising therefore, that many vessels carried a Thames or Trinity House Pilot. All who followed the match in the hired steam boat were offered the opportunity, which they gladly accepted, to place their wagers on the result of the match, at odds for each vessel competing, based on their past performance and the conditions prevailing on the day of the match.

In 1824 two matches were staged, one using the same course as in 1823 and known as 'above bridge' and one starting at Blackwall and proceeding to Gravesend and back - this being a 'below bridge' match. (The 'bridge' referred to is London Bridge). Until 1832 there were just two matches each season except when an additional match was held to mark a special occasion e.g. the Duke of Clarence becoming Patron in 1827, his succession in 1830 and his coronation as King William IV in 1831. It was not until 1830 that the first classification of yachts took place with those over 10 Tons being in the First

Class and those under 10 Tons being in the Second Class.

The courses for the RTYC sailing matches changed little until 1844 when the first race to the Nore Light took place. The 'above bridge' matches all started at Blackfriars Bridge, Southwark Bridge or Temple Gardens while the 'below bridge' matches moved their start to Greenwich Hospital in 1828 (it is no coincidence that the Governor of the Hospital was also Vice Patron of the RTYC) while the turning mark for these matches moved a couple of miles down river from Gravesend to Coal House Point in 1839. By 1841 the number of bigger vessels competing had increased to such a degree that the 'above bridge' matches were abandoned and all matches were 'below bridge' and started from Greenwich or (from 1846) at Erith or (from 1853) Gravesend.

The classification of vessels had to be changed at regular intervals as yachts increased in size and capability. The courses set for sailing matches moved from the confines of the river to the estuary and beyond. Additionally, many members were racing their larger yachts in the open waters of the east coast and west country as well as in the Solent. An upper limit of 25 Tons for vessels competing in RTYC matches was set in 1837 when the earlier first class was divided at 18 Tons; all these changes were made with the objective of producing more level racing. These three classes were maintained until 1843 when they were reduced to two with the division at 12 Tons.

The first extension of the sailing match course out into the Thames Estuary came on 27 June 1844 when an extra match was arranged with entry open to all vessels. The prize was a painting by the Club's marine artist N.M Condy. The course was from Greenwich to the Nore Light and back. The year 1846 saw a number of significant changes occur. Races from Erith to the Nore and back were established as the norm for 'long' courses while shorter races turned at Chapmans Head off Canvey Island. On 19 June 1846 the Club arranged an additional match for a prize of a £70 Silver Cup. Entry was open to vessels of all Royal Yacht Clubs not exceeding 50 Tons - the first time the 25 Ton limit had been exceeded but not the first time that entry had been open to other clubs. The 100 guineas Grand Challenge Cup put up by subscription in 1840, was also open to vessels whose owners belonged to other Royal Yacht Clubs. This 1846 match was also the first where 'compensation for size' was available for the wide range of vessels competing. This took the form of a time allowance of half a minute per ton. The increasing number of larger vessels competing led in 1848 to the creation of a new First Class comprising vessels over 25 Tons and not exceeding 50 Tons,

Cutter Yacht PHANTOM, 25 Tons - Lithograph by T G Dutton

but by 1850 the three classes were First - over 30 Tons, Second - 16-30 Tons and Third - 10-15 Tons, all classes sailing with a $\frac{1}{2}$ min/ton time allowance.

It was only three years later on 1 June 1853 that the Club held its first Schooner Match from Gravesend to the Mouse Light Vessel (off Maplin Sands) and back for a 100 guinea prize. Sadly this historic sailing match was marred by controversy. The first vessel to cross the finishing line was the Swedish built *SVERIGE (280 Tons)* owned by Thomas Bartlett Esq and she was closely followed by Lord Alfred Paget's *ROSALIND (100 Tons)*. The award of the prize was however, withheld while the Sailing Committee heard a protest lodged by Captain H.M. Freeston, owner of the Schooner *VIOLET (60 Tons)* which was involved in a collision with the *SVERIGE*. The Committee upheld the protest and awarded the prize to *ROSALIND*. While the protest was being heard Mr Bartlett wrote to Lord Alfred Paget saying that the evidence was conflicting and no fair conclusion could be arrived at. He therefore proposed that a re-sail should take place between *SVERIGE* and *ROSALIND*. Lord Alfred Paget replied rejecting the proposal and making the point that *ROSALIND* was not involved in the protest and reminding him that the finding of the Sailing Committee would be binding and final. By 24 June Mr Bartlett had made public his rejection of the findings of the Sailing Committee and had given notice that he would take legal action against any member of the Committee who should award the prize to another member. When the Club met again after the 'summer break' it reaffirmed the Sailing Committee's decision as final and deplored Mr Bartlett's letter to Bell's Life in London as uncalled for, insulting and offensive to the Sailing Committee as well as being unworthy of a member of the Club. On 2 November Mr Bartlett refused

to apologise with the result that his resignation was tendered and accepted.

The next significant change in classification came in 1856 when the Cutters were divided into four classes. The First Class was for vessels over 35 Tons, the Second for vessels over 20 Tons and not exceeding 35 Tons, the Third for vessels over 12 Tons and not exceeding 20 Tons while the Fourth class was for vessels of 7 Tons and not exceeding 12 Tons. By this time vessels under 7 Tons were not permitted to participate in RTYC matches. In the following year Schooners were also divided into two classes, the First class being for vessels over 75 Tons and the Second class for those under 75 Tons (the dividing point being changed in 1863 to 100 Tons). The $\frac{1}{2}$ min/ton time allowance was retained for Cutters while Schooners received $\frac{1}{4}$ min/ton. These allowances were further modified in 1858 when neither Cutters over 60 Tons nor Schooners over 150 Tons received a Time Allowance. One of the biggest changes in the racing regulations during this period took place in 1854. The historical method of measuring Tonnage was tied to a law established by Act of Parliament in 1694 (see Appendix 5). By 1850 the familiar problem existed whereby the skill of the yacht designers was making a mockery of the measurement rules especially in respect of length since a heavily raked stern post could significantly increase the measured tonnage. When the Sailing Committee met on 8 February 1854 with the Treasurer, Captain Cornelius Wheeler in the Chair, a motion, proposed by R.S. Wilkinson and seconded by J.L. Craigie, was carried and stated *'that it is the opinion of this Committee that the present plan of measurement has produced results prejudicial to the true interests of yacht building and it is therefore desirable to amend the law'*. Mr Richard S. Wilkinson followed his motion with another one recommending that the Rule for Admeasurement to be adopted by the Club should be as follows:

The length shall be taken on a straight line on deck from the fore part of the stem to the after part of the stern post, from which deducting the breadth, the remainder shall be esteemed the just length to find the Tonnage. The breadth shall be taken from the outside plank in the broadest part of the yacht; then, multiplying the length by the breadth and dividing the whole by 94, the Quotient shall be deemed the true contents of the Tonnage; provided always that if any part of the stem or stern post project beyond the length taken as above mentioned, such projection or projections shall for the purposes of finding the tonnage, be added to the length taken as before mentioned.

The modified formula for measuring tonnage was formally adopted by the Club on 27 February and was used for rating and time allowance purposes for nearly 30 years. As a ready means of recognising yacht size Thames Measurement or Tons T.M. still has some relevance 140 years on.

In 1864 the courses sailed in RTYC matches were extended significantly. On 4 June the first 'Ocean' match was sailed from Thames Haven to Harwich while later in the same month the first 'Channel' match took place and was sailed from Gravesend to Ryde. The arrangements for the Ocean match provide interesting reading. There was to be a Special Train to Thames Haven at 9.0 am. Mr Tatham was to hire Steamboats while the Vice Commodore was to hire Bands. There was to be an Express Train home from Tilbury. This was also an occasion when competing yachts started from their own anchors in two lines - one for Schooners and Yawls and one for Cutters. By an interesting coincidence Mr Alfred Cox, whose suggestion initiated the Ocean Match, proved to be the winner of the £80 prize in the larger class with his Yawl *WHIRLWIND (70 Tons)*, the winner of the £40 Cutter prize being the very successful *VOLANTE (60 Tons)* owned by Mr H.C. Maudslay. The prizes for the Channel Match were more modest and took the form of a sweepstake with competing yachts each putting £5 into the kitty. Four schooners and five cutters took part with Mr J.S Abbot-Dunbar's *MADCAP (70 Tons)* winning the Schooner Class and *VOLANTE* winning the Cutter Class as in the earlier Ocean Match.

These two matches were also included in the 1865 programme when, as in the previous year, the club organised a total of five matches, the most in any year for the period 1823-67. Three of the prizes given in 1865 were donated by members, the most valuable being the 150 guineas prize comprising a Silver Epergne and Cup which was won by Captain Thomas Chamberlayne's Cutter *ARROW (102 Tons)* in the Channel match, again sailed from Gravesend to Ryde. The Ocean Match in that year started from Sheerness and again finished at Harwich, the first prize of £100 being won by Mr George Duppa's Schooner *ALARM (248 Tons)* and the second prize of £50 by Lord Alfred Paget's Yawl *XANTHA (135 Tons)*. No time allowance was given in this match even though it was open to vessels of any rig or tonnage belonging to any Royal Yacht Club. The Channel match continued to feature in the Club's sailing programme for many years. In 1866 it was sailed from the Nore Light to Dover Harbour and the following year from the Nore to Le Havre. A full list of the prizes given and won from 1823 to 1867 is given in Appendix 6 and a list of the various courses sailed is shown in Appendix 7. Where it is known the form of the silver prizes is recorded. Any blanks in the list of winners indicates that the result is not known -

either because it is not contained in the records available or because the match was not sailed for one reason or another.

Successful Yachts and Owners

There are many ways of measuring success and the one selected for these paragraphs is the winning of trophies in Royal Thames sailing matches over the period 1823-67. This was a time when yacht design was changing less rapidly than in later years. The outfit of sails carried changed little and was mainly related to the hull dimensions and the spars appropriate to the rig - the one exception being the emergence of the spinnaker. Hull shape and structure did evolve as did the materials used and nothing influenced this more than the arrival in this country of the *AMERICA*. Perhaps the biggest change during the period was the rapid increase in the yacht population and the number of yacht clubs.

During these years, the presence on board during a match of the owner was by no means certain and in the bigger classes it was more usual that, even if the owner was on board, there would be a professional skipper or sailing master in charge. To attribute success to an owner may, therefore, relate to his ability to engage a successful skipper rather than his own sailing skill. Similarly, success of a particular yacht may more properly reflect the skill of the designer and builder than the owner. To state the obvious, a well designed and built yacht that is skilfully handled is always more likely to be successful. One last comment is that where yachts were successful over many years it is almost certain that they would have been significantly modified, probably several times, during these years.

It is no surprise that the owner winning most Royal Thames prizes during these years was Lord Alfred Paget (with 10 prizes) followed by Samuel Lane and Charles Wheeler jnr with 9 each.

The most successful yacht of the period was unquestionably *PHANTOM* with 12 Royal Thames prizes followed by VAMPIRE (10 prizes) and *LADY LOUISE* and *VICTORINE* with 7 each. Lord Alfred Paget's successes were spread over more than 20 years starting in 1842 with the cutter *SABRINA (21 Tons)*, which had earlier been successfully raced by Henry Gunston. This was followed by the better known cutter *MYSTERY (25 Tons)*, the cutter *BELVIDERE (25 Tons)*, the Inman built schooner *ROSALIND (100 Tons)* and the yawl *XANTHA (135 Tons)* built by Harvey of Ipswich. Lord Alfred Paget's sailing master, John Nicholls, who also sailed *ALARM* for Joseph Weld and George Duppa, was probably the most successful of his era, being equally competent with vessels of any size.

By 1863 Samuel Lane had won 50 prizes although only 9 were given by the Royal Thames. All nine were won by his cutter *PHANTOM (20 Tons)* built by Penney of Poole and frequently modified during her long career. Earlier (1843-44) *PHANTOM* had been owned by A.O. Wilkinson who had been equally successful (he later was to own the schooner *GLORIANA (148 Tons)* built by Ratsey of Cowes in 1852 and which won RTYC prizes in 1865-66).

Charles Wheeler jnr joined the Royal Thames in 1840 having sailed successfully with the Clarence YC and been its Secretary in 1831. With the Royal Thames he won his trophies with *SEA NYMPH (10 Tons)* and with *VAMPIRE (15 Tons)* built by Dan Hatcher at Southampton in 1851 and at times sailed by Henry Truckle of Itchen. *VAMPIRE* was later owned by Captain J.E. Commerell, VC, RN and won a Royal Thames prize in 1864

Schooner Yacht ALARM, 248 Tons - Lithograph painted by C Taylor

while in the years 1865-67 *VAMPIRE* won further prizes when owned by Thomas Cuthbert.

Thomas Smith was one of the earliest members of the Thames Yacht Club having joined in December 1824. His yacht *LADY LOUISA (13 Tons)* won her first Royal Thames prize in 1825 and won the last of her seven prizes in 1842. The Cowes-built boat was one of the most competitive on the Thames in spite of her small size. The other very successful boat in the earlier part of this period was *VICTORINE (18 Tons)* owned by Thomas and Charles Stokes and later by Henry Lord. Between 1835 and 1845 she won 7 Royal Thames Prizes valued at £236. J Thomas Hewes (who was to become the first Commodore of the Royal London Yacht Club in 1838) was also the winner of many prizes during the years 1837-43 with his yachts *BRILLIANT (8 Tons), ADA JANE (18 Tons)* and *FAY (12 Tons)*. There were many other very successful vessels who each won several Royal Thames prizes including *SECRET* owned by J.W. Smith who won outright in 1847 the 100 guinea Grand Challenge Cup. *MOSQUITO (50 Tons)* built, and initially owned, by C.T. Mare at Blackwall won 6 prizes as did *VOLANTE (48 Tons)*, built by Harveys of Ipswich for J.L. Craigie, and QUIVER (12 Tons) owned by Thomas Chamberlayne and later by Denzil Chamberlayne. Any account of successful yachts and owners would be incomplete without mention of *ALARM*. Built in 1830 by Inman at Lymington for Joseph Weld she was cutter rigged and with a tonnage of 193 Tons she was one of the biggest cutters ever built. Having competed in the 1851 match against *AMERICA*, Joseph Weld was greatly influenced by her design and in 1852 he had the bow form of ALARM modified and her rig changed to that of a schooner. Her tonnage now increased to 248 Tons. Joseph Weld became a Royal Thames member in 1859 and immediate-

ly won club prizes in the schooner matches of 1859 and 1861 - in which year he was 86 years old but was still sailing on board his renowned schooner. The yacht was bought by another Royal Thames member, George Duppa, in 1865 and he too won first prize in the schooner match that year and in the Channel Match of 1867.

Finally, mention must be made of the vessels that were emerging as successful prize winners in the last two or three years of the 1823-67 period and were to go on to further success. The cutter *VINDEX (45 Tons)* was built by the Millwall Iron Company and owned by Andrew Duncan. Sailed by J. Downs she won her first Royal Thames prize in 1863. The schooner *MADCAP (70 Tons)* built by Wanhill, owned by J.S. Abbot Dunbar and sailed by J. Harbut jnr was a winner from 1864. The much bigger schooner *EGERIA (152 Tons)* was also built by Wanhill for John Mulholland. She won her first RTYC prize in 1866 and was to become all-conquering in the next decade. The cutter *SPHINX (48 Tons)* was built in 1866 to lines by Hatcher at Maudslay and Field's workshop for Herbert Maudslay as a composite vessel with iron frames and teak planking. As mentioned in Section VII the term spinnaker was derived from her name. Her first success was in May 1866.

Sailing Regulations

The Club's 'year book' was initially divided into two sections: 'Club Laws' and 'Sailing Regulations'. Later, when a Clubroom and ultimately a Clubhouse were acquired, an additional section 'Club Rules' was added.

The conditions under which RTYC Sailing Matches were controlled, were set down partly in the 'Laws' and partly in the 'Regulations' until 1863 when they were placed wholly in the Regulations. This period, 1823-1867, precedes both the Yacht Racing Association (later the RYA) and the IYRU so that clubs were free, indeed obliged, to set their own regulations in the absence of universal regulations.

Many of the RTYC Laws and Regulations have already been recorded, especially those relating to classification, measurement and courses. Those not referred to in detail or only very briefly include the following:

a) No member was permitted to enter an RTYC match if he had not paid his annual subscription or was in any way in debt to the Club.

b) The Commodore was the judge of each match or in his absence the Vice Commodore. If both were competing then the Sailing Committee appointed a President for the match.

c) Protests had to be placed with the Commodore within 1 hour of the first yacht finishing.

d) All wagers made by members had to be registered and the money deposited with the Treasurer.

e) Each yacht had to fly a distinguishing colour at the topmast head, the size being proportional to its class.

f) All yachts had to be at their station within a quarter of an hour after the 'warning' signal, otherwise a yacht was not allowed to compete.

g) All fore and aft rigged yachts could carry only four fore and aft sails. This restriction only applied to Cutters from 1863, when Schooners were limited to eight sails.

h) Should any yacht wilfully foul another, the member steering (or later, deemed to be steering) the yacht so fouling was liable to be expelled from the Club.

i) Ballast must not be changed or moved during a match - a regulation which was the topic of many protests.

j) When sailing to windward the yacht on the larboard (port) tack must give way to the yacht on the starboard tack. Any yacht disobeying the regulation was disqualified.

k) When two yachts are starting for the shore or towards any vessel, and the leeward yacht is likely to run aground or foul the vessel and be unable to avoid hitting the windward yacht, the latter must put about on being hailed by any member of the Club on the leeward yacht.

l) A yacht on retiring must haul down her distinguishing flag.

m) A yacht wishing to protest may hoist the Club Ensign in lieu of the distinguishing flag.

These were the principal sailing laws and regulation in 1841 and the majority stood through to 1867 with no more than minor modification. In 1844 the Captain Marryat's Code of Signals was adopted by the Club - their being no universal code. In 1846 the number of working hands in a crew was limited to eight including the pilot. With the increase in maximum tonnage from 25 Tons to 50 Tons in 1848, vessels over 25 Tons were allowed 3 extra hands. In 1853, with the inclusion of a Schooner match in the sailing programme, they were allowed to carry 1 hand per 5 tons exclusive of the Master, Pilot and 3 members. Also in 1853, the regulation was introduced that the owner of any yacht winning a prize could give a gratuity to each crew member of not more than half a guinea. 1854 saw the introduction of Thames Measurement as a formula for calculating tonnage while in 1864 the crew numbers regulation was again altered to take account of the increasing size of yachts. Cutters could carry 1 hand per 5 tons exclusive of Owner, Master, Pilot and 4 friends while Schooners could carry 1 hand per 7 tons exclusive of Owner, Pilot, master and 6 friends.

Not surprisingly many of these regulations form the basis for today's rules but it is also of note that there were regular bids to revise significantly some aspects of the regulations. On 3 February 1851 the Sailing Committee resolved *'that a Committee be appointed by the Club to open correspondence with the various Royal Yacht Clubs of Great Britain in order to arrive at a Universal Code of Sailing Regulations'* - but nothing further is recorded. On 5 May 1852 the Club received a letter from Commodore Ackers of the Royal Victoria Yacht Club at Ryde *'suggesting the necessity of altering the present classification of yachts'.* He considered that extreme length should be taken as the basis for classification viz.: 40-50 feet for the small class, above 50 feet and not exceeding 60 feet for the second class and above 60 feet for the first class. The RTYC recognised the importance of this proposal but nevertheless deferred the matter for further consideration. Once again nothing appears to have resulted from this except that the Sailing Regulations for the years 1860 to 1863 stated that Schooners shall be classed according to Mr Ackers scale. Mr G H Ackers, who was a member of the RYS devised a system of time allowance calculated on tonnage and the distance of the course which was known as Ackers' Graduated Scale. Notwithstanding the statement in the RTYC Sailing Regulations, Schooners in RTYC matches were classified by tonnage (if at all) and the time allowance (if given) was on the basis of time for tonnage.

On 9 January 1861 a letter from Colonel Henry Brown was read to the General Meeting of the Club. Colonel Brown joined the Club in 1848 and in 1861 owned a 70 Ton Yawl *PLOVER.* In his letter he said *'That the Club Measurement has had a great and pernicious influence on the construction of yachts and the promotion of sport. It appears that the sails carried by the present Racing Yachts approximate to 80 square feet of canvas per ton and it is also evident that the allowance of time should greatly depend on the distance to be sailed over. I therefore propose, as an experiment, that in a race of 20 miles a quarter of a second per square foot of canvas should be allowed; half a second per square foot if the distance be 40 miles; threequarters of a second for 60 miles and one second for 80 miles. The distance to be estimated from point to point as the yachts are required to go both out and home, without reference to the direction of the wind. The sails of the racing yachts to be measured the day before the race. Smaller sails than those measured may be used if the weather should require it, but all sails larger than those measured must be landed previous to the start'.*

Colonel Brown's letter was referred to a Select Committee (including the Commodore) to consider and report back. Good intentions were once again insufficient and appointments to the Select Committee were deferred with the result that the basis for measurement, classification and time allowance was virtually unchanged in the 1860s.

Model of stern of yacht that led to introduction of Thames Measurement

Club Ensign and Burgee

The history of the Club's Ensign and Burgee is fully illustrated in the current Club handbook. The undefaced White Ensign was authorised to be flown by members of the Cumberland Fleet, the Coronation Fleet and then the Thames Yacht Club and Royal Thames Yacht Club until 1834, when it was changed to a defaced white ensign carrying a crown and the letters RTYC in the field in red.

On 22 July 1842 the Lords Commissioners of the Admiralty issued a letter stating:

'My Lords Commissioners of the Admiralty having, by their order of the 6th June 1829 granted permission to the Royal Yacht Squadron, as having been the first recognised club, and enjoying sundry privileges, to wear the White St George's Ensign, and other distinctions, that their vessels might be generally known, and particularly in Foreign Ports, and much inconvenience having arisen in consequence of other Yacht Clubs having been allowed similar colours, My lords have cancelled the Warrant enabling the Royal Thames Yacht Club to wear the White Ensign, and have directed me to send you herewith a Warrant authorising the Vessels belonging to the Club to wear the Blue Ensign of Her Majesty's Fleet, with the distinctive marks of the Club as hitherto worn on the White Ensign, and as it is an Ensign not allowed to be worn by Merchant Vessels, My Lords trust that it will be equally acceptable to the Members of the Club'.

When the Club met on 4 August the Commodore informed the members present that he and the other officers proposed that the blue ensign should carry a white cross with the four letters RTY and C in red and in gothic style, located in the four 'legs' of the white cross and surrounding a red crown in the centre. An amendment to this proposal called for the Blue Ensign distinctive mark to be as stated in the Warrant of 22 July (and which had been issued with the letter). Although the amendment was carried by a large majority, the next meeting of the Club on 6 October referred the matter to the Sailing Committee who met on 10 November. They recommended that the opportunity should be taken to seek Their Lordships approval to discontinue including the letters RTYC in the distinctive marks. The approval was received and it was reported to the Club meeting on 1 December that the new Blue Ensign would be defaced only by a red crown in the middle of the field. By 1848 approval was given to fly an undefaced Blue Ensign - as is the current situation.

The original burgee of the Thames Yacht Club was in red with the letters TYC in white in the centre. On receiving royal patronage this was changed in 1831 to a red burgee with a crown above the letters RTYC, both being in white. In 1834 the colours were reversed while the burgee was completely changed (in conjunction with the change to a Blue Ensign in 1842) to the present blue burgee, with a white cross and red crown at the centre.

IV
Club Administration

The administration of the Club and the expansion of the facilities available to members are recorded in this section under three headings: the committee structure which grew from the most simple to a larger and more complex framework over the period under review; a review of the facilities provided for members and a brief look at the social activities of members and lastly, the rules concerning election to the Club and the rapid growth in the size of the membership.

The Committee Structure

The earliest minute book available shows that it was the custom from 1839 for there to be a General Meeting of the Club on the first Thursday in the month at which the Commodore, William Harrison, was in the Chair. Should he be unable to attend the Captain of the Club or the Treasurer took the chair. These three gentlemen were the only officers of the Club, supported by the Secretary. The only permanent Committee was the Sailing Committee or, to give it the full title of the day, 'The Sailing and General Purposes Committee'. This situation is hardly surprising since the Club's overriding interest was in yachting and it had no permanent Clubhouse. Meetings were held in a room in the British Coffee House in Cockspur Street. The business of the monthly meetings was dominated either by yacht racing or the election of members. Any matter which could not be resolved at a General Meeting was referred to the Sailing Committee. The latter was thus able to exert considerable influence over both the strategic and tactical policies of the Club - a position of strength that was to be eroded in 1860.

The Commodore, in 1839, was a very active 'Chairman' and rarely missed a meeting of the Club, the Sailing Committee or the social functions. The Captain of the Club was responsible for organising the Sailing Matches - a Chief Race Officer of the day; while the Treasurer, quite literally, handled the money passed to him by the Secretary (the Club first opened a Bank Account in 1856). It must be remembered, of course, that the Club's annual income was only about £500, but it was nevertheless a substantial sum at that time.

The first proposal to create a second permanent committee occurred at the Club meeting on 5 February 1846. The motion was 'that a Finance Committee be appointed to consist of seven members of the Club to assist the Treasurer in investigating the Accounts and to superintend its Financial Affairs'. There is no reason to suppose that this motion was inspired by the Commodore, William Harrison, who was about to stand down from office, but it is certain that Cornelius Wheeler, who was a very successful Treasurer over the years

1831-1856, felt that this motion reflected adversely on his stewardship of the Office of Treasurer. He was not alone in this matter; the motion was defeated and Mr R. S. Wilkinson moved 'that this Club feel deeply and beg to express their thanks to Mr Wheeler for his services as Treasurer of this Club and they deeply regret that he should have felt the motion respecting the Finance Committee as offensive in the slightest degree, the same being clearly prospective and meant in the best feeling for the purpose of relieving him of the more onerous position of duty which he has in some degree taken to himself for the purpose of relieving the Secretary'.

The Club may have had only one permanent committee but there was a continuous stream of short term sub committees appointed to investigate and report on specific topics. One such was appointed on 6 November 1845, a time when the Club still held its meetings at the British Coffee House, on a motion by Mr George Reynell 'That it be referred to a Committee of Thirteen members (of which the Commodore, Vice Commodore and Treasurer shall be three) to consider of the propriety and practicability of establishing a Clubhouse for the use of the members of this Club and that it be an instruction to the Committee especially to consider of the mode in which the Club can be better accommodated for the transaction of its public business and that it be a further instruction to the Committee not only to consider and provide suitable temporary accommodation for the Club but to consider generally and report as to the most eligible mode of permanently providing for its want'. The report of this Committee initiated the move to the Piazza Hotel, Covent Garden early in 1846 at which venue the Club had not only a room in which to hold its meetings but also a general Clubroom for use by members in which refreshments were available. Not surprisingly, the second permanent Committee, The House Committee, was appointed a few months later on 26 November 1846 charged with looking after the Club's interests at the Piazza Hotel in co-operation with the proprietor, Mr Cuttriss.

The move to the Piazza Hotel was the first milestone in the broadening of the Club's activities and interests. It also marked the start of greater demands on the Club's financial resources.

The form of Management of the Club's affairs was unchanged over the next 12-13 years in spite of the move to rooms in the nearby Bedford Hotel in 1851 and the further move to the first comprehensive Clubhouse in St James Street in 1857. The latter move inevitably added further to the demands on the Club's finances.

An attempt to establish a Library Committee in December 1859 was unsuccessful on the technical point that the motion proposing this Committee was not presented in the correct form. By the time notice was given that the motion would be re-presented in the correct form it was swept up in a much broader motion seeking a complete overhaul of the Club management and a significant change in responsibilities. On 1 February 1860 at a General Meeting of the Club, Mr James Thomson proposed a motion, that was carried unanimously, *'that there shall in future be elected annually at the March Meeting (of the Club) one Committee to be called the 'Committee of Management' to consist of twenty one members, seven to be a quorum, with power to nominate sub-committees for Sailing, House, Library or such other purposes as they may deem necessary'*. The title of this new all-powerful committee was amended to the *'General Committee of Management'* and was charged to manage the affairs of the Club, subject to the approval of the Club at its monthly General Meeting.

This major change in the Committee structure was open to different interpretations. It could be seen as the Monthly General Meeting 'leasing' many of its responsibilities to the General Committee on a 'report-back' basis or it could be seen as the transfer of responsibilities that previously were the business of the Sailing and General Purposes Committee to the new General Committee. What was clear was that the need for monthly General Meetings of the Club working on the type of agenda it had used in the past would slowly dissolve and the General Meetings were at risk of becoming no more than a rubber stamp for the business of the General Committee, which Committee met at least once a month. This proved to be what happened and in 1862 it was agreed to hold General Meetings only once a quarter. In January 1866 James Thompson proposed that this be changed to a once a year Annual General Meeting to be held in March. Monthly meetings of the Club did continue, however, on a much reduced scale in order to ballot candidates for election to the Club - but these meetings were not chaired by an Officer of the Club and conducting the ballot was their sole business.

The origins of the present Wine and Cigar Committee can be traced to the decision by the Club in January 1863 to relieve the Club Manager of the responsibility for selecting Wines, Beers and Spirits, the members having so poor an opinion of selections available.

The election of Officers in 1863 proved to be difficult as is recorded in Section V. The Club had moved to Albemarle Street in 1860 (a much larger establishment than 49 St James Street) and this had placed even further stress on the Club's resources. This, together with the problems of electing officers, led to the setting up of a Special Committee to resolve these problems. Included in the Special Committee's report were recommendations for the appointment of Club Trustees and the abolition of the Office of Treasurer. Until the presentation of that report all monies had been collected by the Secretary and passed to the Treasurer but no provision had made for the investment and security of Club funds. The funds and property of the Club were now to be transferred into the names of the Trustees. The report also noted that the Office of Treasurer was unusual in associations of this (the Club's) character and deemed unnecessary. All payments by cheque would in future be authorised by the General Committee of Management and cheques would be signed by the Chairman for the time being of that Committee and one other member of the Committee and countersigned by the Secretary. By 1866

the House Committee was expanded to enable it to deal with Financial matters.

While the implementation of these recommendations caused some turbulence it did ultimately establish a structure for management of the Club which prevailed for many years - but could not prevent its sliding down the slippery slope which culminated in the formation of the large splinter group of members who created the New Thames Yacht Club at the end of 1867.

Club Facilities

It should never be imagined that the activities of the Club over this period in the middle of the 19th century were confined, ashore, to central London and, afloat, to the River Thames and its estuary. While they provided the locations for the majority of Club functions and Sailing Matches there is abundant evidence that members sailed in waters far removed from the Thames and that social activity was equally diverse.

Before examining the range of facilities available to members outside London and the Thames it is interesting to note the variety of events that took place in London and formed the Club's annual fixture list. The season started with the Opening Trip in April or May. Members' yachts assembled at Greenwich or Blackwall and cruised in company to Gravesend or Erith where arrangements were made ashore for a Club Dinner. This was a great social occasion, members were appointed Stewards for the trip to ensure that members' expectations were fulfilled and the Commodore led the cruise with his pendant flying. This no doubt equated to today's Fitting Out Dinner as the time to mark the opening of the Sailing Season.

Once the Opening Trip was over the Sailing Matches were started. There were anything from 2 to 6 matches each year and these were held between late May and early July; only occasionally, when a special trophy was presented, did they take place later. This was because members either wished to go away cruising in July August and September or they entered regattas held elsewhere on the East Coast, Solent or West Country. While the number of members actively involved on the competing yachts in these Thames-based sailing matches was quite small, the numbers among the spectators carried either on the steam vessel chartered for the match (and on which was located the Race Committee) or in the 'fleet' that followed the race, were considerable. The ladies who embarked on the steam vessel appear to have had their eyes set on fashion rather than protection against the weather. Colour was further added to the day by the presence on board of a military band to perform popular and martial airs.

The sailing season ended with a 'Closing Trip' in October, an occasion similar to the one that opened the season. Records show this happened until 1847 but after that date this trip appears to have been dropped - yet it still represents the equivalent of the current Laying Up Dinner.

The winter months included two major functions, the Annual Dinner in November and the Annual Ball in February - on or near St Valentine's Day. The latter was held at the Hanover Square Rooms when Mr Adam and his band were in attendance. On 10 May 1844 Mr Adam was appointed Bandmaster of the Club while his band were allowed to be dressed in Royal Thames uniform and were to be called the Royal Thames Yacht Club Band. An Annual Ball was held until February 1861 but it is not mentioned subsequently

- quite possibly the Club was so deeply involved in the pains of evolution after moving to 7 Albemarle Street that the pleasures of an Annual Ball were accorded no priority.

Members who sailed in the Thames estuary or in the Solent were assured of receiving a welcome ashore at many ports. The Club appointed various Hotels and Taverns as Royal Thames 'Clubhouses' where the Club or individual members could dine and wine. The list in 1843 included:

The Medina Hotel, Cowes
The Yacht Tavern, Greenwich
Wates Hotel, Gravesend
The Dukes Head Hotel, Margate
The Royal Oak Hotel, Ramsgate
The Royal George Hotel, Southampton

To this list was added later The Old Ship Hotel at Brighton and The Royal Kent Hotel at Ryde. In later years The Vine Hotel at Cowes and The New Falcon Inn at Gravesend were also given Clubhouse status.

If one should assume that members sailing was confined to the UK waters during this period, there is plenty of evidence otherwise. As early as 1839 the Commodore lead a cruise to Boulogne but the extent of their travel is better indicated by the appointment of agents of the club in ports along the European coast of the English Channel from Rotterdam to Cherbourg and then down to Bordeaux, while further afield agents were appointed in Leghorn, Malta, Lisbon and the Azores. This international aspect of the Royal Thames has always been present even from its early days.

Membership

When the Thames Yacht Club was formed in 1823 it had some 40 members only and few can have foreseen at that time the rapid increase in both numbers of members and prestige of the Club that would take place over the next few decades. By 1827 the numbers had reached 200 and by 1849 there were 400 members peaking to 930 in 1865 before the slump to some 750 at the beginning of 1868 after the secession to the New Thames Yacht Club. While the membership doubled during the decade from 1855, only 20% of the additional members were yacht owners - a clear reflection of the rapidly changing nature of the Club once a permanent Club House was acquired in 1857.

The change of balance between the number of members who were yacht owners and those who were not was recognised by the Club in November 1861 when it was decided to require non-yacht owners to pay a higher entrance fee - 12 guineas instead of 8 guineas.

The turnover of members during the 1850s and 60s was very modest, the number of 'Casualties' each year being remarkably consistent and comprising some 25 resignations, 12 deaths, 10 struck off and 1 or 2 who were bankrupt.

There were also two sad cases of members who became mentally deranged.

Throughout this period, and beyond, election to membership of the Club was by ballot. Whilst the procedural details varied, the general principal was much as it is still shown in the current Club Rules. It is also interesting to note that many other current Club Rules have changed little over the past 150 years, especially those relating to payment of entrance fees and subscriptions, conduct of members, their privileges and matters of behaviour. The question of prompt payment of fees and dues was ever a thorny one and clearly the Treasurer was forever seeking (and receiving) support from the Club to 'bring to heel' non-payers. While the mid-Victorians may have had a different attitude towards indebtedness from that held today, the financial strain put on the Club in 1867 might easily have been assuaged had not some 400 still failed to have paid their 1867 annual subscription of three guineas six months into the financial year (over and above what may have been due from previous years).

As mentioned earlier it is interesting to notice how early in the Club history many of the present rules and practices were established. One such matter is the inclusion of an alphabetical list of members in the Rule Book. This was proposed at a meeting of the Club in 1841 but had a long gestation period, the first such list appearing in 1845. Another practice agreed in 1846 was the numbering of members by seniority. This number enabled members to identify each other when at sea; it also enabled the yacht list, first printed in 1846, to be listed in the order of members' number and cross referenced to the alphabetical list of members.

Letter sent to a member of the RTYC in 1843

Election to membership by ballot was a meticulous process and nomination for inclusion in a ballot at one Club meeting was no assurance of success in the ballot at the next meeting. On the other hand the Club was prepared occasionally to bypass the ballot procedure when distinguished candidates were proposed by senior members. It was also the practice to elect Honorary Members, especially when such membership could be to the advantage of the Club. Two such elections were Mr James Harrison of The Era newspaper in 1843 and Dr Sheridan, Editor of the Morning Advertiser, both of whom could help to promote the Club through the favourable reporting in the press of Sailing Matches and social functions.

Douglas Philips Birt writes in 'The Cumberland Fleet' about the report on Club affairs in The Era newspaper in 1866 that *'the writer seems on the whole well informed on internal matters and on the evidence of some of his remarks it appears he might have been a member'* - it must be highly likely that the writer was James Harrison.

During the period of this review, and beyond, many noblemen were included in the membership, but perhaps none achieved greater fame than the Earl of Cardigan who was elected a member in 1847, seven years before the Charge of the Light Brigade at Balaclava (in which harbour was moored his yacht which he used as his base throughout the campaign).

It might easily be assumed that in the first half of the 19th century the membership would be drawn solely from the London area. This was not so; by 1840 members were elected who lived as far apart as Milford Haven, Poole and Cambridge, while a few years later new members addresses include Tynemouth, Gairloch and Liverpool. By 1865 there was hardly a county in the United Kingdom that did not feature in the membership list while the international nature of the Club is underlined by there being members in more than a dozen countries abroad from Portugal to Singapore and Hong Kong to Russia.

V
Financial and House Affairs

The growth of the Club over the years brought with it, not only increase in membership but also the evolution from simple to the more complex sailing matches. These and the changes associated with the expansion from the days of holding meetings in a coffee house to the availability of a fully equipped Clubhouse, all ensured that the control of the Club's finances needed ever greater attention. In practice, Club's finances were more and more influenced by the scope of the facilities available to members - the 'house' aspect of Club life. All these matters are considered in this section, at times in great detail, in order to show how it came to be that the affairs of the Club grew more and more divisive, reaching boiling point in 1867.

Financial Matters

The financial affairs of the Club were simple and straight-forward for the period 1823-57 during which time income accrued primarily from entrance fees and annual subscriptions; the administrative expenses of the Club were very modest - the Secretary's salary, the hire of rooms for meetings and printing costs. For sailing matches each competing yacht

paid Tonnage Dues of one shilling per ton, while everyone who embarked on the steamboat which followed matches down the Thames paid for a ticket. Set against these sources of income were the cost of hiring the steamboat and the purchase price of the trophies. These elementary accounts showed, in 1839, an annual cash balance in favour of the Club of £91, which figure by 1857 had risen to £598 exclusive of the investment of £2000 in 3% British Consuls.

The annual subscription, originally one guinea, had been increased to two guineas in 1846, three guineas in 1861 and to the controversial five guineas in 1868 (in an endeavour to reduce the annual deficit). Entrance fees were increased more quickly. Having started at two guineas, they were three guineas by 1846, five guineas by 1857 and eight guineas in 1860. In 1862 an entrance fee to be paid by non-yacht owners was introduced at twelve guineas which rose to twenty one in 1865 when yacht owners were charged fourteen guineas. In 1857 the Club's financial position was sound and improving, reaching a peak in 1863 when the favourable cash balance was £1420 exclusive of £4000 of 3% Consuls. This strengthening financial position had enabled the Club to donate trophies

RECEIPTS AND DISBURSEMENTS OF THE ROYAL THAMES YACHT CLUB,

FROM 2ND APRIL, 1845, TO 2ND APRIL, 1846.

Dr.				Cr.			
To Balance in hand	300	18	10	By Prizes given	265	0	0
„ 338 Subscriptions	374	17	0	„ Steam Vessels attending the Matches	175	0	0
„ 122 Entrance Fees	339	3	0	„ Other Expenses of the Matches	124	18	10
„ Tonnage Dues	16	2	0	„ New Anchors, Cables, Slip Ropes, and Flags	26	14	3
„ Admissions on board the Steam Vessels	204	0	0	„ Returned to the Stewards of the Ball their Reserve Fund	11	6	0
				„ Lighting the Club Room, British Hotel	10	0	0
				„ Ball Tickets, presented to Members of the Press and Secretary	5	5	0
				„ Housing Anchors, Cables, &c.	5	0	0
				„ Postage	31	11	4
				„ Printing	44	19	6
				„ Stationery	9	16	7
				„ Various Articles for the Use of Club Room	15	8	9
				„ Newspapers ditto	4	8	6
				„ Sundries	7	2	8
				„ Messenger's Salary	4	3	4
				„ Secretary's Salary and Allowance	86	12	0
					827	6	9
				Balance in hand*	407	14	1
		£1235	**0 10**		**£1235**	**0**	**10**

Audited by { J. J. FORD, J. HUTCHONS.

C. WHEELER,
Treasurer.

* Exclusive of Two Cups in the Hands of the Cup Bearer, value £90.

The Balance Sheet in 1846

for the Club's Sailing Matches worth some £140 in the 1840s, which increased to £500 - £600 in the 1860s. These extremely generous prizes did much to enhance the Club's prestige in both yachting and public circles.

The years of financial confidence to 1857 saw the Club making annual donations to several **CHARITIES**. In March 1846 a motion was carried *'That a Sum of Money, say £5, be set apart as an Annual Donation towards the Mariners and Fishermens Shipwreck Society for the purpose of giving Rewards to those of the Mariners and Fishermen on the Coasts of the United Kingdom who exert themselves in saving the Lives and Property of those who are cast away on the Coasts of England'*. The donation was increased to £10 in 1864.

The Great Exhibition of 1851 that was held in Hyde Park was the subject of discussion at a meeting of the Sailing Committee in July 1850 when it was resolved *'That it is expedient and likely to be very beneficial to the Club to adopt the views of the Commissioners of the Royal Exhibition 1851 by members providing for exhibition models of their vessels which have proved the superiority of their construction by winning prizes'*. A committee was appointed to implement this resolution and a subscription of £50 was made to the Exhibition. In January 1851 the Sailing Committee was amazed to receive a letter from the Metropolitan Commissioner saying *'... that in consequence of the very limited room assigned to 'Section Machinery' they deeply regret that it has been found impossible to concede the space demanded by you ...'*. Since the Club had been encouraged by the Commissioners to exhibit, they wrote a reply to Mr Scott Russell, the Exhibition Secretary: *'The Club, feeling there must be some mistake, beg to refer you to copies of previous correspondence on the subject'*. By February an undefined space had been allocated. Messrs James Hutchons and Charles R. Tatham of the appointed committee contacted selected members and yacht builders to provide models. The Club made available £25 for a Pedestal and Glass Case to cover the models and to pay for other expenses at the Exhibition. It is not clear how many models were exhibited but it is recorded that after the Exhibition the Glass Case was sold for £5.

In December 1854 the Club gave 50 guineas to 'The Royal Patriotic Fund' and agreed that any surplus arising from the Annual Ball should also go to that Fund. The nature of the Fund is not recorded but the date does suggest it might have served to support disabled from the Crimean War.

Another institution the Club supported from 1856 was the RNLI which was given an annual donation of £10. In a letter acknowledging with thanks the RTYC donation, the RNLI Secretary, Richard Lewis, informed the Club that one of its members had offered to pay half the cost of a Lifeboat, provided his co-members contributed the other moiety. In October the Club announced *'that the Subscription List in aid of presenting one of Peake's Lifeboats to the RNLI had successfully closed with the amount of £160.17.0'*. This first lifeboat named *'The Royal Thames Yacht Club'* was located at the Walmer Station and the RNLI reported in February 1857 that it had rescued the crew of the Barque 'Reliance' off Walmer Castle during the terrific gale on 5 December 1856. So began the Club's continuous support of the RNLI – support which is maintained today and provided in 1993 a major contribution towards the cost of the latest lifeboat to bear the Club's name. The other charitable institution supported by the Club from 1858 was 'The Seamens' Hospital Society'

on board the Dreadnought. An annual donation of £5 was approved, which sum was increased to £10 in 1866.

All three charitable institutions benefited in 1861 when the Annual Ball Stewards agreed *'to present contributions from the surplus in The Ball Fund that had accumulated in the past few years'*. £20 went to the RNLI, £20 to the Shipwreck Fishermen and Mariners' Royal Benevolent Society and £10 to the Seamens' Hospital Society.

The years 1857-1867 represented the phase of Club History which takes it from the date it acquired its first Clubhouse at 49 St. James's Street in July 1857 to the date of the formation of The New Thames Yacht Club in December 1867. While the club's finances peaked in 1863, they suffered an operating deficit of over £4000 between mid-1865 and the end of 1867 by which time all the 3% Consuls (which reached a maximum investment of £5750 by the end of 1863) had been sold and tradesmens' accounts were an acute embarrassment. To understand how such a rapid change in fortunes occurred it is necessary to look back over a period of 20 years and to trace the expansion of Club facilities and the broadening of members ambitions.

House Affairs

It was on 3 July 1845 at a meeting of the Club in the British Coffee House that Mr George Reynell gave notice of a motion proposing to appoint a *'Committee to consider the propriety and practicability of establishing a Club House for the use of the members and enable the Club to be better accommodated for the transaction of public business'*. It was four months before the motion was actually considered by a Club meeting by which time the instruction to the Committee had been expanded and required them to consider both temporary and permanent accommodation. A fortnight later members of the appointed committee met at the Piazza Hotel in Covent Garden.

The Committee's report prepared by Mr J.G. Reynell is recorded in full in Appendix 8 as a means of showing the forward thinking of members and as a delightful example of the eloquent, though perhaps verbose, written English of that period. A summary of the Committee's recommendations is *'that the present accommodation at the British Hotel* (when referring to the club's accommodation, there is a frequent interchange of its description either as the British 'Coffee House' or 'Hotel') *is not sufficient for the purposes of the club; that two rooms should be engaged, one for the monthly and special meetings and the other for general use by the members; that Mr Cuttriss, proprietor of the Piazza Hotel, would make available the Great Room of the Hotel for monthly meetings and a second room for members at a cost of £25 per annum. This arrangement was for one year certain'*.

The report was carried unanimously when the Club met on 4 December 1845 - at the Piazza Hotel. The report also shows that the committee recommended that the Club should not embark upon the considerable expense of a permanent Clubhouse until it had evaluated the true cost of a simple arrangement such as had been entered into at the Piazza Hotel.

It is of interest to note in the report the list of newspapers the committee proposed to provide - *'one morning and one evening paper of opposite politics and also three weekly sporting papers viz Bell's Life in London, The Era and The Sunday Times'*.

Start of RTYC Sailing Match from Greenwich (1848).

In concluding their report the committee felt bound to draw attention to the Club's finances. Although the Treasurer had considerable cash in hand, there had been a deficit in the year even though income had reached £700 and the membership had increased by 127. They recommended doubling the then current annual subscription of one guinea. The ready acceptance of this increase is in stark contrast to the high emotions that were generated by many members in 1867 at the proposal to increase subscriptions from 3 to 5 guineas – a proposal that was rejected.

In February 1846 the Commodore received a letter from the Secretary of the Blackwall Railway Company offering the Club use of the upper rooms at the Brunswick Pier on liberal terms. As was the custom, a small committee was appointed to consider the offer. The offer was accepted since it was deemed of value to extend the facilities available to members. Whether, in fact, members put the rooms to use is not apparent and probably they did not since the arrangement was terminated in December 1847.

The one year agreement for the use of the rooms at the Piazza Hotel was due to end on 4 December 1846. At the Club meeting early in November the Commodore, Lord Alfred Paget, advised those present that they must consider the Club's accommodation needs and added that the present terms would not be acceptable to Mr Cuttriss, the Proprietor, should the Club decide to remain at the Piazza Hotel. A committee of no less than 17 members was appointed to resolve the Club's course of action. So began the first of many a series of negotiations about charges for accommodation, all of which increased the Club's expenses though at the same time improving the quality of the facilities available to members. On this occasion the committee obtained quotations from five establishments but concluded that they should remain at the Piazza Hotel, since the quality of the refreshments, the services received and the high standard of

house kept by Mr Cuttriss could not be improved upon for the annual charge he now asked - £200! The new agreement included a revised (and lower) tariff of charges which it was felt would increase use of the Clubroom by members and also a list of improvements and refurbishment to be undertaken by Mr Cuttriss. Again, the agreement was for one year in the first instance.

By the time this new agreement had been concluded the Club had instituted a House Committee which could deal directly with Mr Cuttriss on all matters relating to the Clubroom. There were few recorded problems arising from use of the Piazza Hotel and the Club remained there until early 1851 when they moved to the nearby Bedford Hotel.

The six years when the Club used rooms at the Bedford Hotel were relatively trouble free. The House Committee (chaired by John G. Morgan) made regular reports to the Club and their recommendations were generally accepted. In July 1853 they were authorised to negotiate a two-year agreement with Mr Warren (of the Bedford Hotel) for accommodation at a rental not exceeding £300 per annum - another step towards increased expense.

The arrangement for renting rooms at the Bedford Hotel were due for review or renewal at midsummer 1857. In April that year the House Committee were *empowered to make such Clubhouse arrangements as they may deem advisable for a period of 2 years at a rental not exceeding £400 per annum'*. A month later the House Committee reported that on behalf of the Club they had taken 49 St. James's Street (at present occupied by the Sovereign Life Assurance Company) from midsummer next at the prescribed rental. The report was given unanimous support at the next General Meeting of the Club. This was the second 'turn of the screw' and added further to the Club's financial burden. This fact was well understood by the Officers of the Club as was shown at the June meeting of the Club when a motion proposed by Richard S. Wilkinson to increase the entrance fee from three guineas to five guineas was carried unopposed. The House Committee were only too well aware that additional expenses would not be confined to an increased rental. At a Special General Meeting in July they were authorised to expend up to £600 on the Clubhouse accommodation.

The Club was now established in its first true Clubhouse with a wide range of facilities available to members through-out the day. The membership increased to some 600 members and the importance of making full use of the Clubhouse was clearly understood by the House Committee. As an interesting aside it is noted that the Secretary was *'now required to be in attendance from 1400-1700, Monday to Friday, to receive subscriptions!'*

The Club was now thriving and its financial reserves in the form of 3% Consuls were increasing each year as was the membership which by mid-1859 had reached 750. While the Club's income was increasing, so too were the expenses. When the rental due from Midsummer's day 1859 was agreed it was set at £800 per annum - double the figure of two years earlier when 49 St James Street was taken over. In December the Club was informed by Mr Crockford, Proprietor of the Clubhouse, that they would shortly be given notice to quit on or before midsummer 1860.

At this time the annual subscription was still only two guineas, a figure set 14 years earlier but the entrance fee, set at five guineas in 1857, was again increased, this time to eight guineas from January 1860. The notice to quit 49 St James's Street duly arrived together with the information that should the club wish to renew the lease the rental would be increased from £800 to £1500 per annum.

The Club rejected these terms at its March meeting. That meeting was the occasion when the club first established a General Committee of Management comprising 21 members. The minutes of the meeting record that the 21 gentlemen were *'unanimously chosen'* but the reaction among those chosen was anything but unanimous, especially in respect of one gentlemen - Mr Henry Liggins who had been an elected member of the Club for less than two years. Five other chosen members declined to serve on the new Committee unless Mr Liggins resigned from it. A resolution was passed requesting that resignation. Initially Mr Liggins refused to resign from the General Committee but by May he had changed his mind, withdrew his threat to take legal proceedings and retracted the observations he had made about the five members - peace returned to the newly-formed General Committee of Management.

In the meantime the Club had placed an advertisement in The Times, The Morning Post, The Evening Advertiser and Bell's Life in London which declared *'Wanted a West End Club House'* and a Sub Committee of five had been appointed to manage the search. The Sub Committee needed to act quickly to consider the replies to the advertisement and by mid-April they recommended approaching Mr Grillion of the Clarendon Hotel, Bond Street with reference to his house at No 7 Albemarle Street. They resolved *'that an offer be made to Mr Grillion to pay him £1600 per annum rental, Mr Grillion to provide light, servants and attendance, Billiard Table and all things necessary for the purposes of the Club. Mr Grillion having the advantage of the payments for Billiards, Cards and Bedrooms'.* They also resolved *'that*

with a view to providing the necessary funds for this increased expenditure and also of enabling the Club to expend a proportionate sum upon Prizes and other yachting expenses, the subscription of members be increased from two guineas to three guineas from 1st January 1861'.

Mr Grillion's response to this offer was that the club should pay £1750 a year and provide their own plate at a sum not exceeding £500. At a Special General Meeting of the Club, on 30 April 1860, the proposition from Mr Grillion was unanimously approved together with the increased annual subscription. So opened seven of the most testing years in the history of the Club. These are recorded in some detail in the paragraphs that follow.

The House Committee were left with barely eight weeks in which to be ready to operate out of 7 Albemarle Street. Tickets for the Opening Dinner at the new Clubhouse were priced at one guinea including wine; the dinner tariff was set at 2/6; the charge for a bedroom was one guinea for a week or 4/- each night; the plate and property of the Club was insured for £1000. Mr James Hutchons, the Club Treasurer, signed the agreement with Mr Grillion. The Club in turn, indemnified him from all loss or damage that might arise.

The members of the General Committee and the House Sub Committee found they were having to meet much more fre-quently in order to deal with the problems arising from the acquisition of the new Clubhouse. With the numbers seeking membership increasing rapidly and in view of the need to increase income, the ceiling on membership numbers was raised to 900; a proposal to make available a Suggestion Book was defeated by one vote!; it was agreed that a urinal be placed in the washing room in place of the present chambers and the Hall Porter was instructed not to smoke his pipe outside the front door; he was later reprimanded for taking his meals in the Hall! The annual subscription to Mr Bull's Library was increased to £10 - no doubt the present Club Library benefited from that decision. For the billiards players there was also a bonus in that those who elected to play by candlelight in lieu of gas would pay no additional charge. Such was the business of the day.

So much for the detailed matters of the Club, matters typical of those items that made up the House Sub Committee's agenda. In October 1861 a letter to the Committee from Mr Charles Grillion included an item that constituted the first salvo in what was to be a prolonged battle rather than a brief skirmish. In essence the topic was *'how to operate the Clubhouse profitably and who should direct the operation - a manager or the Club'.* The letter opened pleasantly enough with Mr Grillion (through the manager, Mr Sian) agreeing to consider converting the card room into a third billiard room and also accepting that livery servants wear breeches. He then referred to that fact that during the first year at 7 Albemarle Street the operation of the Club to Midsummer 1861 had resulted in a very considerable loss. This he attributed to management expenses being larger than calculated and the need to employ additional staff to meet the expectations of the rapidly increasing membership. Not surprisingly he sought to revise the terms of the agreement. The House Committee's dismissive reply stated that *'they confidently hoped that a longer experience (of managing the Club) will prove the future to be more remunerative'.* In the meantime the Club approved another measure which would make a modest increase in its income - this was to require non-yachting owners to pay an entrance fee of twelve guineas instead of the eight guineas paid by yacht owners.

The Cumberland Fleet off Sheerness (1780).

Mr Grillion's next letter asked that his loss in 1860-61 of £500 be compensated for by increasing the annual rental to £2200, but the General Committee endorsed the House Committee's view that there should be no revision of rental until more operating experience had been gained. An alternative motion to increase the rental to £2000 was defeated as was a later motion to offer £250 compensation to Mr Grillion for the loss incurred. In February 1862 the Club appointed a Special Committee of five members, including the Treasurer, to employ a Solicitor to aid them in negotiations with Mr Grillion. Their report said that legally the arrangement (with Mr Grillion) was a valid and binding contract and that there should be no revision of contract unless Mr Grillion was prepared to give security against a recurrence of demands for increased rental. The General Committee accepted the report but said that they would consider a revision of the rental if the required security was offered. Yet a further attempt to offer Mr Grillion £250 compensation for loss was defeated by a small majority.

The General Committee was plied with further ammunition in April 1862 by a letter signed by 28 members of the Club complaining about the quality of the wines and spirits. A copy of the letter is at Appendix 9. This letter was passed to Mr Grillion; three members were appointed to discuss the matter with him. After a number of discussions and an exchange of letters, a final letter from the General Committee stated that *'they considered the supervision of the club and servants by The Manager was lax and deficient... and that the loss alleged to have been sustained by Mr Grillion has arisen from inefficient management'*. This terminated the first confrontation with the expectation that the management of the Club would improve and everyone would be satisfied.

The second phase of the 'battle', which had been preceded by more forays by Mr Grillion into the realm of increased rental payment, opened in October 1862 with a letter from the General Committee re-affirming that they would not accede to his requests for increased rental. On the other hand the Club would relieve Mr Grillion of his losses by taking over the running of the Club and would he propose terms for this arrangement. The response to this letter in November 1862 was that he would still prefer the present arrangement to

continue at increased rental but he would not stand in the way of the Club if they wished to have entire control over the premises. He assessed that with 14 years of the lease to run and the value of the furniture and fixtures, he would be seeking a sum in the order of £7500. These terms, the General Committee could not recommend to the Club. This second phase of the 'battle' was resolved in February 1863 when the Club agreed (by a 3 to 2 majority) that Mr Grillion should receive a bonus at the end of each year of £250 provided Clubhouse arrangements were carried out to the satisfaction of the committee; that Mr Grillion signed an endorsement to the Agreement that all plated articles purchased by him for use by the Club shall remain their use during the whole tenancy at no charge for repair but Mr Grillion to be paid £150 for use of the same; that Mr Grillion agree to a revised tariff as prepared by the House Sub Committee and allows the Club to select wines and spirits, while Mr Grillion may charge 25% on cost price for corkage and cellarage. These terms appear to have been accepted and a 'ceasefire' held for the remainder of 1863 - which is hardly suprising since the attention of the Club was focused on the debate over the re-election of Officers as recorded earlier in Section II.

The second half of 1863 saw the club proceeding through smoother waters. The rules of the club were re-written by a Sub Committee of seven members and the appropriate action was taken to transfer the club's investment into the names of the Trustees and to indemnify Mr Hutchons against claims within the terms of the agreement with Mr Grillion (which was signed by Mr Hutchons). This indemnity needed to cover the period to midsummer 1865, the date on which the tenancy could be determined in accordance with the Agreement. Notice of that determination was given on 6 January 1864.

At the first meeting of the General Committee in January 1864 the sum of £250 was paid to Mr Grillion and a reminder given that he must give attention in future to the supply of proper viands, cookery etc. In April Messrs T. Leach, J. Clark and Colonel J. Wilkinson were required to enquire into and report upon the most desirable method to keep the Books and Accounts of the club while Messrs G. Dumergue, C. Smart and Major J. Thomson were asked to discuss, with Mr Grillion, future terms for the lease of 7 Albemarle Street after the determination of the present agreement. The scene was thus set for the third phase of this 'battle' with Mr Grillion.

The discussions with Mr Grillion were of course, taking place after notice had been given to determine the tenancy. This situation inevitably gave Mr Grillion the opportunity to take the initiative in stating terms for selling the residue of his lease of 7 Albemarle Street together with the fixtures and fittings. Whereas in 1862 he had suggested a figure of £7500 he now sought £11,000 and made it clear that he was not willing under any terms to allow the Club's tenancy to continue after June 1865. The Sub Committee had been directed to consider acquiring either the freehold or the lease of 7 Albemarle Street or other suitable premises. Above all they were required to ensure that the Club would in future *'become the purveyor of provisions, wines, servants etc'.*

The Sub Committee invited the Club to consider the property at No 1 Albemarle Street at present occupied by The Albemarle Hotel - a property of similar floor area to No 7 - together with the adjacent shops fronting Piccadilly. The purchase price of No 1 Albemarle Street and the shops was £40,000 (including internal modification) which at 5% represented a rental of £2000 per annum. If the shops were allowed to continue they would produce £800 rental making a nett rental for the premises of £1200. The Sub Committee then reported that their investigations showed that if, as members have indicated, the club should control the 'house' matters then club income must increase from the current £4000 per annum to £6000. It was pointed out that this could be achieved, with the present limit on membership of 1000, by increasing the annual subscription from three to five guineas. If the limit was raised to 1200 the increase would be to four guineas. The General Committee resolved to seek approval from the Club at a Special Meeting to enter into a provisional agreement with Mr Schill for the purchase of the premises at a price not exceeding £32,000. Before that Special Meeting could take place the House Sub Committee had exchanged further letters with Mr Grillion, the Club offering to buy the outstanding lease for £9,000 and Mr Grillion responding with a request for £10,000.

The Quarterly General Meeting of the Club held on 18 January 1865 was chaired initially by Colonel Josiah Wilkinson (and later by the Commodore) who read to the 79 members present the report by the General Committee on accommodation and he was followed by Major (later Colonel) James Thomson who explained in detail the options available, in particular, the choice between purchase of a property and rental of furnished premises. After a protracted discussion Major Thomson moved *'that keeping in view the great aim and object of the Royal Thames Yacht Club viz: The encouragement of yachting and looking at the same time to the rights of non-yachting members - it is essential to the best interests and welfare of the Club, that a permanent Clubhouse should be maintained at the West End, in the best position and of the highest class compatible with the property and income of the Club'.* An amendment moved by Mr Arthur Otway to delete he word 'permanent' was defeated and Major Thomson's motion was carried by a large majority. The question of the Club accommodation was referred back to the General Committee *'with full power to enter into such provisional arrangement or agreement as they may deem most advantageous to the Club - such arrangement being the subject to the approval of a Special General Meeting of the Club to be called for the purpose'.*

In the six weeks that passed before the next Quarterly General Meeting of the Club, the General Committee met no less than five times with accommodation as the central topic of discussion, argument and counter argument. The first meeting was convened at the request of the Commodore to decide how to proceed following the Resolutions passed by the Quarterly General Meeting. Major Thomson moved that the Club should purchase premises and manage them themselves but an amendment moved by Mr Andrew Duncan that no house be purchased was carried by a single vote. A week later the Commodore read to the General Committee *'the friendly opinion of a lawyer to the effect that the Trustees had not the power to dispose of the trust funds of the Club if there were one litigious member of the Club who objected to such disposition'.* By the time of the third meeting the sharp division between members of the General Committee, with respect to Club accommodation, had been heightened by a letter written to Lord Alfred Paget and signed by six members including Major Thomson. The contents of the letter are revealing in that they show the frustration felt by the signatories, all of whom were members of the General Committee and, all but one, members of the House Sub Committee, who for eight months had been involved in negotiations for a future Clubhouse. They were rigorously opposed to the 'amendment' carried at the last meeting of the General Committee and they made the point that it was diametrically opposed to the Resolutions passed by members at the General Meeting - and if persevered in cannot fail to cause dissatisfaction and dissension in the Club. Coupling the content of the 'amendment' with Counsel's opinion in respect of use of trust funds they pressed that either the amendment be rescinded or the whole issue must be referred back to a Special General Meeting of members; the former course being their true wish together with the hope that the Commodore would not stand by counsel's opinion. Lord Alfred Paget's reply was concentrated on his belief that as the Principal Officer of the Club and as a Trustee he would *'not feel authorised to surrender the sum of money which has now been accumulating for many years for any other object than that for which it was originally destined viz Yachting purposes ..... without, in the first instance obtaining the sanction of each and every member .....'.*

These two letters are probably the first documented record of use of the word 'dissension'. James Thomson had joined the Club in 1857 and at that time he owned a 40 Ton schooner. He was therefore a yachting member but he was also a member who joined the club after the date it moved into its first comprehensive Clubhouse in St James's Street. The other emotive element of these letters was Lord Alfred Paget's assertion that the accumulated funds were destined to be used for yachting purposes. This must be open to question since the majority of Club funds invested in 3% Consuls had accrued since 1857, but it was also true that the Commodore's over-riding motivation was the welfare of the Club and complying with the wishes of the members. There is no doubt, however, that the seeds of dissent had been sown though at the time they cannot have foreseen the subsequent events of December 1867, less than three years hence.

At the fourth meeting of the General Committee Major Thomson's motion to rescind the amendment was defeated as was a more flexible motion by Mr Henry Birch (one of the six signatories) which sought approval to rent or purchase the lease of 7 Albemarle Street or purchase other premises (eg 1 Albemarle Street) and use accumulated funds for that purpose. Once again it was the motion of Mr Andrew Duncan that was successful when he sought approval for Mr James Goodson to negotiate with the Charing Cross Hotel Company for suitable accommodation at a rental not exceeding £1500 per annum. This, however, did not help in the search for suitable accommodation as the Hotel Company could not provide what the Club required. The General Committee therefore asked Captain Frederick Clarkson (recently elected to the Committee) to see Mr Grillion and once again discuss terms. It can hardly have come as a surprise when Mr Grillion reiterated the terms that he had sought earlier viz no tenancy and £10,000 for the residual 11 years lease and the fixtures and fittings. With those once again on the table, the Committee set them aside and placed an advertisement for suitable accommodation in the Times and the Telegraph.

It was Mr Arthur O. Wilkinson who chaired the fifth meeting of the General Committee on 27 February 1865 and heard read the replies to the advertisement - no doubt with some dismay, for after a lengthy debate the Committee resolved to report to the General Meeting of the Club two days later that they *'have not yet arrived at any determination with regard to a permanent Clubhouse. They felt it right, moreover, to state that the difficulties in the way of obtaining a House are very great and such as the Committee apprehend can hardly be appreciated by those who have not been party to the enquires and discussions which have taken place on the subject. As it therefore appears impossible to obtain such premises before the expiration of the lease of the present Clubhouse, the Committee recommend the Club to empower them to enter into an Agreement for the rental of furnished Premises for a term not exceeding one year during which time the Committee will use their best endeavours to carry out the Resolution passed by the Club at their last General Meeting'.* Quite extraordinarily, the minutes of that General Meeting record only the Report and there appears to have been no reaction to its content.

Time was rapidly running out if a solution to the accommodation problem was to be found. When the General Committee met on 30 March 1865 it was agreed that Mr A.O. Wilkinson should be authorised to treat with Mr Grillion for the rental of No. 7 Albemarle Street for the remaining 11 years of his lease at a rent of £850 and to agree for purchase of the furniture, linen and plate at a valuation. Four weeks later the Club increased its offer to £1000 and agreed to appoint Messrs Williams and James, Solicitors, to act for them in drawing up an agreement. A Special General Meeting of the Club held on 30 May carried unanimously the motion proposing acceptance of the terms negotiated by Mr A. O. Wilkinson and authorising the use of so much of the Trust Funds as may be required to purchase the furniture. Immediately after that meeting the Commodore chaired a meeting of the General Committee and appointed a Sub Committee of nine *'to consider the best mode of conducting the Coffee Room and House Department'.*

With this Resolution carried the Commodore might well have hoped that his problems were over but this was not to be the case. The solicitors made the new lease agreement available to a meeting of the General Committee on 2 October, a meeting specially convened by Lord Alfred Paget and Colonel Josiah Wilkinson in their capacity as Trustees. While they as Trustees were willing to execute the lease, the third Trustee, Mr James Hutchons, was not and therefore resigned, Mr Henry W Birch being elected Trustee in his place. The meeting concluded by authorising the raising of £3000 from the Club's holding of £5750 of 3% Consols to pay for the valuation cost of furniture

and other club expenses. This was the first step towards the depletion of the Club's finances.

The conflict between the Club and Mr Grillion was once again in full swing with the Club withholding payment (as a bargaining strength in the accommodation negotiations) and Mr Grillion threatening dire consequences. The next meeting of the General Committee two weeks later heard, in his absence, the content of a letter from Colonel James Thomson referring to an earlier letter from the Club's solicitors saying that Mr Grillion had served a Bankruptcy summons on the Secretary, Captain Grant, for £3,006, the alleged amount of the valuation. The solicitors advised that the only way to dispose of the summons was by the immediate advance to Mr Grillion of £2,600 pending the actual execution of the lease by the Trustees. If this was not done Mr Grillion intended to have the whole affair reported in the newspapers. Colonel Thomson, in his letter, had sought approval for the action he had taken (payment of the £2,600) - approval that was readily given by the General Committee. Mr Grillion was also demanding payment of rent due at Michaelmas, but the Finance Sub Committee, now part of the House Sub Committee, declined to pay until Mr Grillion had removed his stock of wines from the cellar of the Club, thus giving the Club full possession of its property.

There can be no doubt that both Lord Alfred Paget and Colonel Thomson were earnestly endeavouring to do all they could for the benefit of the Club and yet there does seem to have been some element of friction between them. The last meeting of the General Committee had been adjourned; when it was reconvened on 24 October 1865 with the Commodore in the chair, a letter from Colonel Thomson was read in which he stated that he had been summoned to attend the meeting in his capacity as a member of the House Sub Committee from which Sub Committee no reports had been received by the General Committee since 29 June. He had been instructed to report on the accommodation arrangements made and to provide an estimate of future expenses of the establishment. He then made the point in his letter that the General Committee has received no minutes of House Sub Committee meetings because, on 30 May, they had superseded its function by appointing nine members to a Special Committee. The central section of the letter might well be described as petulant but equally it is not difficult to imagine the frustration felt by Colonel Thomson. He reminds the General Committee that his views as to the best mode of carrying out the wishes and promoting the interests of the Club are different from the majority of members of the Committee and that the calling of this meeting to discover, as a matter of urgency, the arrangements made, begs the question of why no such meeting had been called in the four months since the *'Special Committee of Nine'* (which included Colonel Thomson) had been appointed on 30 May. The Committee immediately rescinded the Resolution of 30 May, re-instated the original House Sub Committee and expressed their support for all that Colonel Thomson had done, leaving the solicitors to resolve the problem of the quarters rent and Mr Grillion's wine stock.

Over the next few weeks there were indications that the Club's financial position was under some stress as shown by disagreement as to whether accounts should or even could be paid. For all that the Quarterly General Meeting of the Club held in January 1866 with Colonel Josiah Wilkinson in the chair passed without noticeable difficulty and it even included a Resolution *'that the warm thanks of the Club be presented to Colonel James Thomson for the great attention paid by*

Match Race between DON GIOVANNI and SPITFIRE (1824)

him to the interests of the Club.' (It was the last Quarterly meeting, as they resolved to hold in future just a single Annual General Meeting in March).

The financial pressures continued with the result that by mid-February 1866 the General Committee resolved to sell further of the 3% Consuls making the total sold £4000. In addition Colonel Thomson sought approval for the House Sub Committee *'to draw from the Club Funds such sums of money as may be necessary for the payment of servants and other expenses of the Club, such sum not to exceed £1200 from midsummer last'.*

At this stage it is of interest to note some of the expenses to which the Club was committed as well as some of the charges made by the Club early in 1866. The Club Manager, Mr W. Reynolds was paid £156 per annum, The Secretary, Captain Grant, received £280 per annum while the Cellarman's pay was increased from £18 to £21 per annum. Plain breakfast charge was reduced from one shilling and sixpence to one shilling and threepence but there was a surcharge of one shilling for breakfast in bed. The bedroom charge was still four shillings per night or one guinea per week. The table charge in the Coffee Room was increased from sixpence to ninepence and in the Strangers Dining Room from one shilling to one shilling and sixpence. The charges for food and wine were modest and indeed members expected them to be so. On the other hand there was a steady flow of complaints about the quality of meals, wines and servants and a standard sought that the charges made could not finance - not least because the annual subscription was still a mere three guineas as it had been since 1861.

The spring of 1866 saw the Club engrossed in the details of the Sailing Programme for that season and that must have been a breath of fresh air to the hard-pressed Officers and Committee members. In the summer the House and General Committees were largely devoted to the affairs of Mr George Waugh, a member of six years seniority, while the autumn brought back the dark clouds of financial stress.

The exchange of letters between Mr Waugh and the Secretary (on behalf of the House Sub Committee) started in May 1866 when Mr Waugh complained that the Club Manager had not only prevented him from bringing a large package into the Club but had also been rude when addressing him. The Committee's response was that the manager was complying with instructions in not admitting the package and that any impertinence shown by him *'was provoked by your own conduct'.* They also reminded him that he was following the unacceptable practice of not paying his Coffee Room bills. In addition, they had received many complaints from and of him and they wished this to stop. By early June the House Committee were expressing their regret at the offensive nature of his letters and threatened to take the matter to the General Committee. Two weeks later Colonel Thomson, as Chairman of the House Sub Committee, informed the General Committee that Mr Waugh *'had again conducted himself in a manner unbecoming a gentleman and member of the Club'.* It seems that he was in the billiard room in the early hours of the morning with other members and in spite of remonstrances by the Billiard Marker he had persisted in jumping up and down on a settee and ultimately it broke in two! The General Committee then wrote to Mr Waugh seeking confirmation of his intention to resign. Mr Waugh had by now moved from his London address with the result that communications were cut until September, by which time emotions had quietened and the whole affair might have ended without recrimination but for another letter of complaint from a member, that Mr Waugh had, in the Billiard Room, called him a liar and a scoundrel and threatened to throw him over the bannisters and out of the window. Added to this he had, the previous night, acted like a madman, throwing himself on a couch and using disgusting and blasphemous language. Not surprisingly, Mr Waugh was expelled from membership of the Club, but it was gratifying to note from the content of many letters sent to him, that his conduct was entirely the exception.

The Club still maintained its funds in an account at Coutts in the Strand but the House funds were now in a separate account at the City Bank. This was a sensible and logical arrangement but, as the expenses of operating the House built up, there was inevitably pressure to transfer money to the House account. In the year to midsummer 1866 this transfer amounted to a total of £1200. In August a further £400 had to be transferred and in September the General Committee authorised selling sufficient of the remaining £1750 of 3% Consuls to raise £1000 to pay House bills. Among the many expenses to be met were £624 to paint and redecorate the Clubhouse and £105 for new furniture. The House Committee were now struggling to control the operation of the 'House Department' which increasingly was running at a deficit. The control of purchases for the kitchen was at times the responsibility of the Club Manager and at other times of the Chef but neither could produce a profit.

In January 1867 the House Committee resolved to ask Mr S Neale Driver, a member of the Committee, *'to ascertain from Messrs Buckton and Rowlett, Accountants, their charge for balancing the books of the club to 31st December last'*. In February it was reported that Mr Grillion was now a bankrupt and agents for the proprietor of 7 Albemarle Street were requesting payment of the rent due to have been paid by Mr Grillion - this was paid out of the Club funds as was the sum of £450 on account, to the Club Manager to meet some of his expenses. The Committee now instructed Messrs Buckton and Rowlett to draw up a profit and loss account for the House and Coffee Room 'departments'. The House Committee were already having to defer payment of certain accounts. By the end of February the Accountants produced a statement showing that in the eighteen months since the House had been under Club control there was an accrued deficit of £2424. In March the finance element of the House and Finance Sub Committee were critical of Sailing Match expenses in 1866 and they were seeking to impose a lower limit in 1867. Whilst it could be said that the sum spent on prizes in 1866 (£600) was double that spent 10 years earlier, there had been no dramatic increase over the previous years, indeed the increase had been no more than steady throughout. Nevertheless, this criticism, justified or not, was yet another source of division and dissension in the minds of members.

Colonel Thomson now arranged a formal meeting with the Club Manager, Mr Reynolds and as a result the latter tendered his resignation since he found that *'he had failed to give satisfaction'*. In his letter of resignation he drew attention to matters over which he had no control and which lessened profits viz: the high price of provisions; the reduction in the tariff for spirits and wines and the consumption of the latter for cooking and other purposes. On 12 March the House Committee decided to recommend to the General Committee

that the annual subscription be raised *'to such an extent as may meet the deficiency'*. No action was taken before the AGM on 27 March at which it was decided to defer action as regards the accounts until they had been circulated to all members showing what money had been received and expended over the period 30 June 1865 to 31 December 1866. The AGM was adjourned until the 24 April.

During those four weeks the General Committee resolved to recommend that the annual subscription should be increased from three guineas to five guineas. The reconvened AGM decided that the General Committee's resolution should be sent as a circular to every member urging them to signify their agreement to or opposition to the proposed increase in subscription. Several other motions were put to the meeting concerning the Balance Sheet, all seeking to take action to halt the deficit, but the only one that was carried by the 80 members present by a majority of 12 expressed *'regret at the loss sustained in the Manager's department and requested the Committee to adopt more economical management and report the results attained up to the 29 September to a Special Meeting to be called about the middle of November'*.

This mild resolution belied the tension, concern and dissension among many members but it was evident to all who studied the accounts that strong positive action was essential to restore the club's finances to a healthy state. If that had been the only bone of contention the events at the end of 1867 might not have occurred but that was not the position; too many members were dissatisfied with the management of the club and feared that its principal aim - to encourage yachting - was being sacrificed for those members whose sole interest lay in the social and dining aspects of the Club. Over the next six months the Commodore and the Committee did all that they could to stem the increasing operating deficit and to keep every member fully aware of their actions.

By May Mr Neale Driver appears to have succeeded Colonel James Thomson as chairman of the House and Finance Sub Committee while Colonel Josiah Wilkinson brought experience and conciliatory guidance to his chairmanship of the General Committee. When the latter met on 8 May they were advised by Mr Driver that annual Club expenditure exclusive of the House Department would continue to average £3120 while average income would be £3700. In the House Department the wages and keep for the servants amounted to some £1500 per annum but there was no profit from the 'provisions' except on wine, cigars and beds. In their quest for more economical management and being without a Manager, the Secretary was instructed to superintend Mr Grocock, the Head Waiter, while he provisionally acted as Steward. They also called for the most stringent measures to be taken to obtain payment of the annual subscription from the 400 members in arrears. Finally, they authorised the services of a professional accountant to provide a quarterly balance sheet. In June, in order to pay for the prizes given in the 1867 Sailing Matches it became necessary to sell the residual 3% Consuls. By the end of July Colonel Wilkinson and the General Committee, having examined the statements prepared by the Accountants (which showed the House Department having a £582 deficit for the first quarter of 1867 and £417 in the second quarter leading to an estimated annual deficit of £1360) decided that the Special General Meeting must be brought forward to 17 October and a circular prepared for issue to members (see Appendix 10).

In the event 170 members attended the Special General Meeting which was chaired by the Commodore, Lord Alfred Paget. It was Colonel Josiah Wilkinson who addressed the meeting; read a statement prepared by Messrs Buckton & Co, Professional Accountants showing that with a subscription of five guineas from 800 members, the club could be maintained upon its present footing, without exceeding its income. He therefore proposed the increase, a motion seconded by Mr S.N. Driver. An amendment by Mr John Clark, seconded by Mr Arthur Otway MP that the increase apply only to members elected 'after this date' attracted only 9 votes and the original motion was carried by a large majority.

Thus ended what was almost certainly the most difficult and acrimonious period in the entire history of the Club. By the end of December over 170 members had resigned and the actual operating deficit at £1732 was significantly higher than forecast, due entirely to a drop in subscription income of £477 compared with 1866.

The General Committee met on 2 December 1867 to hear the Commodore refer to 'a meeting antagonistic to the Royal Thames Yacht Club having been held on 25 November 1867 at the Freemasons Tavern by certain members of the Club'.

The Committee resolved 'to take no notice' but two weeks later Mr J.D. Lee (who in 1863 had been proposed for the office of Vice Commodore of the RTYC) who had chaired the meeting on 25 November was able to issue a circular referring to the decisions taken that day to form the New Society encouraging Yachting Building and Sailing on the Thames and adding that already 120 gentlemen had indicated their interest to join this New Society including owners of 40 yachts of an aggregate tonnage exceeding 2,200 tons. This society was to be designated The New Thames Yacht Club; an expensive establishment was not contemplated; entrance fee for the first 200 members was three guineas and for subsequent members five guineas; annual subscription was two guineas. The many experienced members of the RTYC now set about putting into practice the lessons learned to the benefit of the new club whose blue burgee, most pointedly, was defaced by a gold phoenix.

The blood letting was over and Lord Alfred Paget was able to lead the Club successfully into the 1870s though financial recovery was not achieved quickly due to the severe drop in membership and the continuing reluctance of too many members to pay their subscription, irrespective of the cost to the Club.

VI
The New Thames Yacht Club

The years during which this club was founded, prospered and then was wound up are, by definition, those which come after the period covered by this volume and it may, therefore, seem inappropriate to include a section about the NTYC. The justification for its inclusion is that the satisfactory progress of the new club was largely achieved by gentlemen who had already contributed much to the Royal Thames and it is of interest to continue to follow their activites.

The circumstances which led to the foundation of the New Thames YC have already been described. From the initial meeting at the Freemason's Tavern, Great Queen's Street on 25 November 1867 further meetings were held at that establishment during which Mr John D. Lee was appointed as Chairman of the Committee while Mr Richard S. Wilkinson was appointed Honarary Secretary and Treasurer. On 3 February 1868 Mr Lee informed the general meeting of the club members that he was confident that a (unnamed) noble lord would accept the post of Commodore. Meanwhile, the meeting appointed Mr Lee to the post of Vice Commodore which he accepted for the time being (and until the Commodore's wishes were known). It was also agreed that until a suitable clubhouse was acquired there was no need to appoint a Secretary. Lastly, the Laws and Regulations for the Club were approved and a Sailing Committee was appointed. A House Committee was also formed and authorised to find accommodation suitable for a clubhouse.

When the club met in March 1868, the Vice Commodore informed the members that while the deputation who waited upon 'the noble lord', now identified as Lord Colville (a member of the government), had been kindly received, his lordship regretted he did not have the necessary spare time that would enable him to accept the appointment. Thus the appointment of a Commodore was set aside for a while. In April arrangements were made for the Club's first sailing matches to be held in June, the first for cutters and the second for schooners. By May the Club had received an Admiralty Warrant to fly a defaced blue ensign; the details for the management of the Club had been established (on lines very similar to those current in the RTYC) and the Club's overiding objective - to promote yacht racing on the Thames - was being energetically pursued by members (largely ex-RTYC) who were among the most successful yachtsmen who raced on the Thames and its estuary. The NTYC was what might be described as a small version of the RTYC but with yachting as it's dominant activity - as had been that of the RTYC until the 1850s. By July the Club had a bank balance in excess of £1000 and with it came the feeling of security and success - much of it due to the drive and skill of both John Lee and Richard Wilkinson.

In October 1868 the Club was still without its own accommodation and its meetings continued in the Freemasons Tavern. In spite of that a Mr F A White was appointed as Secretary with a salary of £60 per annum plus 5% of all funds received for entrance fees, subscriptions and steamboat tickets. In December 1868 the Club took rooms in the Caledonian Hotel, Adelphi as their headquarters at an annual rental of £300 and held their first meeting on 14 January 1869, by which time the membership was some 223. A year later, in December 1869, the Club made two important decisions. Firstly Mr J.D. Lee was appointed Commodore and Mr W.N. Rudge, Vice Commodore. Secondly, agreement was reached to amalgamate the NTYC and the Union Yacht Club in Gravesend for a period not exceeding two years. The appointments were confirmed in January 1870 and the NTYC (House Committee) first met at the Union YC Clubhouse at Gravesend in April. The NTYC, however, retained its use of rooms at the Caledonian Hotel at a rental of £10 per month. In May, the Secretary of the Royal Thames was offered admission to the Gravesend Clubhouse as an Honorary Member.

By 1871 the Club's membership was approaching 400; the sum of £375 was made available for sailing match prizes and the dates for the Club's sailing matches were decided - in conjunction with the Flag Officers of the Royal Thames and Royal London Yacht Clubs (an early indication of the close liaison established between the breakaway New Thames Yacht Club and the Royal Thames). The programme for 1871 comprised two matches for cutters, one for schooners and yawls and an 'Ocean Match' from Harwich to Gravesend. Not surprisingly the Flag Officers and Committee members were still predominantly former members of the Royal Thames but one name that had already come to the fore was that of Robert Hewett who was to become a Flag Officer of both the New Thames and Royal Thames yacht clubs in later years.

A letter from the Commodore, NTYC dated 11 April 1872 and addressed to the Board of Trade provides an interesting insight into a practice current at that time. It said *'I am informed by the Surveyor of Customs that by clauses in the Merchant Shipping Act 1871, it is required that the names of vessels and their draft of water be marked on their bow and stern and that the yacht now building for me by Mr John White at Cowes is not exempt. I am also informed that your Honorable Board have under the powers and authority vested in them, kindly granted exemption to all the craft belonging to the Royal Yacht Squadron. I very respectfully request that they will graciously be pleased to grant similar license to the vessels belonging to the New Thames Yacht Club, the tonnage of which already exceeds 10,000 tons'.*

New Thames Yacht Club Clubhouse, Gravesend.

Sadly, there is no record of the response by the Board of Trade, but it must be likely that it was favourable.

The Club, like many other yacht clubs, spent many hours discussing the question of Measurement of yachts. In April 1874 the Committee approved a proposal that tonnage for measurement purposes should be the product of length, breadth and depth divided by 200 - notwithstanding the general acceptance of Thames Measurement since 1854. This decision was not well received by members and was twice referred back to the Sailing Committee to be reconsidered. (The Club reverted to Thames Measurement in November 1876). It seems probable that it was this apparent *'lack of confidence'* that precipitated in October 1875, the resignation of the Commodore and Vice Commodore. This action quickly closed the ranks among members, who proclaimed their support for the two Officers who, therefore, withdrew their resignations and were re-elected to Office in February 1876 - at which meeting a Rear Commodore was appointed for the first time, Thomas Weeding Weeding.

The division of the Club over the question of measurement would not go away. At a General Meeting of the Club held 13 December 1876 and chaired by Mr William Lake, all the Club Officers and the Sailing Committee tendered their resignations and these were accepted. Two months later A.O. Wilkinson Esq was elected Commodore, W.N. Rudge Esq and T.W. Weeding Esq re-elected Vice Commodore and Rear Commodore and H.J. Baker Esq was elected Treasurer.

The links between the Club and the Royal Thames continued to develop and many yachtsmen were members of both clubs. Lord Afred Paget (then Vice Commodore RTYC) was elected an honorary member of the NTYC in July 1879. In January 1878 a Sub Committee was appointed by each club with the object of assimilating the Sailing Rules of the two clubs. A new joint code was approved in April 1878.

The membership of the Club now stood at 431; the balance sheet was in a healthy state and the Club's sailing matches were highly respected and offered substantial prizes - in short, the Club was already very successful after only 10 years since its foundation. It is interesting to note that the Club's accounts were exclusive of the operation of the Clubhouse at Gravesend which was the financial responsibility of the Clubhouse Manager, Mr Bedford, who leased the property from the Earl Darnley. It is also interesting to note that the original objectives of the Club were still being fulfilled - the funds available for sailing match prizes was now over £600 each year, the largest single item of expense in the club accounts, the next highest being the Clubhouse rental.

In November 1880, R S Wilkinson Esq resigned his membership of the Club. In his earlier days he had been a tower of strength as a member of the Royal Thames but was among the disillusioned who left in 1867 to form the New Thames. Here again as Honorary Treasurer he was in the fore of those who established the club on a sound footing but he was also among the many who resigned office in 1876 and who, in spite of a request from the membership, was not prepared to be re-elected. He had again found himself in the midst of divisive issues and felt he should withdraw.

In February 1881 another NTYC member who was to achieve fame as a member of the Royal Thames, was elected to their Sailing Committee - Theodore Pim, who was a Royal Thames Flag Officer for 22 years including 19 years as Commodore from 1905. Also on the Sailing Committee of the New Thames at that time was Robert Hewett, whom Theodore Pim succeeded in the offices of both Rear and Vice Commodore of the Royal Thames.

The death in 1881 of Mr William Rudge, the Vice Commodore, brought to that office E. Boutcher Esq, owner of the highly successful cutter FIONA, the tiller of which, with its greyhound finial, hangs on the main staircase of the Royal Thames. (By the time of election as Vice Commodore of the New Thames, Mr Boutcher owned an equally successful schooner, *FIONA*).

In 1882 the Club followed the lead given by the Royal Thames and decided to adopt the Sailing Regulations of the Yacht Racing Association. The two clubs were again brought together later in the year when the Royal Thames held a meeting with other clubs and the YRA to consider how to increase the number of entries for Matches held on the Thames and its estuary during the 1883 season.

While the sailing activities of the Club proceeded smoothly and successfully, affairs at the Clubhouse were thrown into disarray in mid 1882 when the Clubhouse Manager went into liquidation shortly before his lease on the property from Earl Darnley terminated. As so often happens when such problems arise, a member comes to the fore to advise and guide the Club. On this occasion, that member was a solicitor named Edward Hilder, a member of the House Committee (and later, a member of the General Committee of the Royal Thames). By the end of the year the Club had acquired a seven year lease on the Clubhouse from Earl Darnley and eleven Club members had guaranteed the cost of purchasing the Club-house furniture and effects. Although this stabilised the Club's affairs it was in fact, the beginning of a period of 26 years during which they were never fully able to re-establish the success of the heady years that followed the founding of the Club. The root of the Club's problems was that the Clubhouse was never profitable and the subscription income could not cover both the cost of the sailing matches and losses made in running the Clubhouse, not least because of a falling membership which, after reaching a peak of 447 in 1875, had dropped to 289 by 1885 and after which year the numbers gradually reduced.

In spite of the problems in the operation of the Clubhouse, the Club's sailing matches continued to attract the leading yachts of the day, but they were concentrated into two days. One day was a 'Channel Match' from Southend to Harwich - often comprising three races for different classes - while the other was a 'River Match' and again open to a number of classes. Prizes were given thanks to the generosity of members who contributed to a prize fund or presented individual trophies; the town of Gravesend also presented prizes. In 1893 the German Emperor's yacht METEOR won the Channel Match (her first victory in UK waters) with the Prince of Wales' BRITANNIA third (in 1894 and in 1895 she won both the Channel and River Matches).

Notwithstanding the pressures on the Club due to lack of funds, the more stalwart members never lost their enthusiasm to keep the Club alive. In 1886 they suspended payment of an entrance fee as a means of encouraging more yachtsmen to join the Club; they constantly sought rent reduction from Earl Darnley; in 1887 a joint committee was formed with the Royal Thames to consider amalgamation of the Clubs, but nothing came of it. By September 1898 it was proposed to wind up the Club but following a Special General Meeting a committee was formed to investigate the chances of the Club continuing to function.

The investigating committee recommend that the Club should continue. A House and Finance Committee was formed to handle Club affairs with its own bank account (the Honorary Treasurer, to continue to manage the bank account into which subscriptions were paid); Trustees were appointed to look after the Club property; it was decided to issue £10 Debentures attracting 5% interest up to a total of £500 and it was agreed to capitalise the fixtures and fittings. In spite of all the energy that was put into attempts to make the club financially sound, the new arrangements did little more than stem the outflow of funds. The death of three Flag Officers between 1903 and 1906 was particularly unfortunate though the Honorary Treas-urer, H J Baker Esq, remained in office from 1881 through to the end (a full list of Club Officers is at Appendix 11).

The death of Earl Darnley in 1901 led to the sale of the Clubhouse to new proprietors in 1906 and although the Club was offered a new lease on an annually renewable basis, the Club's future was bleak since the property was on what had become commercially exploitable land. The consequence was that the owner decided in October 1908 to build a new wharf opposite the Clubhouse. A special General Meeting of the Club on 7 November 1908 was told that there were insupera-ble difficulties in moving to a new site *'and the members agreed that there was no alternative to closing the club when lease expired on 31 December 1908'*. The planned sailing programme for 1909 was abandoned, all debenture holders were able to redeem their investment and all debts were settled - an honourable ending to a short-lived but successful yacht club which found itself in the grip of unre-lenting social and commercial change.

VII
Club Treasures

The Club is particularly fortunate to possess a fine collection of marine paintings and silver trophies. The majority of the paintings of yachts and many of the trophies have a direct connection with the Club and are an integral part of its history. During the period 1823-1867 yachts owned by members and which raced on the Thames, in the Thames estuary and further afield, are shown in some 23 prints at present hanging in various rooms of the Clubhouse. Unfortunately, very few of the large number of silver cups and trophies given by the Club in this period are still in the Club's possession - perhaps over the years a few more will find their way back to the Club when grandmothers' attics are cleared.

Prints of Yachts

Those who own a copy of the book described as an *'Illustrated Catalogue of Prints, Portraits and Oil Paintings in the Clubhouse of the Royal Thames Yacht Club'* which was compiled by Major B Heckstall-Smith (by Order of the Committee) over the period 1935-1938, will already have available much of the information given here, but for the sake of completeness in putting this history together, a modest measure of repetition for some readers can be offset by providing others with a simple guide to these prints. All relate to yachts which competed in RTYC matches in the period 1823-1867. Nearly all the vessels were owned by RTYC members.

Pearl (113 Tons). This print by Lanck shows her winning her match on 28 July 1825. She was owned by the First Marquis of Anglesey (father of Lord Alfred Paget) who, as Lord Uxbridge, commanded the Cavalry at the Battle of Waterloo. During the Battle he had a leg shot away and earned the soubriquet 'One Leg'.

Lady Louisa (13 Tons). Owned by Thomas Smith Esq is shown winning a £30 Cup in a 'below bridge' match held on 23 June 1832. She was a carver-boat, carved out of the solid. He was a very successful owner winning his first Thames Trophy in 1825 in an 'above bridge' match for a £30 Cup. His other successes 'below bridge' were a 50 guineas Cup given in honour of the Duke of Clarence becoming Patron in 1827, £30 Cup in 1829, £30 Cup in 1831 given to mark their Majesties' Coronation and another £30 Cup in 1834.

Brilliant (18 Tons) is shown in this lithograph by G. Rogers Snr winning one of the two cups given by the Club's Patron, King William IV to mark his accession to the throne. The Cups of 50 guineas and 25 guineas were competed for by first class vessels (over 10T) and second class vessels (under 10T) respectively over a 'below bridge' course from Greenwich to Gravesend and back on 28 August 1830. *BRILLIANT* was owned by W O Buckwell Esq. She was later a winner of a 25 guineas Cup in 1832 in an 'above bridge' race from Southwark Bridge to Wandsworth and back to Westminster when owned by Lord Cholmondeley. By 1838 she was owned by J.T. Hewes Esq who won a £25 Cup 'below bridge' and a £30 Cup 'above bridge' from the Temple Gardens to Wandsworth and back.

Alarm (18 Tons) owned by Thomas Wanhill Esq, boat builder from Poole, is shown winning a £25 Cup in a 'below bridge' match from Greenwich to Coal House Point and back in June 1840.

Sea Nymph (10 Tons) in this print by G Lowe is shown winning the Cutter Match (2nd Class) on 29 May 1841 for a prize of a £30 Silver Salver. She was owned by Charles Wheeler Jnr. She won other prizes in RTYC Matches in June 1842 and July 1843 valued at £20, £25 and £30. All the matches were sailed from Greenwich to Coal House Point.

Mystery (25 Tons) was one of the earliest yachts to be built of iron and was owned by Lord Alfred Paget. In her first season she won a £40 prize in June 1842 and in May 1843 won the £50 Cup in a match depicted in the oil painting by N M Condy in the Edinburgh Room of the present Clubhouse, when *BLUE BELLE* went aground at Tulse Point. Her performance in 1844 was exceptional. She won a £50 RTYC trophy in May and the 100 guineas Grand Challenge Cup in June, while in August Lord Alfred Paget led a fleet of RTYC vessels to the Solent and won a prize put up by the RYS for a sailing match competed for in weather conditions which kept most Solent-based yachts in harbour.

Phantom (20 Tons) shown in this lithograph by T.G. Dutton, was originally owned by Arthur O. Wilkinson Esq. In June 1944 he won the match from Gravesend to the Nore Light and back for which the prize was a painting by the Club Artist N M Condy. A month later he won another match from which he was at the centre of the controversy over a protest by the second finisher, *MYSTERY* owned by Lord Alfred Paget, one consequence of which was that the Commodore, W.H. Harrison, resigned (briefly) from office. In 1852 the boat was much altered and then displaced 25 Tons. Its new owner, Samuel Lane Esq, was one of the most successful owners of his day. His victory in June 1863 won him his 50th trophy. Between June 1852 and June 1863 he won six RTYC matches and trophies valued at a total of £350.

Cutter Yacht CYNTHIA, 50 Tons - Lithograph by T G Dutton from painting by N M Condy.

Nancy Dawson (160 Tons) in the lithograph by T.G. Dutton was the Schooner built for Robert Shedden who died in November 1849 while searching for Sir John Franklin's expedition seeking the 'North West Passage'. She is described as *'the only yacht that circumnavigated the globe'*. The print was presented to the Club in 1851 by Robert Shedden's aunt Mrs Robertson of Kelso.

Cynthia (50 Tons) is shown in the lithograph by T G Dutton from a painting by N.M. Condy (Club Marine Artist 1843-1851) winning a £50 purse at Torbay in August 1849. Earlier that year she won a £100 prize in a match from Erith to Nore and back and repeated the success in May 1851. She was owned by John Wicks Esq.

Cutter Yacht SPHINX, 47 Tons - Lithograph by T G Dutton

Mosquito (50 Tons). This is another print by T.G. Dutton of the successful iron cutter built and owned by Charles Mare Esq who won a £100 purse in 1848 and 1850. Later owned by Lord Londesborough, she was again successful in 1850 and 1853 winning prizes of 200 guineas, £100 and £60.

Volante (48 Tons). This lithograph by E T Dolby from a picture by T S Robins (RTYC marine artist from 1851) shows her winning the 200 guineas Challenge Cup in 1852. The Cup was first competed for in 1849 when *CYGNET* was the winner; in 1850 it was *MOSQUITO* who won and since *VOLANTE* had also won in 1851 she won the Cup outright for John L. Craigie Esq (who also won a £100 prize in 1852). Later in 1861 *VOLANTE* was bought by Henry C. Maudslay Esq who lengthened her 10 feet by the bows and continued a successful racing career, winning two RTYC prizes in 1864. Sadly *VOLANTE* was wrecked on Ryde Sands in 1869.

Rosalind (100 Tons) is another lithograph by T G Dutton painted by T S Robins. She won the 100 guineas Schooner Match from Gravesend to the Mouse Light Vessel and back on 1 June 1853 when owned by Lord Alfred Paget. Her win, however, came only following a protest which caused much acrimony within the Club. *SVERIGE,* owned by Thomas Bartlett Esq, crossed the finishing line 25 seconds ahead of *ROSALIND* but was disqualified for having fouled the 60 Ton Cutter *VIOLET.*

Sverige (280 Tons) is also a T G Dutton/T S Robins lithograph. She was built (and owned) in Sweden in 1852 by Nicholas Beckmann and sold to Thomas Bartlett in 1853. She sailed a match starting from Ryde in 1852, against the schooner *AMERICA* (on which she was modelled). After leading by over 8 minutes downwind she was outsailed to windward and lost by 24 minutes.

Arrow (102 Tons). This is a lithograph by T G Dutton painted by Josiah Taylor. It shows ARROW racing in the Solent in August 1854. She was built by Inman at Lymington in 1821 for Joseph Weld Esq. Bought by Thomas Chamberlayne Esq in 1846, the Cutter was modified but continued to race successfully into the 1880s. In RTYC matches she won the Channel Race from Gravesend to Ryde on 21 June 1865.

Osprey (62 Tons). The print is painted by Josiah Taylor and was presented to the Club by him in May 1863. This Cutter was owned by Colonel R.W. Huey and won a £100 RTYC prize in June 1859 and a £50 prize in 1861.

Alarm (248 Tons). This was painted by J M Gilbert in 1852. Owned by Joseph Weld Esq, a founder member of the RYS, *ALARM* was built as a Cutter (193 Tons) - one of the biggest ever built. Once again, the performance of *AMERICA* influenced James Weld and *ALARM's* bow and rig were substantially altered in 1852 after which she emerged as a Schooner of 248 Tons. In July 1853 over a 52 mile course off Brighton she defeated *SVERIGE.* She won both the 1859 and 1861 RTYC Schooner matches for £100 prizes. Later owned by George Duppa Esq, RTYC, she was again successful in the RTYC Schooner and Yawl Class in June 1865 over a course from Sheerness to Harwich and again in the Open Class in July 1867 in a match from the Nore Light to Le Havre, winning £100 prizes in each match.

Audax (59 Tons). A lithograph by T.G. Dutton. Owned by J. H. Johnson Esq, she was built in 1860 by John Harvey of Wivenhoe (it is of note that he was the father of the distinguished actor, Sir Martin Harvey). In RTYC matches she won the 1st Class Cutter match on 14 June 1860 and received a £100 Silver Cup.

Thought (25 Tons). A print of a lithograph painted by Josiah Taylor. She was owned by F Ord Marshall Esq. In June 1857 she won a £50 Claret Jug in a Second Class Cutter match and on 14 June 1860, as illustrated in the Josiah Taylor print, won the Amateur Match (all crew to be RTYC members or Army/Navy Officers; any rig and tonnage not to exceed 35 Tons), the prize being a £50 Silver Tea Service. On 3 June 1861 she won the £100 First Class Prize in a match for first and second class Cutters (at that time, in a mixed match, the first vessel over the finishing line took the top prize regardless of its class).

Marina (65 Tons). Owned by J C Morice Esq this Josiah Taylor print shows her in collision with the Club steamer *Prince of Wales* near the Nore Lightship on 23rd May 1862. An account of the circumstances of the collision is given in Section VIII.

Christabel (43 Tons). Another Josiah Taylor painted lithograph. Built by Edward Aldous of Brightlingsea, owned by Henry H. Kennard Esq. The print shows her winning the First Class Cutter match on 23 May 1862, the prize being a £100 Silver Tea Service. Owned by Arthur C. Kennard Esq from 1865, she won, on 19 June 1865, the 25 guinea Silver Cup, presented by RTYC member Captain P Cosby Lovett, for all classes of Cutter. In May 1866 she also won the Second Class Cutter prize of £100.

Flying Cloud (75 Tons) was also painted by Josiah Taylor. Built by Inman of Lymington and owned by the Hungarian Count Edmond Batthyany who presented the print to the Club in January 1863. She was a very successful Schooner (Second Class) and won the RTYC Match for that Class on 23 June 1862; the prize was £40 in value.

Vindex (45 Tons) by T G Dutton. An iron Cutter owned by Andrew Duncan Esq, she won a prize of £100 in both the May 1863 and May 1864 RTYC First Class Cutter Matches.

Albertine (155 Tons) is also from a lithograph painted by T G Dutton. This Schooner was built by Inman of Lymington and owned by Lord Londesborough. She won the RTYC First Class Schooner Match from Gravesend to the Mouse Light Vessel and back in both June 1863 and June 1864 for £100 prizes.

Madcap (70 Tons). This print was presented to the Club by her owner J.S. Abbot Dunbar Esq. She was successfully raced in RTYC Matches. In June 1864 and June 1866 she won the £50 and £80 prize in the Second Class Schooner Matches and she also won the inaugural Channel Match from Gravesend to Ryde in June 1864.

Glance (36 Tons) was painted by Josiah Taylor. Originally owned by Andrew Duncan Esq and in 1865 by Edward Johnson Esq, she was built by D.G. Hatcher of Southampton. In RTYC matches in 1865 she won the £100 prize for First Class Cutters and the 50 guinea prize donated by Sir Gilbert East in a match open to all Cutters.

Gloriana (148 Tons). This print by Josiah Taylor shows the Schooner racing in the RTYC Schooner Match in June 1869. Built by Ratsey of Cowes in 1852 for Joseph Gee Esq it was later owned and modified by A.O. Wilkinson Esq who raced her successfully in RTYC Matches, winning the £100 prize for Schooner (First Class) in 1865, 1866 and 1868.

New Moon (209 Tons). This print by T G Dutton was presented to the Club in 1866 by her owner Lord Willoughby de Eresby. Built by Mr Tutt at Hastings she was Lugger-rigged, a rig not much favoured at the time. She was the largest yacht with this rig ever built, being 134 feet in overall length. In May 1866 she took part in the Channel Match from the Nore Light to Dover Harbour, competing with a fleet of Schooners, Yawls and Cutters. With her lugger rig *NEW MOON* produced very fast speeds when reaching in a strong wind and left the rest of the fleet far behind; but once the fleet came on to the wind the gaff rigged yachts were able to overtake her. The illustration shows clearly her quadrilateral lugsails.

Sphinx (47 Tons). This is another lithograph by TG Dutton and shows her off Southsea winning the 'Albert Cup' in 1866. She also won the £50 prize for Cutters in the RTYC Match (which had classes for Schooners and Luggers as well as Yawls) from the Nore Light to Dover on 21 May 1866. Built by Dan Hatcher of Itchen Ferry for H.C. Maudslay Esq she copied her cutter rival NIOBE, who in 1865 had carried a sail set from the topmast head to the deck and upon a boom. The sail called a Ni-obe in 1865 became known as Spinker in 1866 and then a Spinnaker. The spelling Spinnaker appeared in 1869.

The location of all these prints, in 1994, is shown in Appendix 12.

Oil Paintings of Club Officers

The majority of the portraits of Club Officers which are hanging in the present Club House are of noblemen and gentlemen who were in Office outside the period covered by this volume (1823-1867). Notwithstanding that, there are four paintings of particular importance since they depict officers who greatly influenced the Club's history.

Robert Williams - The identity of the artist who painted this portrait has often been a subject for disagreement among professional opinion. It has been attributed to J.W.T. Turner but this is almost certainly not true. It is also uncertain as to when the portrait was painted. The Club's records show that Robert Williams died in February 1844 and there is a note recording that the paintings of Robert Williams, William Harrison and Cornelius Wheeler should be hung in the Club Meeting Room in the Clubhouse at the Bedford Hotel. It is possible, therefore, that the painting was completed in the period 1932-43, i.e. after Robert Williams stood down from the office of Treasurer but before his death.

A search of the Club's archives has now thrown light on the identity of the artist. In 1888 the Club was invited to loan the painting to the Royal Academy for their 1888/89 Winter Exhibition at Burlington House. Unfortunately the Club's carriers delivered it a day late and the selection committee could not view it. In spite of that, the Chairman of the Committee, J.C. Horsley RA wrote on 7 December 1888 *'that the Committee are strongly inclined to the opinion that the picture is by Turner'*. As a consequence the Club insured the painting for £2,000.

A year later the painting was again sent to Burlington House and was hung with other Turner paintings in the Winter Exhibition of 1889/90 and praise for it was recorded by all the principal newspapers of the day including such comment as - *'There is a hint of the great master in the mist and cloud perspective in the background'* and *'background with Turner's best sunset colours'*.

While the exhibition was open in January 1890 the editor of the Graphic wrote, seeking the Club's permission for the painting to be reproduced in the issue dated 4 June 1892.

Nine days later a letter was received at the Club from Daniel Pasmore saying he had seen the illustration in the Graphic and noting it was *'stated to be painted by J.M.W. Turner RA. This I hope you will do your best to contradict; the portrait was painted by me for the RTYC, I being introduced by Mr Harwood for the purpose of painting the portrait which was presented through the subscriptions raised by the members'.*

In a further letter on 14 June 1892 Daniel Pasmore stated *'I perfectly remember having painted the portrait in question, being a guest at the Captain's house and can prove by a sketch made by me, having it now and in my possession for years past'.*

The sketches were produced by Daniel Pasmore for inspection by the RTYC Committee on 7 July 1892 when it was resolved *'that the Committee accept Mr Pasmore's statement that he was the artist and are satisfied with the evidence produced'.*

The other interesting section of the letter dated 14 June is that Pasmore says that very soon after painting Robert Williams portrait *'I painted Captain Cornelius Wheeler's portrait'* - that he painted Cornelius Wheeler's portrait has never been in doubt.

This painting which currently is hung on the Quarterdeck of the Clubhouse, is therefore, almost certainly the work of Daniel Pasmore and was probably undertaken around 1840, but the Turner connection remains a mystery.

William H. Harrison - This portrait by Mr C. Ambrose, which today hangs in the Britannia Lounge of the Clubhouse, was commissioned by the Club in 1846 to mark William Harrison's retirement from the Office of Commodore. The silver cup which he is shown to be holding is said to be the trophy given by the Club in 1838 in honour of Queen Victoria's Coronation. It is not recorded at which of the four sailing matches in 1838 the trophy was presented.

An interesting aside to this portrait is the argument between the artist and the Club concerning payment for the commission. In July 1846 Mr Ambrose wrote to the Club seeking payment of an outstanding balance in respect of his commission to paint a portrait of the Late Commodore. The claim was investigated by Mr George Reynell and in January 1847 the Club concluded that no further payment was due. A year later Mr Reynell reported that Mr Ambrose had commenced legal action against him for the balance due - £48.14.6. A Committee was set up, including the Commodore, Vice Commodore and Treasurer, *'to take such measures as they may deem necessary and with power to adopt such proceedings as they may consider advisable to protect Mr Reynell in the action'.* They concluded that while it appeared that Mr Ambrose had no legal claim against the Club they would offer Mr Ambrose a further £25, but this offer was refused. They also agreed that if the legal action was pursued the Club would indemnify Mr Reynell. In December 1848 the Club found itself obliged to pay Mr Reynell £87.16.0!

Cornelius Wheeler - There is no record of when the Club acquired this portrait by Daniel Pasmore but as had been noted earlier it was among those hung in the Bedford Hotel in 1851 and may possibly have been commissioned as early as 1842, when Captain Wheeler was presented with a piece of plate as a testimonial. Currently it hangs in the Queenborough Room of the Clubhouse.

Lord Alfred Paget - At a Special General Meeting of the Club on 8 July 1857, Mr R S Wilkinson in alluding to the valued services of the noble Commodore, begged to move *'that a Committee be formed to wait upon the Commodore, Lord Alfred Paget, MP, for the purpose of ascertaining whether his Lordship will sit to Mr Grant RA for his portrait'.* The Committee consisted of no less than 18 members and it was decided that a Subscription List for the portrait would be opened to which members could contribute a sum not exceeding one guinea.

This fine portrait by Sir Francis Grant is to be seen in the present Clubhouse on the Quarterdeck. It was exhibited at the Royal Academy Exhibition of 1859.

Oil Paintings of Yachts

There are only a small number of oil paintings depicting Sailing Matches or individual yachts during the period 1823-1867. Nearly all the paintings from that period are the work of **Nicholas M. Condy** and are located in the Edinburgh Room of the present Clubhouse. Four of these paintings feature Lord Alfred Paget's iron yacht *MYSTERY*. N.M. Condy, a West Countryman, became the Club's Marine Artist in 1843 and was given Honorary Membership of the Club; he then became a member in his own right the following year and remained so until his death in 1851 when he was succeeded by **Thomas Sewell Robins** whose work is well illustrated in many prints displayed in the Clubhouse. Another yacht portrayed by Condy is Arthur O. Wilkinson's *PHANTOM*, which is shown racing with Lord Alfred Paget's *BELVIDERE* in an RTYC match in 1845 from Greenwich to Coal House Point for a £60 silver cup presented by a member of the Club, Earl Fitzhardinge. Another painting in the Edinburgh Room by the Belgian artist Louis Verbouchoven and dated 1847 shows the RTYC Cutter *VICTORINE* owned at that time by Henry G. Lord. In 1845 he had won the £30 Stewards Cup. Earlier owners of *VICTORINE* were Thomas and Charles Stokes who were 'founder' members of the Thames Yacht Club in 1823. Their success in RTYC Sailing Matches included a £30 Cup in August 1835 and other prizes in July 1837, July 1838, June 1839, August 1840 and July 1841, a total of over £200 in prizes.

Silver Trophies

During the period covered by this volume, 1823 - 1867, no other Club could match the quality and generosity of the trophies donated by the Royal Thames Yacht Club. Over 220 trophies valued at nearly £12,000 were competed for over the 45 sailing seasons. It is sad to reflect that only seven of those trophies are to day in the Club's possession.

RTYC Grand Challenge Cup 1840. When the Club met on 7 May 1840, Mr William Pegg proposed *'That a Challenge Cup of the value one hundred guineas be given by the members of this Club, to be sailed for by yachts belonging* *to any Royal yacht Club (upon conditions to be hereafter determined upon) which could materially conduce to the prosperity of this Club and tend to promote good feeling among the Yacht Clubs in England'.* By the end of the meeting 24 members had contributed £77.13.0 towards the £105.0.0 required. The first match for the Challenge Cup made by The Bernards was to take place on 7 September 1840 and would be for yachts not exceeding 25 Tons and be sailed from Greenwich to Coal House Point and back. Any yacht that should win the event in consecutive seasons would win the Cup outright. The first winner was *GAZELLE* (Henry Gunston) and in subsequent years:

1841 *CHAMPION* (Thomas & James Wanhill), 1842 *ADA* (Hon M H Upton), 1843 *ENIGMA* (W Head), 1844 *MYSTERY* (Lord Alfred Paget), 1845 *PRIMA DONNA* (C R Tatham). In 1846 and 1847 - it was won by *SECRET* owned by J W Smith who thus won the trophy outright.

The Belvidere Cup. - When the Club met on 2 January 1845 the Commodore, William Harrison, read a letter received from a member, Lord Saye and Sele, in which His Lordship *'proposes to give a cup value, 100 guineas, to be sailed for by yachts belonging to the Club (not exceeding 25 Tons) during the 1845 season at such time as may be appointed, to commemorate Mr Harrison's return to the Office of Commodore'.* He also donated *'a case of champagne for the day of the match so that the Commodore's health and the prosperity of the Club may be drunk'.* Having read the letter to the members present the Commodore received unanimous support to his proposal that the Cup be called 'The Belvidere Cup' in honour of His Lordships seat on the banks of the Thames.

The *'return to the Office of Commodore'* refers, of course, to the unforeseen outcome of the protest between *PHANTOM* (Arthur O. Wilkinson Esq) and *MYSTERY* (Lord Alfred Paget) which ultimately caused the Commodore to resign his office. The Cup, made by I.S. Hunt, was competed for on 3 May 1845, there being nine vessels entered. The match was won by the Cutter *BLUE BELLE* owned by Twisden Hodges Esq.

Robert Williams Salver was presented by the Club to Robert Williams on 5 April 1832 in recognition of his service to the Club as Treasurer 1823-1830.

EMMET Challenge Trophy was won by the Cutter *EMMET* (Edward Gibson Esq) in the RTYC Second Class Cutter match from Erith to the Nore Light and back on 22 May 1858. This, large Tankard, worth £50, was made by C.F. Hancock and presented to the Club in 1974 by Mr Gibson's great grandson.

Nautilus Cup was won by the Cutter *VINDEX* (Andrew Duncan Esq) in the RTYC First Class Cutter match from Gravesend to the Nore Light and back on 31 May 1864. This £100 trophy was presented to the Club in 1953 by Andrew Duncan's daughter Mrs Mitchell.

Holt Challenge Cup was won by *PHANTOM* (Samuel Lane Esq) who was second to *QUEEN* (Captain T E Whitbread) in the Second Class Cutter match from Erith to Nore and back on 7 June 1862. The silver claret jug made by Garrards was originally valued at £20. Currently available records do not explain how the trophy acquired the name Holt.

The Ice Bucket was won by *SPHINX* (H.C. Maudslay Esq) who came first in the Cutter Class in the Channel Match on 21 May 1866 from the Nore Light to Dover. This £50 trophy was presented to the Club in October 1927 by Mr Maudslay's son Algernon Maudslay.

It is probable that more of the 220 trophies given in this period are in the possession of families related to the winners or in the silver vaults of countries in Europe or America. The only one that has been heard of in recent years was a silver tea service won by *SECRET* (J.W. Smith), the outright winner of the Grand Challenge Cup, on 11 May 1847 - this prize was in the possession of a lady in Canada who was a distant relative of J.W. Smith.

What is known about many of the trophies of this period that were given by the RTYC is which **SILVERSMITHS** created the cups, claret jugs, epergnes, tankards, tea services etc. Once the number and value of the prizes to be given was agreed it was the custom of the Sailing Committee (and later on, the General Committee) to invite several silversmiths to compete for the privilege of making the trophies. A considerable number of the trophies given were made by four silversmiths:

Garrards, Haymarket
Smith & Nicholson, Dukes St, Lincoln's Inn Fields
C F Hancock, 39 Burton Street
Bensons, Ludgate Hill

Other silversmiths who acted for the Club were:

Gass & Co, Regent Street
Hunts & Roskill, New Bond Street
Widdowson & Veak, 73 The Strand
Elkingtons
Storrs and Beard
Angell
Thomas
The Barnards

VIII
Anecdotes

It will surprise no one that threaded through the network of the Club's history are little incidents worthy of recording whether they be of a serious nature or are just diverting. This section brings together, in chronological order, some twenty such incidents with the aim of providing light relief for readers as well as reflecting the attitudes and manners of the period.

7 June 1828
This was the day of a below bridge sailing match won by *DAISY, 19 Tons* (J G Irwin) from *LADY LOUISA, 13 Tons* (T Smith) in a closely-fought match with a strong wind prevailing throughout. *WILL O' THE WISP, 16 Tons* (W H Harrison) had broken a gaff soon after the start and was forced to retire. Included in the report of this match in the Sunday Times of 8 June is a sentence which informs us that: *'Pigeons were sent off to London to communicate the positions held by boats during the race'.*

Comment: In what was an exciting but otherwise insignificant match one could hardly imagine who received the messages carried by the pigeons and what their purpose was - to alert the bookmakers?

3 July 1838
The winner of the prize for second class vessels in the match from Greenwich to Gravesend was *VICTORINE* (T & C Stokes) but after the match Mr W. Lyon (ALERT) reported that a scandalous manoeuvre had prevented him from winning. When he was leading the class on the return through Blackwall Reach a skiff belonging to a lighterman named Sommers had rowed across his bows on no less than 3 occasions and a member of the skiff's crew had informed him that their express purpose was to prevent ALERT from winning. Mr Lyon produced, in evidence, a scull seized from one of the skiff's crewmen. The committee advised Mr Lyon to prosecute!

Comment: It would seem that the wagers had been placed on *VICTORINE* and not on *ALERT*.

3 September 1840
At a meeting of the Club Mr William Egan, Captain of the Club, proposed that the Waterman accidently struck by the wadding from the (starting) gun fired from the Royal Sovereign (committee boat) at the last sailing match and thereby slightly injured should be remunerated. The proposal was carried unanimously and it was resolved that the Treasurer be requested to pay him the sum of one guinea.

Comment: It seems strange that the word 'remunerated' was used when recording this occurrence; the word 'compensat-

ed' would seem to be more appropriate!

7 September 1840
This was the day when the Club, for the first time, held a sailing match from Greenwich to Coal House Point and back for a 100 guineas Grand Challenge Cup. The opening sentences of the report on the match set the scene:

'The last match of the season of this highly popular and spirited Club was sailed on Monday under circumstances of a truly gratifying and pleasurable nature, which reflect the utmost credit on the members. For many years the Club has displayed a liberality in the promotion of yacht sailing but seldom equalled and certainly never surpassed by any similar institution in the United Kingdom; on this occasion however, the members determined, if possible, to excel all their former doings, and a subscription was set on foot amongst them for the purpose of giving a Grand Challenge Cup, value 100 guineas, to be sailed for by gentlemen's yachts, not exceeding 25 Tons, belonging to any royal yacht club in the world.'

The report then continues:
'On the return leg of the match the GAZELLE and ALARM built up a considerable lead over the other competing yachts and it is recorded that 'The crews of the FORTUNA, ADA JANE and one or two of the other yachts, we believe, on finding that they could not win, paid little or no attention to sailing, but proceeded below for 'cabin comforts', and if all fared as well as some whom we saw at the conclusion of the match, we should imagine that the lockers yielded a vast quantity of something very pleasant to the taste'.

Comment: There is no reason to believe that such activities were necessarily the norm, but it did show a keen sense of priorities.

6 February 1845
This was the occasion of a Club meeting at the British Coffee House in Cockspur Street. Among the proposals tabled was one by Mr Josiah Wilkinson *'That in order to ensure due attention to the Business of the Club, no refreshments be introduced nor smoking be permitted until the Commodore has announced from the chair that the business of the evening is concluded'.* When put to the vote the proposal was defeated by 30 votes to 16.

Comment: Little changes over the years! It is interesting that the acceptability of smoking should be questioned 150 years ago.

3 May 1845

At this meeting, Captain Thomas Meeson, who was Captain the Club, stated that he wished to know whether the working of a small engine containing about five pails of water to wash the sails would be an infringement of the (Club) law prohibiting water ballast. He added that it would not be shifted from one side of the yacht to the other. No objections were raised to Captain Meeson having such a machine on board.

Comment: It is fascinating to learn of this method of wetting the sails instead of the customary method using skeets.

16 May 1845

This was the date of the first sailing match of the 1845 season. Following an occurrence during the match, Mr Henry Gunston (owner of *ANTAGONIST*) wrote to the Club Secretary complaining about the unfair sailing of Mr John D Lee in *MYSTERY* (owned by Lord Seaham). In his letter he said that *'When MYSTERY overhauled me, in consequence of the balloon jib getting foul of the other jib in shifting, and which acted as a backsail, I do most positively declare that I never bore up for the purpose of preventing her from going by me to leeward, that after passing round the Flag Boat I kept my luff on the weather shore and did not alter my course till I came within my draught of water, and then only bore up to avoid getting aground'.* Mr John Lee also wrote to the Club Secretary saying *'That I must decline meeting Mr Henry Gunston (and the Sailing Committee) until he has retracted the term of 'damned scoundrel' applied to me on the day of the match in question. That done I am ready to produce evidence which will prove his charge as frivolous as his abuse is vexatious'.*

Mr Gunston retracted the expression complained of by Mr Lee and the Sailing Committee were then able to take evidence from and on behalf of each gentleman. The Sailing Committee reported that in their opinion no rule in the sailing regulations had been violated by either party (though it is clear that both yachts went aground) and therefore the Committee has no findings to report but advise gentlemen to avoid putting each other ashore in future.

Comment: Today's Judges and Protest Committees might have found the complaint somewhat frivolous and have given advice in stronger terms.

31 May 1848

was the day when the Vice Commodore moved *'That an artillery man from Woolwich should be employed on board the Steam Vessel on Match Days to load and fire the guns'.*

Comment: As explained elsewhere the Steam Vessel served as Committee Boat and platform for spectators to view the sailing matches. The incident with wadding on 3 September 1840 may have occurred again and prompted this action.

1 June 1853

was the date when the first Schooner Match was sailed by the Royal Thames from Gravesend to the Mouse Light Vessel and back. This landmark in the Club's history of racing on the Thames was marred by the protest between the *SVERIGE* and the *VIOLET* and the decision by the Sailing Committee to award the prize to *ROSALIND*, all of which is described in the section on Sailing Matches. Controversy was abroad, however, even before the day of the match in the form of correspondence between Mr Jos.C Bankworth of the Royal Western Yacht Club and the Secretary of the Royal Thames.

This started amiably enough with a simple enquiry as to whether entry to the match was open to vessels belonging to clubs other than the Royal Thames.

On being informed that entry was for vessels of the Royal Thames only, Mr Bankworth wrote *'I regret to find that the illiberal spirit of your committee should curtail the interest which would otherwise attach to the amusement of the day and I should be obliged by your informing me whether the practice of excluding members from other clubs from competing for prizes given by the Royal Thames is the rule or the exception; if it be the rule I shall feel it my duty to canvas the yachting world to exclude the Thames Club from participation in the amusements held out by other clubs'.* The Secretary confirmed that exclusion was the (general) rule, to which Mr Bankworth wrote *'I beg to say that it is my wish that all gentlemen having the direction of the Royal Thames Yacht Club Regattas should know the views entertained by members of another club in reference to the limited competition permitted to owners of vessels not being members of the RTYC.'*

'On referring to your rules I am lead to suppose the whole object is to oblige everyone possessing a vessel to sail her under the burgee of the Royal Thames Yacht Club and I only regret that a race in which the whole of the yachting world would otherwise take a deep interest should be devoid of the only incident requisite to create that interest' and followed that by yet a further letter saying *'I beg to say I have conferred with our Secretary who informs me it is the custom annually with the clubs you have named, to present prizes open to all other Yacht Clubs unfettered (as I am informed the Thames Challenge Cups are) with certain conditions rendering comparatively useless the prize when obtained'.*

The RTYC Sailing Committee met on 17 May 1853 and instructed the Secretary to reply to Mr Bankworth with a letter saying *'I have laid your letters before the Sailing Committee of the Royal Thames Yacht Club and am directed to inform you that the time is too short to allow of any alteration of the regulations which have been made with regard to the Match on 1 June next. I am also directed to state that the Committee are always most anxious to take into consideration any question that may be submitted to them with the view of promoting competition for their prizes, but that the tone of your letters preclude them from carrying on any further correspondence with you on the subject'.*

The postscript to this eventful sailing match was that the cutter yacht *QUEEN (27 Tons)* owned by Mr Thomas Alston of the RTYC and which was one of the many vessels which followed the competitors, ran down a fishing boat, but saved the man and boy on board, for whom £5 were at once subscribed.

Comment: The records do not say whether Mr Bankworth was writing on his own behalf or for the Royal Western Yacht Club. What is certain is that the correspondence did no lasting harm to relations between the RTYC and the RWYC. It is of note that it was not until 1859 that the annual Schooner Match was opened to vessels of any Royal Yacht Club. As for the unfortunate fishing boat it is to be hoped that the vessel was salvaged, otherwise £5 was scant compensation unless it was fully insured!

26 June 1856
A Special General Meeting of the Club, with Captain
Cornelius Wheeler, (who had recently stood down as
Club Treasurer) in the chair, was called on this day.
Mr R S Wilkinson, proposed a resolution *'That this Club
congratulate their Commodore, Lord Alfred Paget MP, upon
the fortunate escape of himself and his crew upon the
occasion of his Lordship's vessel being run down by the
DIAMOND, mail steam packet, in the service of the Belgian
Government, and trust that the Belgian Government will
see the justice of making proper compensation to his
Lordship for the loss he has sustained'.*

A further resolution which, like the one above, was carried
unanimously, was *'That the Vice Commodore be requested
to forward a copy of the above resolution to His Majesty, the
King of the Belgians (a Patron of the RTYC) and to their
Royal Highnesses, the Duke de Brabant and the Count de
Flanders, both members of the RTYC'.*

Comment: The Commodore's 'vessel' was the yawl *ALMA 66
Tons,* a large yacht by any standard but nevertheless it would
seem to have been unsighted by the mail packet. Unfortunately
the Club's records do not reveal what one would like to know
- how did the collision occur and were the resolutions
successful in obtaining compensation for the Commodore?

4 February 1857
was the occasion when, at a General Meeting of the Club, Mr
John N Wilson brought forward a motion *'That as it appears
that the plan sent up by the Metropolitan Board of Works to
the Government for the main drainage of the Metropolis
contemplates a discharge of undeodorised sewage into the
River Thames on its north side at Rainham Creek and on its
south side at about a quarter of a mile higher up the river
than Erith, the immediate attention of the Club should be
called to a project so seriously affecting the interests of all
engaged in yachting pursuits upon the River Thames'.*

The 58 members present at the meeting discussed this
important but unsavoury topic at great length and ultimately
decided to set up a committee of six members to decide
*'What steps, if any, should be taken by memorial or
otherwise to express the sentiments of the Club'.*

The report of the committee, chaired by Mr James Hutchons,
the Treasurer, made three recommendations. Firstly that the
plan if carried out as contemplated would materially affect
the comfort and pleasure hitherto enjoyed by members of the
RTYC. Secondly, that the time for action had arrived. Thirdly,
that a memorial be forwarded to Sir Benjamin Hall, calling the
attention of that gentleman to the serious effect which the
plan proposed will have upon the comfort and pleasure of
the members of the RTYC; of others making use of the River
Thames as a means of recreation and upon the shipping
interest generally.

Comment: Since the club continued to start their sailing
matches from Erith for many years afterwards it seems
reasonable to assume that either the plan was abandoned
or a suitable deodorising plant was installed for use prior
to the discharge of the metropolis' sewage.

4 January 1860
saw Mr James Thomson propose a motion *'That with a view
to aid the government in its measures for increasing the
efficiency of our National Defence, and more particularly for*

*the purpose of inducing seamen to join the Reserve Force of
Royal Naval Volunteers about to be established, the yacht
owners of the Club be requested, in manning their vessels
for the ensuing season, to give the preference to men who
have enrolled or are willing to enrol themselves in the RNVR
and as far as practicable select their crews exclusively from
that body'.*

Comment: The close bonds between yachtsmen and the Royal
Navy has existed for many years and have provided the latter,
at all levels, with a pool of able and experienced seafarers.

14 June 1860
was the day for the first 'amateur' sailing match organised by
the RTYC. The crews of the vessels, not exceeding 35 Tons,
had to be members of any Royal Yacht Club or Officers in
the Navy or Army - a pilot could be carried to provide advice.
The race from Erith to the Nore Light Vessel and back was
won by the cutter yacht *THOUGHT (27 Tons)* owned by
F O Marshall Esq.

The introduction to the description of the race provides
fascinating reading not only because of its prose style but
also because of the importance attached to providing suitable
entertainment for the considerable crowds of spectators
(frequently five or six hundred) who followed the competitors.
The extract from Hunt's Yachting Magazine is reproduced in
full so that readers, like the spectator on the day, may enjoy
the scene at the start of the match.

The Corinthian crews were scanned with much attention,
and went about their work after a fashion which showed that
novices in yachtsmanship had no business there; there was but
one feeling, however, with regard to them, and that was that
the vessels were not matched evenly enough, so that a better
opportunity might be afforded of testing the abilities of the
respective crews; (the tonnage varied from 9 to 27 Tons with
half minute per ton time allowance) they all looked well, and
were evidently selected with care; but if a selection could
be made, it was in favour of the crew of *THOUGHT,* their
physique was splendid, and there was a dash, an esprit about
them unmistakeable, that told they were fit to handle or take
a vessel anywhere in any weather; in addition to which they
were all attired in a neat and serviceable uniform, which not
a little added to their thoroughbred appearance; and apropos
to this we would beg to say a few words about racing crews.
Why is it that they in general select a heterogeneous attire of
used up garments which upon other occasions are stowed
away in out of the way clothes bags; not of course that it
makes an iota of difference in the success of the vessels,
but still to the eye of the spectator it presents anything but
a picturesque effect, besides which, some such distinctive
characteristic would have much weight in keeping the respective vessels in the mind's eye during the various changes of
a close contest, and would be a pleasing adjunct to the racing
flag; jockeys do not appear in strapping jackets and overalls at
the starting post; cricketers turn out in appropriate style; and
in the hunting field the brilliant scarlet bespeaks the 'going'
men. Why then should the gallant spirits who are the thews
and sinews of our noblest and manliest national pastime,
garb their stalwart forms after such a dubious fashion; salt
water harms not, it merely takes the gloss off, and imparts
a 'service' look.

Comment: The writer of the above would be pleased to
know that yachtsmen and uniform are still a feature of the
crew of today's vessels though he would probably join in the

dismay at the pyjama outfits worn by cricketers on Sundays.

4 July 1861
the date for that season's Schooner Match from Rosherville to the Mouse Light Vessel and back to Greenhithe. The £100 prize was won by *ALARM (248 Tons)* owned by Mr Joseph Weld.

Included in the report on the match is the content of a letter from the owner of *ALARM* in which he relates these extraordinary circumstances: *'On putting the ALARM ashore to clean her bottom, we found that the rope which is called a spring, in getting the vessel round after the gun had fired for the yachts to start, had got between the rudder and the stern post. This spring is 27 fathoms in length, and was made fast to the hawser which she rode by, and in casting around at the start she broke this 6 inch hawser, which is thrown overboard at the time; but it being made fast to the spring, she towed the whole away after her in the race. The spring was 3 inch rope, and 27 fathoms long, the hawser 6 inch rope and 24 fathoms long. The whole 51 fathoms she dragged not only in the race, but round to Southampton'.*

Comment: Throughout the race there was a strong south westerly blowing otherwise it is doubtful whether *ALARM* would have moved from her mooring. That she not only moved but won the race is almost as remarkable as the fact that no one noticed anything unusual in her sailing characteristics!

23 May 1862
was the day of the first sailing match of that season. The match was for 1st Class Cutters (over 35 Tons); the competitors included *MARINA (65 Tons)* owned by J C Morice Esq while the Race Committee and Supporters were aboard the steamer *PRINCE OF WALES*. All who were present are unlikely to forget an incident involving those two vessels.

The race, from Erith to the Nore Light Vessel and back, was sailed in a strong SW wind. As *MARINA* was drawing near to the Nore, the club steamer had stopped about 100 yards to leeward of the Light Vessel, but it was considered that her position might be improved by placing her in a line with, but above, the Light Vessel, so that yachts might pass on each side, giving a better view to the members, and she began to steam ahead, when the *MARINA* with immense speed came dashing along, and it was evident the Steamer could not get into her intended position. *'Turn her astern'* was shouted from some score persons, but before that could be established the *MARINA*, not for one moment imagining that *'a club steamer would ever get in the way of a racing craft'*, came tearing round the Light Vessel, supposing the way clear, and was taking the usual course after rounding, when to their great surprise there was the steamer; the crew shouted, and the helmsman jammed the tiller hard down to ease the avoidable shock, the *MARINA* answered her helm quickly, but still the steamer was too close to prevent being run into, and the yacht's bowsprit struck her about four feet from her stem, driving a hole into the iron plate. Then, fortunately, the bow-sprit, instead of becoming fixed in the steamer's bows, was driven with immense force, straight on her own decks, carrying away bitts, windlass, and everything it came in contact with. Her stem was split, and much other damage done. The *MARINA* having thus got clear of the steamer, her powerful canvas drove her across the latters bows, twisting it considerably, opening the deck planking, and carrying away the ornamental woodwork, both port and

starboard, rendering the steamer a mark of derision with the rabble on her upward course.

The crew of the steamer were quickly on the alert, and several jumped into the forecastle, where the breach had been made, and after some half hour, effectively prevented by tow and other materials the further increase of the water.

Fortunately no one was hurt, except one man on board the *MARINA* slightly. He was, it appears, below, and hearing the shouting, put his head up through the fore hatch, but luckily drew it down in time, so that the bowsprit in passing only cut his face and ear. It was a most miraculous escape from sudden death, for had it struck him on the head it would have been smashed to atoms. On board the steamer there were two or three sent down on their beam ends. At the time of the collision there were some forty or fifty persons on the fore part of the steamer, and had the top hamper of the *MARINA* given way many would have been injured and perhaps some swept overboard.

Some parties considered this accident an exceeding good diversion from the usual routine of yacht sailing, but we attribute that to a species of pretended courage, which carries a certain degree of contempt of any reflecting mind, for such weak-minded persons. Had the breach been five or six feet further aft it would have been in the fore saloon, which might have placed the steamer in a perilous position, but thank Providence it was otherwise.

Comment: MARINA, in spite of the collision, was still seaworthy but when the steamer caught up with her a line was passed and she was towed back to Gravesend for repair. From the limited information available it appears that blame could be laid against both vessels. It is interesting to note that shortly afterwards the Commodore proposed that a cup of the value of £100 be presented to Mr J C Morice in consequence of the accident which befell the *MARINA* during the sailing match on 23 May.

11 June 1863
This was the day when the renowned cutter *PHANTOM (27 Tons TM)* owned by Samuel Lane Esq won her fiftieth prize - a handsome silver loving cup and cover valued at £50. The match was sailed in strong SW winds, though the direction of the wind varied throughout the race. At the start the competitors' progress was hampered by a great number of merchant vessels and barges but it was also reported that *'There were many moving incidents during the day, and among others two or three vessels went ashore. Just before starting, a large schooner ran into another and carried away her jib-boom; and a brig put her bowsprit through the mainsail of the MARS, nearly tearing it in half. There was a party of ladies on board the MARS, and sooner than disappoint them, her owner Mr Haines set a storm trysail, and accompanied the match. Many other yachts also went down the river with the racers, and the squalls were so frequent that several of them, as well as some of the vessels engaged, returned with their racing flags and burgees torn'.*

Comment: It has to be remembered that the 'incidents' referred to above related to members' yachts that were following the match as spectators, but such was the stalwart nature of both the ladies and gentlemen, that nothing would deter them from their sport. Such also was their enthusiasm and spirit that when the Commodore, Lord Alfred Paget, sailed past the club steamer Prince of Wales the band 'saluted' him by playing 'Auld Lang Syne' and 'There's a good time coming'. On board the steamer it was noted that *'The Captain gave his company a good view of the race and the comestibles provided by Watt, the steward, were all that could be desired'* - all of which no doubt supplemented the air of well being.

31 May 1864

On this day matches for first and third class Cutters were held, the former being from Gravesend to the Mouse Light Vessel and back (light airs caused the race to be shortened and turned at the Nore Light Vessel). Among the entries were *ASTARTE (75 Tons)* built by Day & Son and owned by Thomas Seddon Esq, *SURF (54 Tons)* built by Fife and owned by George Harrison Esq and *VOLANTE (60 Tons)* built by Harvey's and owned by Herbert C Maudslay Esq - all three owners were RTYC members. All three had also competed the previous day in a closely ought match organised by the Royal London YC and which *ASTARTE* won from *VOLANTE* by just 5 seconds on corrected time, with SURF a close third. The result was confirmed only after the hearing of a protest by *SURF* against *ASTARTE* following contact between the latter's bowsprit and the former's boom. Once the result of the hearing was announced, George Harrison declared that he would never again sail in a race where *ASTARTE* was entered. The consequence was that SURF did not start on 31 May and as the report on the match observed *'If we can judge by SURF not starting, the two will never meet again'.*

ASTARTE and controversy were never far distant at this time since during this match on 31 May *'All was going well, when, in the Hope, ASTARTE and VOLANTE came suddenly in contact - when going about, the ASTARTE's boom-end caught the VOLANTE's backstay, broke the topmast, which, with topsail-yard falling heavily on the gaff about the middle, broke that also, thus disabling VOLANTE to continue the race - she therefore immediately bore up and returned to Gravesend. ASTARTE continued and was first to cross the finishing line but was third on corrected time'.*

Comment: George Harrison's *SURF* certainly did not compete again against *ASTARTE* that season but Mr Harrison soon solved his problem by selling *SURF* and buying the Schooner *CIRCE (133 Tons)* for the 1865 season. In contrast to Mr Harrison, Mr Maudslay took no antagonistic stand in spite of the extensive damage caused to *VOLANTE* by the collision with *ASTARTE*. It was recorded that *'Mr Maudslay generously abstained from claiming any compensation for damage received from Mr Seddon and the latter withdrew his protest against VINDEX - the winner of the first prize'.*

21 May 1866

was the date for the opening match for the season *'Of this great Club'* and it is recorded in Hunt's Yachting Magazine as a match that excited extreme interest among yachtsmen. It was in fact the Channel Match from the Nore Light Vessel to Dover and attracted an entry of 6 Schooners, 9 Cutters, the Yawl *XANTHA* (Lord Alfred Paget) and the Lugger *NEW MOON*, a gigantic open boat of 209 Tons.

The race started at 0807 in a fresh wind and by 1035 *XANTHA* has taken a lead she was never to lose - she took the winners' gun at Admiralty Pier, Dover at 1455, twenty minutes ahead of the Schooner *EGERIA*. It was a highly competitive race and many boats sustained damage and were forced to retire. The Cutter *CHRISTABEL*, which finished third just 30 seconds behind *EGERIA*, was disqualified for leaving the North Sand Light Vessel to port instead of starboard, *'CHRISTABEL having no paper instruction on board'*. As the finish approached *'EGERIA soon passed SPHINX (4th and winner of the Cutter prize) like a racehorse, and being extremely anxious to come in before CHRISTABEL, sent up her balloon jib, under which she went along almost as fast as the steamer in which Mr Churchward had brought out a select party to see the race, and came on CHRISTABEL like a huge dolphin on a flying fish, she went too fast for her, but the way was short and it was only in the boat's last jump that, to the great interest of the spectators, collared and passed the little beauty, which to the great astonishment and delight of all who admire pluck, had two young ladies on board, who deserve to be recorded as thorough heroines, and they passed the winning flag boat off the Admiralty Pier to finish second'.*

Comment: Well done the young ladies - their 'heroism' would hardly attract attention in these 'liberated' days.

It is noteworthy that *'not less than 10,000 persons were present to witness the finish'* a level of support that today would hardly ever be attracted unless it were to welcome the victor in an America's Cup series.

9 June 1866

The opening paragraphs of the account in Hunt's Yachting Magazine of the sailing match held on that day make interesting reading: *'The schooner match of this powerful club was held on 9 June, and combined with it was that for yawls, a rig that seems to be obtaining much more favour among yachtsmen than formerly'.* The prizes offered were: for schooners over 100 Tons, 100 sovereigns; under 100 Tons, 80 sovereigns; and yawls exceeding 50 Tons, 80 sovereigns. Much dissatisfaction was expressed that a club with such ample funds at command should not have given prizes for the second vessels in each class; and there is no doubt the entries were much affected by it.

Comment: The conclusion was certainly borne out by the entry - three Schooners in each class and only two Yawls. What perhaps is more relevant is the view held that the Royal Thames at that time was a club with *'ample funds at command'*. While the winners on the river were happily collecting their respective purses the House Committee were frantically trying to reduce their operating deficit and were seeking to constrain sailing expenses. As has been voiced in an another section of this record, there is no evidence to support the claim that this nadir in the club's financial fortunes could be laid at the sailing activities - and it is interesting to note that second prizes were offered in the 1867 schooner match (but entries were still only six!).

Appendix 1

*Notice in the Public Ledger and Daily Advertiser
Saturday 19th July 1823*

HIS MAJESTY'S CORONATION

The Subscribers and Members of the Old Cumberland Fleet
will dine together at the Ship Tavern, Water Lane, Tower Street
this day at four o'clock precisely, to celebrate the Coronation
of his Most Gracious King George IV; when the superb Silver
Cup, sailed for in honour of that event, on Thursday last, from
Blackwall to Coal House Point, below Gravesend, and back,
by Gentlemen's Pleasure Vessels, will be presented to Captain
George Keen, the winner of the prize; and to arrange the
articles for the Sailing Match to take place on Wednesday
afternoon the 30th instant, and to start at three o'clock from
Blackfriars Bridge, and sail to Putney and back to Cumberland
Gardens, under the especial patronage of the proprietors of
the Royal Gardens, Vauxhall.

Notice in the Public Ledger Tuesday 29th July 1823

**SUPERB GALA
ROYAL GARDENS, VAUXHALL
TO-MORROW EVENING,
WEDNESDAY, JULY 30**

GRAND SAILING MATCH for a SUPERB SILVER CUP and
COVER, weighing 61 ounces under the especial Patronage
of the PROPRIETORS of the ROYAL GARDENS, VAUXHALL,
will take place TO-MORROW, WEDNESDAY JULY 30, by the
following Gentlemen's Pleasure Vessels:-

Vessels Names	Owners Names	Place Belonging	Tons
Antelope	Capt. C Clementson	Adelphi	6
Venus	Capt. T Groves	Horselydown	13
Swallow	Capt. R Williams	Paul's Wharf	5
Mentor	Capt. E Jones	Stairgate	6
Fortitude	Capt. M Martin	Millbank	7
Spitfire	Capt. T Bettsworth	Chelsea	5
Trial	Capt. J Jones	Rotherhithe	5
St George	Capt. W Brocklebank	Deptford	10
Swift	Capt. W Field	Arundel Stairs	4
Ludlow	Capt. R Wilks	Arundel Stairs	4
Eclipse	Capt. R White	Vauxhall	6
Waterloo	Capt. J Tomkins	Lambeth	8

The vessels will start from Blackfriars Bridge at Three o'clock
in the afternoon precisely.

Several Bands of Music from the Royal Gardens will be
upon the River. The superb Silver Cup and Cover will be
presented to the fortunate Winner in the Royal Gardens
the same evening.

The other amusements of the Evening will consist of:

The concert - Cosmoranas - Fantoccini - Hydraulics - Revolving
Evening Star - Mount Vesuvius - French Theatre - Tight and
Slack Rope - Illuminated Fountain - Grand Ballet of Cupid and
Psyche - Fire Works and Ascent of the Rope etc etc

Notice in The Public Ledger dated 11th August 1823

HIS MAJESTY'S CORONATION FLEET

THE MEMBERS and FRIENDS of this SOCIETY intend celebrating the Birthday of His Most Gracious Majesty King George IV To-morrow by a trip to sea, on board that beautiful Steam Packet the *LORD MELVILLE,* and which will leave the Tower at half past seven o'clock in the morning precisely; proceed down the River, round the Nore Light, pass the Royal Dock Yard, Sheerness, into the River Medway, join His Majesty's Fleet, lying there, when a Royal Salute will be fired upon the occasion; the Packet will return to the Tower in the evening.

The supurb Silver Cup, sailed for by Gentlemen's Pleasure Vessels, on the 30th July, given by this Society, and exhibited subsequently at the Royal Gardens, Vauxhall, will be on board, and duly presented after dinner to the fortunate winner, William Brocklebank, Esquire, owner of the Saint George.

Double Ticket (admit on board a Gentleman and a Lady)
£1.10.0
Single Ticket for a Gentleman
£1.0.0

The above Terms cover every possible expense of the day, (out and home) breakfast, dinner, wine, desert (consisting of fruit and confectionary), also tea and coffee.

A first- rate Band of Music will attend on board.

Appendix 2

Letter from Lord Alfred Paget dated 27th April 1863

Sir,

I have received an intimation from the Secretary that it is the wish of the General Committee of the Royal Thames Yacht Club that I should inform them not later than Monday week whether I will accept the honourable Post which the Club have again conferred upon me.

I had intended delaying that answer until the next General Meeting when I could have better explained in person not only the deep regret I feel at relinquishing the proud position I had held amongst them for so many years but the motives, which after mature deliberation, have induced me to take that step. I think I need hardly assure the committee that it has not been without sincere regret that I have arrived at that determination, for I can truly say that the welfare and prosperity of the RTYC has for many years been one of the dearest objects in my life.

When I first joined it some 23 years ago, we were few in number and comparatively an insignificant yachting club; we were however, a united and happy community. We have risen by degrees to be the largest and most respectable Club of the kind in the world; it has been my pride to foster and witness its advancement and to induce any influential persons I could to patronise and become members of it.

Events have taken place of late which (though I am bound to say, not of a personal character against myself) have

convinced me that there has not been displayed that confidence in my old colleagues with whom I have been associated in the general management of the Club, which I hold to be so essential to its welfare, and as I feel that my confidence in them was not diminished, I considered myself in honour bound to resign with them.

The Club however, at the adjourned meeting, paid me the compliment to elect me unanimously again, for which I felt deeply grateful, but their next step was to elect an entirely new set of Officers to act with me (one of whom has only entered the Club a few months) and a General Committee of Management excluding most of those gentlemen with whom I had acted for so many years and held in such great esteem; this without a word of consultation with their Commodore, a courtesy which has for many years past been invariably extended to me.

I have felt that under these circumstances that, however painful to myself, it was only my duty both to myself and to my late colleagues respectively to decline the honour conferred upon me. In doing so however, I hope I shall still retain the kind remembrances of the Members of the Club, and though my official connection with the Club now ceases, be assured I shall still cherish the recollection of my long association with so many sincere friends and still feel the greatest interest in the welfare of the RTYC.

I am, Sir
Your obedient Servant
Alfred Paget

To:
The Chairman of the General Committee, RTYC

Appendix 3

1. The anomalous position of the club in being left without Flag Officers naturally engaged the immediate attention of your committee. The removal of that anomaly was considered by them of the utmost importance and the first step to be taken in discharge of the duty imposed upon them. The general feeling of the club evinced by the unanimous re-election of Lord Alfred Paget to the Office of Commodore and by the regret expressed upon his subsequent refusal to accept the Office, led your committee to the conclusion that it was essential to the interests of the Club that he should be prevailed upon to resume the Office of Commodore. Your committee accordingly put themselves in communication with him and they have the satisfaction of reporting that Lord Alfred Paget is ready to undertake that Office. Your committee have annexed to this Report a letter from his Lordship explanatory of the grounds upon which he had acted and they take this occasion of acknowledging the co-operation they have received from the late committee of management, who together with a large number of members addressed a written requisition to his lordship to resume his position.

2. The Club has on its list so many members well qualified for the Office of Vice Commodore, that your committee felt great difficulty in making a selection. They have, however, been relieved from any embarrassment by the consent of Lord de Ros, one of the oldest members and supporters of the Club, to be nominated as Vice Commodore. Your committee cordially recommend this appointment in the belief that it will be acceptable to the Club and they have the satisfaction of adding that Lord Alfred Paget entirely concurs in the proposal.

3. The twelfth section of the Rules prescribes that all monies collected by the Secretary shall be paid over to the Treasurer, but no provision is made for the Investment and Security of the Funds and Property of the Club. Your committee strongly recommend that this comission be now rectified by the appointment of five Trustees into whose names the funds and property of the Club shall be transferred and that the Commodore, Vice Commodore and Mr James Hutchons, the late Treasurer, whose long and able services have tended so materially to the prosperity of the Club, should be three of such Trustees.

4. The Office of Treasurer is unusual in associations of this character and is, in the opinion of your committee, unnecessary; they therefore recommend that all monies collected by the Secretary shall be paid by him, as soon as practicable, and without any deduction, to the account of the Club with the Bankers and that no payment shall be made except by the orders of the General Committee for Management and by cheques signed by the Chairman for the time being and one other member of such Committee and countersigned by the Secretary.

5. In the opinion of your committee the Secretary, being a paid Officer, should be appointed by the General Committee of Management and hold Office during good behaviour. They therefore recommend that the General Committee of Management should have the absolute power of appointing and dismissing this Officer under such regulations as may hereafter be sanctioned by the Club.

6. In order to ensure co-operation in the performance of the duties respectively entrusted to the Commodore, Vice Commodore and General Committee of Management, your committee recommend that the Commodore shall in the month of March in every year appoint seven of the General Committee to act as the "Sailing Committee".

7. The attention of your committee has been necessarily directed to the Rules and though they are unwilling to lengthen their Report by further allusion to them, they are of opinion that the General Committee should be requested to revise and make such alterations in the Rules as may properly carry out the foregoing recommendations should the club approve them.

66

Letter from Lord Alfred Paget dated 15th June 1863

Gentlemen,

I feel proud that the committee appointed by the RTYC to take into consideration its present position should have done me the honour to inform me that they had resolved "That it is essential to the interests of the Club that their late Commodore should resume his office". I need scarcely assure you and the Club generally that I shall never forget the kind feelings which have been displayed towards me on all occasions.

Before I acceded to your request I felt bound to submit your Resolution to those old colleagues with whom I had acted for many years and I beg to enclose a copy of their

views on the subject with the signature of the committee, together with a list of 140 names, which it appears have been appended to their resolution.

I wish to avoid on the present occasion all reference to the original cause of disturbance in the harmony which had previously existed amongst us and to waive all personal feelings - considering alone the welfare of the Club.
It remains to me therefore but to express my willingness to defer to the wishes of the Club, and of the Special Committee and to serve them again to the very best of my ability in the Office of Commodore.

I beg to remain
Gentlemen
Yours most faithfully
Alfred Paget

To The Special Committee

Appendix 4

Patrons and Vice Patrons 1823-1867

Patrons

1827-1837	The Duke of Clarence Later HM King William IV
1837-1901	HM Queen Victoria

Vice Patrons

1833-34	Admiral Sir Richard Keats
1835-39	Admiral Sir Thomas Hardy
1840-41	Admiral The Hon Charles Fleming
1841-48	Admiral The Hon Sir Robert Stopford
1848-53	Admiral Sir Charles Adam

Additional Patrons

1841-1861	HRH Prince Albert
1847-	HM The King of the Belgians
1852-	HM The King of the Netherlands
1855-1863	HM The King of Sardinia
1855-	H.I.M. Napoleon III
1864-	HM The King of Italy
1865-	HRH The Prince of Wales

Appendix 5

That for the purpose of ascertaining the Tonnage of ships or vessels; the Rule for Admeasurement shall be as follows (that is to say) the length shall be taken on a straight Line along the Rabbet of the Keel, from the Back of the Main Stern Post to a Perpendicular Line from the Fore Part of the Main Stem under the Bowsprit, from which, subtracting Three Fifths of the Breadth, the Remainder shall be esteemed the just length of Keel to find the Tonnage; and the Breadth shall be taken from the Outside of the Outside Plank, in the broadest part of the Ship, whether that shall be above or below the Main Wales, exclusive of all manner of Doubling Planks that may be wrought upon the Sides of the Ship, then multiplying the length of the Keel by the Breadth so taken, and that Product by half the Breadth, and dividing the whole by ninety four, the Quotient shall be deemed the true contents of the Tonnage.

$$\text{Tonnage} = \frac{(L - 3/5\ B) \times B \times 1/2\ B}{94}$$

$$\text{Tons TM} = \frac{(L - B) \times B \times 1/2\ B}{94}$$

where L is defined differently

Appendix 6

Date	Course (see Appendix 10)	Prize Value	Silver	Winning Yacht	Owner
10.09.23	1	25 gns	Cup	Spitfire (5T)	T Bettesworth
19.06.24	2	25 gns	Cup	Venus (13T)	T Groves
26.08.24	1	25 gns	Cup	Don Giovanni (11T)	J M Davey
23.06.25	2	25 gns	Cup	Greyhound (12T)	Vink
30.08.25	1	£30	Cup	Lady Louisa (13T)	T Smith
27.06.26	2	£30	Cup	Sylph (12T)	E Codd
17.08.26	1	£30	Cup	Don Giovanni (11T)	J M Davey
03.07.27	2	£40	Cup	Rob Roy (16T)	Herbert
23.08.27	1	£30	Cup	Venus (13T)	G Keen
27.09.27	2	50 gns	Cup given by Duke of Clarence on becoming Patron	Lady Louisa (13T)	T Smith
07.06.28	3	£30	Cup	Daisy (19T)	J G Irwin
28.08.28	4	£30	Cup	Fairy (13T)	E N Lewer

Date	Course (see Appendix 10)	Prize Value	Silver	Winning Yacht	Owner
11.06.29	3	£30	Cup	Lady Lousia (13T)	T Smith
18.08.29	4	£30	Cup	Royal Eagle (13T)	C Stokes
15.06.30	3	£30	Cup	Rob Roy (16T)	W Fitch
19.8.30	4	£30	Cup	Fairy (13T)	C Hasledon
28.08.30	350 gns	25 gns	Cup1st Class (over 10T)	Matchless (19T)	J Hyatt
			Cup - 2nd Class	Brilliant (8T)	W Blackwall
			Both given by William IV on his Accession		
18.06.31	3	£30	Cup	Ellen (17T)	G Keen
13.08.31	4	£30	Cup	Emulation (13T)	A Milne
15.09.31	3	£30	Cup - 1st Class	Lady Louisa (13T)	T Smith
		£20	Cup - 2nd Class	Water Witch (8T)	J Unwin
			Both given in honour of Coronation of William IV		
23.06.32	3	£30	Cup - 1st Class	Lady Louisa (13T)	T Smith
01.08.32	4	25 gns	Cup - 2nd Class	Brilliant (8T)	Lord Choldmondely
21.08.32	3	£30	Cup - 1st Class	Alert (16T)	J Ford
25.06.33	3	£30	Cup - 1st Class	Ellen (17T)	G Keen
05.08.33	4	£25	Cup - 2nd Class	Vestris (8T)	J Weston
24.08.33	3	£30	Cup - Open	Sabrina (21T)	G & H Gunston
24.07.34	5	£25	Cup - 2nd Class	Lady Emma (8T)	W & R C Bucknall
14.08.34	3	£30	Cup - 1st Class	Alert (16T)	J Ford
21.05.35	3	£30	Cup - 1st Class	Sabrina (21T)	G & H Gunston
14.07.35	5	£25	Cup - 2nd Class	Selina (9T)	J Southam
18.08.35	3	£30	Cup - 1st Class	Victorine (9T)	T & C Stokes
26.05.36	3	£30	Cup - 1st Class	Ada Jane (17T)	G W Sweeting & W Malby
18.07.36	5	£25	Cup - 2nd Class	Wave (10T)	J Christian
28.08.36	3	£30	Cup - 1st Class	Gazelle (25T)	G & H Gunston
29.05.37	3	£30	Cup - 1st Class	Widgeon (20T)	T E Snook & H Cassell
13.07.37	3	£30	Cup - 1st Class	Victorine (18T)	T & C Stokes
21.07.37	5	25 gns	Cup - 2nd Class	Malibran (10T)	W Sawyer
12.08.37	3	£30	Cup - Open	Alert (18T)	W Lyon
19.05.38	3	£50	Cup - 1st Class	Sabrina (21T)	G & H Gunston
03.07.38	3	£50	Cup - 1st Class (Over 20T)	Gazelle (25T)	G & H Gunston
		£31	Cup - 2nd Class (11-20T)	Victorine (18T)	T & C Stokes
		£25	Cup - 3rd Class (Up to 10T)	Brilliant (8T)	J T Hewes

Date	Course (see Appendix 10)	Prize Value	Prize Silver	Winning Yacht	Owner
26.07.38	3	£48	Cup - 2nd Class	Ada Jane (18T)	J T Hewes
14.08.38	3	£48	Cup - 2nd Class	Ada Jane (18T)	J T Hewes
23.05.39	6	£50	Cup - 1st Class	Success (22T)	R Hope
22.06.39	6	£50	Cup - 2nd Class	Victorine	T & C Stokes
30.07.39	5	£35	Cup - 3rd Class	Ripple (9T)	W Holt
25.06.40	6	£30	Cup - 1st Class	Sabrina (21T)	Lord Alfred Paget
		£25	Cup - 2nd Class	Alarm (18T)	T Wanhill
16.07.40	5	£20	Cup - 3rd Class	Bermudian Maid (7T)	H Bailes
08.08.40	6	£30	Cup - 1st Class	Gazelle (25T)	H Gunston
		£25	Cup - 2nd Class	Victorine (18T)	T & C Stokes
		£20	Cup - 3rd Class	Ripple (9T)	W Holt
07.09.40	6	100 gns	Grand Challenge Cup Open to all Royal YC Vessels up to 25T	Gazelle (25T)	H Gunston
29.05.41	6	£40	Salver - 1st Class	Champion (25T)	T & J Wanhill
		£30	Salver - 2nd Class	Sea Nymph (10T)	C Wheeler jnr
		£20	Claret Jug - 3rd Class	Alarm (18T)	R H Forman
28.06.41	6	100 gns	Grand Challenge Cup - Open	Champion (25T)	T & J Wanhill
29.07.41	6	£40	Salver - 1st Class	Victorine (18T)	T & C Stokes
		£30	Salver - 2nd Class	Ada (25T)	Hon H Upton
		£20	Claret Jug - 3rd Class	Little Vixen (10T)	R Wright
04.06.42 no wind re-sailed 07.06.42	6	£40	Breakfast Service - 1st Class	Mystery (25T)	Lord Alfred Paget
		£30	Salver - 2nd Class	Lady Louisa (12T)	T Smith
		£20	Claret Jug - 3rd Class	Sea Nymph (10T)	C Wheeler jnr
05.07.42	6	100 gns	Grand Challenge Cup - Open	Ada (25T)	Hon H Upton
01.08.42	6	£40	Tea Service	Champion (25T)	H Gunston
23.05.43	6	£50	Cup - 1st Class (over 12 up 25Tons)	Mystery (25T)	Lord Alfred Paget
		£25	Tankard - 1st Class, 2nd Prize	Phantom (20T)	A O Wilkinson
		£25	Tankard - 2nd Class (up to 12 Tons)	Dolphin (10T)	T & J Wanhill
08.06.43	6	100 gns	Grand Challenge Cup - Open	Enigma (25T)	W Head
07.07.43	6	£50	Cup - 1st Class	Blue Belle (25T)	A Fountaine
		£25	Tankard - 2nd Class	Fay (12T)	J T Hewes
11.05.44	6	£50	Tankard - 1st Class	Mystery (25T)	Lord Alfred Paget
		£25	Claret Jug - 2nd Class	Curlew (12T)	W H Rees
10.06.44	6	100 gns	Grand Challenge Cup - Open	Mystery (25T)	Lord Alfred Paget
27.06.44	7	Painting by N M Condy of Winning Yacht		Phantom (20T)	A O Wilkinson
10.07.44	6	Cup	Presented by Captain Cocksedge	Phantom (20T)	A O Wilkinson

Date	Course (see Appendix 10)	Prize Value	Silver	Winning Yacht	Owner
25.07.44	6	£50	Salver - 1st Class	Blue Belle (25T)	T Hodges
		£25	Cup - 2nd Class	Sea Nymph (10T)	C Wheeler jnr
16.06.45	6	100 gns	Grand Challenge Cup - Open	Prima Donna (25T)	C R Tatham
30.06.45	6	£60	Cup presented by Earl Fitchardinge Crew of Club Members only	Belvidere (25T)	Lord Alfred Paget
16.07.45	6	£30	Stewards Cup - 1st Class	Victorine (18T)	H G Lord
		£30	Cup - 2nd Class	Sea Nymph (10T)	C Wheeler jnr
20.05.46	8	£30	Cup - 1st Class, 1st Prize	Primma Donna (25T)	T Harvey
		£30	Cup - 1st Class, 2nd Prize	Vixen (25T)	T Heighington
		£30	Cup - 2nd Class	Ranger (12T)	E W Roberts
05.06.46	6	100 gns	Grand Challenge Cup - Open	Secret (25T)	J W Smith
19.06.46	9	£70	Cup - Yachts up to 50T	Heroine (35T)	Sir J Carnac Bart
04.07.46	8	£60	Cup - 1st Class, 1st Prize	Secret (25T)	J W Smith
		£30	Cup - 1st Class, 2nd Prize	Ino (25T)	H Gibson
		£30	Cup - 2nd Class	Enchantress (11T)	R Atkinson
11.05.47	8	£60	Tea Kettle - 1st Class, 1st Prize	Secret (25T)	J W Smith
		£30	Tea Service - 1st Class, 2nd Prize	Ino (25T)	H Gibson
		£30	Punch Bowl - 2nd Class	Ranger (12T)	E W Roberts
08.06.47	6	100 gns	Grand Challenge Cup (outright winner of Cup having successive wins)	Secret (12T)	J W Smith
07.07.47	9	£100 purse	For Yachts up to 50 Tons	Eclipse (50T)	T Wickham
29.05.48	9	£80 purse	1st Class (over 25T up to 50T)	Daring (31T)	G Cook
		£60 purse	2nd Class (over 12T to 25T)	Secret (25T)	J Wicks
		£30 purse	3rd Class (up to 12T)	Frolic (12T)	A Cox
13.06.48	9	£100 purse	Open up to 50T	Mosquito (50T)	C Mare
11.07.48	9	£80 purse	1st Class	no entries	
		£60 purse	2nd Class	Secret (25T)	J Wicks
		£30 purse	3rd Class	Frolic (12T)	A Cox
30.05.49 no wind re-sailed 16.06.49	9	£20 (£80 purse)	Cup - 1st Class	Cynthia (50T)	J Wicks
		£10 (£40 purse)	Cup - 2nd Class	Foam (20T)	R Antrem
29.06.49	9	200 gns	Challenge Cup - No tonnage limit open to all Royal YC	Cygnet (35T)	H Lambton
05.06.50	9	£100 purse	1st Class (Over 30T)	Mosquito (50T)	C Mare
		£50 purse	2nd Class (15T up to 30T)	Whisper (19T)	T Eveleigh
		£30 purse	3rd Class (10T up to 15T)	Mazeppa (12T)	C Bromley
05.07.50	9	200 gns	Challenge Cup - Open	Mosquito (50T)	Lord Landesborough

Date	Course (see Appendix 10)	Prize Value	Prize Silver	Winning Yacht	Owner
26.05.51	9	£100 purse	1st Class	Cynthia (50T)	J Wicks
		£50 purse	2nd Class	Mazeppa (12T)	C Bromley
				finished ahead of all 2nd Class	
		£30 purse	3rd Class	Whisper	T Eveleigh
25.06.51	9	200 gns	Challenge Cup - Open	Volante (48T)	J L Craigie
08.07.51	9	100 gns	Cup presented by Queen Victoria (Patron)	Cygnet (35T)	H Lambton
14.05.52	9	200 gns	Challenge Cup - Open (wins Cup outright)	Volante (48T)	J L Craigie
12.06.62	9	£100	Model of Eddystone Lighthouse 1st Class	Volante (48T)	J L Craigie
		£50	Silver Vase 2nd Class	Phantom (20T)	S Lane
		£30	Tankard 3rd Class	Vampire (15T)	
03.05.53	9	£100	Epergne - 1st Class	Mosquito (50T)	Lord Landesborough
		£50	Ewer - 2nd Class	Phantom (20T)	S Lane
01.06.53	10	100 gns purse	Schooners - Open	Rosalind (100T) (after Protest)	Lord Alfred Paget
30.06.53	9		1st and 2nd Classes		
		£60 purse	1st Prize	Mosquito (50T)	Lord Landesborough
		£40 purse	2nd Prize	Volante (48T)	J L Craigie
		£30 purse	3rd Prize	Phantom (20T)	S Lane
			3rd Class		
	11	£30 purse	1st Prize	Vampire (15T)	C Wheeler jnr
		£10 purse	2nd Prize	Vesper (15T)	P Roberts
22.05.54	9	£100 purse	1st Class	no entries	
		£50 purse	2nd Class	Phantom (20T)	S Lane
		£30 purse	3rd Class	Vampire (15T)	C Wheeler jnr
06.07.54	10	100 gns purse	Schooners	no entries	
26.05.55	12	£100	Epergne - 1st Class (Over 35T)	Phantom (20T)	S Lane
		£50	Epergne - 2nd Class (Over 20T to 35T)	Marina (26T)	W J Foster
		£30	Punch Bowl - 3rd Class (Over 12T up to 20T)	Vampire (15T)	C Wheeler jnr
26.06.55	12	£100	Vase - Schooners - Open	Shark (175T)	W Curling
09.07.55	13	£20	Jug - 4th Class (7T to 12T)	Julia (7T)	W P Bain
14.05.56	9	£100	Cup - 1st Class Cutters	Amazon (46T)	A J Young
		£70	Epergne - 2nd Class Cutters	Thought (25T)	G Coope
14.06.56	4	£100	Epergne - Schooner - Open	Wildfire	J T Turner
08.06.56	11	£50	Claret Jug - 3rd Class Cutters	Quiver (12T)	T Chamberlayne
		£30	Tankard - 4th Class Cutters	Flirt (5T)	R M Dunn
02.06.57	9	£100	Tankard & Salver - 1st Class	Mosquito (50T)	T Groves
		£50	Claret Jug & 6 Cups - 2nd Class	Thought (25T)	F Ord Marshall

Date	Course (see Appendix 10)	Value	Prize Silver	Winning Yacht	Owner
19.06.57	14	£100	Ewer - 1st Class Schooners (Over 75T)	Vestal (74T)	F Ord Marshall
		£50	Soup Tureen -2nd Class Schooners (under 75T)	Zouave (105T)	R Arabin
18.07.57	11	£40	Claret Jug - 3rd Class	no entries	
		£30	Punch Bowl - 4th Class, 1st Prize	Quiver (12T)	T Chamberlayne
		£10	Tankard - 4th Class, 2nd Prize	Violet (10T)	J R Kirby
22.05.58	9	£100	Tea & Coffee Service - 1st Class	Amazon (46T)	J H Johnson
		£50	Tankard - 2nd Class	Emmet (28T)	E Gibson
22.06.58	15	£100	Cup - 1st Class Schooners	no entries	
		£50	Tea Service - 2nd Class Schooners	no entries	
06.07.58	11	£40	Jug - 3rd Class	Vampire (18T)	C Wheeler jnr
		£30	Cup - 4th Class, 1st Prize	Emily (8T)	R Hewitt
		£10	Tankard - 4th Class, 2nd Prize	Julia (7T)	P Turner
		£40	Vase - 2nd Class not having won a prize previously	Pearl (24T)	Hon A Annesley
26.05.59	1	£40	Tea Service - 3rd Class, 1st Prize	Quiver (12T)	D T Chamberlayne
		£15	Cup - 3rd Class, 2nd Prize	insufficient entries	
		£30	Claret Jug - 4th Class, 1st Prize	Swallow (16T)	Captain F H Sykes
		£10	Cup - 4th Class, 2nd Prize	Violet (10T)	Rt Hon Lord de Ros
10.06.59	9	£100	Epergne - 1st Class	no records	
		£50	Tea Service - 2nd Class		
25.06.59	9	£100	Tea Service - Open	Osprey (59T)	Colonel R W Huey
		50 gns	Jug & 2 Goblets - RTYC crewed vessel up to 35T. Presented by T Broadwood	Whisper (19T)	B Greenhill
09.07.59	15	£100	Cup - Open to Schooners 75T and over	Alarm (248T)	J Weld
30.05.60	11	£50	Claret Jug 2nd Class, 1st Prize	Phantom (25T)	S Lane
		£20	Cup 2nd Class, 2nd Prize	insufficient entries	
		£40	Tea Service 3rd Class, 1st Prize	Quiver (12T)	Captain D Chamberlayne
		£15	Cup 3rd Class, 2nd Prize	insufficient entries	
		£30	Tankard 4th Class, 1st Prize	Kitten (13T)	R Leach
		£10	Tankard 4th Class, 2nd Prize	Folly (12T)	W L Parry
14.06.60	9	£100	Cup 1st Class, 1st Prize	Audax (59T)	J H Jackson
		£30	Salad Bowl 1st Class, 2nd Prize	insufficient entries	
		£50	Tea Service Amateur Match up to 35T, 1st Prize	Thought (25T)	F Ord Marshall
			Claret Jug Amateur Match up to 35T, 2nd Prize	insufficient entries	
29.06.60	14	£100	Shield Schooners Open, 1st Prize	Alarm (248T)	J Weld
			Claret Jug Schooners Open, 2nd Prize	insufficient entries	

Date	Course (see Appendix 10)	Value	Prize / Silver		Winning Yacht	Owner
03.03.61	9	£100		Cutters & Yawls		
			1st Class	1st Prize	Thought (25T)	F Ord Marshall
				2nd Prize	Christabel (43T)	H H Kennard
			2nd Class	1st Prize	Osprey (59T)	Colonel R W Huey
				2nd Prize	Phantom (25T)	S Lane
18.06.61				Cutters		
		£40	3rd Class	1st Prize	no entries	
		£15		2nd Prize	no entries	
		£30	4th Class	1st Prize	Folly (12T)	W L Parry
		£10		2nd Prize	Don Juan (10T)	W Cooper
		£50	Mixed Rig up to 50T, no previous prize & built pre 1860		Eva (22T)	W R Gade
04.07.61	15	£100	Schooner - Open 1st Prize Alarm (248T) 2nd Prize insufficient entries		J Weld	
23.05.61	9	£100	Tea Service, Cutters 1st Class, 1st Prize		Christabel (43T)	H H Kennard
		£40	Claret Jug & 2 Goblets, Cutters 1st Class, 2nd Prize		Glance (36T)	A Duncan
		£40	Tankard, Cutters 3rd Class, 1st Prize		no entries	
		£20	Basket, Cutters 3rd Class, 2nd Prize		no entries	
07.06.61	9	£50	Claret Jug - Cutters, 2nd Class, 1st Prize		The Queen (25T)	Captain T W Whitbread
		£20	Claret Jug - Cutters, 2nd Class, 2nd Prize		Phantom (25T)	S Lane
		£30	Claret Jug - Cutters, 4th Class, 1st Prize		Folly (12T)	W L Parry
		£10	Butter Dish - Cutters, 4th Class, 1st Prize RTYC Yachts not won before & 20T or above:		Octoroon (12T)	C Lang
		£10	Claret Jug - 1st Prize		Violet (32T)	J R Kirby
			Tea Pot - 2nd Prize		Oriole (26T)	J W Ledger
03.06.62	10	£100	Shield - Schooners Open 1st Prize		Flying Cloud (75T)	Count E Batthyany
		£40	2 Claret Jugs 2nd Prize		Leanora (105T)	R B Hesketh
28.05.63	9	£100	Tea & Coffee Service, Cutters 1st Class 1st Prize		Vindex (45T)	A Duncan
		£50	Tankard - 2nd Prize		Phryne (56T)	T Seddon
		£40	Punch Bowl & 2 Goblets - 3rd Class, 1st Prize		no entries	
		£20	Claret Jug - 2nd Prize		no entries	
11.06.63	9	£50	Loving Cup - Cutters - 2nd Class, 1st Prize		Phantom (25T)	S Lane
		£20	Cup - 2nd Class, 2nd Prize		insufficient entries	
		£30	Punch Bowl - 4th Class, 1st Prize		Octoroon (12T)	C Long
		£10	Cup - 4th Class, 2nd Prize		Quiver (12T)	Captain D Chamberlayne
		£40	Tankard, RTYC Yachts not won before, 1st Prize		no entries	
		£10	Cup, RTYC Yachts not won before, 2nd Prize		no entries	
27.06.63	10	£100	Tankard & 6 Goblets Schooners 1st Class (over 100T)		Albertine (155T)	Lord Landesborough
		£50	Claret Jug - 2nd Class (up to 100T)		Intrigue	F K Duncan

Date	Course (see Appendix 10)	Prize Value	Silver	Winning Yacht	Owner
31.05.64	10	£100	Epergne - Cutters - 1st Class, 1st Prize	Vindex (45T)	A Duncan
		£50	Plate - 1st Class, 2nd Prize	Mosquito (50T)	T Houldsworth
	12	£40	Epergne - Cutters - 3rd Class, 1st Prize	Vampire (19T)	Captain T E Commerell
		£20	2 Goblets - 3rd Class, 2nd Prize	Dudu (15T)	W Rudge, Capt E Bladock
04.06.64	16		Ocean Match open to Schooners, Yawls and Cutters		
		£80	Cup - 1st Prize	Whirlwind (77T)	A Cox
		£50	Cup - 2nd Prize	Volante (60T)	H C Maudslay
15.06.64	12		Cutters - 2nd Class		
		£50	1st Prize	no entries	
		£20	2nd Prize	no entries	
		£30	Punch Bowl - Cutters - 4th Class 1st Prize	Quiver (12T)	Captain D Chamberlayne
		£10	Cup - Cutters - 4th Class 2nd Prize	Folly (12T)	W L Parry
16.06.64	10	£100	Epergne - Schooners - 1st Class (over 100T)	Albertine (155T)	Lord Landesborough
		£50	Plate - 2nd Class	Madcap (75T)	J S Abbot Dunbar
—.06.64	17	4 x £5	Sweepstake - Schooners Channel	Madcap (75T)	J S Abbot Dunbar
		5 x £5	Sweepstake - Cutters Match	Volante (50T)	H C Maudslay
03.06.65	9	£100	Wine Cooler Cutters - 1st Class, 1st Prize	Glance (36T)	E Johnson
		£50	Water Jug & 2 Goblets Cutters - 1st Class, 2nd Prize	Vindex (45T)	A Duncan
		£50	Cup Cutters - 2nd Class, 1st Prize	no entries	
		£20	Fruit Stand Cutters - 2nd Class, 2nd Prize	no entries	
12.06.65	18		Ocean March open to Schooners, Yawls and Cutters		
		£100	Tureen - 1st Prize	Alarm (248T)	G Duppa
		£50	Tea & Coffee Service - 2nd Prize	Xantha (135T)	Lord Alfred Paget
19.06.65	10	£100	Epergne Schooners - 1st Class, 1st Prize	Gloriana (148T)	A O Wilkinson
		£50	Ice Dish Schooners - 1st Class, 2nd Prize	insufficient entries	
		£50	Cup 2nd Class, 1st Prize	Intrigue (82T)	F K Dumas
		£25	Claret Jug 2nd Class, 2nd Prize	insufficient entries	
		25 gns	up - Presented by Captain P Cosby Lovett	Christabel (51T)	A C Kennard

Date	Course (see Appendix 10)	Prize Value	Prize Silver	Winning Yacht	Owner
21.06.65	17	150 gns	Epergne & Cup - Presented by Mr Geo. Salt Open to all Royal YC Yachts, Channel Match	Arrow (102T)	Captain T Chamberlayne
		50 gns	2 Claret Cups - Presented by Sir Gilbert East Open to all Cutters	Glance (36T)	E Johnson
04.07.65	9	£40	Ink Stand - Cutters - 3rd Class 1st Prize	Vampire (19T)	T Cuthbert
		£20	Claret Jug - 2nd Prize	insufficient entries	
		£30	Claret Jug - Cutters - 4th Class, 1st Prize	no entries	
		£10	Cup - 2nd Prize	no entries	
05.07.65	12	50 gns	Presented by H F Smith & H C Maudslay Amateur crew in Cutters 10T to 35T	Vampire (19T)	T Cuthbert
21.05.66	19		Channel Match -		
		£100	Schooners & Luggers	Xantha (135T)	Lord Alfred Paget
		£50	Yawls	Egeria (152T)	J Mulholland
		£50	Cutters	Sphinx (48T)	H C Maudslay
24.05.66	10		Cutter Match		
		£100	1st Class	Christabel (51T)	A C Kennard
		£50	2nd Class	no entries	
19.06.66	10	£100	Schooners over 100T	Gloriana (148T)	A O Wilkinson
		£80	Schooners up to 100T	Madcap (70T)	J S Abbot Dunbar
		£80	Yawls over 50T	Xantha (135T)	Lord Alfred Paget
23.06.66	9		Cutters Match		
		£30	3rd Class	Vampire (19T)	T H Cuthbert
		£20	4th Class	no entries	
30.05.67 protests re-sailed 07.06.67	10		Cutter Match		
		£100	1st Class	Vanguard (60T)	Captain W N Hughes
		£50	2nd Class	no entries	
10.06.67	19		Schooners Open to any Royal YC or NYYC Ocean Match		
		£100	1st Prize	Egeria (152T)	J Mulholland
		£50	2nd Prize	Pantomine	Colonel Markham
29.06.67	12		Cutter Match		
		£30	3rd Class	Vampire (19T)	T H Cuthbert
		£20	4th Class	Buccaneer (12T)	Captain E H Bayly
04.07.67	20		Channel Match		
		£100	1st Prize	Alarm (248T)	G Duppa
		£50	2nd Prize	Julia (122T)	G F Moss

Appendix 7

(See charts on page 96)

Sailing match courses

1. Blackfriars Bridge to Wandsworth and back to Cumberland Gardens

2. Blackwall to Gravesend and back

3. Greenwich to Gravesend and back

4. Southwark Bridge to Wandsworth and back to Westminster

5. Temple Gardens to Wandsworth and back

6. Greenwich to Coal House Point and back

7. Greenwich to Nore Light Vessel and back

8. Erith to Chapmans Head and back to Greenwich

9. Erith to Nore Light Vessel and back

10. Gravesend to Mouse Light Vessel and back

11. Erith to Chapmans Head and back

12. Gravesend to Nore Light Vessel and back

13. Erith to Sea Reach and back

14. Gravesend to Mouse Light Vessel and back to Rotherhithe

15. Rosherville to Mouse Light Vessel and back to Greenwich

16. Thames Haven to Harwich

17. Gravesend to Ryde

18. Sheerness to Harwich

19. Nore Light Vessel to Dover

20. Nore Light Vessel to Le Havre

Appendix 8

Report by the Committee on Club Accommodation (1845)

That having regard to that part of the Resolution which directs them *'to consider of and provide suitable accommodation for the Club'* they have after much consideration decided that the monthly and other meetings of the Club shall no longer be held at the British Hotel, the committee being unanimously of opinion that the premises are not sufficiently extensive and commodious for the wants of this Society. Your committee have therefore after much consideration entered into an arrangement with Mr Cuttriss the proprietor of the Piazza Coffee House, Covent Garden, by which that Gentleman has consented to place the Guest Room of his Establishment at the entire disposal of the Club on the usual monthly meeting nights as well as on the occasion of special meetings. Your committee have consequently instructed the Secretary to summon all future Club meetings to the Piazza Coffee House in pursuance of that arrangement.

Your committee with regard to that part of the Resolution which directs them to consider the propriety and

practicability of establishing a Clubhouse and of the mode in which the Club can be better accommodated for the transaction of its public business, feeling some difficulty in recommending the Club to enter upon so large an expenditure as would be involved in the establishment of a Clubhouse, without some data to proceed upon showing the proportion of members likely to support it, have thought it more prudent to recommend the Club to try to experiment upon a small and inexpensive scale and have therefore entered into a further arrangement with Mr Cuttriss whereby that Gentleman in consideration of the small payment of Twenty Five Pounds per annum agrees to provide the Club with a Room for their exclusive use with fire, lighting and attendance. Your committee have further agreed upon a Tariff of Prices with Mr Cuttriss for the supply of Dinner to members, a list of such prices is in the Clubroom for the inspection of members.

The arrangements with Mr Cuttriss have been made for one year certain. Your committee have further directed that the Clubroom shall be furnished with stationery and one morning and one evening paper of opposite politics and also three weekly sporting papers viz: Bell's Life in London, The Era and The Sunday Times and they have also passed certain Rules to be observed by members using the room, a strict compliance with which they feel persuaded, members will cheerfully accord, and by which the committee trust that the comfort of all parties will be ensured.

The arrangements having been entered into for one year certain. It is presumed that before the expiration of that period a test of the practicability of establishing a Clubhouse will have been afforded and as your committee conceive, at a very trivial expense.

Your committee cannot close their report without adverting to a subject which although not specially referred to them to consider of, has yet been brought incidentally under their notice. The annual income of the Club last year reached the large sum of seven hundred pounds but notwithstanding, the expenses exceeded that sum, and that upon a balance of the Receipts and Payments of the year, a deficiency arose. The growing importance of this Club and its large annual increase in numbers (last year reaching 127 members) has rendered a more lavish expenditure necessary. Your committee therefore conceive that although a considerable balance appears to be remaining in the Treasurer's hands, yet that

to place the Club upon a secure footing it does appear to the committee to be extremely desirable to increase the Annual Subscription from one guinea to two guineas. The committee cannot doubt but that this small increase will be cheerfully submitted to, for in no club are such extensive privileges afforded to members for so small an annual payment as one guinea.

In conclusion your committee desire to congratulate the Club upon the extraordinary success of their last season. It cannot fail of being gratifying to the members to see this popular Club so rapidly increasing in importance, indeed it is conceived that its success in latter years has been altogether unprecedented. To its extreme liberality, its excellent management and its undeviating faith, are to be attributed so pleasing a result and your committee trust that the members will not hesitate to strengthen the hands of their Officers of the Club, by placing at their command the means to carry out those measures which may be deemed necessary to support its hitherto well sustained credit.

Appendix 9

Letter dated 4th April 1862 by 28 members concerning Wines and Spirits

As members of the RTYC who are in the constant habit of dining and frequenting the Clubhouse, we feel called upon to draw your attention to the unsatisfactory supply of Wines and Spirits.

In passing we may allude to the prices which in many cases are such as are not met with on the Wine Carte of any leading Restaurant with which we are acquainted

- it is however, to the wines themselves that we must strongly object, as they are of so inferior a class as materially to check their consumption. As no reliance can be placed on the character of the wines supplied we are prevented to a very great degree from using the Clubhouse as a place where we can exercise hospitality to our friends. We consider this matter one of equal importance to the Club and to the Contractor to the Club as seriously affecting the comfort of the members and to the Contractor as materially diminishing his profits. There are many other points in the management of the Club to which we take exception, but we are unwilling to diminish the force of this protest against the present conduct of the Refreshment Department by entering upon other points.

Appendix 10

Royal Thames Yacht Club
Albemarle Street
Piccadilly, W

9th October 1867

Sir,

The GENERAL COMMITTEE have felt it necessary to anticipate the Resolution passed at the General Meeting of the Club in April last and to obtain from Professional Accountants an estimate of its working for a whole year, to 31st December 1867, based upon the actual profit and loss account for the first half of the year.

From this statement it results that the Club cannot be carried on, even with the strictest economy, without an increased Annual Subscription.

The Income derived from paying members amounts to £2,740, of which about one-third is appropriated to Prizes and Expenses incidental to yachting. The Rent of the Club-house absorbs £1,000 per annum, leaving between £800 and £900 only (exclusive of Entrance Fees) for salaries and House Expenses. The proportion of the Expenditure appropriated to the yachting interest exclusively should not, in the judgment of the Committee, be reduced; although by the addition of many members who are not Yacht Owners, the character of the Club has been somewhat modified, yet care has always been taken to maintain the objects for which it was originally established, and to preserve its distinctive features. The following details are submitted in evidence of this:-

The Entrance Fee for Yacht Owners is Fourteen Guineas, for non Yacht Owners it is Twenty Guineas. The Club numbers amongst its 900 members 219 Yacht Owners, with a fleet of 241 yachts of 14,000 Tons - constituting the largest Fleet, with the greatest amount of tonnage of any Yacht Club in the world. The Subscription of Yacht Owners, and the receipt from Steamboat Tickets, amount to £815, this year - and it appears from an average of three years - that the amount on Prizes and incidental expenses of the Matches is £851. The Committee also draw attention to the circumstances, that without the prestige afforded by the gift of Royal Cup, the Club has for many years past given a larger sterling value to be sailed for than any other Club in the Kingdom.

The Yacht Owning Members are in the ratio of one-fourth of the total number of the Club, and it has been ascertained after careful investigation, that the proportion of Yacht Owning to General Members using the Clubhouse is about the same as that of their relative numbers in the Club, - viz, one fourth.

Since the present Committee have been in office, they have effected important reductions; but they are still of opinion that an increase of Two Guineas in the Annual Subscription is absolutely indispensable and necessary, to maintain the Club in its present position.

Under these circumstances the Committee consider it essential to the existence of the Club that a Special General Meeting be forthwith held to consider its position, to re-consider the Resolution passed at the meeting of the 24th of April, and to decide at once upon the expediency of increasing the Annual Subscription, and altering the Rules in conformity therewith.

A SPECIAL GENERAL MEETING will accordingly be held on THURSDAY, OCTOBER 17th, at 5 pm at which the attendance of every Member of the Club is most earnestly requested.

Should you unfortunately be unable to attend, you are invited to communicate to the Secretary, in writing, on or before the 17th Instant, your views upon the subject.

I am
SIR
Your most obedient Servant,
P.C. STUART GRANT
Secretary

The following is the resolution referred to:-

That this meeting be adjourned until the middle of November, at 8 o'clock pm; in the meantime the Secretary shall forward (fourteen days at least before said meeting) a Circular to each member residing in the United Kingdom, begging the favour of him to reply in writing without delay, whether he assents or dissents to the recommendation of the General Committee to increase the Subscription on the 1st January next from three to five Guineas per annum, and that a printed Form be sent with each Circular for the member to sign.

Appendix 11

Officers of the New Thames Yacht Club

Commodore

1870 - 76	J.D. Lee
1876 - 91	A.O. Wilkinson
1891 - 03	R. Hewett
1903 - 08	C. Arkcoll

Vice Commodore

1868 - 70	J.D. Lee
1870 - 81	W.N. Rudge
1881 - 89	E. Boutcher
1889 - 95	E.W. Buller
1895 - 03	C. Arkcoll
1903 - 05	R.H. Simpson
1905 - 08	C.F. Southgate

Rear Commodore

1876 - 81	T.W. Weeding
1887 - 88	E.W. Buller
1889 - 91	R. Hewett
1891 - 95	C. Arkcoll
1899 - 03	R.H. Simpson
1903 - 05	C.F. Southgate
1905 - 07	H. Borrass

Honorary Treasurer

1868 - 81	R.S. Wilkinson
1881 - 1908	H.J. Baker

Appendix 12

Location in Club House of Prints described in text

PEARL	Cabin 7	*OSPREY*	Cabin 12A
LADY LOUISA	Cabin 50	*ALARM (248 Tons)*	Paget Room
BRILLIANT	Cabin 16	*AUDAX*	Mountbatten Suite
ALARM (18 Tons)	Queenborough Room	*THOUGHT*	Cabin 42
SEA NYMPH	Cabin 5	*MARINA*	East Cabins Corridor
MYSTERY	Mountbatten Suite	*CHRISTABEL*	Coffee Room
PHANTOM	Cabin 14 and Mountbatten Suite	*FLYING CLOUD*	West Passage
NANCY DAWSON	Coffee Room	*VINDEX*	Mountbatten Suite
CYNTHIA	Cabin 12	*ALBERTINE*	Mountbatten Suite
MOSQUITO	Coffee Room	*MADCAP*	East Cabins Corridor
VOLANTE	Cabin 11 and Mountbatten Suite	*GLANCE*	Cabin 12
ROSALIND	Coffee Room	*GLORIANA*	Cabin 12A
SVERIGE	Queenborough Room	*NEW MOON*	Mountbatten Suite
ARROW	Cabin 10	*SPHINX*	West Passage

Cornelius Wheeler, Treasurer, 1831-1855 - Painting by
Daniel Passmore

His Royal Highness The Duke of Cumberland.

Robert Williams, Treasurer, 1823-1830 - Painting by
Daniel Passmore.

82

Paintings by N M Condy incorporating Lord Alfred Paget's Mystery.

MYSTERY overtaking Bluebell.

MYSTERY winning at Falmouth 1843.

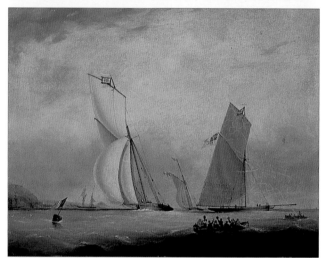

MYSTERY winning at Plymouth 1842.

MYSTERY under sail.

Lord Alfred Paget, Vice Commodore 1845 - 1846 and 1874 - 1888, Commodore 1846 - 1873
- Painting by Sir Francis Grant.

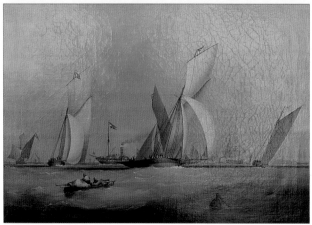

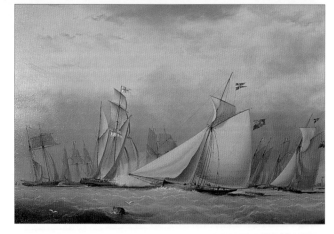

(Top) Gaff Cutters racing inshore by N M Condy.

(Above) Yacht Racing 1844 by N M Condy.

(Above right) The Start by N M Condy (1844).

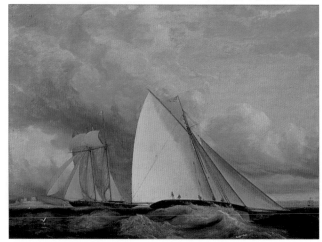

(Right) PHANTOM (A O Wilkinson) and BELVIDERE (Lord Alfred Paget), 1845 by N M Condy.

William Harrison, Commodore 1831 - 1846 - Painting by C Ambrose.

MYSTERY by N M Condy.

(Right) The Cumberland
Fleet passing St Paul's
Cathedral (1175)
- Painting by D Turner.

(Below) The Cumberland
Fleet at the first regatta held
in England, 23 June 1775 -
Painting by Francis Swaine.

Lord Queenborough,
Rear Commodore 1905-1910,
Vice Commodore 1911 - 1923
and 1932 - 1935, Commodore
1924 - 1931 and 1936 - 1945
Painting after Arthur Hacker.

Theodore Pim,
Rear Commodore 1902 - 1903,
Vice Commodore 1904,
Commodore 1905 - 1923 -
Painting by William Llewellyn.

CAMBRIA (above) leading DAUNTLESS at end of Trans-Atlantic Race, passing sandy Hook light vessel 1870. CAMBRIA (below) wins Anglo-American Race round the Isle of Wight in 1868.

J S Highfield, Rear Commodore 1924 - 1925,
Vice Commodore 1936 - 1945 - Painting by
Frederick Whiting.

Earl Mountbatten, Commodore 1946 - 1970,
Admiral of the Cumberland Fleet 1971 - 1979
- Painting by William Apap.

Elmer Ellsworth Jones, Rear Commodore 1964 - 1966,
Commodore 1970 - 1974 - Painting by M Duyn (after
Frank Eastman).

AMERICA winning Round the Island Race 1851.

SVERIGE (Thomas Bartlett) and ROSALIND (Lord Alfred Paget) - First RTYC Schooner Match 1853.

(Left) VOLANTE, 48 Tons -
Owned by John L Craigie
(1852).

(Right) FIONA, 78 Tons
- Owned by E Boutcher
(1865).

Start of Round Britain Race (1877), held to celebrate Quenn Victoria's Golden Jubilee.

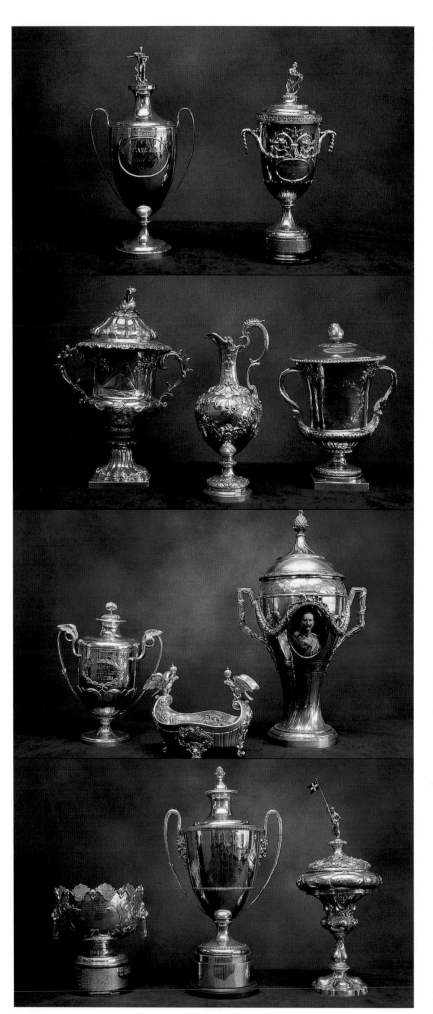

Cumberland Cup 1777 (right) and
Vauxhall Cup 1802.

Glazebrook Cup (left), Holt Cup and
Muir Cup.

Queen Victoria Cup (left), Emperor of
Russia Rosebowl and the Heligoland
Cup (1906).

Cory Cup (left), Quennborough
Cumberland Cup and the Docker Cup.

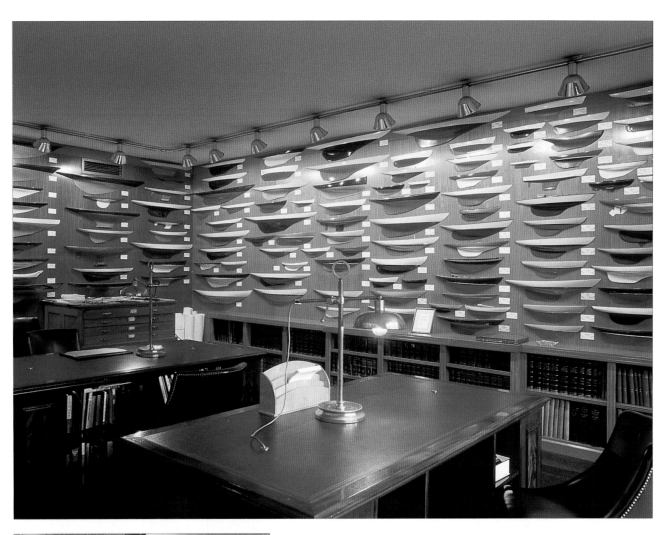

The Model Room.

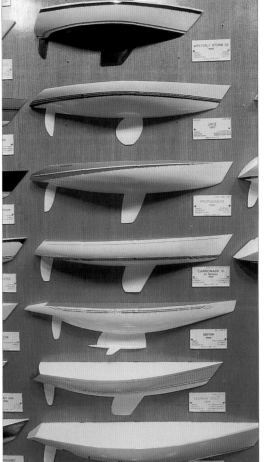

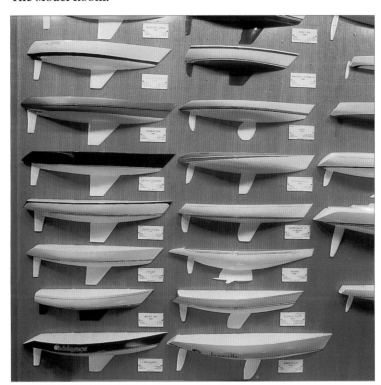

One of the two stone lions at the entrance to the Britannia Lounge.

(Above) The entrance hall of the Clubhouse.

The entrance to the club-house.

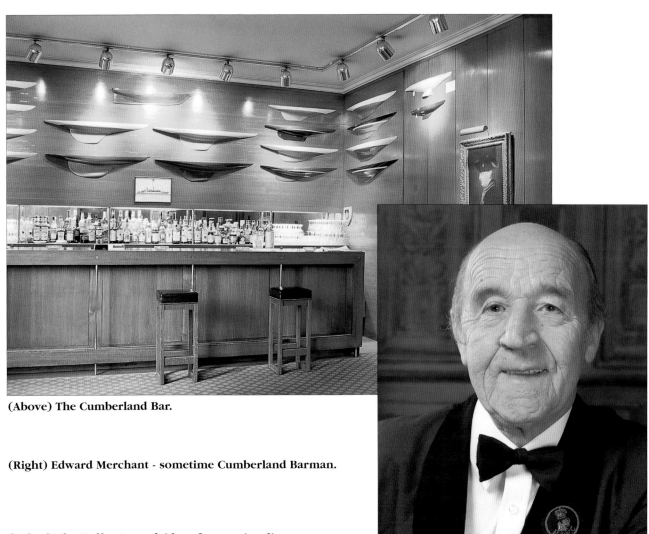

(Above) The Cumberland Bar.

(Right) Edward Merchant - sometime Cumberland Barman.

(Below) The Coffee Room laid up for a major dinner.

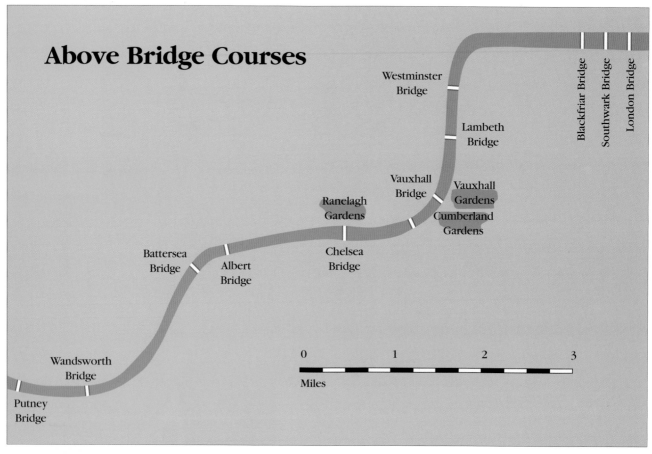

Above Bridge Courses

Westminster Bridge

Lambeth Bridge

Vauxhall Bridge

Vauxhall Gardens

Ranelagh Gardens

Cumberland Gardens

Blackfriar Bridge

Southwark Bridge

London Bridge

Battersea Bridge

Albert Bridge

Chelsea Bridge

Wandsworth Bridge

Putney Bridge

0   1   2   3

Miles

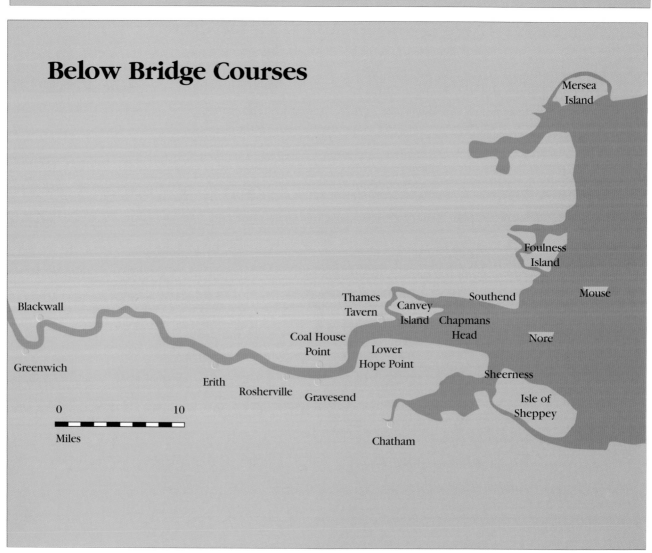

Below Bridge Courses

Mersea Island

Foulness Island

Blackwall

Thames Tavern

Canvey Island

Southend

Mouse

Coal House Point

Chapmans Head

Nore

Greenwich

Lower Hope Point

Erith

Sheerness

Rosherville

Gravesend

Isle of Sheppey

Chatham

0   10

Miles

The Chronicles
of the
ROYAL THAMES YACHT CLUB

Volume II

1868-1918

Introduction

The fifty years covered by this volume, 1868-1918, can rightly be called the golden era of yacht racing. For the Royal Thames Yacht Club, it was a period when its influence over the sport diminished, but that in no way detracts from the Club's pre-eminence in yacht racing both in the United Kingdom and in many countries overseas.

Historically these 50 years saw the spiralling expansion of the industrial revolution and its effect on modes of transport; the advances in communications with the invention of the many techniques of telephone and radio communications and, above all the great advances in scientific and medical knowledge. At the turn of the 19th century Britain was filled with fervent patriotic support for what many considered to be an ill-advised war in South Africa that took many lives but which was soon overshadowed by the appalling loss of life in the unproductive trench warfare of 1914-18.

Against such a vast backdrop the affairs of the Royal Thames may seem a trifle trivial, but perhaps less so when it is recalled that many members of the Club were deeply involved in the component parts of that backdrop. This volume has been compiled to record the continued development of the Club during half a century and to try and re-create the atmosphere of those years as it existed both on the water and in the Clubhouse.

While the Royal Thames' river matches continued throughout the years 1868-1914, those years did see the beginning of the end of sailing matches on the River Thames. The Royal London Yacht Club took a Clubhouse at Cowes, the New Thames Yacht Club was wound up, the Royal Corinthian Yacht Club left Erith and operated from Burnham and the Royal Thames established a station on the Solent. The foundation of the Yacht Racing Association and, later, the International Yacht Racing Union led to frequent changes in measurement rules and consequently to changes in yacht design. Big schooners were largely replaced by big cutters and the International Rule brought out many more smaller classes and so opened yacht racing to many more people.

For the Royal Thames this period saw the Club complete 50 years of residence at their Clubhouse in Albermarle Street and then move to more commodious premises in Piccadilly. Although the financial fortunes of the Club fluctuated their general trend was one of consolidation and improvement. The level of membership of the Club also fluctuated but the figure of 750 in 1868 had reached 1072 by 1918.

Perhaps the greatest influence over life for members of the Royal Thames came from the Prince of Wales, both afloat and ashore. His Royal Highness's interest in and support of yachting had a profound effect in widening the public interest in that sport in the last quarter of the 19th century. Perhaps even greater was his influence over Society circles. The rigid attitudes of his father, Prince Albert; coupled with the constraints placed upon him by his mother, Queen Victoria, meant that he was given little opportunity to be constructively employed. It is hardly surprising therefore that he indulged in a hectic and extravagant social life at a pace few others could maintain; but for many he set standards they chose to follow. Philip Magnus in his fine biography of King Edward VII reproduced a confidential memo from Prince Albert to the Royal Equerries setting down the way in which the young Prince should conduct himself (the memo was written in 1858 when the Prince of Wales was aged $16^1/_2$ years). A copy of the main elements of the memo are at Appendix I. It provides very interesting guidelines on the manners of that time. Many of the strictures would not come amiss if followed by today's society. Judging from Club records it seems that certain members of the Royal Thames chose to follow the Prince of Wales' lead rather than the advice sent out by his father.

Overall this was a very successful period for the Royal Thames Yacht Club and the sections that follow have been compiled in the hope of reflecting the progress of the Club and the progress of yachting against an ever-changing historical and social background.

I
Officers of the Club

Flag Officers

During the 50 years covered by this volume of the Club History only ten members held office as a Flag Officer of the Club, even though for most of the period there were three officers in post at any one time. This is even more remarkable when compared with modern custom whereby Flag Officers serve for only two or three years. The reason for this disparity is not hard to identify: in the period under review the Office holders had to devote a relatively limited time to Club affairs leaving the day-to-day business of the Club to the Chairman of the Committee, the Committee members and the Secretary. Additionally, the majority of the Flag Officers were not tied down by business commitments and therefore were happy to be re-elected to office at the Annual General Meeting. Finally, from 1874 it became the custom for Flag Officers to progress from Rear Commodore to Vice Commodore and, when the timing of succession permitted, to Commodore. Today's Officers would find such protracted periods of commitment both impracticable and exhausting when imposed on top of an already pressurised business life. A vignette of each of the ten Flag Officers is set out below.

LORD ALFRED PAGET, by 1868, had been a Flag Officer continuously for 23 years of which all but the first year was as Commodore. He was still to serve a further seven years as Commodore and over five years as Vice Commodore until his death in August 1888. His prowess as a yachtsman had long been established though by now he had taken to steam yachting. His loyalty to the Club and his leadership of it were of the highest order as shown by his successful navigation of the Club through the turbulence of the 1860s into the calmer waters that followed. He never wavered from his aim to place the Club at the heart of British Yachting and in spite of long periods of travel abroad on Royal duties he invariably chaired meetings of the Sailing Committee right up to the last years of his life. A member of the royal household - he was Clerk Marshal to the Queen - he was a great favourite of Queen Victoria and represented her abroad, as when accompanying HRH The Prince of Wales on a visit to India between October 1875 and March 1876. He owned many steam yachts named *VIOLET* and it was in the last of these - built specifically for him in 1886 by Ramage and Ferguson, to enjoy sea fishing - that he died at Inverness on 24 August 1888; his funeral was held at Hampton Court five days later. His portrait was already hanging in the Clubhouse and a suitable tablet was affixed to it. The deep sorrow felt by the members was expressed in a letter of condolence to Lady Paget; a letter which had to be sent to her in a box since she was spending some time in Cannes.

LORD de ROS was elected to the Club in September 1841 and became Vice Commodore in 1863, which post he held until his death in January 1874. At that time The Committee resolved to ask the Commodore to pass to the family of Lord de Ros *'their sense of the great services rendered for 33 years to the Club by his lordship and of the uniform kindness and consideration shown by him to the members. His memory will always be held in grateful respect as a nobleman who, by his personal example, as well as by his judicious advice most signally promoted the best interests of yachting and, by his kindness and courtesy, commanded the personal attachment of all the members of the Club'.*

Lord de Ros owned many yachts and raced his small cutters in Club Sailing Matches but was not a foremost racing member. He came to office after a period of several months of turbulence when the Club was virtually without a Flag Officer following the death of Richard Green, Vice Commodore and the resignation of the Commodore, the Treasurer and the General Committee. Once the Club had put its affairs in order Lord deRos was in a position to give tremendous support to the re-elected Commodore, Lord Alfred Paget, throughout the traumas of 1867 and the financially-stretched years that followed.

Unfortunately his health deteriorated during his last two years in office and he tendered his resignation on three occasions but he was asked to continue. It must be probable that Lord Alfred Paget was reluctant to elect a new Vice Commodore until the Prince of Wales succeeded him as Commodore.

HRH THE PRINCE OF WALES was elected Commodore of the Club in 1874 and remained in that office until his accession to the throne as King Edward VII in 1901, after which he was Patron of the Club (see Appendix 2) until his death in November 1910. The Prince of Wales was little involved in the administration of the Club but he was always consulted when the Sailing Committee were arranging the dates of club sailing matches and he presided over the Annual General Meeting of the Club in 1875 and 1887. He accorded his patronage to the Club from 1865, the year in which he acquired his first yacht *DAGMAR (36 Tons)* and it must be reasonable to assume that it was Lord Alfred Paget' s influence that persuaded him to accept the office of Commodore in 1874. This assumption is supported by the letter sent to Lord Alfred Paget by Francis Knollys who was the Prince of Wales' Secretary from 1870. The letter was written from St Petersburg on 19 January 1874 at which time the Prince was attending the wedding of his brother Alfred, Duke of

Edinburgh to Marie, daughter of Emperor Alexander II of Russia. A copy of the letter (the original of which is in the Club Archives) is at Appendix 3.

The Prince of Wales was not a practising yachtsman but did enjoy sailing nevertheless. Of the many yachts he owned, two were by far the most successful racing vessels. The 210 Ton schooner ALINE, which regularly entered Royal Thames sailing matches, was named after the daughter of his friend Baron Gustav de Rothschild. A reproduction of the print of *ALINE* (which hangs in the present Clubhouse) was used for the keeper-prize plates given to winners of Club trophies in the 1980s. It was, however, his next yacht with which both he and his son (later King George V) are most closely associated. The G.L.Watson designed cutter *BRITANNIA (221 Tons)* was ordered in 1882 and commenced racing in 1883; during that year she won 32 prizes from 43 starts. The big cutter was exceptionally successful throughout more than 50 years of racing. In July 1895, after she had defeated Barclay Walker's *AILSA* and Lord Dunraven's *VALKYRIE,* the Prince of Wales wrote to the Duke of York (later King George V) *'To-days victory indeed makes BRITANNIA the first racing yacht afloat'.* Unfortunately, the Prince's stretched financial circumstances forced him to sell *BRITANNIA* in 1897 but he bought her back on becoming King Edward VII - for sentimental reasons - though personally never raced her again.

The Prince's involvement in yachting through being Commodore of the Royal Thames Yacht Club and of the Royal Yacht Squadron (1882-1900), as well as being President of the Y.R.A, lifted the sport to unprecedented heights of popularity.

EARL BRASSEY was elected to membership of the Club as Thomas Brassey Esq in May 1857. When he died in March 1918 he had been the senior member of the Club for two years. He was a Flag Officer of the Club for 30 years from 1874-1903 and a trustee for over 40 years, from 1878 until his death. In 1874, when the Prince of Wales became Commodore of the Club and Lord Alfred Paget reverted to the office of Vice Commodore it was agreed that there should still be two working Flag Officers with the consequence that the office of Rear Commodore was instituted and Thomas Brassey Esq M.P. was elected to that office. At that time, prior membership of the General Committee of Management of the Club was not a prerequisite for election to Flag Officer and it certainly did not inhibit Thomas Brassey's considerable contribution to the Club. His services to the country were recognised by his appointment as a KCB in 1881; he became Lord Brassey in 1886 and Earl Brassey in 1911. He was much devoted to maritime affairs and is best remembered through Brassey's Naval Annual which was first published in 1890. He served as Secretary of the Admiralty and established a force that was later to become the Royal Naval Volunteer Reserve, in which so many yachtsmen served with distinction. For yachtsmen, however, he is always associated with his schooner *SUNBEAM (532 Tons).* In her day she was the best-known cruising yacht in the world. She sailed nearly a quarter of a million miles over 40 years, including a circumnavigation of the world and trips to India and Australia.

His parliamentary duties and his long absences on his cruises (unlike the Prince of Wales he was very much the practical sailor and master of *SUNBEAM)* kept him from Club duties at times, but such was the support he received from the membership of the Club that he was elected Vice Commodore in 1889 after the death of Lord Alfred Paget. In 1901 the Prince

Robert Hewett, Rear Commodore 1889 - 1901, Vice Commodore 1902 - 1903.

of Wales became King Edward VII and accepted the appointment of Patron of the Club in succession to Queen Victoria. At the AGM in March 1901 it was decided to ask the General Committee to recommend who should fill the newly-vacant office of Commodore. A Sub Committee was appointed to consider this and its recommendation in November 1901 that Lord Brassey be elected was confirmed in March 1902, but in the September he tendered his resignation. This was accepted with much regret though he agreed to stay in office until the AGM in March 1903.

After his death many tributes were paid to his services to the Club but in other fields an interesting tribute was contributed by Mr Alfred Gollin at the Annual General Meeting of the Club when he *'testified to the great respect in which Lord Brassey was held in Australia while he was Govenor of Victoria and Commodore of the Royal Victoria Yacht Club'* - of which club Mr Gollin was Vice Commodore.

ROBERT HEWETT became a member of the Club in October 1854. He owned the North Sea fishing fleet based at Gorleston and gave the Club many years of distinguished service. He served for many years on the Sailing Committee and later on the General Committee before being elected Rear Commodore and Trustee in 1889 following the death of Lord Alfred Paget. With the Prince of Wales accession to the throne he became Vice Commodore in March 1902 but sadly died on 25 January 1904 from a heart condition - one which today would have been dealt with by a by-pass operation. He was also a Flag Officer of the New Thames Yacht Club, being elected Rear Commodore in 1889 and Commodore in 1901

**Sir James Pender, Rear Commodore 1904,
Vice Commodore 1905 - 1910.**

and was also a Flag Officer of the Royal Corinthian Y.C., which was at that time based at Erith. His wide range of responsibilities made him a major influence over sailing in the Thames Estuary where his cutter *BUTTERCUP (10 Tons)* was a champion of her class - he designed and built her with a (novel) clipper bow in an era of straight-stemmed cutters.

THEODORE PIM was elected to the Club in October 1871. A stockbroker by profession he came from a rich Irish yachting family who lived in County Dublin. He was the owner of several yachts called *ROSABELLE;* the first of these - an 88 Ton yawl built in 1875 - competed regularly in RTYC matches. In 1885 he owned the first of two steam yachts which bore the name *ROSABELLE* while the second one, of 614 Tons and acquired in 1901, was much used for cruising. A model of the latter is still to be seen in the Mountbatten Suite of the present Clubhouse in Knightsbridge.

Theodore Pim was elected Rear Commodore of the Club in 1902. Although he had not served on either the General or Sailing Committees of the Club he had been a member of the Sailing Committee of the New Thames Yacht Club. After serving for two years as Rear Commodore he became Vice Commodore in 1904 and Commodore in 1905, which office he held until his retirement from office in March 1924. He was also a Trustee of the Club from 1904.

SIR JAMES PENDER was elected to the Club in June 1902 and became Rear Commodore in 1904, while a year later he was elected Vice Commodore and held that office until he asked to stand down in 1910. He was also a Trustee of

the Club from 1904. When he joined the Club he owned the 153 Ton yawl *BRYNHILD* which he sold in 1905 and replaced with the 165 Ton cutter *KARIAD* in 1906, the 170 Ton cutter *BRYNHILD* in 1907 and the 263 Ton steam schooner *LAMORNA* in 1912. A model of the latter is displayed in the present Coffee Room of the Knightsbridge Clubhouse.

THE DUKE OF BEDFORD became a member of the Club in July 1900. In 1903 he acquired the 1023 Ton screw schooner *SAPPHIRE.* He was elected Commodore of the Club at the AGM in March 1904 after a protracted period during which there were two other nominations for the office, but both gentlemen nominated declined to accept the office. It all started with the death of Queen Victoria in January 1901 and the Prince of Wales, who was Commodore, became instead the Patron (as King Edward VII). By November 1901 the appointed Sub Committee recommended that Lord Brassey (the Vice Commodore) be elected Commodore, that Robert Hewett (Rear Commodore) be elected Vice Commodore and that Forrester Brittan be elected Rear Commodore. At the AGM in March 1902, the two former recommendations were accepted but the office of Rear Commodore was not filled and the Sailing Committee was instructed to make the election - which they did in April by appointing Theodore Pim as Rear Commodore. This did not, however, lead to a period of stability for the Flag Officers because in September Lord Brassey indicated his wish to resign the office of Commodore. The General Committee expressed their regret at his wish to resign and asked that he remain in the office until the 1903 AGM. In November the Sailing Committee were invited to select a candidate for Commodore. Their first choice was the Prince of Wales (later King George V) but by February 1903 he had declined to accept the election and the Sailing Committee recommended that Robert Hewett be Commodore, Theodore Pim Vice Commodore and Almeric Paget Rear Commodore.

The March 1903 AGM did not take up this recommendation but simply re-elected Robert Hewett and Theodore Pim as Vice and Rear Commodore, then appointed another Sub Committee (this time comprising two members of the General Committee and three members of the Sailing Committee) to consider the election of a Commodore. In December 1903, the Duke of Connaught was proposed for the office but he too declined to accept. Matters were further complicated in January 1904 by the death of Robert Hewett.

Four weeks later it was recommended that the Duke of Bedford be elected Commodore, Theodore Pim, Vice Commodore and Sir James Pender, Rear Commodore. These recommendations were confirmed at the March 1904 Annual General Meeting. Even these elections proved only a short term solution since the Duke of Bedford wrote a letter in January 1905 resigning the office. The Sailing Committee now proposed that Theodore Pim be Commodore, Sir James Pender Vice Commodore and Almeric Paget Rear Commodore. These proposals were adopted by the March 1905 AGM and led to five years of stability for the Flag Officers.

LORD QUEENBOROUGH (Almeric Hugh Paget) was the son of General Lord Alfred Paget and was made Baron Queenborough of Queenborough in 1919. He became a member of the Club in January 1901 and started his long period of service to the Club as a Flag Officer four years later. During the years covered by this volume he owned several racing yachts including *CAPRICE (37 Tons)*, *MA' OONA (49 Tons)* and *CORONA (106 Tons)* as well as the steam schooner *BLANDUSIA (148 Tons).*

THE MARQUIS OF ANGLESEY became a member of the Club in June 1905. At the Annual General Meeting held in March 1911 he had the unusual experience of being elected a member of the General Committee (there were only eight candidates nominated to fill the eight vacancies on the Committee) while later in the same meeting he was made Rear Commodore of the Club following the resignation of Sir James Pender and the election of Almeric Paget to succeed him as Vice Commodore. In 1910 he became the owner of the steam schooner *SEMIRAMIS (1797 Tons)*

Patrons and Patronage

The **PATRON** of the Club throughout the years covered by this volume was the reigning monarch, i.e. HM Queen Victoria, HM King Edward VII and HM King George V. All these were generous in presenting trophies for the Club Sailing Matches but Queen Victoria had virtually no direct contact with the Club. On the other hand Edward VII, as will already be apparent, was actively involved and was a member from 1865 until his death 1910. George V was little involved with the Club but was a member from 1894 and was, of course, a practical and accomplished yachtsman in his beloved *BRITANNIA*.

ROYAL PATRONAGE of the Club was considerable throughout the period 1868-1918. Successive Kings of the Belgians gave their Patronage to the Club from 1847 as did the King of the Netherlands (1852-1890), the King of Italy (1864-1909), the Emperor of Russia (1874-1917) and the King of Spain from 1910. Additionally the King of Sweden and Norway gave his Patronage from 1856 until 1905 (when Norway became independent) and as King of Sweden until 1909. The King of Norway's patronage was first recorded in 1909. Several of the Patrons owned very large yachts and as members of the Club it was the practice to include these in the Club's list of yachts. The total tonnage of yachts owned by the Club's members was an important status symbol. For example, in 1900 the total tonnage of yachts owned by Royal Thames Members was some 50,000 Tons but nearly 9,500 Tons related to the *'Royal Members'* and not least to the Emperor of Russia; two of his yachts accounted for 7,368 Tons.

In addition to the Kings and Emperors referred to above the Club's list of members included many other Royal Persons. These are listed in Appendix 4. It will be noted that those of German and Austrian origin were quickly removed from the list after August 1914.

The considerable number of foreign *'Royals'* who were members of the Club during this period or who gave patronage to the Club may seem to be remarkable, but is readily explained by the inter-marriage of the Royal Families of Europe. Queen Victoria's uncle became King Leopold I of the Belgians; the Prince of Wales' (King Edward VII) daughter married King Haakon VII of Norway, his brothers the Duke of Edinburgh and the Duke of Connaught had daughters who married King Alfonso of Spain and King Gustav VI of Sweden, while his sister Alice married the Grand Duke of Hesse and their daughters married Prince Louis of Battenburg, Prince Henry of Prussia and Nicholas II, Emperor of Russia.

The office of **CUP BEARER** during the years 1868-1918 was filled for all but 15 of those 50 years by Colonel Josiah Wilkinson. He became a member of the Club in 1844 and reference to him has been made already in the previous volume, paying tribute to his loyalty and service to the Club during the difficult times in the mid 1860s. He was elected

Cup Bearer in March 1868 and retained that office until his death in 1903 at the age of 93. His tact and vision were greatly respected, not least since he guided members into the realisation that a London-based Club combining yachting and social interests was entirely feasible. It is possible that he never sought office as a Flag Officer but it is certain that should all Flag Officers be unavoidably absent at the Annual General Meeting it was to Colonel Wilkinson that the meeting turned to be chairman in the sure knowledge that he would guide the meeting safely through the agenda. Special tribute was paid to him by the Chairman of the Committee at the 1904 AGM when he reminded those present that in his early days Colonel Wilkinson raced his cutter *ENIGMA* successfully and how his son Leonard R Wilkinson was now a member and the name *ENIGMA* had re-appeared in the Club's yacht list. His successor as Cup Bearer was Lt Col Sir George Leach who, in 1904, had been a member for some 31 years. He remained in office until his death in 1914 when he was succeeded by Rear Admiral, the Hon. Victor Montague, who in turn died 10 months later to be replaced by Mr Adrian Hope in March 1915.

The **TRUSTEES** of the Club in 1868 were Lord Alfred Paget, Colonel Josiah Wilkinson and Henry W Birch Esq, the two former being two of the three Trustees appointed when such offices were first created in 1863. Henry Birch had became a Trustee in 1865. Throughout the period covered by this volume only five other members were appointed as a Trustee since it was the custom that Trustees remained in office until their demise. Thus it was that Henry Birch, who died in 1878, was succeeded by Thomas Brassey who remained in office until 1918 when he was succeeded by Lord Queenborough. When Lord Alfred Paget died in 1888 he was succeeded by Robert Hewett and in 1904 by Sir James Pender. Colonel Wilkinson on his death in 1903 was succeeded by Theodore Pim. All but two of these Trustees were also Flag Officers of the Club during part or all of their period in office but none would have found the tasks relating to the office of Trustee particularly strenuous since the Club's financial state was reasonably stable and the Club changed its Clubhouse only once in the 50 years. The appointment of a member to be both a Flag Officer and a Trustee may appear to raise problems from a conflict of interest, but it did not.

The practise of appointing members as **AUDITORS** to the Club was maintained throughout the nineteenth century. A resolution was placed before the Annual General Meeting in March 1901 which proposed to end the practice of appointing annually two or three members as auditors and instead to appoint a firm of chartered accountants. This led to the appointment of Deller and Benwell as Auditors in 1901 but by 1905 the Committee had little confidence in the thoroughness and accuracy of the audited accounts and they appointed Collins and Tootell to audit the Club accounts at an annual fee of 30 guineas. Outstanding among the members who served as auditors was W L Hooper Esq. who was presented in 1871 with a piece of plate valued at £25 and a gold watch in recognition of his services. Others who gave long service as auditors were Martin J K Becher Esq. (16 years) and William H Harvey Esq. (10 years) while Sir George Leach who later became Cup Bearer was an auditor for 5 years.

There were seven holders of the office of **SECRETARY** during the years covered by this volume of whom three were obliged to retire due to ill health and two others resigned in unsatisfactory circumstances. During these years the salary paid increased from £200 per annum to £300 and the

Secretary additionally received commission for arranging the sale of yachts for members - in 1886 this was 5% on the first £1,000 and $2^1/_2$% on the remainder. This was changed in 1912 when the commission taken became 4% up to £1,000, $3^1/_2$% over £1,000 and up to £5,000 and 3% over £5,000. The bigger change was that only 4/7th of the commission went to the Secretary while 1/7th went to the General Club fund and 2/7th to the Regatta Fund.

Captain P C Stuart Grant' s long and often controversial period in office ended after 18 years when ill health forced him to retire at the end of 1871 - he died in February 1872. A subscription list for his widow and children raised nearly £200. His successor H W Mellis was the Secretary for 10 years but again ill health brought an end to his time in office in January 1882 though, unlike Captain Grant, he survived in retirement for many years. While the detail was not recorded, it is evident that there was a conflict between Mr Mellis and the Committee; not least there is an inference that money received by Mr Mellis from members paying their subscriptions had not been paid into the Club accounts by the time he resigned. The Club was in a strong position, however, since it was the custom to require the Secretary, on appointment, to deposit a security of at least £500. In March Mr Mellis was proposed for membership of the Club by Mr E W Buller but was not elected. In April the Committee considered a letter from Mr Buller saying that *'In consequence of the kindly remarks made from the chair by the Rear Commodore (Thomas Brassey) at the Annual General Meeting (March 1882) many of Mr Mellis's friends have expressed a wish to raise a Testimonial Fund in recognition of his services to the Club and it appears to them that this movement might also afford a satisfactory termination of the questions that have arisen between Mr Mellis and the Committee. With this object in view, Mr Mellis has now instructed his solicitors to withdraw the letters written by them on his behalf and will himself abstain from any further action in the matter'.* The Committee' s response was to pass, unanimously, a terse resolution that *'The Committee are of the opinion that under the circumstances they should not be asked to take action in the matter'.*

As is noted later on in Section IV, Mr E W Buller' s intervention may not have been in Mr Mellis' s best interests bearing in mind his own uncertain relationship with the Committees but it is clear that whatever the details of the problems, the acrimony continued and it is recorded, with displeasure, that as late as November 1884 a member complained that Mr Mellis had entered the Clubhouse.

When the Club advertised for applicants for the office of Secretary in succession to Mr Mellis there were some 236 who applied, including six RTYC members - who had been informed by the Committee that they must resign their membership of the Club if they wished to be considered. The Sub Committee formed to select a new Secretary required four ballots before appointing Mr Edward Grimston from the short list of five candidates. He was not one of the six ex-members who had applied and all six were re-instated as members of the Club. Edward Grimston served in office for only three years. He resigned in February 1885 and departed to Ceylon with what appears to have been almost indecent haste. Certainly there were many financial claims on his surety over the next nine months. If the number of applicants in 1882 seemed huge it was dwarfed by the 354 who applied in 1885, from whom the Committee selected Captain Thornton Scovell.

Captain Scovell served the Club for over 14 years during which time his loyalty to the Club, his administrative skills and his relationship with members of the Club were all of a high order. In July 1900 he gave six months notice of his wish to retire, which was greatly appreciated, and allowed the Committee ample time to select his successor Lt Col CBG Dick. A Testimonial Fund for Captain Scovell was contributed to by members and resulted in his been given silver coffee pots and a salver as well as the sum of £200. A keen yachtsman, Colonel Dick found it increasingly difficult to decide where his loyalties lay. By July 1904 he was openly criticised by the Committee for not devoting sufficient time to his duties at the Club and in October he resigned and was succeeded by Lieut. F.W. Chaine, Royal Navy. Lieutenant Chaine seems to have been very much in the same successful mould as Thornton Scovell but ill-health prevented him serving as Secretary for more than five years. The last Secretary to be appointed during the years covered by this volume was Captain John E H Orr, late of the Royal Artillery. He had the very difficult task of maintaining the very necessary continuity of Club administration during the move of the Clubhouse from Albemarle Street to Piccadilly in 1910-11, but his own continuity of service as Secretary was interrupted in October 1914 when he was called to serve in the Royal Horse Artillery. He was given leave of absence from his duties at the Club. He remained in office however, until 1925.

While the Flag Officers were all ex-officio members of both the General Committee and the Sailing Committee and although one of them would frequently chair the Sailing Committee, the **CHAIRMAN OF COMMITTEES** was elected by the members of the Committee who in turn had been elected to the General Committee at the Annual General Meeting in March of each year. In addition to chairing meetings of the General Committee of Management they chaired the House Committee and the many special Sub Committees that were set up. They therefore had considerable influence over the election of members, finance and the management of the Clubhouse, while the Flag Officers, although very alive to the affairs of the General and House Committees, exercised more direct influence over the Club' s sailing activities. During the 50 years covered by this volume relatively few members served as Chairman of the Committees since each served for many years - not necessarily in succession once the Club rules were changed to make retiring General Committee members ineligible for re-election until a year after their retirement. Additionally, these Chairmen would have served for very long periods as members of the General Committee as is shown:

W Frederick Moore was Chairman for five years (1871-75) and was on the General Committee for 15 years. He died in 1887 following an accident in the Clubhouse. The coroners report contained *'suggestion from the jury relative to the staircase balustrade!'*

Walter F Stutfield was Chairman for eight years (1876-83) and was on the General Committee for 17 years. He died in 1888.

E R Handock was Chairman for 10 years during the period (1884-98) and was on the General Committee for 21 years. He died in 1900.

John McNeile Miller was Chairman for six years during the period (1900-08) and was on the General Committee for 11 years.

II
The Club and Yacht Racing

Introduction

This section records the Club's involvement in yacht racing, its organisation of sailing matches for its members and members of other selected Clubs and the evolution of yacht racing, during the race seasons 1868-1914. For the Royal Thames, these years saw the change in the control of yacht racing in the UK from individual clubs (not least the Royal Thames) to National and International bodies; it saw the start of the move by the Royal Thames from racing on the Thames and its estuary to racing in the Solent - not only by individual members but by the Club itself. Over this period there was a succession of changes in the classification of yachts and in the measurement of yachts, all aimed at improving the quality and equality of racing - but not necessarily achieving it and certainly not creating formulae free from loopholes that soon became apparent to lynx-eyed yacht designers. For all the changes in rig, rules and design many consider that, for sheer magnificence, the years in the early part of those covered by this volume were supreme. This was certainly the view of that most knowledgeable of yachtsmen, Dixon Kemp. Writing in The Graphic on 2 August 1894 he proclaimed in an article on British Yachtsmen:

'The period 1860-1880 may be called the Golden era of yacht racing, and although we may know a great deal more now as to what it is possible to get out of a yacht, it is unlikely that we shall ever again witness such contests as took place within the period named.'

Over a hundred years later that observation is still true in terms of both the size and numbers of the yachts competing at that time - the twentieth century has seen nothing like it; not even when 'J' Class and similar large yachts were competing in the 1920s and 30s.

Yacht Racing Topics 1868-78

The problems of 1867 which ended with the breakaway members forming the New Thames Yacht Club in no way undermined the Royal Thames' commitment to sailing matches on the Thames. A full programme of matches took place in 1868. Once the break had occurred the relationship between the Royal Thames and the New Thames was certainly one of co-operation and probably friendship on most occasions. An interesting incident involving both Clubs occurred in December 1870. Lord Alfred Paget convened a meeting of the Flag Officers of the 'Thames Yacht Clubs' from which a circular was written and sent out to each member of these leading Yacht Clubs (see Appendix 5).

The aim of the proposals in the circular is quite clear - the formation of a single Thames Yacht Club to provide better racing, more economically and to have Clubhouses in the West End and on the Solent at Cowes. An instant reaction to the circular was an anonymous letter in the weekly paper *BELL' S LIFE IN LONDON* on the 17th December, signed by 'Vigil' who purported to be an RTYC member. In this letter he states that the claim in the circular that it was sent to members of the three leading Thames Clubs is untrue, i.e. it was not sent to members of the three oldest clubs: Royal Thames Yacht Club (1823), Royal London Yacht Club (1838) and the Prince of Wales Yacht Club (1851), but had been sent to members of the New Thames Yacht Club formed only three years ago by those Royal Thames members who broke away in December 1876 *'in order to supplant the Royal Thames - but have failed'.* He then described the Commodore of the NTYC, John D Lee, as *'tradesman who was flag-maker to the Royal Thames'* and the Vice Commodore, William M Rudge as *'gentleman from whose chambers the circular was issued'.* He then called for a Special General Meeting of the Royal Thames to deal with the circular. In publishing 'Vigil's' letter the editor of *BELL' S LIFE* wrote *'In publishing this letter it must not be assumed that we share the writer' s tone or sentiments but we do support the concept of an amalgamated club. It will, however, be difficult to achieve when the concept is opposed by those with vested interests and in whose eyes sport is subordinate to sociability. If the bona fide yachtsmen of the RTYC, RLYC, and NTYC agree there is hope for the project'.*

The next edition of *BELL'S LIFE* published on 24 December 1870 carried a letter from Lord Alfred Paget explaining the proposals set down in the circular and deploring 'Vigil's' sneer at John Lee whom he considered to be *'gentleman in feeling and behaviour'.* He added that the response of the members of the three clubs to the circular showed that of the 1150 members (those who were members of more than one club could respond only once) 311 were in favour of amalgamation, 49 were opposed but 800 failed to respond. Even though 27% were in favour this did not give the support needed to proceed with amalgamation and the scheme had therefore been abandoned. Over the next few weeks other members wrote to *BELL'S LIFE* some in favour and some against amalgamation, including further letters from 'Vigil' in one of which he suggested that since the Royal London considered themselves to be *'top of the tree'* on the Thames, separate clubs would be good for yacht racing and provide healthy competition.

Another letter came from R S Wilkinson (ex RTYC) and now Honorary Treasurer of the New Thames Yacht Club. Whilst he too deplored 'Vigil's' original letter he also made it clear why he was in the van of those who seceded from the Royal Thames where, he said, strong financial resources had been squandered on a badly-managed Clubhouse.

When the General Committee next met on 10 January 1871 it seems they had received several letters from members all enquiring whether the Committee had prior knowledge of the circular and should not a meeting of members be called without delay? The Committee's response was that *'the circular to which you allude has not been issued with either our knowledge or consent, nor has it as yet in any recognisable form, been officially brought before us'.*

As regards to 'Vigil's' letter in *BELL'S LIFE* the Committee responded with the following letter to the editor of that newspaper: *'Lt Col Wilkinson and Mr Birch, trustees of the Royal Thames Yacht Club brought under the notice of the Committee certain letters which had appeared under the signature of 'Vigil' in BELL'S LIFE. They resolved unanimously that an insertion in your next impression should state that the Committee notice with the greatest indignation the personal and unjustifiable attack made upon Lord Alfred Paget, the Commodore, by an anonymous letter in BELL'S LIFE in London, signing himself 'Vigil' and professing to be a member of the Club. The Committee, without pronouncing any judgement upon the merits of the proposal to amalgamate the various Thames Yacht Clubs are of opinion that the Commodore in bringing the matter forward was influenced only by a regard for Yachting interests generally and for this Club. The Committee repudiate in the strongest terms the assumption by ëVigil' that he represents the feelings of the majority of the members. They are confident, on the contrary, that nothing has occurred to alter the very high feeling of esteem and confidence with which the Commodore has been for so many years regarded by this Club'.* This strong and somewhat lengthy rebuttal seems to have been effective and the topic was raised again only at the Annual General Meeting in March 1871 - it was raised by Lord Alfred Paget personally when he said that if, because of the letter in the press, members did think he was not a fit person to be re-elected Commodore he should be happy to resign. He was, of course, re-elected with the unanimous support of the 87 members present and a testimony by Lt Col Wilikinson expressing gratitude for his services to the Club over so many years.

This was a strange affair which, in the end, did no harm to individuals or to the Club; but it did illustrate the potential dangers of the Flag Officers taking action unbeknown to the Committee no matter how well intentioned that action may be.

This contentious subject was brought into the open once more nearly 18 years later in a regular feature *'Topics of the Week'* in the edition of the magazine *FIELD*, published on 29 September 1888. This was 18 months after the attempted amalgamation of the RTYC and NTYC. The article suggested that amalgamation of these two clubs could be advantageous if they were joined by the Royal London. It then went on to review the events in 1870 and noted that the RLYC was largely opposed to amalgamation at that time because, firstly, there would be difficulty in 'placing' all the Flag Officers (although their Vice Commodore, Thomas Broadwood offered to stand down) secondly, because the RTYC finances were stretched while those of the RLYC were sound and thirdly they considered the amalgamated club title would be more imposing if 'Royal London' were used rather than 'Royal Thames'. The Committee of the RTYC decided to ignore this article!

Only a few months before the 'Vigil' letter was published, James Ashbury MP had been making history for the Club by his successful transatlantic race in *CAMBRIA* against the American *DAUNTLESS* and by making the first challenge for the America's Cup - a challenge which was both courageous (though unsuccessful) and controversial (an aspect of that event which has been present in many succeeding challenges). That Mr Ashbury's schooner was a fast boat was never in question and he must have enjoyed winning the Anglo-American race round the Isle of Wight in August 1868. He entered *CAMBRIA* in most of the Royal Thames matches during the three seasons 1868-70 and won several prizes, but they included only one 'first' though he did cross the finishing line first on other occasions only to be pegged back by time allowance.

In the 1870s the pattern of sailing matches arranged by the Royal Thames each season was based on a Cutter match, a Schooner and Yawl match and the Nore to Dover Channel Match. The two former were sailed from Gravesend to the Mouse Lightship and back. To these was added a Nore to Boulogne match in 1868 and Dover to Boulogne and back in 1870. These matches were dominated by the cutter *FIONA* (E Boutcher) and the schooners *GLORIANA* (A O Wilkinson), *EGERIA* (J Mulholland) and *FLYING CLOUD* (Count Batthyany), each of which achieved many successes. A table showing Club sailing matches and prizewinners is included as Appendix 7. The courses sailed are shown in Appendix 6. These results, in which unfortunately, there are one or two gaps, have been taken from Club records, Hunt's Yachting Magazine, The Yachtsman, Yachting Monthly, and the Illustrated London News. In the June 1889 edition of the latter magazine there is an interesting note saying that the illustrations of the Royal Thames River Matches are *'reproduced' from photographs taken by Messrs W.W. Rouch and Co. with their Patent Eureka Detective Camera'.* Most matches were open to other yacht clubs (especially those with royal patronage) as well as the New York Yacht Club and from 1873 the Havre Yacht Club. Although not an active yachtsman, HRH The Prince of Wales, whose patronage of the Royal Thames started in 1865, was enthusiastic about yachting and regularly attended Royal Thames sailing matches in the 1870s and 80s. In most seasons he was present at one sailing match aboard Lord Alfred Paget's yacht, while occasionally he was afloat in a competing yacht.

The well established 'Channel Match' was, at this time, considered to be a severe test of the seamanship of the crews and the seaworthiness of the yacht, should the weather conditions be unfavourable. This was certainly the case on 11 June 1870 when four schooners, a yawl and five cutters started from the Nore Light Vessel, on the usual course down the Thames estuary through the Oaze Deep and the Alexandra and Princes Channels to the Tongue Light Vessel, where they turned for Dover going outside the Goodwins. The wind appears to have been some force 5-6 gusting to 8 from between West and South West and once round the Tongue the sea was decidedly unpleasant. Most yachts suffered ripped canvas and broken spars but the unfortunate schooner *PLEIAD*, 181 Tons (J D Gibb) shipped a huge sea and two crew members were swept overboard, only one of whom was recovered. In spite of all this, most of the competitors came to the start for the race from Dover to Boulogne and back less than 48 hours later, a match to be sailed in a stiff breeze but generally more pleasant conditions. Even so, the report of the match in Hunt's Yachting Magazine includes these lines:

Lugger Yacht NEW MOON, 220 Tons - Lithograph by T G Dutton

Who can forget the crossing over
From Calais to the Strait of Dover?
Prostrate upon the Cabin floor
The Wanderer lies with stomach sore,
And utters many groans pathetic
While undergoing his emetic.
His mind is full of fancies drear -
Shipwreck, he sees, death hov'ring near!

Fortunately, fatal accidents were extremely rare but crew members being swept overboard occurred a little more frequently. In the cutter match in 1871 the well known boat builder Dan Hatcher who was at the helm of *GLANCE*, 35 Tons (J R Rushton) got entangled in the mainsheet while rounding the Club steamer (which had re-located to shorten the course) and was carried overboard. Happily he was able to swim to a lifebuoy and was rescued by the Club steamer dinghy. In the Channel Match of 1874 the schooner *CETONIA*, 202 Tons (W Turner) lost a crewman off the bowsprit in a very nasty sea, after rounding the North Sand Light Vessel but quickly rescued him. An accident of a different nature occurred in the Cutter match held on 1 June 1876 from Gravesend to the Mouse Light Vessel and back. The cutter *NEVA*, 62 Tons (R Holmes-Kerr) led from the start but after passing Southend and approaching the Mouse was caught by *IONA*, 66 Tons (J Ashbury). When they met, *NEVA* was on starboard, while *IONA* was on port tack. The latter did not give way and as a result *NEVA's* bowsprit was carried away and she had to retire. Those on board *IONA* blamed the pilot, claiming he was the only man 'on look out' and gave the helmsman a succession of conflicting pieces of information as to the relative bearing between the two yachts. On *NEVA* the crew said that they held their course (being on starboard tack) until they realised that a collision was inevitable. At that moment their helmsman luffed up to reduce the impact which would otherwise probably have sunk *IONA*. Clearly the blame rested on *IONA* and this was acknowledged by Mr Ashbury as soon as the race was over in a letter to Mr Holmes-Kerr when

he expressed his regret that the accident had occurred. In view of this no action was taken by the sailing committee but a careless 'look out' had put both boats at risk.

The ability of the Sailing Committee and the Race Committee to plan and control yacht racing on the Thames was never questioned - indeed it was much praised. Even so they had their shortcomings on occasions. The match for schooners and yawls on 5 June 1874 needed to start not later than 10.00 if the yachts were going to benefit from the ebbing tide and reach the Mouse. Regrettably the club steamer did not arrive at Gravesend until 10.30 and the race committee, travelling independently, until 11.00! The late start necessitated the course to be shortened off Southend and only a last-minute breeze come to the aid of the competing yachts becalmed two miles up the river and in risk of being driven back and failing to reach the steamer for the turn.

A very different problem arose in 1882. In October 1881, when the 1882 sailing programme was arranged, the Cutter Match was fixed for 29 May. In March 1882 this was changed to 12 June (the same day as the Schooner & Yawl Match) because the tides were unsuitable on 29 May. In April the Sailing Committee were advised that the 12 June was not convenient for the Commodore, HRH The Prince of Wales, who asked for these river matches to be sailed on 13 June - a date already selected by the Royal London for their river matches. Royal Thames cutter owners had already entered for the Royal London match on 13 June so that the only starter in the Royal Thames match was *ANNASONA*, 40 Tons (J D Hedderwick). The Sailing Committee found themselves in a cleft stick. While they had informed the Royal London of the now unavoidable clash of dates, their hands were tied. What they could not have foreseen was that *ANNASONA* would start (in order to avoid forfeiting her entrance fee) and would subsequently claim the cutter prize. The Sailing Committee response was in a letter to Mr Hedderwick saying: *'The Sailing Committee are of opinion that the owner of the*

ANNASONA cannot claim the prize offered for Second Class Cutters on 13 June in as much as having made a start to save entrance fee he sailed back again and left the race and afterwards sailed in the match of the Royal London Yacht Club. The Sailing Committee feel bound to express their regret that such a claim should be made and that a member of the Royal Thames Yacht Club should have, in the presence of HRH The Commodore and a large company assembled to witness the race, deserted his own Club in order to compete for a prize in another Club meeting on the same day'. Whether the tidal information available between October and March changed is not clear, but the Sailing Committee were always obliged to seek concurrence from the Commodore for the Sailing programme - on this occasion they could neither foresee the unfortunate outcome of this obligation nor the action of one misguided member!

The Yacht Racing Association

In the early 1870s it was still the practice for yacht clubs to act independently in drawing up sailing regulations for their club, especially in respect of measurement, classification and time allowance. The Royal Thames in particular and the Royal Yacht Squadron considered themselves to be the leading authorities in this respect and set standards which others often chose to follow - but by no means always. By this time many yacht owners competed in regattas organised in many locations and under many different sets of regulations. It was hardly surprising, therefore, that in 1875 a body seeking to establish national standards was formed and called the Yacht Racing Association.

The first recorded contact between the new Association and the Royal Thames was early in 1876 when, on 23 March, the Sailing Committee met and took note of a letter from the President of the YRA (Lord Exeter), a member of the Club, putting forward a national set of sailing regulations. The sailing committee postponed consideration of the letter until the return from India of the Vice Commodore, Lord Alfred Paget.

His Lordship was present at the next meeting of the Sailing Committee on 27 April and once again the matter was discussed but no decisions were taken until a further meeting on 12 May. At this meeting it was proposed *'that the peculiarities of the Thames courses render it impracticable to adopt the rules of the YRA as a whole; but that the committee recognises the desirability of uniformity and will recommend the Club to adopt them as far as may be practicable'.* Before this proposal could be considered an amendment was tabled *'that this committee regret they cannot recommend the Club to adopt the rules of the Yacht Racing Association as many of them are so much at variance with those of the Royal Thames Yacht Club'.* The amendment was carried by a show of hands of the nine members present.

On 14 February 1877 the Sailing Committee were again discussing this subject following receipt of a letter signed by 24 members. The committee replied through the Secretary with a letter stating *'I have laid before a meeting of the Sailing Committee, specially convened for the purpose, your letter having reference to the adoption by this Club of the code of rules prepared by the Yacht Racing Association and I am instructed to inform you that the Sailing Committee, after more careful consideration, regret they are unable for many reasons to recommend the club to adopt the rules of Association or modify the decision arrived at last year'.*

Although the Sailing Committee were adamant in their stand against the YRA rules (and some other clubs took a similar stand) they did agree in May 1877 *'that where a vessel cannot conveniently attend at the appointed day and place to be measured, she may enter and race upon the certificate she holds from the YRA, it being open however to any competitor to claim to have such vessel measured by the RTYC.'* Some no doubt felt that the Royal Thames was taking an arrogant stand but the Sailing Committee felt strongly that their long years of experience gave them a special place in yacht racing and a standard against which others could be judged. For all that, a Sub Committee did review the Club's sailing regulations but the proposed and agreed changes for the 1878 season were not significant.

By the end of the 1881 season the pressure for change in the Club's attitude to the YRA rules was increasing. In October the Secretary was instructed to write to the Secretary, RYS to ascertain whether their Committee would send delegates to meet members of the RTYC Sailing Committee to *'discuss any alterations in the sailing laws which may be deemed necessary to meet the wishes of racing yacht owners'.* In December Lord Ailsa sent a letter to the Sailing Committee *'enclosing the names of those yacht owners who decline to sail their vessels except under the rules of the YRA.'* The Sailing Committee decided that a circular on this topic should be sent to every member of the Club seeking their views (see Appendix 8). A special meeting of the Sailing Committee on 15 February 1882, having considered the replies received, proposed a Resolution for the AGM that was moved by Robert Hewett and seconded by Walter Stutfield *'That this committee do, at the Annual General Meeting of the Club in March next, recommend to the Club that the Sailing Rules of the Yacht Racing Association be adopted for the ensuing season of 1882'.* An amendment to this was proposed by Ernest Buller but was not seconded and the resolution was carried. Mr Buller was given permission to have his amendment recorded in the minutes of the meeting and it makes very interesting reading. His amendment was:

(1) That this meeting has been informed that the circular inviting the adoption of the Yacht Racing Association Rules was issued to all the members of this Club representing a Yacht Tonnage of, say, 25,000 Tons.

(2) That the adoption of the Rules has only been recommended by, say, 20 members representing, say, 2,000 Tons.

(3) That this result proves that the adoption of the Yacht Racing Association Rules is only recommended by a small portion of the Club.

(4) That to alter the Sailing Rules in subservience to the wishes of a small minority would be opposed to the ancient traditions, detrimental to the present position and injurious to the future interests of the Club.

(5) That these resolutions be communicated to the next Annual General Meeting of the Club and that no further steps be taken in the matter.

The logic of Mr Buller's argument is hard to discount and bearing in mind the Sailing Committee's opposition to the YRA rules over the years it is perhaps surprising that Robert Hewett's resolution was agreed. Tactically Mr Buller was probably ill-advised in his item (5) to try to shut out for all time a change to the YRA rules. When the Annual General Meeting took place on 22 March 1882, Rear Commodore Sir Thomas Brassey proposed adoption of the YRA rules for 1882, he was seconded by Walter Stutfield, Chairman of the Committee and the resolution was carried by the 97 members present. Although the resolution referred only to the 1882 season the rules were adopted from that season onwards - and despite his opposition Mr Buller continued his membership of the Sailing Committee.

Although the Sailing Regulations of the Club from 1882 were 'According to the Rules and Time Allowance of the Yacht Racing Association' by no means all races organised by the Royal Thames were sailed under these strictures. From 1883 the annual programmes started to include Handicap Matches - the handicaps being set by the Sailing Committee. An increasing acceptance of a National Body for the sport was inevitable and Royal Thames members were soon to be included on the YRA Council. In 1887 the YRA comprised 107 members of whom 44 were members of the RTYC (including 10 who were founder members). The 44 included the President, Vice President and eight of the 24 Council members (including the Honorary Treasurer).

By 1900 the YRA comprised not only individual membership but also club membership. When the Sailing Committee met on 21 January 1901 they *'decided that this club should join the YRA and that Messrs R H Simpson and M H Mills should be the Club representatives'*. It could be said that by July 1906 the Royal Thames was fully integrated with the YRA since at that time the General Committee gave unanimous support to the propositions by the Vice Commodore, Sir James Pender, *'to invite the Council of the YRA to use one of the Club-rooms for their meetings'* - an arrangement that still stands today. By 1908 Augustus Manning, a member and former Chairman of the Royal Thames Sailing Committee, was Vice President of YRA - a situation that ensured that the policies supported by the Royal Thames would be heard in the YRA council. In spite of the early difficulties for the Royal Thames to accept the YRA and its rules it is interesting to note that as early as November 1882, when the Sailing Committee felt the need to take action to reverse *'the paucity of entries for matches sailed on the Thames during the past few seasons'*, they resolved to discuss this matter at a meeting they called and invited attendance of representatives of the New Thames YC, the Royal London YC and the YRA!

By 1899 the Royal Thames chaired annual fixture meetings to agree a joint programme for river matches to be held during the following year's season. By 1908 that programme was submitted to a meeting chaired by the YRA for integration into a national programme and at which the Thames Clubs were represented by the Royal Thames.

Yacht Racing Topics 1879-1914

The format for Royal Thames sailing matches had changed little over the period 1868-78 with courses for the 'River' Matches starting at Gravesend, Rosherville or Erith and turning at the Nore or the Mouse Light Ships while the 'Channel Race' was established on the Nore to Dover course. When the Sailing Committee met in January 1879 it was agreed that it would be advisable to start the Schooners and Yawls in the more spacious waters of the Lower Hope - by 1883 virtually all River Matches started from Lower Hope. Another topic

raised at that meeting centred on a report from the Secretary that several racing yacht owners had requested the Committee to consider the advisability of adopting 'flying starts' on the Thames. No doubt these owners were concerned by the difficulty in controlling large yachts in confined waters subject to variable winds from a moored position with no sails set - a situation ready-made for collisions, damaged spars and torn sails. The committee decided to seek the views of racing owners in general. A mere 10 replies were received of which seven were opposed to flying starts - probably because there would be no time compensation for late starters! In spite of this negative response flying starts were agreed for the 1881 season except for the cutter matches starting from Gravesend.

The meeting between the RTYC, RLYC and NTYC in November 1882, that was held in order to agree a joint programme for 1883 resulted in their river matches being on successive days, where possible, thus providing more racing opportunities when yachts were assembled on the river. For the Royal Thames, the Channel Match continued every season, but they introduced more multi-rig matches, handicap matches and for 1883, Amateur Matches. The crews in the latter were made up entirely from 'Amateurs' who were defined as *'Gentlemen who have never received pay for sailing in a fore and aft vessel, Officers of the Royal Navy and Mercantile Marine excepted'*. The Club made modest funds available for the Amateur Races which also catered for small yachts - the Sailing Committee, and the Club as a whole, were regularly criticised for failing to provide racing for small (under 10 Tons) yachts.

While there were good entries for the Amateur Matches the experiment was not repeated and in following seasons matches were held for varying classes (by tonnage) together with Handicap Matches and the Channel Match. The programme meeting with the representatives of the Royal London and New Thames Yacht Club was found to be beneficial and by 1898 representatives from the Royal Harwich and the Royal Cinque Ports Yacht Club also attended. The inclusion of Handicap Matches in the annual programme - the handicaps being set by the Sailing Committee - was to provide the Club with a continuing degree of independence from the everchanging YRA classifications; an arrangement which was well received by opponents of the YRA, while the Class races run under YRA rules and time allowances suited the equally strong-minded supporters of the YRA.

Perhaps the most overt critic of the Royal Thames as it passed through the unsettled sailing waters of the 1880s was Edward Fox. In April 1885 he published a pamphlet entitled *A Suggestion to the Members of the RTYC and YRA in the interests of Yachting'*. His early remarks point out that *'the RTYC perhaps more than any other Club may be taken as the parent institution under whose Flag our National Sport first received substantial support in England...'* and citing 1873 as the year when *'this Club may be said to have reached the height of its prosperity'* (from the point of view of influence over yachting affairs). He continues by suggesting that over the following 10 years, when the sport of yachting had seen extraordinary growth, the Royal Thames position had, at best, remained stationary. He notes that membership is declining, less money is voted to yachting each year, its influence over yachting threatens to become provincial and isolated; while the Clubhouse *'no longer offers those increasing requirements and luxuries which, if possessed, would have enabled it to hold its own as a first-class London Club quite independently of yachting income, upon which*

RTYC enclosure on Ryde Pier (1930).

the house expenses now make constant and vexatious inroads...'. He continues in that vein, deploring the failure of the Sailing Committee to modernise 'Thames Measurement' and he sees the YRA undermining what authority the Royal Thames had retained. On the principal that 'if you can't beat them, join them', his proposed remedy was to form an all powerful National Yacht Squadron, based in London, by combining the RTYC and YRA. His detailed proposals for financing it are given as is an extraordinary hierarchy of world and national heads of state as Patrons, The Prince of Wales as Admiral of the Fleet and some 40 or so Flag Officers of Royal Clubs as Vice Admirals and Rear Admirals as well as an enormous Council.

When the General Committee met on 2 June 1885 and considered the pamphlet, the Secretary was instructed to reply that *'the scheme suggested was advocated in a manner so disparaging to the Club and contained, in the opinion of the Committee, so many passages contrary to fact that they must decline to consider the matter in its present form'.* In spite of the rebuff Mr Fox continued his membership for another 15 years.

While the administrators and organisers of yacht racing in the 1880s were constantly changing the rules in the expectation that they could create more competitive and attractive racing, the designers, and probably the owners, were moving away from large schooner rigged to big cutter rigged yachts. This is well illustrated by entries for the Royal Thames annual Channel Match from Nore to Dover. In 1879 the entry of 18 yachts comprised equal numbers of schooners, yawls and cutters. In 1886 the 12 entries were made up of nine cutters and three yawls. For the Royal Thames, however, the outstanding sailing match of the 1880s was the Jubilee Race in 1887, held to mark 50 years of the Queen's reign.

The details of the Jubilee Race are fully written up in several documents including Douglas Phillips Birt's 'The Cumberland Fleet' the March and July 1887 issues of Hunt's Yachting Magazine and by Captain E du Boulay in the 1908 volume of The Yachting and Boating Monthly. To simply record these well known accounts here is quite unnecessary but it may be of interest to note some of the salient issues. No one doubted that a maritime nation seeking to mark such an important anniversary should include in the celebrations a unique

nautical occasion and the Royal Thames felt that its wealth of experience in yacht racing made it well qualified to promote and organise a 1,520 miles race circumnavigating Great Britain and Ireland, leaving both islands to port. The concept was received with great enthusiasm and the Commodore, HRH The Prince of Wales, immediately entered his schooner *ALINE* and agreed to start the race off Southend from the *NORHAM CASTLE,* which was chartered by the Club as committee boat. There was to be a single prize of £1,000 for the winner at Dover. When the race was announced many thought there would be an entry as large as 80 yachts. As owners and their advisers studied the charts of the rock-strewn Pentland Firth and its powerful tides, together with the potential dangers from the full weight of the Atlantic bearing down on the west coast of Ireland, coupled with the general lack of experience of yachtsmen in true ocean racing, it is not surprising that on the day only 11 yachts came to the start line - three schooners, three yawls, two ketches and three cutters.

Hunt's Yachting Magazine was very critical of the whole concept. They clearly subscribed to the view that, above all else, yacht races were there to provide entertainment for the spectators who followed the competitors and this race could not provide that opportunity. They also rigorously opposed such a huge prize for one owner in one race feeling that such a notion would deprive many of smaller prizes.

The competitors ranged from Lord Francis Cecil's cutter *SLEUTHHOUND (40 Tons)* to the schooner *SELENE (255 Tons)* owned by T Henderson Esq. This made it difficulty to agree a scale for time allowance. Eventually it was decided to adopt a 'time-on-distance' system based on a course of 2,000 nautical miles, this length to be increased by 100 miles for each day under 10 days and decreased by 100 miles for each day over 10 days, the time to be taken from the first yacht to finish. (No time allowance to be given if the first yacht took more than 30 days). If the enthusiasm of owners waned, that of spectators did not and a huge flotilla of craft assembled to witness the start shortly after midday on 14 June. The competing yachts were a mixture of racers and cruisers and many an old salt felt the latter would succeed in the open sea. It was not to be and Sir Richard Sutton's cutter *GENESTA (80 Tons)* took an early lead (2 years earlier he had challenged unsuccessfully for the Americas Cup) - this lead he never lost and in fact they never sighted any other competitor throughout the race. *GENESTA* crossed the finish at Dover in the early hours of 27 June followed, 19 hours later by *SLEUTHHOUND* and over the next 19 hours by *GWENDOLIN (170 Tons)* owned by Major Ewing, *SELENE* and *ALINE (191 Tons)*. The old salts favourite *STET (98 Tons)*, the ketch owned by the redoubtable Ernest Buller, finished the course some days later having been becalmed in the Channel; the other five competitors retired.

The circumstances of Captain du Boulay's involvement in the race are also worthy of note. He recalls that: *'GENESTA's owner, Sir Richard Sutton, was High Sheriff for the county of Berkshire in 1887, and, having carefully studied all the frightful penalties that might be inflicted on him by an irate judge should he be absent from the next assizes that were to be held in June, he was reluctantly compelled to give up the idea of being able to sail on board his vessel during the race. But what is one man's misfortune is anothers luck, so at the last minute he asked me to take his place and represent him on board and keep the log. Hence I had the most interesting race it has ever been my good fortune to sail'.* It is history's good fortune that his extrapolation of the log he kept provides an illuminating account of the race and the conditions under which it was sailed as well the particular experiences of the *GENESTA* and her crew.

While the 1880s may have been a decade when the Royal Thames was struggling to find the basis for accepting the rules of the newly established YRA and a time when it was proving difficult to encourage sufficient entries for the river matches, it was still a period when members of the club achieved many successes in Royal Thames and other club matches with outstanding yachts. Particularly successful were George C. Lampson with his schooner *MIRANDA (140 Tons)* and John Jameson with his yacht *IREX (85 Tons)* and his cutter *SAMOENA (90 Tons)*; the latter owner continued his prize-winning achievements into the next decade with his outstanding cutter *IVERNA (152 Tons)*. The winner of more first prizes in the 1890s than any yacht was the Prince of Wales' Fife-designed cutter *BRITANNIA (221 Tons)* - a success she maintained throughout her long career. Other successful owners were Myles B. Kennedy's cutter *MAID MARION (72 Tons)*, Colonel Villiers Bagot's cutter *CREOLE (54 Tons)*, Peter Donaldson' s cutters *CALLUNA (258 Tons)* and *ISOLDE (81 Tons)* and, although not elected a member of the Royal Thames until 1911, W B Paget's yachts *NAMARA (102 Tons)* and *COLUMBINE (81 Tons)*. Also worthy of mention are the Marquis of Ailsa's trio of 'hounds' *FOXHOUND, BLOOD-HOUND*, and *SLEUTHHOUND (40 Tons)*, which were successful not only for him but for later owners. *CREOLE* continued to be the most successful yacht in Royal Thames matches right up to 1914, by which time she had won more than 30 prizes over 25 years. The other most successful yachts at the beginning of the twentieth century were Sir James Pender's yawl *BRYNHILD (153 Tons)*, the cutter *VANITY (50 Tons)* owned by J R Payne and I H Benn (who was to become the club's Cup Bearer in 1942), the cutter *GAUNTLET (37 Tons)* owned by F. and C H Last and lastly A K Stothert's yawl *ROSAMOND (63 Tons)*, all of which were regular winners of their class.

The start of the twentieth century brought to an end Queen Victoria's long reign and the Commodore of the Royal Thames, HRH The Prince of Wales, succeeded to the throne. It also brought many changes to the Club sailing matches and the location of the matches entered by members of the Club. In 1901 it was decided to start and finish the river matches off Southend, though starts from Lower Hope were restored in 1907. With the demise of the New Thames Yacht Club, the

Royal Thames took over their annual Southend to Harwich match and thus extended their historic programme of River Matches and the Channel Match. Perhaps the biggest single change was the involvement of the Club and its members in regattas outside the United Kingdom. In 1903 the Channel Match from Nore to Dover was followed by a match from Dover to Ostend, attendance at the Ostend Regatta and an Ostend to Dover match. In 1904 there was a match from Dover to Calais and back together with attendance at the regatta at Ostend and Boulogne. In 1906 members attended the regattas at Havre, Ostend and Antwerp followed in 1912 by participation in the Dover to Heligoland match.

The first European International Regatta under the patronage of HM King George V was held on 7 and 8 August 1911 at Spithead. This was an extremely successful venture which provided races for the A Class and nine classes between 6 and 23 metres under the International Rule. Members of the Royal Thames were present in strength and featured among the prize winners. Myles B Kennedy won a magnificent trophy (still in the club's possession) in the 23 metre class with his cutter *WHITE HEATHER II (178 Tons)* - in fact he was only required to 'sail over' the course, while Frederick Milburn's cutter *NORADA (106 Tons)* won the 19 metre race on both days, winning the German Emperor's Cup and the Irish Cup. During the two days club members won a total of 11 prizes including two seconds in the 10 metre class for Herbert Marzetti with his cutter IREX (17 Tons).

The year 1912 saw many club members taking passage on the chartered liner SS Aragruaya to attend the Kiel Regatta, while in 1913 the South Eastern Railways turbine steamer was chartered for the International Regatta at Havre, provided 250 members and their friends took tickets at six guineas each - this cost covered the passage from London via Folkestone to Havre and back with luncheon and a tea on board and daily cruises at Havre.

It was also in 1912 that the club challenged for the two premier French trophies - The Coupe de France and the One-Ton Cup. Established in 1891, the Coupe de France was sailed in the International 10-metre class. The races of not less than 20 miles each were continued until one yacht had won three races. The Yacht Club de France selected the challengers or defenders but a recognised club in any other country could challenge. In 1912 it was Herbert Marzetti's 10 metre *IREX* that the Royal Thames selected to challenge - and challenge successfully. In 1913, when defending, the Royal Thames again selected the Fife-designed *IREX* after selection races against Richard Hennessy's *PAMPERO*. Once again *IREX* was successful but in 1914 it was to be Richard Hennessy' s opportunity to defend successfully the Coup de France with *PAMPERO*.

The One-Ton Cup was established in 1898 by members of the Circle de la Voile de Paris following the sale of their shares in the yacht *ESTEREL* which had been built to defend the Coupe de France. Originally the cup was for small inshore keelboats rating at One Ton under the 1892 French tonnage rules but, following the International conference of 1906, at which the IYRU was formed, the One Ton Cup was presented to the new Six Metre class. When the Royal Thames challenged the German holders in 1912 it was with *BUNTY* owned by the brothers E G and C P Martin. They were successful after seven days of racing. The following year the club was once more successful - this time as the defender - with Algernon Maudslay's *CREMONA*.

Another success for the club in 1914 was achieved when the Circle de la Voile de Paris invited the Royal Thames to challenge for the King of Spain's Cup to be sailed for in the Six Metre class at Menton. On the day it was Captain R T Dixon's VANDA that came first and N Clark Neill's *SANDRA* that came second after three days of competitive racing.

It was in 1913 that the whole direction of sailing matches held under the Royal Thames burgee took a significant change from the River Thames to the Solent. As recorded under 'Waterside Premises' in Section IV, the Club acquired a pavilion on Stokes Bay Pier and held matches off there that season, including the successful defence of the Coupe de France and the One Ton Cup. The outbreak of war in August 1914 limited the use of Stokes Bay to two seasons. By the end of the war the Admiralty still retained use of the pier at Stokes Bay but fortunately the club was able to lease the pavilion on Ryde Pier at a rent of 103 guineas per year.

Classification

In the early period of the years covered by this volume the classification of yachts was by tonnage (from 'Tons' TM) coupled with time allowance and was often changed annually. In 1868 there were four classes of cutter by tonnage varying from 7-12 Tons 'to greater than 35 Tons' and a time allowance for cutters. There were also two classes of schooner above or below 100 Tons and their associated time allowance. By 1874 this had changed to three classes of cutter with a range of four time allowances in the 1st class and one for each of the 2nd and 3rd classes. For the schooners also there were two time allowances for vessels under 100 Tons and four for those over 100 Tons.

From 1882, when the club agreed to sail their 'non-handicap' races under YRA rules, it might have been hoped that greater stability in this field would have taken place but it was not to be. When the YRA was formed in 1875 it used the Thames Measurement as the basis for tonnage but amended that formula in 1880. In 1887 a totally different and simple tonnage formula was adopted and classified yachts as '20 Raters' or '60 Raters' etc. This formula survived for nine years when, in 1896, a complex 'linear formula' was introduced which classified yachts in 'feet' - five years later this was modified, with the introduction of 'rating' and later 'feet', the Sailing Committee of the Royal Thames decided each year the range of rating or feet for the classes for which races were held.

This ever changing scene must have made life difficult for yacht designers and yacht owners when trying to anticipate the requirement for succeeding seasons; especially since America, Scandanavia, Germany, France, and Switzerland each evolved their own formulae. It was therefore, a considerable achievement in 1906 when the International Conference was able to agree a single international formula and the classes which would stem from it. A list of the measurement formulae used in the United Kingdom is given in Appendix 9

Prizes

From 1868 to 1878 the club continued its policy of selecting prizes/trophies for the club sailing matches from a selection provided by nominated silversmiths. This was a somewhat open-ended policy in that the cost of prizes was not subject to quantitative control. The policy was changed in 1878 when prize winners were allocated a sum of money and then

selected a trophy, subject to the approval of the committee that it was to Royal Thames standards. Throughout the second half of the nineteenth century there was always an undercurrent of criticism from members who felt that the club devoted too large a sum to prizes, while yacht owners believed that attractive prizes encouraged the top yachts to enter Royal Thames sailing matches. Fortunately, during the years covered by this volume, there were always benefactors among the members who presented generous prizes. These included HM Queen Victoria, HRH The Prince of Wales, Lord Brassey, George Duppa, Colonel Peters, MA Muir and the daughters of the late A O Wilkinson. As described in Section V the club eventually established a Regatta Fund in 1905 to which many members made annual donations. This gave the Sailing Committee a large measure of financial independence when organising the annual sailing programme.

In spite of the financial constraints placed on the Sailing Committee and the criticism of their alleged profligacy or their failure to maintain control over yacht racing in the United Kingdom, the Royal Thames did retain its pre-eminent position in the sport and when regattas could restart in 1919 they were well-placed to take a lead.

Minutiae

Having reviewed the major aspects of 50 years of yacht racing in the Royal Thames Yacht Club, it may provide an appropriate contrast to end this section by recording half a dozen minor issues that exercised the Sailing Committee.

In July 1888, club member and successful yacht racing owner Sir George Lampson informed the committee to *'take notice of the reported intention of the War Department to buoy off a part of the Solent at Browndown for the purpose of rifle practice'*. The Committee decided to protest at once to the Board of Trade against the project - but it fell on unsympathetic ears.

In February 1890 a petition to the board of Trade to prevent the deposit of dredgings from Southampton Docks inside the anchorage at Calshot Castle was forwarded to the club by Captain Hughes of Hamble and signed by the Vice Commodore on behalf of the Sailing Committee after full discussion.

Another member, Mr F G Fitch, wrote to the Committee in May 1896 asking them to apply to the Royal Yacht Squadron *'for leave for RTYC members to come ashore at their landing stage at Cowes'*. The Committee felt that the stage was required by the RYS and declined to lay themselves open to a refusal of the application!

Later, in November of the same year, the Committee considered a letter from the Royal Corinthian Yacht club asking the RTYC to join them in *'petitioning the War Office to stop firing across the fairway from the Sheerness and Grain Forts which was found very dangerous to yachts cruising in the vicinity.'* Not surprisingly the Committee agreed to join RCYC in a protest.

Finally, in March 1899, the Committee received a letter from the Board of Trade stating that a Light Due of one shilling per registered ton would be collected on or soon after 1 April. While this is an all too familiar, and at times, contentious subject the Committee seemed to be unconcerned and decided to *'acknowledge the letter and place it in the front hall'*.

III
Club Administration

Committee Structure

In 1868 the Club had two executive committees - the General Committee of Management (constituted in 1860) and the Sailing Committee. The latter had always existed and prior to 1860 it was all-powerful, but with the acquisition of successively more expensive Clubhouses the Sailing Committee became answerable to the General Committee on matters of financial expenditure. Members who had been proposed and seconded as candidates were elected to the General Committee at the Annual General Meeting of the Club in March each year (and by ballot if the number of candidates exceeded the number of vacancies). It was the responsibility of the Commodore to nominate members to serve on the Sailing Committee.

The General Committee comprised 21 members who were appointed for one year. At the next AGM the 21 members who received the most votes comprised the new General Committee. This rather haphazard method was soon changed and one-third of the Committee were then required to retire each year - but could immediately be re-elected and members could, therefore, serve continuously. This revised rule was still unpopular, especially by members who felt the Club was being run by a small, almost self-appointed, group of members. In 1884 the rules were again altered and retiring members became ineligible for re-election until a year after their retirement. Another interesting amendment to the rules was approved in 1876 - this required that any General Committee member who had not attended six committee meetings ceased to be a member of the Committee. This requirement lapsed after 1879.

While the members comprising the Sailing Committee were invariably yacht owners, the 21 who formed the General Committee were predominantly non-yacht owners (at times there were only one or two yacht owners and rarely more than five or six). Perhaps this is not surprising since the General Committee dealt largely with House and Financial matters and balloting of members for election. This did not meet the approval of all members. At the 1903 AGM a proposal was tabled that of the 21 members of the General Committee 10 should be yacht owners. A protracted discussion by the 162 members present took place but when put to the vote the proposal was rejected by a large majority.

The Sailing Committee in 1868 comprised the Flag Officers (ex-officio) and seven members. This latter number was soon increased to 12. With the appointment of the Prince of Wales as Commodore in 1874 the rules were altered to allow the Commodore or Vice Commodore to nominate members for the Sailing Committee. This procedure was retained until 1903 when it was changed such that *'The General Committee appointed not less than nine members of the Club who, with the Flag Officers, shall form the Sailing Committee, who shall retire in rotation in the same manner as the General Committee but shall be eligible for re-election'.*

The General Committee was authorised *'to nominate Sub Committees for such purposes as they may deem proper'.* In 1868 there were two 'permanent' Sub Committees, the House and Finance and the Wine, the former frequently being referred to in the abbreviated form 'House Committee' . The numbers of members on the House Committee varied considerably and at one stage reached 15 but the majority of meetings were attended by no more than five or six. The Wine Committee numbers also varied but rarely exceeded five or six.

The responsibility of the House Committee was to oversee the operation and management of the Clubhouse and to ensure that the standard of the service provided to members equated to their expectations; a balance that was never going to be an easy one to achieve. Making a profit from the operation would always be particularly difficult. By 1884 membership numbers had dropped significantly and the annual accounts showed that the Club had made a 'loss' for several years. It is no surprise, therefore, that when the General Committee met on 4 November 1884 they passed a resolution *'that the House Committee be dissolved and that in future the General Committee do meet weekly for the general management of the affairs of the Club and monthly as heretofore for the ballot'.* Since both the General and House Committees were chaired by the same person and since the latter committee comprised members of the former, it is difficult to understand what this resolution achieved. In practice the business conducted at the weekly meetings bears a very close resemblance to that at the earlier House Committee meetings while the monthly ballot meetings did far more than elect new members and there was much duplication between the two meetings. In fact what was happening was that the General Committee were meeting weekly, and once a month the ballot was added to the agenda. What is certain is that after 1884 the membership numbers increased, the financial position improved and the resolution of 4 November seemed justified. Over the next few years the weekly meetings became fortnightly meetings and when, in April each year, the General Committee made appointments to Sub Committees the term 'House' reappears. In 1893, however, appointments were made to the 'General Purposes' Sub Committee which seems to have replaced the House and Finance Sub Committee of earlier years.

The wheel eventually turned full circle and in October 1898 the General Committee *'considered the question of the House Committee and it was agreed that the House Committee should have full powers in all domestic arrangements of the Club'* (even though in April that year appointments had been made to the General Purposes Sub Committee!). The final change came in 1905 when separate House and Finance Sub Committees were established.

The Wine Committee, formed in 1863 to improve the selection of wines for the membership, continued to make a valuable contribution to the affairs of the Club and seems to have been successful in balancing modest prices and adequate profitability without undermining quality. In 1909 they formed a combined Sub Committee with the Cigar Sub Committee which had been established in 1876. Thus was formed today's Wine and Cigar Committee.

In 1859 there had been an unsuccessful attempt to form a Library Sub Committee and it seems that no further action was taken to care for the Club's collection of books until 1878 when the Rev F H Addams (a member since 1864) accepted the appointment of Honorary Librarian. The General Committee resolved *'that a quarterly allowance of four guineas be granted from the Club funds for expenses with reference to keeping in good condition the books in the Club Library'*. The Rev Addams resigned from the Club in 1887 and no mention of a new librarian appears in Club records until ten years later when Mr F R Fisher was appointed. At the same meeting of the General Committee (when the appointment was announced), a donation of £10, from Club funds, was made to the 'Library Fund' while in the following month the Committee agreed to open a subscription list for the Library with a maximum donation limited to ten shillings - three months later when the list closed £13.10.0 had been given. Mr Fisher's membership ended in 1907 and no doubt the Committee were too much involved in the prospect of moving to a new Clubhouse to spend time selecting a new librarian. As soon as the Clubhouse in Piccadilly was occupied, however, a meeting of the General Committee in June 1911 appointed three members to a Library Sub Committee who were granted £50 for the purchase and binding of books. Six months later in January 1912 the General Committee *'inspected the new Library Catalogue and a unanimous vote of thanks was passed to Mr A Underhill and the Library Sub Committee'*. Mr Arthur Underhill is referred to again in March 1914 as the Honorary Librarian and he was granted a further £20 towards the Library expenses. After years of uncertainty the Library had been established on a sound footing.

Medical Officer

When one realises that it was the custom for many of the Club servants to be accommodated in the Clubhouse it is surprising to find that it was not until August 1900 that reference is made to a Medical Officer who was contracted to attend Club servants. The first gentleman named is a Dr Dutch whose fees for his service were *'one guinea for three visits but for a single visit to be half a guinea'*. This rather confusing statement on the doctor's fees is presumably referring to the number of visits in a specified period of time, e.g. per week or month. In December 1911 a Dr Northcote *'was appointed Medical Officer to the Club on the same pro rota terms as the late Medical Officer, the engagement to be terminable quarterly'*.

Club Rules/Members List

The Club rules and the format of the members list changed infrequently but some interesting proposals (some of which were approved) and changes occurred during the years covered in this volume. Some of the more relevant matters are included below in chronological order.

In August 1874 Mr J Spencer Price proposed *'that until increased accommodation be provided in the Clubhouse only yacht owners be elected members'*. Nothing came of this proposal and it is less than clear whether he was referring to the general shortage of rooms or of the particular shortage of bedrooms. What is surprising is that Mr Price was not a yacht owner!

Today it would be unacceptable to make members addresses readily available but in the nineteenth century, when instant data transmission was still far away in the distant future, it was the practice to include the home addresses of members in the members' list. This practice was stopped at the Royal Thames with the issue of the members' list for 1875 - the first issue for many years due to the financial constraints imposed in the period 1868-74.

The information contained in the members' list included a member's 'number' and a member's 'yacht number'. Until 1893 the member's number was decided by his position in the alphabetical list of members' surnames. As the sequence in the list changed when new members were elected and existing members resigned or died, so the member's number was liable to change each year. The object of the member's number was defined in the laws and regulations of the Club, paragraph 27, to be *'so as to enable one yacht to signal to another when at a distance, what members they may have on board'*. In 1883 it was resolved that the constant changing of a member's number was unsatisfactory and members were given permanent numbers. This 'permanent' arrangement did not last long. In 1890 a members number was determined by the member's date of election - a reversion to a varying number and a system continued and accepted since that date.

The direct connection between the Cumberland Fleet and the Royal Thames Yacht Club was always known and accepted within the Club. In spite of that the frontispiece of the members' handbook simply stated *'Royal Thames Yacht Club, instituted August 1823'*. It took a meeting of the General Committee in April 1900 to alter the frontispiece so that it read *'Cumberland Fleet 1775, Thames Yacht Club 1823, Royal Thames Yacht Club 1830'*.

While all candidates seeking election to the Club had to be proposed and seconded by members, a former member could apply for re-election simply by making the request in writing to the Committee. This was changed from December 1904 when the General Committee resolved that anyone seeking re-election to the Club must be proposed and seconded and follow the same procedure as new candidates.

Lastly, in December 1911, the Vice Commodore, Lord Queenborough asked the General Committee if they would agree to include in the members' book a seniority list of members in addition to the alphabetical list. This the committee accepted and the seniority list appeared in the 1912 edition. No doubt many of today's members would appreciate this 'extra' in the current handbook.

Schooner Yacht FLYING CLOUD, 75 Tons - Lithograph by Josiah Taylor.

Lady Members

In the second half of the twentieth century until 1992 the
term 'Lady Member' has had a specific meaning and is defined
as a category of membership of the club open to ladies.
The rules of the Club have never been written in terms that
made membership available exclusively to men and no doubt
the current climate of political correctness could insist that
the qualification for membership must allow both sexes to
be eligible to apply. During the period covered by this volume
the wording of the Rule (No: 7), relating to application for
membership, said *'That every candidate for admission to
the club shall be proposed by one member and seconded by
another; that his name, address, profession or business, with
the names of his proposer and seconder, shall be inserted in
the 'List of Candidates' Book ten days at least before such
a candidate shall be eligible for ballot by the Committee'.*
The inclusion of the word 'his' in Rule 7 was almost certainly
because it was assumed that applicants would be gentlemen
rather than that applicants could not be ladies.

The early records of the Club provide no evidence of a lady
applying for membership. The first evidence is however,
available in the minutes of the special meeting of the General
Committee held on 13 May 1874 under the chairmanship of
W F Moore, when a letter was read from Baroness Meyer de
Rothschild asking permission to become a candidate for
admission to the Club. On a vote she was elected by 15 votes
to 3. Later, on 12 May 1875, it was recorded that *'The case
of Mrs Hamilton who was desirous of joining the Club was
postponed for further enquiries!'* This was followed by
a special meeting of the General Committee (again under the
Chairmanship of W F Moore) on 8 June 1875 when, after the
ballot and an item concerning the manner in which the Derby
Sweep should be drawn, it is noted that *'Mrs C Hamilton was*

unanimously elected a member of the Club'. As was the case
for most ladies who became members, she was the owner of
a substantial yacht.

This election was quickly followed by another on 27 July
when the minutes note that *'The Secretary conveyed
a message from Lord Alfred Paget, Vice Commodore,
recommending that Mrs Caroline Anne Gamble of Ashburn,
Gourock, owner of steam yacht 'Cecile' be elected a member
of the club to fly the club colours and Mrs Gamble was
unanimously elected a member'.* A further two ladies
were elected to membership by ballot before the turn of
the century and ten more by 1914. A full list of ladies elected
and the yachts they owned is at Appendix 10.

Perhaps the most notable of these distinguished ladies was
Miss Isobel Napier, who ultimately became the most senior
member of the Club in 1970 and who was a relative of
Richard Green, Vice Commodore 1851-62.

Distinguished Members

The members selected here have been arrived at on the
premise that they represent a wide range of professions
in which they excelled; some were elected Honorary
Members in recognition of their achievements; others
were distinguished people who applied for membership
of the Club and were duly elected.

On 29 June 1870 the Committee offered Honorary Membership
to **Ferdinand de Lesseps** the great French engineer who had
been responsible for the recently opened Suez Canal. When it
is recalled that the British Government of the day were decidedly luke-warm in their support for the project, it is to the
credit of the Club that they should have made this gesture.

In 1894 the Committee elected to membership on 2 August, **Arthur Charles Harmsworth**, owner of the 450 Ton Barque *WINDWARD*. The duration of his membership may have been just a few years, but his reputation as a newspaper proprietor grew over the years to make him one of the giants in that field. Just two years later on 6 August 1896, **Sir Hubert Parry**, Director of the Royal College of Music and distinguished composer became a member. At that time he owned the 21 Ton yawl *LATOIS* and later replaced it by the 88 Ton Ketch *WANDERER*.

On 14 October 1909 the Commodore, Theodore Pim proposed and the Vice Commodore, Sir James Pender seconded the election of **Sir Thomas Lipton**, Chairman of the company of that name. At that time he was owner of the 1,242 Ton screw schooner *ERIN* - a large photograph album from that yacht is included in the present Club Library. He is best remembered, however, as the owner of a succession of cutter yachts named *SHAMROCK* and with which he unsuccessfully challenged for the America's Cup between 1899 and 1930. By the time of his election to the Royal Thames he had already made three challenges with *SHAMROCK I, II* and *III* through the Royal Ulster Yacht Club and was to make a further two in 1920 and 1930 with *SHAMROCK IV* and *V*.

It was Sir James Pender who proposed for membership on 8 June 1911 **Dr Douglas Mawson** owner of the 816 Ton screw barquentine *AURORA*. Born in Bradford in 1882, Douglas Mawson emigrated to Australia in his youth to become a brilliant scientist. In 1908 he accompanied Shackelton to the Antarctic and was one of the same party who discovered the South Magnetic Pole on 16 January 1909. On the return journey he was fortunate to be rescued after falling into a deep crevasse. It was in 1911 that he led the Australian Antarctic Expedition and by the summer of 1912 he took forward a party comprising two members of the expedition and two dog teams. After travelling 315 miles in 35 days he lost one companion, a dog team and virtually all their equipment in another deep crevasse. Mawson and his other companion together with an emaciated dog team turned back for their base camp. One by one the dogs died and with 100 miles still to travel his second companion became ill and died. Mawson, facing death and with virtually no food struggled on pulling a sledge carrying a tent, a lamp and oil. His remarkable courage enabled him to defy death and he eventually reached his base only to discover that his ship *AURORA* had sailed, leaving five men and stores to sustain him through the Antarctic winter. In the following spring *AURORA* returned and he was able to return to civilisation. On 2 June 1914 the Royal Thames gave a dinner in his honour having already made him an Honorary Member of the Club - his membership, not surprisingly, had lapsed. The courage of (Sir) Douglas Mawson must surely rank alongside that of Captain Scott. In January 1915 he presented the Club with the RTYC burgee which he had flown from AURORA and which now hangs in the present Clubhouse on the stairs leading to the Secretariat offices.

It was the Vice Commodore, Lord Queenborough who proposed for membership in December 1911 **Rear Admiral David Beatty** who was to own in 1913, the screw schooner *SHEELAH, 679 Tons*. In making this election no one could know that they were electing a naval officer who was to become instantly recognised and a hero of the Battle of Jutland in 1915 where he commanded the Battle Cruisers in the last major set-piece sea battle. In November 1918 he was made an Honorary Member of the Club. Admiral Sir John Jellicoe, the

Commander of the British Fleet at Jutland, had been made an Honorary Member in February 1917.

It was Ian Hamilton Benn (who was to become Cup Bearer of the Club in 1942) who proposed for membership in May 1912 the distinguished marine artist **Norman Wilkinson** who owned an 11 Ton cutter *WILD ROSE*. His name is well known by today's members through his fine painting of King George V's historic yacht *BRITANNIA* (in its Bermudan rigged form) which hangs in the present Clubhouse.

The penultimate selection for this all too short list of distinguished members is **Edward Keble Chatterton**. He achieved international recognition as an author and writer on yachting. Many of his better known books are included in the present Club Library. At the time of his election in January 1914 he owned a 5 Ton cutter *VIVETTE*. It is interesting to note that the seconder supporting his candidacy was Norman Wilkinson. Finally, it is perhaps surprising to realise that another famous author and playwright was elected to membership in April 1915 and that was **Arnold Bennett** whose novels, centred on the five towns of the Potteries, brought him great success. He owned the 50 Ton motor vessel *VELSA*.

Discipline

The application of disciplinary procedures against members who fail to conform with the rules of the Club has been a duty which the Committee have always exercised with great competence. The standards of behaviour expected of members and the rules prescribing them have changed little in the past hundred years in spite of changes in social behaviour over that period. Nevertheless the nature of the failure of members to conform has changed in many ways and these brief paragraphs have been included to illustrate that point.

In May 1877, Mr Maurice Howard's name was one of many who were struck off the list of members because of failure to pay their annual subscription - a not uncommon situation leading to a predictable outcome. In the case of Mr Howard, however, the Committee received a letter from him in October 1878 requesting re-admission to the Club. In reply the Committee wrote *'that they regret they are unable to entertain his request favourably as they disapprove of his having forced his way into the Clubhouse and played at Billiards, though warned that he was no longer a member by both the Hall Porter and Billiard Marker'*.

In February 1891 Mr Edward Brock, like Mr Howard, had failed to pay his subscription and he was one of several members who received a circular drawing this to his attention and requesting payment. His response, however, was very different from that of Mr Howard. The Secretary informed the Committee on 5 March that *'the circular had been returned with a memo from the Manager of the Lea Valley Distillery Co. (Mr Brock was a Whisky distiller) which stated that Mr Brock had absconded'*.

Mr John P Bigelow's problem was of a very different nature. He had joined the Club in 1879 (and like many members at that time had inserted in his application under the heading 'profession or business' - none). In December 1891 it came to light that *'in July he had borrowed from one Club Servant £2 and later on £3 from another and that these sums still remained unpaid'*. The Secretary was instructed to write to Mr Bigelow. His reply was available at the next committee meeting. This refers to the 'alleged' debt of £5 and the

Committee deferred action for six months. This suggests that either Mr Bigelow contested his indebtedness or, more probably, that he was unable to pay. What is certain is that Mr Bigelow's membership of the Club was terminated and in July 1892, when there still was no expectation that the debts would be settled, the Club reimbursed the servants. In the meantime the Secretary had issued a written order to the Club servants that *'on no account, on pain of dismissal, were they ever to give cash unless they received a member's cheque for the amount at the time'*. This seems to be a somewhat optimistic directive!

Mr William Tranter was elected to membership of the Club in January 1910. He owned the 229 Ton screw schooner *SEA BELLE* and, like Mr Bigelow entered 'none' under 'profession or business'. In June 1912 the Club chartered the SS Araguaya to convey members on a cruise to the Kiel Regatta in which the Club was well represented. Mr Tranter was among those present (as will be seen from the photograph of the cruise ship, hanging in the Secretary's Office, which is signed by many members attending). In November 1913 a notice was issued to members calling a Special General Meeting on 11 December (see Appendix 11). As will be seen Mr Tranter had incurred debts amounting to about £25 and these were still outstanding. The 41 members present at the SGM voted by a large majority to expel Mr Tranter from the Club and to approve payment of the debt by the Club.

It is noteworthy that the heading of the Notice calling the SGM to deal with Mr Tranter's indebtedness includes the Club's registered address *AMPHITRITE*. This was first registered in April 1892 and was retained for some 100 years by which time the Telex and Fax superseded the telegram. There is no indication as to why this particular 'lady' from Greek Mythology should have been chosen for the Club's registered address. In 1892 a member of the Club did own a schooner named *AMPHITRITE* but the more probable reason is her place in Greek Mythology. She was married to Neptune (the Italian sea-god known to the Romans as Poseidon) and was the most famous of the fifty daughters of Neseus (the Nereids, who were the sea nymphs of the Mediterranean).

IV

Clubhouse Affairs

Management Of The Clubhouse

In 1868 the Club was recovering from the schism of 1867 and taking action to stabilise its affairs - particularly in regard to the operation of the Clubhouse at 7 Abermarle Street. The Club's sailing programme proceeded smoothly but the need to review the financial control and the efficiency of the running of the Clubhouse was clear to everyone. One urgent need was to reduce radically the high level of unpaid subscriptions but it was not until 1872 that the sum outstanding was reduced to a reasonable level.

Under the guidance of Colonel Josiah Wilkinson the Committee decided in March 1869 to advertise for a manager to 'farm' the Club - an interesting description which would seem to draw on the management of country estates. The accountants advised the Committee that such a manager should be offered £1,000 per annum to undertake the task. Eventually Mr John Webb was contracted to take up the duties on 1 June. He was a young man who had served as Butler for two years at the Carlton Club where his father was manager. Immediately prior to coming to the Royal Thames he had been managing the Medical Club. After careful study of the Club's books with the accountants, John Webb believed he could make a profit of £150 to £200 per annum having paid all his expenses out of the £1,000. These expenses included the cost of coal, gas, coke, wood, washing, Billiard repairs, Stewards' expenses such as brushes, soap and candles as well as the wages, liveries and board of servants and the maintenance of kitchen utensils and bedroom linen. Mr Webb was also required to provide a security of £1,500.

The optimism surrounding the appointment of John Webb soon dissipated and by April 1870 the Club was again advertising for a manager to replace him. The new manager was to be Mr Joseph Powell who came from the Caledonian United Services Club in Edinburgh and was to stay with the Royal Thames for six years. The letter inviting him to attend an interview is at Appendix 12 and is of interest in that it re-affirms the range of duties mentioned earlier and gives an insight into the facilities available in the Clubhouse and the expectations of the members.

The House Committee must have found it difficult at times when having to decide between support for the members and support for the manager and his servants. If a member had a complaint about the quality of a meal or the price charged it was the custom that he should note this on his dinner bill or write a letter to the Committee and return his dinner bill unpaid until the matter was resolved. The extent to which the Committee had to go in order to reach a balanced and fair decision is illustrated by complaints dealt with in June 1871. In the first case the Secretary was instructed to write to the member concerned saying *'that the Committee have examined your complaint of the Dinner by having fish served to you brought before them. They are bound to state they consider the fish served to you well cooked and of the best quality. The Manager has made a complaint that you used language to him in the presence and hearing of his servants and a member of the Club, which, without repeating here, the Committee consider most unwarrantable and uncalled for and but for the Manager's consent to withdraw his complaint they would be compelled to take further notice'.* It is to be hoped that the Committee were able to examine the offending portion of fish very shortly after the complaint was made or their task would have been very difficult to carry out without bias. In the second case the member appears to have complained of his selected joint and to have then ordered a chop. The Committee again found the meat well cooked and of best quality and added *'As there was a choice of three joints including the one served to you the Committee think the Manager was entitled to charge you extra for the chop you ordered'.*

Difficulties with dinner bills continued and by October 1871 the House Committee decided that all Bills would be brought before the Committee. Two members of the Committee, Mr W H Mogford and the Rev F H Addams, were detailed for this task. It is unfortunate but true that complaints are always recorded and praise rarely, if ever. Certainly Mr Powell had his problems. In November 1872 five members wrote complaining of *'the low quality of the provisions supplied'* while in December a very respected member complained that the Manager had been unwilling to cash cheques for him and had made offensive remarks to the members. The Committee called for and received an apology from Mr Powell who added that *'he had not the least intention of offending the member'.*

In June 1874 a new 21 year lease of 7 Abermarle Street was completed at a rental of £1,000 per annum. This encouraged the Committee to embark on a refurbishment of the Clubhouse in the Autumn of 1874 at a cost of £1,835 plus £1,250 for new furniture. This expenditure together with the cost of negotiating the new lease was in part offset by a £2,000 loan from Coutts Bank. The Clarence Club offered use of their Clubhouse during most of the three month period of refurbishment.

It was expected that the refurbished Clubhouse would encourage members to make greater use of it. In support

RTYC Nore to Dover 'Channel' Race (1874).

of this Mr Powell introduced a hot lunch comprising of soup and joint at a charge of one shilling and ninepence but by November 1875 the average number of hot lunches served each day was only two and the practice was discontinued.

By the Spring of 1876 a Sub Committee led by Walter F Stutfield Esq, Chairman of Committee, recommended that *'they should confer with Mr Powell so as to terminate the present agreement and draw up a fresh one more in the interests of the Club'*. They had reached this decision *'partly from being in possession now of certain ascertained facts which were not within the reach of the Committee who were acting at the time when that agreement was drawn up in July 1870, and partly form conclusions they have drawn on other points by comparative examination of the Balance Sheets of other London Clubs'*. The alterations in the manager's contract put to Mr Powell found little favour with him. In particular he felt he would require an additional £200 p.a. and also he felt that his health would not withstand the responsibility of even greater superintendence of the Club. The latter point especially, determined the Committee to terminate Mr Powell's contract at the end of the year. His successor was a Mr Beckett. It is clear that the Committee were not happy with Mr Powell' s performance but they did instruct the Secretary to write to him and inform him of their appreciation of the way he had looked after the furniture and other fixed assets. It is noteworthy that the annual allowance sought by Mr Beckett was £960 compared with £1,200 paid to Mr Powell. The Committee would have welcomed this reduction in expenditure since again membership numbers (and therefore income) were falling and the club finances were once again sliding from profit to deficit.

In January 1878 a Sub Committee was appointed to examine Mr Beckett's accounts. When they reported to the General Committee in May they required the Manager to lower his charges for wines and spirits and requested the Trustees to give Mr Beckett three months notice to terminate his agreement as Manager and Caterer. In seeking a new manager to

take office from 1 September 1878 the Committee proposed an allowance of £1,100 and set the profit margins to 20% on spirits; 20% on wine; 50% on mineral water; 10-15% on cigars and about 30% on malt liquors. The Committee considered nine candidates for the post of manager from whom they selected Mr H Burrows but he declined the appointment since the accommodation offered in Stafford Street *'was not commodious enough for his family'*. Five of the candidates were again considered with the result that Mr J Downe was appointed. It was also decided to increase the fee paid to the accountant Mr Rudler, by £50 p.a. and to direct him to make a monthly examination of the Manager's books. Mr Downe appears to have run the Club satisfactorily for over four years but in December 1882 members were complaining about the quality of both the service and the dinners provided. As a consequence Mr Downe was invited to improve standards within a month or he would be given three months notice to leave. In January 1883 Mr Downe asked that his allowance be increased from £1,100 to £1,200 p.a. Once again a Sub Committee was appointed under the Chairmanship of W F Stutfield to investigate the grounds for such an increase. They reported in February and advised that the increase be paid *'as it would be inconvenient that he (Mr Downe) should leave whilst the busy season is coming on and that if any alteration should be made necessary in consequence of continued dissatisfaction, such alterations should take place in the Autumn'*. The Sub Committee also reported that they *'are of opinion that should it become necessary or advisable the Club can, with proper supervision, take the Management into its own hands without loss'*. In the event, Mr Downe tendered his resignation in May and it was accepted. As a consequence yet another Sub Committee (of six members), again chaired by W F Stutfield, was appointed to make recommendations for the future management of the Club. Their report in June simply reinforced the opinion put forward in February and the Committee gave unanimous support to a resolution that the Club assume responsibility for the Management of the Club at the termination of Mr Downe's engagement.

Thus ended the long period of 'farming' the management of the Club and a new era opened with the appointment of Mr Hilton as Superintendent - to supervise the engaged staff. He presented to the House Committee particulars of the staff necessary to carry on the business of the Club. Many existing staff were retained but considerable new appointments were made including a gentleman named Girardin as Chef - he survived less than 24 hours having been *'drunk and unfit to attend to his duties on the evening he started his appointment'*. He was discharged immediately. Among the many appointments made were a Sergeant Major as Hall Porter, a Hall Boy, a Clerk to the kitchen, a Head Marker and Under Marker for the Billiard Rooms, a Butler and Under Butler, Waiters for the Coffee Room and House Maids. Wages varied from £12 pa for the Under Still-Room Maid to £60 for the Head Waiter. The House Committee set out a new tariff for the Coffee Room and opened a special 'Provisions' Account at the City Bank in Bond Street.

The House Committee were soon able to identify problems with running the Club. By April 1884 increases were approved for Coffee Room charges, while in May wine prices were revised - upwards. The General Committee had already put an upper limit of £600 on expenditure for Sailing Match prizes and in June they appointed a Sub Committee *'to examine the present position of the Club'*. The report to the General Committee in July was referred to the House Committee for implementation but they in turn referred it back to the Sub Committee to deal with!

Regrettably, details of the report are not available but it is not without relevance that in July the accountant was instructed to produce a quarterly Balance Sheet; that in October E.W. Buller (a member of the Sub Committee) resigned his membership of the General Committee; that in November the General Committee resolved *'to dissolve the House Committee and that the General Committee do meet weekly for the General Management of the affairs of the Club and monthly as heretofore for the ballot'* (for candidates for election to membership) and that at a Special General Meeting in November a resolution to reduce the entrance fee to 10 guineas and to increase the annual subscription for yacht owning members to seven guineas was challenged by an amendment proposed by E.W. Buller and seconded by Sir Charles Bright that 'there should be no further alterations to the Rules of the Club (e.g. in particular, to the levels of entrance fee and subscription) until effect be given to the alteration to Rule IV which was carried at the March 1894 AGM (this was a resolution proposed by Sir Charles Bright that the seven members who retire from the 21 strong General Committee at each AGM cannot be re-elected to the Committee until 12 months has elapsed)' . When this amendment was put to the members present the vote was 41-41 and the whole matter was adjourned to the next AGM.

It seems quite apparent that not only was farming of the management of the Club to an appointed Manager less than satisfactory but also, the effectiveness of control through the House Committee was being challenged as was the Rule that in effect permitted a member elected to the General Committee to stay on the Committee for an indefinite period provided he was nominated and seconded at the AGM every three years.

The March 1885 AGM chaired by the Vice Commodore, Lord Alfred Paget, was attended by over 100 members. The papers for the meeting reported that not only were membership numbers falling but use of the Clubhouse was not at the level needed to provide sufficient income and therefore the Club accounts in 1884 would show a deficit of £300. Members were asked to increase their support in order that the management of the Club by Committee (rather than through a contracted manager) could be successful. Lastly, members were advised that following the Special General Meeting in November 1884 the General Committee as a whole proposed to tender their resignation at the March 1885 AGM - this they did. Their Chairman E.R. Handcock in tendering the resignation added *'that if it was the wish of the majority they would be willing to continue their services'* - a proposal to that effect was carried by a large majority. This support for the Committee seems to have led to beneficial results since the Club became profitable and membership rose once more and remained in the region of 800 over the next 10 years.

After resigning from the General Committee Ernest W Buller seems rarely to have been out of the limelight. In June 1885 he reported the loss of £20 - part of a parcel of bank notes sent for him from his bank and delivered to the Clubhouse. They were accepted by the Club messenger and then passed to the Hall Porter from whom the parcel was handed to Mr Buller (short of £20). Unfortunately for Mr Buller the Hall Porter was drunk at the time and was consequently given a month's notice. Later the same month Mr Buller wrote complaining that members were bringing Yacht Skippers into the Clubrooms. The response by the Committee to this complaint was a masterpiece of verbosity and read *'The Committee were not desirous of going further into the matter than to say they consider such matters as bringing Servants into the Clubrooms and seating them there are best left to good taste and discretion of the members themselves and they do not believe it is necessary to do more than draw attention to the fact that such proceedings are distasteful to the majority of the members of the Club'*.

Mr Buller next engaged the attention of the Committee in February 1890 when they received a letter from a member, A E Craven Esq, complaining that Mr Buller had insulted his guest, Colonel Brown RA, in the Club and, further, that when he remonstrated with Mr Buller, he called him a liar and refused to retract his words. The Committee directed the Secretary to write to Mr Buller requiring him to attend a special meeting of the Committee in a week's time when he would be expected to provide either a satisfactory explanation or an ample written apology for Mr Craven. Mr Buller chose to ignore the request and instead wrote asking for certified copies of Mr Craven's letters. With these in his possession Mr Buller wrote to the Committee a week later describing Mr Craven's letters as *'disgraceful and absolutely untrue'*. A second special meeting of the Committee held a week later and attended by Colonel Brown concluded, on the basis of his recollections and the evidence from the letters of Messrs Craven and Buller, that *'Mr Craven's charge against Mr Buller of having greatly insulted Colonel Brown was not borne out, but are of opinion that Mr Buller was most rude'*. Lack of a witness prevented the Committee from considering Mr Craven's second charge that Mr Buller insulted him.

It might be supposed that this conclusion by the Committee would end the matter - but not so. Further letters were exchanged and yet another special meeting held on 26 March. It was attended by Colonel Brown and Mr Muir, the latter giving evidence to support Mr Craven's charges. The Committee resolved to request Mr Buller to send in his resignation. Once again Mr Buller side-stepped the Committee

and was present at their meeting on 2 April when he served
a writ on the Committee and the Secretary. A further special
meeting was called on 21 April to consider the expulsion of
Mr Buller under Rule 29. The Committee heard that Mr Buller
had in court tendered an apology to Colonel Brown and that
the Committee Chairman, Mr E R Handcock, had satisfactorily
settled Mr Buller's action against the Club. Mr Craven's conduct
meanwhile had attracted the dissatisfaction of the Committee
and he had been so informed. On 15 May Mr Alfred E Craven
wrote resigning from the Club and stated that *'he was not in
a position to pay the costs incurred by the Club in the late
actions for injunction'* - his resignation was accepted.

Five years later on 19 September 1895 Mr Buller was one
of three members to be 'struck off' for not paying his subscription but once again he survived and was reinstated on
7 November having paid his arrears - what is more he repeated
the process in 1896 but the Committee took note that he
had been very unwell and unable to attend to his affairs.
Mr Buller's name does not appear in the 1897 list of members
and it must be probable that even his remarkable power's of
'recovery' could not overcome ill health. It would be wrong
to end this long account of Ernest Buller's activities on a tone
that implied he was just a thoroughly tiresome member,
always causing trouble. All the evidence available shows him
to have been a loyal, hard-working supporter of the Royal
Thames and trusted by his fellow members who elected him
to the senior committees of the Club. In addition, as a member
of the New Thames Yacht Club, he was elected to the offices
of Rear Commodore (1887-88) and Vice Commodore (1889-95)
- which placed him in the same situation as many distinguished
members of the Royal Thames who also served both Clubs.

It has already been recorded that the lively AGM of March
1885, which had taken place a few months after Ernest Buller
resigned from the General Committee because his recommendations had been swept aside, had taken actions to improve
the management of the Club. With the Club performing
effectively the lease of the Club premises came under
discussion in January 1896. (The 21 year lease signed in
June 1874 at £1,000 pa had been renewed from 25 December
1897 for a further 21 years at the same rent). The protracted
negotiations continued for over two years with the outcome
announced at the March 1899 AGM. The new 21-year lease
was to run from 25 December 1897 at an unchanged rent
for three years after which it would be increased by £50 to
£1,050 - the first effective increase since the Club moved
to 7 Abermarle Street in 1860.

At the turn of the century the Club appeared to be running
smoothly and there was no cause for concern. Therefore it was
a little surprising that in January 1904 the General Committee
found it necessary to set up a Committee of Enquiry into the
management of the Club, the Committee consisting of their
Chairman, J McNiele Miller, and five others who were required
'To enquire into Finance and the Management of Servants'.
The recommendations they made were unanimously accepted
in July. Their report is regrettably not available but it is not
without significance that the then Secretary, Colonel Dick,
was the subject of criticism as was the Club Steward.
Both had resigned before the year ended.

Although the lease of 7 Abermarle Street had been re-negotiat-
ed in 1899 (for 21 years) it may have included an option to
terminate after 11 years. What is certain is that in March 1910
the General Committee agreed to inaugurate a 'Sinking Fund'
as a provision against the expiring of the lease and credited

it with the sum of £100. (Yachtsmen do not usually welcome
the title 'Sinking'!) By June the possibility of moving to new
premises was raised at a General Committee meeting by the
Rear Commodore, Almeric Paget. A Sub Committee of four
was appointed to go into the subject.

The Sub Committee was chaired by Edward Hilder (he was
also chairman of the General Committee). Edward Hilder was
a solicitor and although he had not been elected to membership of the Club until April 1909 and to the General Committee
in March 1910, he was a former member of the now lapsed
New Thames Yacht Club where he had done sterling work
in negotiating the lease of their Clubhouse. The immediate
recommendation of the Sub Committee was to accept an offer
by Mr Scott of 24 Abermarle Street to take over the lease of
No 7 (the Clubhouse actually gave up the lease on 6 September
1910) and an offer from Lord Bristol for the Club to lease
6 St James Square. A special General Meeting of the Club was
called for the 26 July (see Appendix 13). The few members
who responded by letter were in favour of the move. The 102
members who attended the SGM had no doubts about the
benefits of the proposed move and gave unanimous support
to the Resolutions. The improved facilities were clearly
attractive especially the increase in the number of bedrooms
available from three to eleven. Unfortunately, by mid-September
negotiations, for 6 St James Square had failed and the Club had
vacated 7 Albermarle Street. Meanwhile, members were able
to use the Raleigh Club, the New Oxford and Cambridge Club,
the Junior Athenaeum and the Badminton.

The Sub Committee had by now become aware that many
members of the Isthmian Club at 105 Piccadilly were very
dissatisfied with the management of their Club and might
well welcome its being taken over by the Royal Thames
as a private members' (rather than a proprietary) club.
Two members of the Royal Thames, Messrs J H Clutton
and A Troughton, valued the property and recommended
an offer of not more than £22,000 be made for the lease of
105 Piccadilly, which was owned by Lord Walsingham, the
lease expiring in 1930. It was forecast that many Isthmian
Club members would join the RTYC, boosting Club membership to 1,200 and making the move financially viable. An offer
of £20,000 was made but although the bid would have been
accepted it seems that others who had a prior option found
the money needed at the last moment. Undeterred, the Club
turned its sights on the Lyceum Club at 128 Piccadilly where
the leaseholder, Mr Smedly, had suggested a figure of £40,000
would be needed to buy out the lease.

By early December the lack of a firm negotiating figure
persuaded the Club to abandon this option and turn their
attention to 80 and 81 Piccadilly owned by Mr Burdett-Coutts.
A letter was circulated to members before Christmas (see
Appendix 14) informing them that they proposed to take
a three month tenancy of 81 Piccadilly at a cost of £400 with
the option during the three months to take a lease of 80
and 81 Piccadilly at an annual rental of £1500 for a period of
13 years from 2 January 1911. A resolution to this effect was
put to a Special General Meeting of the Club held on the 31
January 1911 and carried unanimously. The accommodation
available at 80/81 Piccadilly comprised a basement for staff
accommodation, kitchen and stores; a ground floor with
Smoking Room and a Billiard Room, a First Floor with Coffee
Room, Writing Room, Card Room and another Billiard Room;
while the third and fourth floors had 13 bedrooms. Finally, the
AGM in March 1911 resolved to lease 1 Bolton Street (around
the corner from 80/81 Piccadilly) as additional bedroom

RTYC Clubhouse, 80/81 Piccadilly (1911 - 1923).

accommodation at £250 annual rental. The latter acquisition reduced the structural alterations needed at 80/81 Piccadilly but they would still cost some £2,000.

At long last the quest for an improved and more commodious Clubhouse was over and the members were once again able to return to their own headquarters. To help finance the increased costs yachting members' subscription was increased from six to eight guineas at the 1911 AGM (i.e. to the same figure as paid by non-yachting members since 1896).

The benefits arising from the move to Piccadilly were impressive. The membership at the end of 1910 was 781; two years later it had increased to 1032. By 1912 the Club was once more able to build up an investment portfolio for the first time in over 40 years. 80/81 Piccadilly was to be the Club's home for the period of the 13 year lease.

Waterside Premises

A feature of Club life over the 50 years of this volume is the number of occasions when either the Club sought a second clubhouse with waterside facilities, or other water-side-based yacht clubs sought to amalgamate with the Royal Thames; a further variation was for a yacht club to invite the Royal Thames to share their facilities while the clubs remained independent.

In January 1877 the Sailing Committee appointed a Sub Committee led by A O Wilkinson to consider the possibility of obtaining suitable club accommodation at Gravesend. Nothing came of this but it seems strange that the Club did not approach the New Thames Yacht Club who had been established in their clubhouse at Gravesend since 1870, bearing in mind the number of yachtsmen who were members of both clubs as well as recognising that the ill-feelings of 1867 had subsided. In December 1883, Captain Percy Hewett of the Royal Victoria Yacht Club at Ryde wrote to the Club suggesting an amalgamation of the two Clubs at Ryde. Once again the Sailing Committee did not pursue the proposal. In October 1885 the Committee received a letter urging them *'to buy the old Clubhouse of the Royal Southern Yacht Club'* but the offer was quickly declined.

In December 1886, almost 10 years after the Club considered arranging accommodation at Gravesend, a far more specific proposal was considered by a special meeting of the General Committee chaired by Lord Alfred Paget. The proposal was that the Royal Thames should consider the desirability of amalgamating with the New Thames Yacht Club - which at the time was in a weak state financially. The Sub Committee appointed to investigate and report back was this time chaired by Colonel Josiah Wilkinson, the Cup Bearer. The Sub Committee comprised three members of the General Committee and three from the Sailing Committee - the latter including the redoubtable Ernest W Buller and it was he who, on 27 February 1887, read to the Sub Committee a 'Memorandum and Scheme' - subject to satisfactory financial investigation and report on both sides. The seven clauses in this proposal (see Appendix 15) were agreed by the Sub Committee who laid it before a joint meeting of the General and Sailing Committees chaired by Colonel Wilkinson on 8 March. They too adopted the report with the exception of Clause 5 and proceeded to nominate four members to meet a similar number from the NTYC. The meeting took place at the Caledonian Hotel but no agreement was reached and the attempt to amalgamate was abandoned. When one reads the Royal Thames proposed terms for the amalgamation it is not difficult to imagine that on this occasion it was the New Thames who found no advantage to be gained from the proposal!

Three years later, in February 1889, the Club received a letter from the Nautilus Club at Ryde proposing an amalgamation but the Sailing Committee once more could find no advantage to be gained by this proposal. No further proposals were made for 11 years when, in January 1900, a member, Captain H C Fox placed before the Committee photographs of a house called 'Ferncote' at Westcliff-on-Sea with the suggestion that *'the place might make a seaside annexe for the Club!'* The Committee was not disposed to avail themselves of his suggestion. A more positive step was taken two years later when it was agreed to hire a room for the 1902 season at the Marina Hotel, Cowes, at a rental of £35. Again, in May 1903, the Vice Commodore, Robert Hewett, obtained the support of the General Committee to his proposal *'that it was considered desirable by the Committee that the RTYC should have a station at the mouth of the Thames at Dover'*. A Sub Committee was set up to deal with this scheme which included the Vice Commodore, the Rear Commodore Theodore Pim, the Chairman of the Committee, J McNeile Miller and Lord Euston. A letter on the subject was sent to all members seeking their support - by October it was evident that adequate support for the scheme by the members was not being given and it was abandoned.

The subject was before the Committee once again in May 1906 when the Royal London Yacht Club made proposals for an amalgamation but the Committee's response was that it *'was unable to negotiate on the terms put forward'*. This proved to be no more than a relatively short-term setback. When the Committee met in February 1909 the Chairman, J McNeile Miller, informed them that - following negotiations between the Flag Officers of the Royal Thames and the Royal London - an agreement had been drawn up providing a form of amalgamation between the two clubs (see Appendix 16). The Committee gave unanimous support to the proposal and authorised the Flag Officers to sign it subject to the approval of the Annual General Meeting. That meeting took place on 16 March and was attended by 134 members. The Vice Commodore, Sir James Pender, proposed the adoption of the agreement and J McNeile Miller seconded it informing the members present that certain beneficial amendments to the agreement had been made and supported by both Clubs. A long and somewhat acrimonious discussion followed when those opposed to the agreement made remarks such as *'I condemn Cowes as a port of no value to members of the Club'* and another member said he *'had much experience of Cowes and referred in disparaging terms to that port'*. A member who supported the scheme said he *'considered Cowes a useful port and the use of the Cowes Clubhouse of great advantage'*. The matter was

eventually put to the vote when a show of hands saw 57 in favour and 73 against adoption of the agreement. Several members demanded that a poll be held and this was accepted and took place a week later. Again the members rejected adoption, this time by 93 to 52, and the agreement became void.

Two years later, in February 1911, the Royal Victoria Yacht Club at Ryde wrote yet again suggesting a working arrangement between the two clubs (it was last raised 27 years earlier) and while the Royal Thames was prepared to consider the suggestion it was felt unlikely to lead to anything useful and the RVYC decided to drop the matter for that year. The period between New Year and the start of the sailing season was always a fruitful time when new ideas for the coming season were brought forward. 1913 was no exception. In November 1912 the Sailing Committee had unanimously agreed to extend the RTYC race programme to the Solent. By January 1913 they agreed to racing in Stokes Bay on 1 August that year and a month later negotiations with the London and South Western Railway company had begun with the aim of the Club renting from the company a Pavilion to be built on Stokes Bay Pier. The cost of the pavilion was estimated at £550. The General Committee proposed to accept this price provided the rental for the first 10 years did not exceed £120 and, once more, subject to approval by the AGM to alter Section 1 of the Club Law which limited the Club to holding regattas on the River Thames. The AGM in March gave unanimous support to the Resolution to amend Section 1. When the Sailing Committee met on 18 April the Commodore was able to report that *'the proposed agreement with the L&SWR with regard to their building a pavilion on Stokes Bay Pier for the use of the Club was sanctioned'*. At long last the Royal Thames was to have a waterside station. The Facilities available in the pavilion are not on record but it was almost certainly a situation from which racing could be controlled and may well have had limited 'social' facilities. The pavilion appears to have been completed in time to be open for use in 1914 from 8 June until 30 September, though the outbreak of war in August probably curtailed that 'open' period. The General Committee was informed in June 1914 in a letter from the Vice Commodore that *'he and the Commodore were respectively giving £200 and £100 towards extinguishing the debt on the Pavilion at Stokes Bay'*. The Committee placed these donations at the head of a subscription list inviting members in general to contribute.

Clubhouse Services

The evolution of the services for the Clubhouse provides an interesting commentary on the technological advances during the nineteenth century. On the other hand some of the problems experienced at that time have a striking similarity to those that arise in the later years of the twentieth century! Some of the more interesting, and perhaps surprising items have been taken from the Club' s records and described in the paragraphs that follow.

One of the more surprising items is recorded following a meeting of the House Committee in January 1875 when it was reported that *'approval has been given for a contract for a constant supply of water on the meter system in place of paying £20 a year for a partial supply'* - one could be forgiven for assuming that water supply by meter was only a contemporary topic for discussion.

The method of lighting available in the public rooms of the Clubhouse in the 1870s appears to have been a combination of oil lamps and gas burners. Even these relatively simple items of equipment could raise problems - problems remote from technicalities. In March 1875 the Secretary expressed his great concern to the House Committee that *'the lamps for the drawing room consumed 18 gallons of oil in 4 weeks at a cost of 3/9 a gallon being at a rate of £40.10-0 per year. Further, the manager had declined to pay for the same and apparently there is no clause in his agreement to compel him to do so'*. This matter was soon resolved by the arrival of a new manager - with a modified agreement! Shortly before Christmas 1879 it became necessary to fix the new gas burners in the Dining Room - a task that would take four days to complete much to the dismay of the Committee. It may have been that in spite of having such inconveniences in mind the General Committee in January 1881 *'after some discussion relative to a proposal to light the Clubhouse with Electric Light, agreed to postpone the matter for fuller consideration'*. Five months later a letter to the Electric Light Company referred to lighting a portion of the Clubhouse temporarily.

It is doubtful whether the temporary trial ever took place and no reference to electric lighting appears again until November 1887 when a Sub Committee comprising of Sir Charles Bright and Messrs Henry Rutter and Albert Morson was set up to again *'consider the question of lighting the Club by electricity to be supplied from the Grosvenor Gallery in Bond Street'*. Tenders to provide electric light in the public rooms and entrance hall were all in the order of £155. It seems that the Royal London YC clubhouse in London already had electric lighting installed since their Secretary, Mr Charlwood, informed the Sub Committee *'that the cost per lamp, making allowance for the decrease in consumption in the Summer months, would be over £4 per lamp per annum'*. The Sub Committee report did not recommend installing electric light at that time. It was April 1891 before the subject was yet again considered. Once more the Secretary obtained estimates for the cost of installation and a Sub Committee comprising Mr Thomas Breen and Colonel Peters was appointed to make recommendations. In May the General Committee accepted the estimate of £142.15-0 from Messrs Woodhouse and Rawson of 88 Queen Victoria Street. The lighting was installed during the 'closed period' in August and notices were placed inviting members to be economical in their use of the electric lighting. A subscription list was opened to pay for the installation including all fittings. Some 100 members subscribed £195. The annual cost of operating the installation was a little over £200. The membership welcomed this innovation which probably, in spite of the many deferments, was achieved long before it was available in their homes. The technically minded may be interested to learn that the original installation was based on a 100 volt system, changing to 200 volts in October 1897.

Other landmarks in the provision of improved facilities for the Club included the purchase of refrigeration in May 1879. In June 1879 the General Committee *'agreed to accept the tender of the National Telephone Company for the erection of a Telephone at a charge annually of £17'*. In February 1902 it was decided to purchase a weighing machine from Mr W Wilson for £10 - this venerable equipment was in use in the gentlemen's cloakroom until 1997. Lastly, in February 1910, *'sanction was given for the purchase of a Vacuum Cleaner at a cost not to exceed £16'*. No one could ever suggest that the Clubhouse was other than up-to-date with technology.

The standards of hygiene frequently left much to be desired and in spite of improved materials the problems experienced in the nineteenth century can still occur. Two typical examples occurred - one in 1879 and the other in 1905. In the former instance the Club received a letter from the City Bank (adjacent to the Clubhouse) drawing the attention of the Committee to the offensive smells from the Club drains! A surveyor discovered that they were open brick drains, untrapped and, beneath the servants' WC. In close proximity to the City Bank he discovered a large cesspool containing the accumulation of years! That this unpleasant situation was not apparent at an earlier date is beyond belief. The problems in 1905 were equally revolting and far from uncommon. In August it was decided to employ HG Wood & Co. to clear out the cockroaches at an expense not exceeding £2. Later in the month they were again employed, this time to catch rats - the Secretary was instructed to pay a further £2 for this service provided the number of rats was substantially reduced!

Social Activities

In the 1840s and 50s there had been a regular pattern of social events for Club members. In February there would be the Club Ball; in April the 'Opening Trip' marked the start of the sailing season when the Commodore led members' yachts in company from Greenwich to Gravesend where they proceeded ashore for dinner. The 'Closing Trip' followed similar lines at the end of the season in October while in November the Annual Club Dinner was held. Such a regular pattern of events did not occur during the years covered by this volume. While Rule 30 of the Club's rules (deleted in 1914) prescribed an Opening Trip or Cruise each year on a date to be agreed at the AGM, there is no record that such trips actually took place. Indeed, the only reference to an Opening Cruise appears in the Minutes of the Sailing Committee held in February 1870 when that Committee recommended *'that there should be no Opening Cruise that year'*. In 1872 the same remarks were applied to the Club Ball when it was agreed that the Club would not hold one that year - or any other year apparently. In fact, only a year earlier five members had written to the Committee proposing a Club Ball and the General Committee agreed to the proposal - but there is no record of it's having taken place. As for both the Closing Trip or Cruise and the Annual Dinner, these seem to have lapsed entirely, except that at the AGM in March 1905 a member proposed that a dinner be held at the end of the Sailing Season and this suggestion was well-supported. When the General Committee met in May a Sub Committee of five was appointed to consider the proposal and report. In the event the dinner took place at the Café Royal on 24 October and was attended by nearly 150 members and guests. The ticket price was half a guinea - club cigars were available at 6d, 1/- and 1/6. The sum of ten guineas was made available for music during the dinner. This successful venture was not repeated in the years following.

None of this is meant to infer that there were no social activities during this period. Certainly, there were periods when monthly Club dinners took place but they seem to have been of an informal nature. Additionally, dinners were held to mark special occasions. In December 1870 a member, Colonel E T Gourlay MP wrote to the Commodore concerning his fellow MP, James Ashbury (*CAMBRIA* - first challenger for the America's Cup) and said *'relative to the desire of giving Ashbury a Banquet or Club Soirée - I was in New York when he was there, and think that he deserves public recognition at the hands of the Club, for the able and enterprising manner in which he represented the Thames and also the Country'*. This proposal was accepted and there are several references to *'members of the Club who had met to carry out the details of the complimentary Dinner to Mr Ashbury'* - but there is no record of the date when it was held. What is perhaps more interesting is that the Dinner was not in recognition of his unsuccessful challenge for the America's Cup but for his successful transatlantic race in *CAMBRIA* (immediately prior to the America's Cup Challenge) against the American schooner *DAUNTLESS* owned by J G Bennett, Vice Commodore of the New York Yacht Club - the finish of which is portrayed in the painting in the Coffee Room of the present Clubhouse.

In October 1885 following another unsuccessful challenge for the America's Cup by Sir Richard Sutton (*GENESTA*) the Committee informed him *'that it was the unanimous wish of the Members of the Royal Thames Yacht Club to entertain him at dinner on a day to be fixed later'*. Sir Richard thanked them *'for the honour they had done him in asking him to dinner - and regretting that he was unable to accept it'*. A testimonial to him was placed on the Club notice board!

After years of resisting its introduction, it was finally conceded in December 1870 to purchase a *'Book of Complaints and Suggestions'*. The printers from whom the book was ordered were required to print on the cover the inscription *'Any member who may feel cause for Complaint, or may wish to offer a Suggestion with reference to any matter in connection with this Club, is invited to make a note of the same in this Book, appending to it his signature. The subject will then come before the Committee at their next weekly meeting and will be by them duly considered'*. There is ample evidence that the Committee did indeed scan the Suggestion Book and respond. Over the years, however, the frequency of Committee meetings decreased and attention to suggestions became correspondingly infrequent.

Extra-mural social activities were uncommon except that in 1894 the Committee agreed to place a notice in the hall of the Clubhouse *'regarding an enclosure at Henley called 'Club Land'. Tickets for the same to be sold in the Clubhouse'*. Since Henley Regatta has always been an element in the social round it is not surprising that the Royal Thames members should be a part of it, as they still are today. While there is no evidence of members (as a group) attending the Derby meeting at Epsom there was invariably a Derby Lottery (sweepstake) held each year in the Clubhouse. Another minor landmark in 1894 was the decision of the Club to take a copy of Yachting World for the smoking room (two years earlier it had been agreed to take a copy of The Yachtsman).

Members in-house entertainment was largely found in the Card Room and the Billiard Rooms. The rules concerning use of those rooms were very strictly maintained - not least in respect of their use by visitors to the Club. The Card Room was solely for use by members, no gambling was allowed and the only card game permitted (in 1876) was whist. Play after 1.00am attracted a charge of two shillings and sixpence. The 'front' billiard room (in the Albermarle Street Clubhouse) was for use by members only but a member could introduce two friends to play in the Strangers Billiard Room provided they had dined in the Clubhouse on that day. Again 2/6 was charged to each player after 1.00am - the Club closed at 2.00am. Even playing chess with a 'stranger' was not permitted as a Mr Z Turton discovered in 1873 when he was rebuked for doing just that. A year later four members were reported for failing to pay the 2/6 fee (or fine) for playing whist 'after hours'. By 1879 the Card Room rules had been modified to permit the games of whist, piquet and écarté to be played. The charges levied are certainly interesting by virtue of the relatively large sum due - *'The charges for two packs of Whist cards is one shilling each player (minimum charge 4 s.). The charge for two packs of Piquet cards is 3 s. The cards after the play to be taken to the Card Room Waiter and may be had from him or in the Secretary's office at 6d per pack. Fresh cards are to be used on each occasion of playing'*. In spite of these charges, the net income accruing to the club from cards was never more than a few pounds each year.

Billiards was the game that seems to have been most popular and to which the Committee devoted far more of their time at meetings. One of the problems constantly requiring attention by the Committee was how to ensure that the Club rules prevented any member from monopolising use of the table. In the 1870s no member was allowed to play more than two games of 50 points or one of 100 if the table was required by other members. Should a member arrive in the Billiard Room when no other member was present it was customary for him to play with the Billiard Marker. This necessitated a rule change in 1892 saying *'that no member may play with the marker should two members wish to play, but if a member is playing with the marker he may finish the game but not beyond a score of 100'*. In January 1893 a Sub Committee was set up to review the rules for billiards. Members were permitted to use the billiard tables to play not only billiards but also pool and pyramids. Pool was played using the 'colours' as are today seen on a snooker table, while Pyramids used the 15 red balls. Both alternatives were strictly 'potting' games and when combined formed the modern game of snooker. Visitors were permitted to play only billiards in the Strangers Billiards Room. Perhaps the highlight of this period took place in April 1872 when the Rev. F H Addams was given permission to introduce Monsieur Izaz, the celebrated French billiard player, into the club billiard room.

V

Club Finances

When the Club met for the Annual General Meeting in March 1868, members learned that the forecast excess of expenditure over income in 1867 of some £1200 had, in fact, been exceeded and was found to be over £1700. In spite of this deficit and the heavy loss of members (171) to the newly formed New Thames Yacht Club, the Flag Officers and their advisers informed the 74 members present that they believed the Club could continue to maintain its high standards in the Clubhouse and support their usual programme of Sailing Matches and associated prizes. Notwithstanding these aspirations, a voluntary subscription list was opened with the aim of paying off the deficit, though the money offered by members would not be called upon until the total sum had been contributed. In spite of this it was to be 1872 before a favourable balance was achieved, while from 1870 until 1895 it was necessary for the Club to carry a loan from their bankers, Coutts, of up to £2000. Fortunately, with interest rates being so low, the annual interest paid on the loan was never more than £85 (of an annual expenditure of £5000-£8000).

In 1869 the Club membership dropped to 681, the lowest figures for the 50 years of this volume, and it was not until 1875 that the membership again exceeded 800 (this was quite an achievement since the annual subscription for non-yachting members had just been increased from five guineas to seven guineas on 1 May 1874). In spite of this increased subscription income, the Club returned to an operating deficit of £200-£300 from 1878 until 1886. After the membership peak of 1875, the numbers again declined and by 1883 were approaching 700. In addition the annual cost of sailing prizes and other sailing expenses had risen to over £1000. It was decided that prizes must not exceed £600; in fact the total sailing costs in subsequent years were kept below £600 - not least due to the generosity of many members who donated trophies or prize money each year.

The financial improvement in 1886 was largely due to a significant increase in membership which in turn had responded to a resolution carried at the 1886 AGM to suspend the payment of an entrance fee. When payment of an entrance fee was re-introduced following a Special General Meeting in 1889, the fee payable by yachting members was reduced from 15 to 7 guineas and for non yachting from 21 to 10 guineas. This had little adverse effect on membership which remained in the region of 800 for a while. By 1893, however, membership was again going down and the AGM once more suspended payment of an entrance fee. A proposal in 1900 to re-introduce it was defeated and re-introduction had to wait until 1907. The decision in 1896 to increase subscription from 5 to 6

guineas for yachting members and 7 to 8 guineas for non-yachting started a sequence of years when income exceeded expenditure and from 1897 the Club was able to start each year by putting £2000 or more on deposit and use it to sustain the cash flow.

Over the years there were constant changes in the arrangements for management of the Clubhouse. This was because the Committee sought to achieve the high standards expected by members while at the same time keeping charges low enough to be acceptable to members. A profitable operation was always going to be difficult in the relatively small Clubhouse in Albermarle Street but once the move to Piccadilly was achieved in 1911 there was a rapid upsurge in it's use. 236 members were elected in 1911 and 119 in 1912 which took the membership up to 1032. Although it was necessary to arrange an overdraft from Coutts from 1911 this was not expensive and the Club was able once again to build up an investment portfolio which had exceeded £3000 by 1915.

In an attempt to encourage profitable management of the operation of the Clubhouse a separate 'provision' account was opened at the Bond Street branch of the City Bank in September 1883, but within nine months it was necessary to transfer money from the Club's general account with Coutts to the City Bank and in January 1886 the City Bank account was closed as the experiment had been a failure and was not tried again. Later in 1903 a separate 'Prize Fund' was instituted for the sailing activities into which members were invited to make annual contributions; additionally at each AGM the meeting authorised a sum (usually £200-£300) to be allocated to sailing from the General Club Fund. This arrangement enabled the Sailing Committee to organise the Club's sailing matches on the basis of known (and limited) funds. By 1905 a separate account (within the Club's audited accounts) was created and called the Regatta Account. In that year the Club made a grant of just £200 and members donated £179 in cash and £367 in prizes. By 1914 well over 200 members subscribed to the Regatta Fund which had a balance of over £1500.

The state of the Club's finances in 1914 and the quality of the management of the finances was as good as it had been at any time in the Club's history. This was particularly fortunate in view of the difficult financial circumstances of the Club during the years 1914-18.

The Club's support of charities during these years was confined to the Seaman's Hospital who received an annual donations of five guineas. When the Club's financial circumstances improved St George's Hospital was also given five

guineas from 1897, while the following year the Club
re-introduced a regular donation to the RNLI of two guineas -
over the previous 30 years any donation was in response to
an appeal letter from the RNLI. The lifeboat at Walmer, which
had been given by the RTYC in 1857, was transferred to the
nearby station at Kingsdown in 1870 and a tablet was placed
in the Walmer boathouse saying that first lifeboat on the
Walmer station had been so donated. It was noted that the
replacement lifeboat would cost £500 but the Club does
not appear to have reacted to that information - which is
hardly surprising in view of the stretched condition of the
Club's finances at that time. This is not to suggest that the
Club had become miserly but rather to note that the edict
'Charity begins at home' was being followed while the Club's
financial position was, to say the least, uncertain.

Albert Morson, Cup Bearer (1935 - 1940).

VI

1914 - 18

General Matters

Britain declared war on Germany on 4 August 1914. That same day a special meeting of the General Committee was called, chaired by Joseph Temperley with the Vice Commodore, Lord Queenborough in attendance. The Secretary read to those present a copy of a notice posted in the Carlton Club dealing with the effect on members and staff of the declaration of war. It was quickly agreed that a similar notice should be posted in the Royal Thames. It read:

The Committee has made arrangements whereby members can make a deposit with the Club (either by cheque or otherwise) against which all expenses incurred in the Club will be charged, thus obviating the difficulty in giving change; and it is hoped that all members will fall in with this arrangement.

Until further notice no cheque or cheques will be cashed. It has also decided:
(1) Not to economise by reducing the staff of servants employed
(2) To provide for the servants' families in case of need

By reason of the above considerations and of the probable rise in the cost of food a slight extra charge for meals to members may have to be made.'

This section is included in this volume of the Club's history in order to highlight the effect on the Club and its members of a major global war using weapons not invented in time for earlier conflicts and involving direct attacks on cities and towns of Britain, as well as taking away from the Club significant numbers of members and servants for active service in the Army and Navy.

The intent of the notice posted on 4 August was soon put into practice. In October 1914 the Committee agreed to pay half-wages, when asked, to all members of staff on active service who have dependants. They also decided that instead of seeking a bank overdraft, they would transfer £1050 from the Regatta Fund to the Club's current account - the sum to be repaid in January 1915 and to bear interest at 5% p.a. - a surprising financial arrangement but carried out to the letter when 10 guineas was added to the sum 'repaid'. At this meeting the Committee also decided to consider taking out insurance against 'aerial risks' - most definitely a novel problem for them. The insurance was taken out in August 1915 to provide cover for £21,000.

The effect of the war on the Club's affairs and on its members was soon evident. At the 1915 Annual General Meeting it was announced that there would be no regatta that year. In fact the Sailing Committee having met on 24 March 1914, were not to assemble again until 20 November 1918 when they made tentative plans for some racing in 1919 but noting that no large yachts had been built during the war. A year later the involvement of the Club in the war was apparent when the chairman reported that 15% of the members had enlisted in the Army and the Royal Navy as well as 18 members of staff. Inevitably many lost their lives during the war and later, in 1916, a Roll of Honour was posted.

The major problem facing those responsible for the administration of the Club was a financial one although in the last 18 months of the conflict food shortages created a further problem. In spite of these and other difficulties the Club remained buoyant as is well-illustrated by the remarks of the Commodore, Theodore Pim, to the 1917 AGM when he said that he *'congratulated the members on the healthy position of the Club and reminded them that it had already weathered the heavy storms of the Napoleonic Wars and of the Crimean War, and that he was confident of its success in the present period of stress'.*

The financial problems of the Club were easily identified - falling income and increasing expenditure - but a solution was not so simple. A report by the House and Finance Sub Committee in June 1916 examined ways and means of dealing with the problem. Their recommendations were, however, modified by the policies decreed by the General Committee who were very conscious of its obligation to make (subscription) concessions to members serving in the forces and they were unwilling to increase general subscription levels since this would penalise the many who were unable to use the facilities of the Club. These factors, together with some inevitable drop in membership numbers, were the causes of the loss of income. As far as costs were concerned, food shortages caused rapid increases in the cost of provisions. The other principal increase in costs was servants wages - great difficulty was found in acquiring and retaining efficient staff - and in services such as coal, electricity and telephones. The report recommended that members who are able to use the facilities of the Clubhouse should be required to pay increased charges for meals, bedrooms and drinks to compensate for some of the increased costs. Some economies were proposed such as reducing the number of newspapers and periodicals provided, by not printing members' lists in 1918 and 1919 and by foregoing the annual painting of the exterior of the Clubhouse. Their opposition to drastic changes was

well-justified. The forecast loss of £800 in 1916 was followed
by profits being achieved in 1917 and 1918 - not least because
of an increase in the membership and careful investment of
the reserve funds available and their sale later in the war years.

The increased charges agreed by the General Committee
meant that bedrooms were now 6/- per night; a four course
dinner cost 4/- and a luncheon comprising joint, vegetables
and cheese was increased to 2/-. A war tax of 3d and 6d was
levied on luncheon and dinner respectively. A glass of brandy
or whisky was now 10d but the Club was always seeking
economical purchases. Thus, in April 1915 they acquired
140 gallons of whisky at 21/10 per gallon! In an attempt to
enhance use of the Clubhouse and so increase income it was
decided in December 1915 to offer honorary membership
to all Naval Officers serving in the Admiralty. Unfortunately,
food shortages in 1917 led to the need to inform those Naval
Officers that they may no longer bring guests to the Club.
Three months later their honorary membership was reluctantly
cancelled. This is entirely understandable bearing in mind that
from March 1917 the Club ordered 'that Friday each week
was to be a meatless day and that the third week in each
month was to be a potatoless week'. Perhaps even more
alarming was the report by the Secretary in February 1918
'that he had been unable to obtain from the Officials of the
Custom House a licence to purchase a larger quantity of
spirits proportional to the increase in consumption!'

If there was difficulty in getting permission to buy more spirits
the same was not true of German wines, the purchase of
which was deliberately stopped earlier in the war years.
For the same reason alien members of royalty and other
alien enemy members were struck off the list of members.
In a more positive mode the Club and its members were very
supportive of charities supporting those who were serving
and those who suffered as a consequence of the war.
Two examples of this are that in January 1915 the
Committee resolved to purchase two photographs of the
King and Queen of the Belgians at 2/6 each in aid of the
Belgian refugee fund. Later that year it was agreed to accept
a collection box for the YMCA to help provide funds to
support 'Concerts at the Front' .

The custom by members of donating gifts to the Club was to
continue in spite of the war. Four, somewhat 'different gifts' ,
were received - mostly during the earlier months of the war.
In November 1914 Miss Amy Paget, daughter of Lord Alfred
Paget, presented a box of specimens of submarine cables,
while in June 1915 Admiral Sir Alfred Paget presented
a German mine and six months later the Secretary,
Captain Orr, presented an incendiary bomb!

Rowhedge Cottages

When the General Committee met on 15 April 1915 they
considered a letter form the Vice Commodore, Almeric Paget,
concerning cottages at Rowhedge near Colchester. A small
Sub Committee was set up to consider the Club's response to
the content of the letter. The Sub Committee's report was
presented to the General Committee on 10 June and its
recommendation adopted. A letter of thanks was ordered to
be sent to Major George Paget (elected to the Club in 1882).

In the absence of the content of both Almeric Paget's letter
and the Sub Committee report it is impossible to know what
came about. Some light can be shed on the subject thanks to
documents in the Club archives. These include a plan of land
for building purposes drawn up by Messrs Sexton and
Grimwade and in particular identifying Plot 10 in Church
Road. Letters between Messrs Howard Ellison and Morton
and Lady Cecilia Paget of Upper Lodge, Bushey Park,
Teddington refer to the purchase of this plot for £75 in
October 1888 on her behalf. Other letters dated October 1908
and October 1913 from G N Scrutton, Builder and Decorator,
refer to the repairs carried out for Lady Alfred Paget to the
'Paget Memorial Almshouses' at Rowhedge, Colchester.
It will be recalled that Lord Alfred Paget died in August 1888
and it must be probable that the Almshouses were a memorial
to him - but why at Rowhedge and what was the purpose of
Almeric Paget's letter - the search continues.

Peace

When peace came in November 1918 the Flag Officers and
Committee could rightly feel well pleased with their stewardship of the Club throughout the war years. The membership
at 1072 was almost identical to the 1914 figures and the Club
was in a sound financial position and could look to the future
with confidence. This view was clearly expressed by the
Vice Commodore, Lord Queenborough, at the AGM in March
1919 when he said 'that it must be a matter of pride to
the members that they have weathered the storm, that
a period of peace was ahead and that the Club remained
the great yachting centre'. He added 'that the Committee was
trying indefinitely to find a house more suitable to the
increasing membership and was glad to say that the Club
was strong enough financially to take a larger house and
to pay more rent'.

On that high note ended 50 years of Club History; a half
century that had started with uncertainty after the troubled
times of 1867. The intervening years had seen the Club's
fortunes rise and fall, but strong direction of the Club's affairs
ensured that its future was never in doubt; nor was its declared
objective to stay in the forefront of yachting lost to sight.

VII

Club Treasures

Introduction

Throughout the period covered by this volume the Club continued to benefit from the generous donations by members of prints, oil paintings, silver and other memorabilia. Unfortunately, the Club acquired relatively few prints or paintings of the many yachts which had outstanding success in Royal Thames sailing matches. The shortage of paintings of successful yachts is all the more surprising because throughout most of this period the Club appointed a marine artist.

Many of the 'Treasures' that were presented to the Club, are regrettably, no longer in the Club's possession. These gifts formed part of the Club's heritage and history and the history of the Royal Thames is also a major part of the history of yacht racing in the United Kingdom, especially during the nineteenth century. The Club, therefore, should recognise that it has a responsibility to protect and preserve that history by continuing to keep full records of its affairs and by carefully maintaining its existing records in good order.

Marine Artists

It has already been recorded in the previous volume that the Club appointed **Nicholas Matthew Condy** as its marine artist on 7 September 1843 and many of his fine paintings are on display in the Edinburgh Room of the present Clubhouse. Following his death the Club appointed **Thomas Sewell Robins** on 3 December 1851. Again his works are displayed through yachting prints hanging in the Clubhouse. The next recorded appointment of a marine artist was that of **Barlow Moore** on 28 January 1885. It is of note however, that the marine artist **C.R. Ricketts** became a member of the Club in 1857 and two of his oil paintings hang in the Clubhouse today viz: *CAMBRIA* winning the Transatlantic Race against *DAUNTLESS* prior to the first challenge for the Americas Cup in 1870 and *LIVONIA,* with her bowsprit broken while weathering a storm when crossing the Atlantic in 1871 prior to the second challenge. There is no record to show whether Ricketts was ever appointed as the Club's marine artist. It is much more likely that both paintings were commissioned by the yachts' owner John Ashbury. Examples of Barlow Moore's watercolour paintings are currently displayed in the Paget Room of the modern Clubhouse. These are of the yacht *LATONA (165 Tons)* owned by Herbert Greystone and presented to the Club by him in January 1895 and the yacht

VOL-AU-VENT (104 Tons) owned by R. Ingham Clark and presented by F W F Clark. There is evidence of some friction between Barlow Moore and the Committee, so it comes as no surprise to discover that on 2 April 1891 the Committee resolved *'that the appointment of 'Marine Artist' be abolished and omitted in the Members' List for 1891'.* Barlow Moore continued his membership of the Club until 1897. On 17 March 1898 a new marine artist **Robert Taylor Pritchett** was appointed (he was mainly a watercolour artist; he died in 1907). Pritchett sought permission from the Club in October 1892 to make sketches of prints in the Clubhouse for use as illustrations in 1894 Badminton Library - Yachting Volumes (in which he also wrote chapters on yacht design and yacht club histories) a copy of which is in the present Club Library. Pritchett had a very different background from most artists. His father had been head of the Enfield firm of gunmakers to the East India Company and he too was taught his father's trade. Later he was to develop the rifled-gun, so much more effective than the smooth bored musket. For some reason he abandoned his early profession to become a watercolour artist and his work was later introduced to Queen Victoria for whom he created paintings of many state occasions. The last artist to be appointed during this period was **Louis Nevill** on 29 March 1911 but, once again, none of his paintings are now displayed in the Clubhouse.

Prints and Paintings of Yachts

It is unfortunate the Club's present collection of prints and paintings of yachts includes, with a small number of notable exceptions, few of the many very successful racing yachts of the period. Those exceptions are the oil paintings of *CAMBRIA* and *LIVONIA* which made the 24-day crossing of the Atlantic in order to make respectively the first and second challenges for the America's Cup in 1870 and 1871. Both vessels were owned by James Ashbury a member of Parliament for Brighton, a member of the Royal Thames and a Commodore of the Royal Harwich Yacht Club. There are watercolour paintings by Barlow Moore of *VOL-AU-VENT* and *LATONA* and among the prints are those of E. Boutcher's famous cutter *FIONA*, Count Batthyany's *KRIEMHILDA* and also *CAMBRIA* and *ALINE* (owned at one time by the Prince of Wales).

The schooner *CAMBRIA (199 Tons)* was built in 1868 by Michael Ratsey at Cowes for James Ashbury. It was his relative

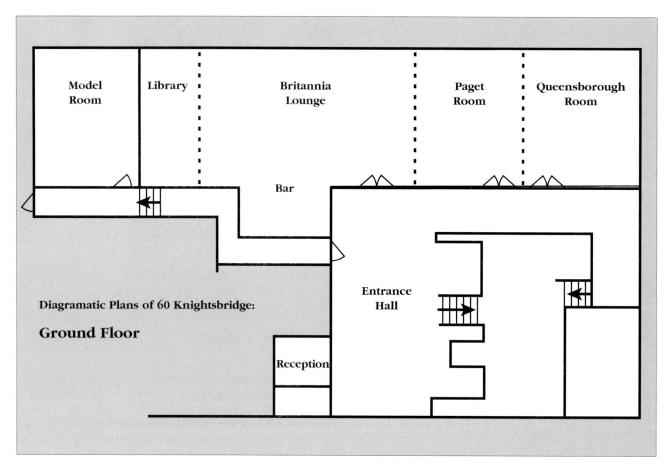

Diagramatic Plans of 60 Knightsbridge:

Ground Floor

success against the visiting American schooner *SAPPHO* that persuaded James Ashbury to challenge for the America's Cup. The two oil paintings of *CAMBRIA,* however, show the finish of her Transatlantic Race in July 1870, against the other visiting American schooner *DAUNTLESS,* the finishing line being the Sandy Hook Lightship, New York. The dates when these paintings were given to the Club and their respective artists are not wholly clear, but the following points are relevant. The 1988 inventory of Club paintings identifies the artists as P Ouless and C R Ricketts. At a meeting of the General Committee on 2 January 1872 it is recorded that Mr. Ashbury (a member of the Committee) *'proposes to present to the Club an oil painting of CAMBRIA winning the Atlantic Yacht Race and a photograph of the first two vessels entering the Red Sea (from the Suez Canal), the CAMBRIA flying the RTYC colours.'* The earlier minutes of the Annual General Meeting held on 23 March 1871 records that *'a painting of CAMBRIA and OIMARA rounding the winning Flag Boat off Dover on completion of the Nore to Dover, RTYC Channel Race, 11 June 1870, was exhibited'.* The proceeds from subscriptions to the latter painting, at £1 each, were to be used to purchase a silver prize for the winner of the Dover to Boulogne Race on 17 June 1871 (the winner of this prize was *GUINEVERE (294 Tons)* owned by Captain C S A Thelluson). This picture was painted by Charles Robert Ricketts (Lieutenant, Royal Marines and an RTYC member 1857-76) immediately prior to *CAMBRIA's* departure for the Atlantic Race and it might be assumed, therefore, that Ricketts painted the picture of CAMBRIA presented by James Ashbury in January 1872.

The two paintings of James Ashbury's second America's Cup challenger *LIVONIA (280 Tons)* depicts her with a bowsprit broken in heavy weather in mid Atlantic on her way to New York for the challenge. Constructed in 1871, the builder was again Michael Ratsey at Cowes. The 1988 inventory identifies

the artists of these two paintings as Charles Gregory and C.R. Ricketts. In his 1938 Catalogue of RTYC paintings, Brooke Heckstall-Smith refers to the four paintings of *CAMBRIA* and *LIVONIA* identifying one painting of each yacht as 'originals' and the other two as copies by C.R. Ricketts - though he did not identify the artists of the originals. He also records that the oil painting of *LIVONIA,* (signed by C.R. Ricketts and dated 1872) which was presented to the Club by James Ashbury in 1887, as being 'inferior to the original.' In the present Clubhouse the Ricketts painting of CAMBRIA hangs in the passage between the Coffee Room and the Mountbatten Suite while his LIVONIA painting hangs in the Edinburgh Room. Inferior his paintings may have been, but on 13 May 1886 the Committee had been happy to accept from Edward Ricketts (RTYC member 1845-1891), father of 'C R', a painting by his son of HRH The Prince of Wales visiting HMS 'London' in the Bay of Naples. Whatever conclusions one draws about the identity of the artists of these four oil paintings, they do represent an important part of yachting history and the history of the Royal Thames.

As for prints now located in the present Clubhouse, the most successful yacht depicted is undoubtedly E. Boutcher's *FIONA (77 Tons).* Built in 1865, she was the winner of many prizes in Royal Thames matches. The print (now hung in the Mountbatten Suite) shows the Fife-built cutter winning the Queen's Cup on 17 June 1868. The print is taken from a chromolithograph by Josiah Taylor.

The print of Count Batthyany's cutter, *KREIMHILDA (106 Tons)* also depicts the winning of another Cup presented by HM Queen Victoria six years later on 24 June 1874. The print of the successful Ratsey-built cutter is taken from a lithograph by C.R. Ricketts. Built in 1872, she was the most successful cutter in 1873. The print now hangs in Cabin No. 9.

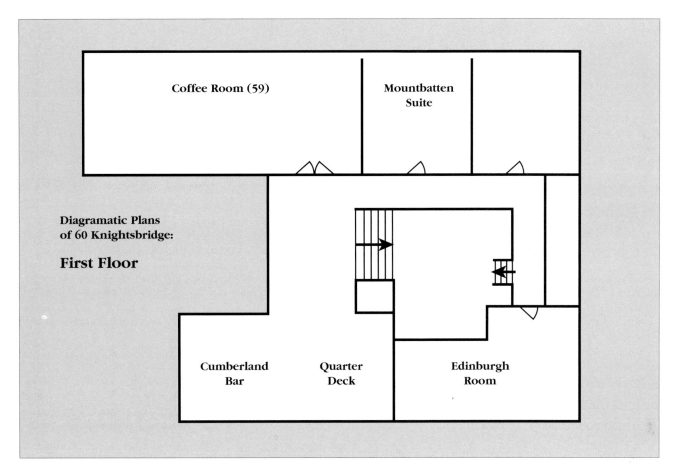

Diagramatic Plans of 60 Knightsbridge:

First Floor

Coffee Room (59)

Mountbatten Suite

Cumberland Bar

Quarter Deck

Edinburgh Room

The schooner *ALINE (216 Tons)* was built by Camper and Nicholson in 1860. The print (in Cabin No. 18) is by T.G. Dutton. *ALINE* had only modest success in Royal Thames matches. Included among her owners were Sir Richard Sutton and HRH The Prince of Wales (1882-1895).

The watercolours of yachts of this period which are still hanging in the Clubhouse include the two by Barlow Moore already referred to and two by Tomasco De Simone of *GUINEVERE* and *CAMBRIA* which are located in Cabin No. 15. The Nicholson-built schooner *GUINEVERE (294 Tons)* was owned by Captain Charles Thelluson. She was particularly successful in the 1871 season winning both the Nore to Dover 'Channel Match' and the 100 guineas prize donated by C R Ricketts, the prize being the proceeds from subscriptions to his painting of the 1870 Channel Match. Another watercolour is that showing *CAMBRIA* passing Port Tewfik at the southern end of the Suez Canal. *CAMBRIA* had been part of the vast flotilla of vessels that passed through the canal to mark the ceremonial opening of Ferdinand de Lesseps, creation on 17 November 1869. The opening was performed by the French Empress Eugenie who sailed in the Imperial Yacht *AIGLE* which led the flotilla from Port Said followed by the P & O vessel *DELTA*. Where *CAMBRIA* was placed in the line of vessels is not known but it is of interest that 36th in line was Thomas Cook (founder of the travel company that bears his name) in the Levant Line paddle steamer *AMERICA*. The artist responsible for this watercolour is also not known but it is for speculation whether the 'photograph' of *CAMBRIA* leaving the Suez Canal presented by James Ashbury was subsequently coloured or copied in watercolour. Whatever the truth about the painting it is once again a record of an event with a permanent and important place in World History and an interesting place in Club history.

Another photograph (by Beken of Cowes) of a very successful

yacht hangs in Cabin No. 3. This is the 23 metre Fife built yacht *WHITE HEATHER II*, built in 1907 for Myles B. Kennedy. She won no fewer than nine Royal Thames prizes over the years 1907-12. These successes were often at the expense of Sir Thomas Lipton's America's Cup challenger *SHAMROCK*.

Lastly, a print of historic interest to the Club and still hanging in the present Clubhouse was presented by a Mr. Newton-Robinson and acknowledged at a committee meeting held on 6 March 1890. This print shows the Cumberland Fleet competing for the last silver cup presented by the Duke of Cumberland on 23 July 1782.

Portraits of Club Officers

During the years covered by this volume four more oil paintings of Officers of the Club came into the club's possession. The Officers concerned were The Prince of Wales, Earl Brassey, Robert Hewett and Lord Queenborough. The circumstances under which they were acquired are described in the paragraphs that follow.

HRH The Prince of Wales. In January of 1881 a letter was circulated to members informing them that it was proposed to commission a portrait of the Commodore (HRH The Prince of Wales) and inviting subscriptions of not more than one guinea. There appears to have been a modest response to the letter since a second circular proved to be necessary in December of that year. On 9 May 1882 it is noted that the amount received, *'£45 - 3 - 0, had been put into a separate account with Messrs Coutts called 'The Commodore' Portrait Fund'*. On 23 May, the artist, Mr. Augustus Savile, informed the committee that the portrait was finished. It is not recorded how much was paid for the portrait or how much was eventually subscribed. The portrait now hangs in the Paget Room.

When the committee met on 7 June 1894 it was announced that the Vice Commodore, **Lord Brassey** had promised to present to the Club a copy of a portrait of himself painted by Frank Hall and this was completed by October. At the same meeting it was resolved to open a subscription list for commissioning a portrait of the Rear Commodore, **Robert Hewett** (subscriptions to be limited to £1). In August the commission was offered to A. Chevalier Taylor for 100 guineas. This portrait was also complete by October. Both these portraits now hang in the Queenborough Room (in half length form as distinct from their original three-quarter length, the reduction having been made when the Clubhouse in Knightsbridge was re-built in 1963).

The last oil painting of a Club Officer to be presented to the Club in this period was of the then Vice Commodore, **Almeric Paget (Lord Queenborough)**. This painting (after Arthur Hacker) was presented in March 1914. Appropriately it too hangs in the Queenborough Room.

Lieutenant Colonel Josiah Wilkinson gave more service to the club than almost any other member who did not become a Flag Officer. It is recorded in November 1898 that he 'presented his portrait' to the Club - implying that it was a portrait of himself. If that was the case then it is particularly sad that that portrait of a gentleman who gave so much to the Club is no longer among the portraits that hang in today's Clubhouse.

Club Silver

The trophies listed below are all part of the Club's collection at this time. Where known, details of their origin and when they came into the Club's possession, are given. The conditions to be met for inclusion in this volume's silver trophy list is either that the trophy was presented by the Club or donated to the Club during the years 1868-1914 or that the trophy was won during those years but presented to the Club at a later date.

Belvidere Cup. This trophy is included even though it was listed in the previous volume of these chronicles. The cup was presented to the Club in 1845 by Lord Saye and Sele, and sailed for on 9 May 1845 in a race won by *BLUE BELLE* owned by Twisden Hodges Esq. When the General Committee met on 10 April 1913, the Vice Commodore, Almeric Paget, said he wished to present the cup to the Club in commemoration of his father, Lord Alfred Paget, who had raced his yacht *BELVIDERE* for the cup, and who was the first Vice Commodore of the Club and elected to that office in 1845.

Twining Shield This trophy was presented to the New Thames Yacht Club in 1868 by the Earl Twining and first won by the cutter *SPHINX* (of Spinnaker fame) owned by J.S. Earle, in a race on the Thames held on 1 June 1868. It was presented to the Royal Thames by Miss A.M. Twining in 1936 and to-day is presented to the member who puts forward the best log of his voyages.

Ascot Plate This massive Victorian salver, made by Garrards, was the gift of HM Queen Victoria to Ascot in 1882. On 10

October 1907 a member, Horace Dixon Esq. (also referred to as Lt. Cdr. H. Harcourt Dixon), presented this salver - known as 'The Ascot Gold Vase 1882' - to the Club. How it came into his possession is not disclosed.

Queen Victoria Cup was made in 1805 by William Fountain. It was presented by H.M. Queen Victoria and awarded to the winner of the Nore to Dover Channel Match held on 12 June 1885. The match was sailed in light airs which favoured the smaller vessels and was won by *ULERIN (10 Tons)* owned by E. Vincent Esq. - the smallest yacht to win this prestigious race. It was re-presented to the Club in 1963 by R.H. and F.D. Corfield.

Muir Cup was made by John Bridges in 1824. It was presented to the Club in 1891 by M.A. Muir Esq. It was won in a River Match for yachts rating 20 to 40 by *REVERIE* owned by A.D. Clarke. It was re-presented to the Club by Mrs. Cecil F.A.Walker in 1955 in memory of her husband's yacht *MARIEKE* which he had built in Holland in 1912. Mr. Walker was elected a member of the Club in 1914 and served in the Grenadier Guards.

Records are frequently at variance when searching for confirmatory evidence and the following is a typical example. A handwritten note by the Club Secretary, Thornton Scovell, says the 60 guinea cup was George III and dated 1784, weighing 90 oz. and was in perfect condition when presented by M.A. Muir Esq. in 1891.

Staples Trophy This vase was presented by H.I.M. The German Emperor to the winner of the Ocean Race held to mark the opening of the Kiel Canal in 1895. The race was held on the 24th June and won by the cutter *DOROTHY (22 Tons)* owned by RTYC member Sydney F. Staples.

Beverley Cooper Challenge Cup The inscription on this trophy states that it was won by the yacht *MARIGOLD* in 1896 and presented to the RTYC by the owner's daughter, Mrs. Kennedy, in 1961. There is little doubt that the owner of *MARIGOLD* was George Beverley Cooper but confusion does arise since it is said that the trophy was made in 1913!

Howard Taylor Bowl Little is known of this large punch bowl made by Johnson, Walker and Tolhurst in 1800 and presented by John Howard Taylor in 1901 to the Union des Yachtsmen de Cannes.

Alfred Gollin Cup This two handled bowl was also made by Johnson, Walker and Tolhurst in 1907. It was presented to the Royal Thames in 1946 in memory of Alfred Gollin, who was elected an RTYC member in 1902. It is of interest to note that Alfred Gollin himself presented a cup for the winner of a handicap match during the River Matches held on the 6th June 1902. The cup was described as the Melbourne Coronation Cup - Alfred Gollin being Commodore of the Royal Yacht Club of Victoria.

Seymour King Trophy This 1896 trophy was presented to the Royal Thames in 1985 by F.J.P. Chitty Esq. of Charlottesville, Virginia, U.S.A. (together with the Ryde Coronation Town Cup - see below). Mr. Chitty was a descendant of J.A. Sanderson Esq. (an RTYC member) who won the trophy with his cutter PALMOSA at the Royal Temple Yacht Club regatta at Ramsgate on 14 July 1902. The trophy was presented by the Commodore of the Royal Temple - Sir Henry Seymour King (who was an RTYC member 1897-1901).

Ryde Coronation Town Cup This bowl was made by Joseph Rodgers at Sheffield in 1902 and was presented at the Royal Victoria Yacht Club regatta held on 14 August 1902 by the inhabitants of Ryde to mark the coronation of H M King Edward VII. It too was won by *PALMOSA* owned by J.A. Sanderson Esq.

Marzetti Cup This massive silver cup is another trophy presented originally by HIM The German Emperor. It was won, at the R.Y.S. Regatta at Cowes in 1902, by the cutter *IREX (88 Tons)* owned by Herbert Marzetti (a Royal Thames member 1880-1927) who was a successful yachtsmen and active member of the General and Sailing Committees of the Club.

Heligoland Cups These two huge, waisted trophy cups were again presented by HIM The German Emperor in 1904 and 1906 to winners of the Dover to Heligoland Race. Each has two enamel panels, the former cup depicting King Edward VII on one side and the Kaiser and Kaiserin on the other, while the latter cup omits the Kaiserin. The 1904 trophy was won by the yacht *VALDORA (107 Tons)* owned by RTYC member J.G. Douglas Kerr Esq. MP and presented to the Club by R.R. Davies Esq. in 1935. The 1906 trophy was won by the yacht *BETTY (92 Tons)* owned by I H Benn Esq. and who later, as Sir Ion Hamilton Benn, was to be the Club's Cup Bearer. It seems probable that he presented the trophy to the Club when he stood down as Cup Bearer in 1961.

Southampton Corinthian Yacht Club Cup This trophy, made in Birmingham in 1904, was won by the yacht *NYAMA* - probably in 1909. The yacht can almost certainly be identified as the cutter *NYAMA (11 Tons)* owned by Herbert Marzetti (owner of *IREX*).

Minema Bowl This trophy was made in Sheffield in 1907. It too was won by *NYAMA* in 1910 in a race run by the Solent division of the now defunct Minema Yacht Club.

Emperor of Russia Rosebowl This splendid, valuable trophy by Fabergé was presented by H.M. The Emperor of Russia to Almeric Paget on 5 August 1909 during Cowes Week for winning the 15 metre class in *MA' OONA*. The latter (as Lord Queenborough) presented the trophy to the Club in 1936 to mark his re-election as Commodore.

Irex Trophy This large two-handled cup was made in 1910 by Walker and Hall of Sheffield. It was presented to the winner of the 10 metre class in the First European Festival of Yacht Racing held at Cowes on 7 - 8 August 1911. HM King George V, a keen and successful yachtsman, was Patron of the Festival. On both days the 10 metre class was won by the Fife designed *TONINO* owned by HM The King of Spain. Second on both days was IREX owned by Herbert Marzetti (she was also Fife-designed). The cup was awarded for the race on 7 August and a report on that race in the September 1911 issue of Yachting Monthly comments that '*IREX, rather handicapped since her re-measurement, was not good enough for the King of Spain's TONINO, another clever Fife*'. Both owners were members of the Royal Thames but presumably the cup came to the Club via Herbert Marzetti.

White Heather Cup This massive trophy Flagon made by Elkington was also presented at the First International Regatta at Cowes in 1911 and went to the winner of the 23 metre class. In the event only *WHITE HEATHER II* owned by Royal Thames member Myles B. Kennedy Esq. entered - and sailed over the course.

Allan Messer Challenge Cup Made in 1903 the cup was presented to the Club in 1954 as a memorial to Allan Messer who was elected to the Royal Thames in 1907 and served as Cup Bearer 1940-41. The trophy was originally presented to the winner of the Open Handicap Race in the Southend to Harwich Match held on 7 June 1913 and won by the yacht *CARIB (37 Tons)* owned by Allan E. Messer Esq. A week earlier he had won the Rait Memorial Cup in the Handicap Race of the Nore to Dover Channel Match.

King of Spain's Cup In March 1914 the Sailing Committee received a letter from the Circle de la Voile de Paris asking for a challenge for the King of Spain's Cup in a match for 6 metre boats to be held at Menton. In June it was recorded that the trophy given for the races, held on 30 - 31 May and 1 June had been won by *VANDA* owned by Captain R.T. Dixon. *SANDRA* owned by Norman Clark-Neill was second thus making it a highly successful challenge by the Royal Thames who had been represented on the Race Committee by Norman C. Craig KC, MP. The trophy carries this engraving '*Coupe Challenge Offerte au Circle de la Voile de Paris par S M Alphouse XIII Roi d' Espagne*'.

Memorabilia

In addition to paintings and silver trophies, other items of historic interest were presented to the Club, not all of which are still to be seen in today's Clubhouse, those that are can be seen on the walls and in the display cabinets in the entrance area of the Clubhouse.

In October 1886 it was decided that the **Ivory Mallet** formerly used by 'The Cumberland Fleet' should be put into a glass case and kept in the Smoking Room. It is interesting to note, in view of the above date, that the evolution of the Royal Thames from the Cumberland Fleet was not included at the front of the Rule Book until 1900.

When the General Committee met on 4 June 1891 the Secretary informed them of a letter he had received from Thomas Taylor FRCS, who was the grandson of Thomas Taylor, Commodore of The Cumberland Fleet 1780-1816. Included with the letter were several items including a cap worn by one of the oarsmen from the crew of the barge in which the Commodore of the Cumberland Fleet sailed on race days. There was also an oarsman's uniform button, two notices of race and a paper depicting the signals used in 1793. The Secretary also produced three pictures presented by Robert Castle and Edward Walter Castle. One picture was of Commodore **Thomas Taylor** and the other two were of the cups won by him and presented by the Duke of Cumberland. Two weeks later a Sub Committee of three was formed to arrange for the '*framing of the Cumberland Fleet relics and to determine where the pictures should be placed in the Clubhouse*'. At the same time it was agreed to make the donor of the relics, Thomas Taylor, an Honorary Member of the Club.

Although the date of presentation is not recorded, it is evident from the Committee record for 5 November 1891 that R and E W Castle had presented two further prints to the Club and the Secretary was instructed to write and thank them for the prints of the **Duke of Cumberland** and the **Duke of Clarence** (William IV) - who respectively inspired the forma-tion of the Cumberland Fleet and gave the Thames Yacht Club

RTYC Race Committee (1910).

its royal patronage. A note in the archives says that Robert Castle found the picture of the Duke of Cumberland in the shop of Mr. Macfarlane, 32 Wych Street, Strand but it was promptly purchased by Mr. William Yates (elected to RTYC 1892) and presented by him to the Club in 1895!

It was fifteen months later that the Secretary informed the Committee of a letter from Robert Castle enclosing one from Richard Taylor, another grandson of Commodore Taylor, in which he presented to the Club six of the **flags** used by his grandfather. The Committee immediately asked for estimates of the cost of acquiring two airtight glass cases (for the flags) to stand in the Smoking Room either side of the Cumberland Fleet collection. Richard Taylor was made a Life Honorary Member in October 1893.

The flow of memorabilia continued and on 7 December 1893 the Secretary received a further letter from Robert Castle enclosing one from yet another Commodore Taylor grandson - Robert Taylor - presenting 10 scale **drawings** of yachts of the Cumberland Fleet. Robert Taylor was given Life Honorary Membership in February 1894. It is of note that the 'Cumberland Fleet Collection' was loaned to the International Yachting Exhibition at the Royal Aquarium in 1894.

Robert and **Edward Walter Castle** (presumed to be brothers) were elected to membership of the Royal Thames at the same Ballot Meeting in December 1888 and were joint owners of the yacht *LACERTA (34 Tons)*. It is clear that they had a great interest in the history of the Club. The 1894 edition of the Badminton Library of Sports and Pastimes contains in the Yachting section, Volume II, a comprehensive account of the activities of the Cumberland Fleet written by the Castles. A letter dated 13 October 1892 written by the then Club Secretary, Thornton Scovell, to George Paget Esq. says that *'The History of this Club from 1775 (Cumberland Fleet days) is, and has been for the past 3 years, being drawn up by two members - the Messrs Castle'.* The purpose of the letter was to ask George Paget if he would ask Lady Paget, widow of Lord Alfred Paget, whether she still had in her possession records of the Cumberland Fleet which it was understood had been passed to Lord Alfred by Mr. Taylor (deceased) - presumably the son of Commodore Thomas Taylor. There is no record of a reply, regrettably. Robert Castle died in 1898.

From time to time members donated books to the Club for the library. It is evident that not all such donations were recorded, and certainly not all that were donated are still in the Club's library - such as The Times edition of the **Encyclopedia Britannica** for which the committee authorised the payment of £10 into the Library Fund in May 1898 (and which reached the end of its useful life in 1990). Not all donations came from club members and a particular (and surprising) example is a book containing details of the Royal Thames' Nore to Dover **Channel Matches** from 1866 which was given by a Mr. J.G. Poderin. This interesting, hand-written book is very definitely on the shelves in the current Club library as is a volume of **'British Yachts and Yachtsmen'** which was donated anonymously in October 1907. Mr. Arthur Underhill, who chaired the Library Sub Committee, produced in February 1912 the design of the **Book Plate** which is still used by the Librarian. In February 1898 Mr. T H Miller presented a wheel from a **gun carriage** from Lord Nelson's flagship *FOUDROYANT*. This is still to be seen in the Clubhouse entrance hall with a clock mounted in it. The pair of **brass guns** located on the quarter deck of the present Clubhouse were presented by Mr. F. Smith in December 1911. **The Barograph**, also in the entrance hall, was presented in April 1914 by Mr. W.E. Cain (later Sir William Cain, Bart.).

An especially important gift came from Charles Arkcoll Esq. in February 1910. He was the last Commodore of the New Thames Yacht Club and he gave to the Royal Thames the **records of the NTYC** which are still in the RTYC archives and add greatly to our knowledge of the rise and fall of the NTYC and its relationship with the Royal Thames.

The **carved tiller** of the cutter *FIONA*, originally owned by E Boutcher Esq. and later by H M Rait Esq., is one of most admired artifacts in today's Clubhouse, hanging, as it does, on the wall of the staircase leading to the Quarterdeck. The circumstances which led to its being presented to the Club are worthy of recording in these chronicles.

Henry M Rait died in May 1907 and the following month the Secretary received a letter from Messrs Fladgate & Co. informing the Club that the late Mr. H.M. Rait had left his yacht *FIONA* to the Club to be used as a Club Yacht. A Sub Committee of four was appointed to consider whether the Club could accept the legacy. Their report, presented to the General Committee on 12 September, recommended that the

Club accept the legacy but, since the Club had no water-side premises, management of the yacht would be difficult. They proposed that members be invited to take over, fit out and sail the yacht for the season; Messrs Domoney and Andrew Gibbs being given preference. One Sub Committee member, Henry Marzetti, dissented from the recommendation. Overall, however, the Sub Committee thought that the best course to adopt would be to explain to the executors of Mr. Rait's will that the Club could not accept the yacht and suggested that the yacht be sold, the proceeds invested and the income used to provide a Cup to be raced for annually and to be known as 'The Rait Memorial Cup'.

A year passed before the legalities involved were finalised. Thus, on 10 September 1908, the Secretary was able to report that he had arranged the sale of FIONA to Mr. Thomas Oliver of 15A High Street, Grays, Essex for the sum of £650 less 5% commission. It was resolved that the purchase money be placed in a separate account at Messrs Coutts to be called the 'Rait Memorial Account'. After payment of all expenses, one moiety of the money was to be paid to Mr. Rait's residuary legatees and the other moiety placed on deposit to provide cups in addition to a money prize at the discretion of the Sailing Committee and in such a manner to provide cups over a period of seven years. (Race results in Appendix 7 show that this was done from 1909 when a cup valued at £35 plus £20 cash were given to the winner of the 15 metre class in the Nore to Dover, Channel Match). In the event, the residuary legatees received £269.6.7 while the sum of £258.10.5 was placed on deposit as the Rait Memorial Fund. Due to the absence of regattas during the war years 1914-18, the Fund did not close until 1922.

So much for the Rait Memorial Fund and the cups it generated, but how did the tiller come into the Club's possession? The answer came only a month after the sale of FIONA to Mr. Thomas Oliver who, on 8 October 1908, gave the original tiller of FIONA to the Club and it was hung in the outer hall of the Albermarle Street Clubhouse (over the hat rack).

Finally, it is interesting to read original **letters** that can be seen among the archives. Reference has already been made to the letters associated with the painting of the portrait of Robert Williams and the proof that it was Daniel Pasmore and not Turner who was the artist. Several letters were 'resolutions of condolence' sent on the death of the Monarch or Members of the Royal Family together with a reply from the appropriate member of the Royal Household. An interesting example of these replies concern the death of HM King Edward VII - Patron and former Commodore of the Royal Thames. This reply dated 4 August 1910 came from the Home Office, rather than a royal residence, and is signed by the then Home Secretary, Winston S. Churchill. Another aspect of this source of memorabilia is the availability of a few original telegrams such as those sent to the Club in January 1904 informing the Club of the death of the Vice Commodore, Robert Hewett.

It is recorded in Section II of this volume that the Club attended the International Regatta at Kiel in June 1912 and that members travelled to Kiel on the chartered SS ARAGUAYA. In May that year an Admiralty letter authorised the Club to fly the Blue Ensign from the chartered ship. Even more interesting are the copies of the text of the speeches made at the regatta by Theodore Pim, Commodore, Royal Thames Yacht Club and HIM The German Emperor. The occasion for these speeches was the presentation by the Commodore to the German Emperor of a replica of a Cumberland Cup (as given by the Duke of Cumberland over the years 1775-81). The Commodore's speech ended with these words: *'We ask you, Sir, to accept this, not only as a memento of the visit of the Royal Thames Yacht Club to the first International Regatta in German waters, which we consider it a privilege to have taken part in, but also of the (silver) jubilee of the Kaiserlicher Yacht Club (founded 1887) and as a personal mark of admiration and esteem which we hold for your Majesty's continuing efforts in the course of Yachting generally. This feeling, Sir, is shared not only by us individually, but by yachting men throughout Great Britain and the entire British Empire'.*

The German Emperor after expressing his gratitude for the Cup and the presence of the Royal Thames Yacht Club members and their ladies ended with these words: *'May this week form a new link in the chain of personal and sporting friendship between our two Clubs and Countries. May the Cumberland Cup stand here as a visible pledge of this friendship so natural and valuable to Great Britain and Germany.'*

Just over two years later this country was at war with Germany.

On 21 August 1914 a letter from the Admiralty informed the Club that My Lords (of the Admiralty) have now ordered that so long as hostilities may last all warrants, issued to yacht clubs authorising their members to fly the Blue Ensign, must be regarded as non-effective. No one at that time anticipated that this order would last for over four years or that they would witness the tragedies that befell their countrymen on the battlefields of France and Belgium.

Finally, the Club received several gifts of commemorative **Medals** during these years but regrettably these are no longer in the Club's possession. These included those issued at the time of the Royal Thames Round Britain Jubilee Race in 1887 and from the 1911 International Regatta at Cowes and also one presented to the Commodore (Theodore Pim) by the Yachts Club of Cannes on the occasion of the unveiling there of a statue of King Edward VII. One medal of this period that is still in the Club's possession is one presented by the Vice Commodore (Almeric Paget) to W Bratspiel Stamp, owner of the 15 metre yacht MAUDREY, in 1913 on the occasion of the first RTYC Regatta held at Stokes Bay.

VIII

Anecdotes

Once again this section has been included as a postscript. In most cases the incidents tell of unusual or unacceptable behaviour by members of the Club or of the staff. This record is in no way included as a vehicle for criticism of individuals but purely to illustrate the matters that may have caused a ripple through meetings.

10 June 1873 was the date in that year for the annual Nore to Dover 'Channel Match' . There were no less than 18 yachts entered including seven schooners, five yawls and six cutters ranging from 51 Tons to 267 Tons. The weather was ideal for a competitive race and by the time the fleet was passing through the Prince's Channel, north of Margate, it was noted that the yawl *FLORINDA (140 Tons)* was leading and that the schooner *GWENDOLIN (190 Tons)* was 'threatened' by the schooner *CAMBRIA (188 Tons)* who braced up squaresail and square topsail for a try at the *GWENDOLIN's* weather wind. Nothing, however, came of the attempt, but the *GWENDOLIN,* making a similar shot at the *FLORINDA's* breezy side, had the effect of bringing down the topmast, topsail, flying jib and spinnaker of Mr William Jessop's yawl and giving her crew half an hour's diversion. In spite of this *FLORINDA* was first across the finishing line off the Admiralty Pier at Dover $6^1/_4$ minutes ahead of Mr E. Boutcher' s renowned cutter *FIONA (79 Tons).* Such a lead was insufficient to prevent the first prize going to *FIONA* on time allowance (15 seconds per ton). Hunt's Yachting Magazine considered this to be *'one of the finest races ever sailed, the 52 mile course from Nore to Dover being completed in 7 hours and 43 minutes'.*

Comment: This was indeed a remarkable achievement by *FLORINDA*. She deserved to have her efforts recognised by allowing her to receive the £100 first prize. Even more remarkable perhaps, is that no protest was raised!

20 June 1887 was the date on which a special meeting of the House Committee was called to consider a report from the Secretary that the Night Porter had informed him that Mr F P Conolan had used the Club without having paid his subscription following his election to the Club on 7 June. It also was reported that he had behaved in an extraordinary manner in the Clubhouse. He had taken off his coat on Saturday night in the Smoking Room and torn both sleeves off his shirt. He had ordered claret and soda and been unable to pay for it; he had borrowed money for cabs and owes the night porter nine shillings and sixpence. His behaviour had been offensive to many members who had raised complaints. In addition a member, Mr Charlwood, had written complaining that Mr Conolan had taken off his shoes and put them under the table in the Smoking Room. The Secretary had written to Mr Conolan and in the reply was enclosed a post-dated cheque.

The committee directed that the cheque be returned and that the Hall Porter be instructed that Mr Conolan should be denied admittance to the Club.

Comment: This gentleman's membership of the Club must be one of the shortest on record. It is assumed, but not recorded, that the Club reimbursed the unfortunate night porter from the petty cash.

7 May 1891 The Secretary informed the General Committee of the death of Samuel Wyatt, one of the Club waiters. The Committee authorised the ordering of a wreath of flowers for the funeral and the purchase of two bottles of ammonianised quinine for the servants. They also ordered that the room in which he died be re-papered and thoroughly purified.

Comment: This gruesome report poses the questions: what horrible disease caused the death of the unfortunate Samuel Wyatt and were members using the Coffee Room put at risk?

5 November 1891 The Secretary was directed to write to the Brighton Aquarium with reference to the RTYC Burgee being flown from that establishment. Two weeks later he was able to report that the burgee had been hauled down.

Comment: A fertile imagination can conjure up all sorts of improbable reasons for this incident.

19 July 1900 Another curious event came to light on this date. The death of the cellarman, Thomas Eldridge was reported - and the cause of death as given by the Coroner's Jury was strongly commented upon by the Committee.

Comment: Once again the cause of death is not recorded but it is a possibility that the very nature of his duties were to blame.

16 May 1901 It is noted that Mr Barclay Walker's offer of a Polar Bear (stuffed and mounted) was accepted with thanks. The House Committee were directed to find a place for it.

Comment: One can imagine that the task of locating this (presumably, full size) animal may have been 'passed down the line' .

22 April 1907 On this day the House Committee ordered that £1 advanced by the Steward to the Under Billiard Marker on account, should be refunded, the sum being irrecoverable from the Under Marker who had absconded!

Comment: This appears to be a very modest sum but it probably represented two week' s wages for the Under Marker.

Appendix 1

Extract from the biography of King Edward VII by Philip Magnus

Memo from Prince Albert to the Royal Equerries describing how a Gentleman should conduct himself:

Appearance, Deportment and Dress

A gentleman does not indulge in careless, self-indulgent, lounging ways, such as lolling in armchairs or on sofas, slouching in his gait, or placing himself in unbecoming attitudes with his hands in his pockets.

He will borrow nothing from the fashions of the groom or the gamekeeper, and whilst avoiding the frivolity and foolish vanity of dandyism, will take care that his clothes are of the best quality.

Manners and Conduct towards Others

The manners and conduct of a gentleman towards others are founded on the basis of kindness, consideration and the absence of selfishness (a Prince must always be scrupulously courteous, attentive, punctual and on guard against the temptation to use harsh, rude or bantering expressions). Anything approaching to a practical joke would be inpermissible.

The Power to Acquit Himself Creditably in Conversation or whatever may be the Occupation of Society

Gossip, cards, billiards were to be regarded as useless; but some knowledge of those studies and pursuits which adorn society and make it interesting was essential. The Prince of Wales must be induced to be a persevering example, to devote some of his leisure time to music, to the fine arts, either drawing or looking over drawings, engravings etc., to hearing poetry, amusing books or good plays read aloud; in short to anything that whilst it amuses may gently exercise the mind.

Appendix 2

Letter from the Keeper of the Privy Purse

Marlborough House
Pall Mall S.W.
25th March, 1901

Sir,
I have the honour to inform you that I have submitted to the King your letter of the 20th February and, in reply, I am commanded to say that His Majesty is pleased to accede to the request contained in it to become Patron of the Royal Thames Yacht Club.

I have the honour to be, Sir
Your obedient servant
Lt. Col. C.B.G. Dick
Secretary
Royal Thames Yacht Club

Appendix 3

St. Petersburg
19 June
1874

**Letter from Francis Knollys,
Private Secretary to the Prince of Wales**

My dear Lord Alfred,

The Prince of Wales desires me to say that it will give him great pleasure to become the Commodore of the Thames Yacht Club.

I would write you a longer letter but I am just off to a dinner at the Palace and as a messenger starts early tomorrow morning I think it would be a pity to miss the opportunity of writing to you by him.

Yours sincerely,

Francis Knollys

Appendix 4

Royal Members of the Club 1868-1918

1874-1880
His Imperial Highness the Grand Duke Alexis

1874-1894
His Royal Highness the Duke of Edinburgh

1880-
His Royal Highness Prince Henry de Bourbon

1882-1914
His Imperial Highness Archduke Stefan of Austria

1855-1904
His Royal Highness the Count de Flanders

1894-1901
His Royal Highness the Duke of York

1897-1907
His Royal Highness the Duke of Abrizzi

1909-
Field Marshall, His Royal Highness, the Duke of Connaught

1910-1914
His Royal Highness Prince Henry of Prussia

1911-1914
His Imperial Highness the Crown Prince of Germany

1911-1915
His Highness Prince Leopold of Battenberg

1913-1915
His Serene Highness Prince Louis of Battenberg

Appendix 5

No. 9 St. James Street, London
December 7th
1870

Dear Sir,

At a meeting of Flag Officers of 'THAMES YACHT CLUBS'
convened by LORD ALFRED PAGET, the following PAPER
was read and agreed to be forwarded to each member of
the three leading Yacht Clubs.

YACHTING ON THE THAMES

There are several Yacht Clubs on the River Thames, below
London Bridge, and experience has shown, that during the
short summer season in which all the Regattas of these
Clubs take place, great inconvenience arises from there
being so few days on which the tides suit for matches, so
that the fixtures of the different Clubs often clash, or follow
too closely on each other; that great expense is incurred by
each Club in rents of Club Houses, salaries of Secretaries
and Servants, hire of Steamboats; Bands, storing and laying
down moorings etc. And that there is also a risk of jealousy
in the matter of naming the days and other arrangements
for the matches; all of which inconvenience, expense and

risk of ill-feeling it is desirable to avoid. With a view to this,
with the object of giving more sport in Yachting on the River
Thames, and an opportunity arising which may never occur
again; it is suggested to amalgamate the present Clubs and
thus form one Grand Yacht Squadron on the Thames, and
to solicit His Royal Highness the Prince of Wales to become
its Commodore. If this suggestion were carried out, a Club
would be established in every respect worthy of the great
metropolis to which it would belong, and it would be able
to give more important matches, with larger and better
prizes for Yacht Owners, and to have good Club accommo-
dation for its members, both on the River and in London.
The present Flag Officers of the Amalgamated Clubs might
be a Sailing Committee, all carrying the same distinguishing
Burgee, and would have power to appoint officers and
Working Committees and arrange the matches and general
business of the Club.

Before any further step is taken, will you kindly inform us
here on or before the 15th instant, if you approve of the
suggestions, when, if we find a majority in favour the
detailed arrangements will be gone into and a meeting
of the respective Clubs will be called by their Flag Officers.

We are, Dear Sir,
Yours very faithfully,

FORRESTER BRITTEN and
ROBERT HEWETT
Hon. Secs.

Appendix 6

Courses sailed in RTYC Matches
(See charts on page 96)

1. Erith to Nore Light and back to Gravesend.

2. Gravesend to Mouse Light and back to Gravesend.

3. Nore to Dover
   (O = Outside Goodwins I = Inside Goodwins).

4. Nore to Cherbourg.

5. Dover to Cherbourg.

6. Dover to Boulogne and back.

7. Dover to Liverpool.

8. Gravesend to Southend and back to Gravesend.

9. Ryde to Cherbourg and back.

10. Lower Hope to Mouse Light and back to Gravesend.

11. Gravesend to Nore and back.

12. Erith to Middle Blyth and back to Erith.

13. Erith to East Blyth and back to Erith.

14. Lower Hope to Nore and back to Gravesend.

15. Lower Hope to West Oaze Buoy and back to Gravesend.

16. (First Circuit) Southend to Nore Light to West Oaze Bury to Mouse Light and back to Southend.
    (Second Circuit) Southend to Nore Light to West Measured Mile Buoy and back to Southend.

17. Course round Dover Bay - 22 miles.

18. Dover to Calais and back.

19. Dover to N.E. Varne Buoy to South Goodwin Buoy and back to Dover.

20. Flushing to Deal.

21. Southend to Harwich.

22. Nore to Deal.

23. Stokes Bay 'Round the Buoys'

24. Lower Hope to West Oaze Buoy to Mouse Light to East River Middle Buoy to Nore Light to Southend.

Appendix 7

Date	Course	Prizes		Winning Yachts'	Owners
18.05.68	1	£100	1st Class Cutters	FIONA (77T)	E. Boutcher
	1	£30	3rd Class Cutters	LUNA (25T)	R.A. Daniell
02.06.68	2	£100	1st Class Schooners	GLORIANA (133T)	A.O. Wilkinson
		£50		EGERIA (152T)	J. Mulholland
17.06.68	2	£105	Cup presented by Queen Victoria	FIONA (77T)	E. Boutcher
		£50	Cup	EGERIA (152T)	J. Mulholland
30.06.68	3(0)	£100	Channel Match	CONDOR (129T)	Capt. W. Ewing
		£50		GLORIANA (133T)	A.O. Wilkinson
03.07.68	4	£100	Cup presented by George Duppa, Esq.	GLORIANA (133T)	A.O. Wilkinson
		£25		CAMBRIA (188T)	J. Ashbury
		£10		ALBERTINE (156T)	Capt. J. Ormsby Phibbs
24.05.69	1	£100	Vase 1st Class Cutters	SPHINX (46T)	J.S. Earle
		£50	Cup and Goblets	MURIEL (40T)	H. Bridson
05.06.69	2	£100	Gilt Vase 1st Class Schooner	EGERIA (152T)	J. Mulholland
		£30	1st Class Schooner	GLORIANA (133T)	A.O. Wilkinson
	2	£50	Cup and Goblets 2nd Class Schooner	FLYING CLOUD (75T)	Count Batthyany
21.06.69	3(0)	£100	Channel Match	JULIA (113T)	G.F. Moss
		£50		EGERIA (152T)	J. Mulholland
23.06.69	5	£20	Sweepstake	GUINEVERE (294T)	C. Thellusson
			2/3 to First, 1/3 to Second 5 Entered	EGERIA (152T)	J. Mulholland
23.05.70	2	£100	Vase	MURIEL (40T)	H. Bridson
		£30	1st Class Cutters	VINDEX (45T)	A. Duncan
		£20		CHRISTABEL (52T)	Rt. Hon. Earl Anglesley
08.06.70	2	£100	Vase	GLORIANA (148T)	A.O. Wilkinson
		£30	1st Class Schooners and Yachts	EGERIA (161T)	J. Mulholland
		£20		CAMBRIA (199T)	J. Ashbury
	2	£5	Jug and Goblets	FLYING CLOUD (75T)	Count Batthyany
			2nd Class Schooners and Yachts		
11.06.70	3(0)	£100	Vase Channel Match	EGERIA (161T)	J. Mulholland
		£50	Tankard	JULIA (122T)	G.F. Moss
13.06.70	6	50gns	Dover Town Cup	CAMBRIA (161T)	J. Ashbury
			Presented by Dover Regatta Committee		
		£15		JULIA (122T)	Lord Lennox
29.05.71	2	£100	1st Class Cutters	VANGUARD (59T)	W. Turner
		£40		VOLANTE (60T)	H. C. Maudslay
	2	£50	2nd Class Cutters	FOXHOUND (35T)	Marquis N. Ailsa

Date	Course	Prizes		Winning Yachts'	Owners
13.06.71	2	£100	1st Class Schooners and Yachts	EGERIA (152T)	J. Mulholland
		£50		GLORIANA (133T)	A.O. Wilkinson
16.06.71	3(0)	£100	Channel Match	GUINEVERE (294T)	Capt. C.S.A. Thelluson
		£50		VANGUARD (60T)	W. Turner
17.06.71	6	100gns	Presented by Mr. Ricketts, being the proceeds of his painting 'Finish of Channel Race 1870'.	GUINEVERE (294T)	Capt. C.S.A. Thelluson
20.06.71	7	50gns	Presented by Thomas Brassey	LIVONIA (280T)	J. Ashbury
01.06.72	2	£100	Cup 1st Class Cutters	ALCYONE (39T)	Lt. Col. Sir W. Topham
		£40	Cup	MYOSOTIS (40T)	T.G. Freke
	2	£50	Cup 2nd Class Cutters	FOXHOUND (35T)	Marquis of Ailsa
12.06.72	3(0)	£100	Cup Channel Match	EGERIA (152T)	J. Mulholland
		£50	Vase	FIONA (77T)	E. Boutcher
17.06.72	2	£100 Epergne	1st Class Schooners and Yachts	EGERIA (152T)	J. Mulholland
		£50 Tea Urn	2nd Class Schooners and Yachts	FLYING CLOUD (75T)	Count Balthyany
	2	£25		GERTRUDE (68T)	
21.05.73	2	£100	Cup 1st Class Cutters	KRIEMHILDA (107T)	Count Balthyany
		£40	Waiter	VANGUARD (60T)	W.P. Miller
	8	£25	Tea Set 3rd Class Cutters	VAMPIRE (19T)	T. Cuthbert
		£12.10.0 100		VANESSA (20T)	H. Bailie
05.06.73	2	£100	Cup 1st Class Schooner & Yacht Match	EGERIA (161T)	J. Mulholland
	2	£50	Tankard 2nd Class Schooner & Yacht Match	GERTRUDE (68T)	Major Tharp
10.06.73	3(0)	£100	Cup Channel Match	FIONA (79T)	E. Boutcher
		£50	Vase	EGERIA (152T)	J. Mulholland
25.05.74	2	£100	Cup 1st Class Cutters	ARETHUSA (60T)	T. Broadwood
		£6	2nd Class Cutters	BLOODHOUND (40T)	Marquis of Ailsa
	2	£30		NORMAN (40T)	Major Ewing
10.06.74	2	£100	1st Class Schooners	CETONIA (202T)	W. Turner
		£50		PANTOMIME (142T)	J.F. Starkey
	2	£100	1st Class Yachts	FLORINDA (136T)	W. Jessup
	2	£40	2nd Class Yachts	SURF (54T)	F.D. Lambert
		£20		GERTRUDE (68T)	J. Watts
24.06.74	3(0)	100gns Cup	Presented by Queen Victoria	KRIEMHILDA (106T)	Count Batthyany
		£50	Channel Match	SEA BELLE (142T)	H. Taylor
		£50		FLORINDA (137T)	W. Jessup
24.07.74	9	100gns Cup	Presented by George Field Esq.		
Although this match was included in the programme for 1874 there is no record showing that it took place.					
01.06.75		Cutter Match Prizes not known			
	2	1st Class		NEVA (63T)	R.K. Holmes-Kerr
	2	2nd Class		BRITANNIA (40T)	Capt. Hartwell
14.06.75		Schooner Yacht Match Prizes not known			
	2	1st Class Schooners		EGERIA (153T)	J. Mulhollan
	2	2nd Class Yachts		FLORINDA (136T)	W. Jessup
18.06.75	3(0)	100gns Channel Match		SEA BELLE (142T)	H. Taylor

Date	Course	Prizes		Winning Yachts'	Owners
01.06.76	2	£100	1st Class Cutters	FIONA (77T)	E. Boutcher
		£40		VOL-AU-VENT (102T)	Col. W. Markham
	2	£60	2nd Class Cutters	MYOSOTIS (40T)	H.D. Macmaster
		£30		BRITANNIA (40T)	W.C. Quilter
17.06.762	2	£100	1st Class Yachts	FLORINDA (136T)	W. Jessup
		£40	2nd Class Yachts	NEPTUNE (51T)	N.B. Stewart
		£100	1st Class Schooners	EGERIA (153T)	J. Mulholland
		£50	2nd Class Schooners	PHANTOM (175T)	A.O. Wilkinson
21.06.76	3(0)	100gns Cup	Channel Match	EGERIA (152T)	J. Mulholland
		£50		FLORINDA (136T)	W. Jessup
		£50		CUCKOO (93T)	H. Hall
23.05.77	2	£100	1st Class Cutters	NEVA (63T)	R. Borwick
		£40		VOL-AU-VENT (104T)	Col. W. Markham
	2	£60	2nd Class Cutters	BLOODHOUND (40T)	Marquis of Ailsa
		£30		MYOSOTIS (40T)	H.D. Macmaster
08.06.77	2	100gns 1st Class Schooners		MIRANDA (140T)	G.C. Lampson
		£50		SEA BELLE (142T)	H. Taylor
	2	£100	1st Class Yachts	FLORINDA (136T)	W. Jessup
		£40	2nd Class Yachts	VERONICA (86T)	T.G. Freke
22.06.77	3(0)	£100		NEVA (63T)	R. Borwick
		£50	Channel Match	FLORINDA (136T)	W. Jessup
		£50		CORINNE (160T)	N. Wood
27.05.78	2	£100	1st Class Cutters	VOL-AU-VENT (104T)	Col. W. Markham
		£40		NEVA (63T)	F. Cox
	2	£60	2nd Class Cutters	CORALIE (40T)	Sir F. Gooch
		£30		MYOSOTIS (40T)	H.D. Macmaster
11.06.78	2	£100	1st Class Yachts	JULLANAR (128T)	A.D. Macleay
	11	£25	3rd Class Cutters	MAGGIE (15T)	L. Wheeler
		£12.10		LILY (10T)	E.F. Quilter
15.06.78	3(0)	£100	Channel Match	FLORINDA (136T)	W. Jessup
		£50		NEVA (63T)	F. Cox
		£50		MIRANDA (140T)	G.C. Lampson
31.05.79	2	£60	1st Class Cutters	BLOODHOUND (40T)	Marquis of Ailsa
		£40		BRITANNIA (40T)	W. C. Quilter
	11	£25	3rd Class Cutters	VANESSA (20T)	R. Borwick
		£12.10		SAYONARA (20T)	G.W. Richardson
14.06.79	10	£70	Handicap Match 1st Class Schooners	MIRANDA (136T)	G.C. Lampson
		£70	2nd Class Yachts	SURF (54T)	Williams
	10	£30		FLORINDA (136T)	W. Jessop
19.06.79	3(0)	100gns Cup		FORMOSA (103T)	F.S. Stanley
			Presented by Thomas Brassey Esq.		
		£50	Channel Match	FLORINDA (136T)	W. Jessop
		£50		MIRANDA (140T)	G.C. Lampson
05.06.80	2	£100	1st Class Cutters	VANDUARA (90T)	J.Clark
	2	£50	2nd Class Cutters	BLOODHOUND (40T)	Marquis of Ailsa
		£30		NORMAN (40T)	Major Ewing
	11	£30	3rd Class Cutters	FREDA (20T)	T.G. Freke
		£20		MAGGIE (15T)	F. Taylor
21.06.80	10	£100	1st Class Schooners	MIRANDA (135T)	G.C. Lampson

Date	Course	Prizes		Winning Yachts'	Owners
23.06.80	3(0)	100gns Cup	Presented by Queen Victoria	LATONA (163T)	A.B. Rowley
		£50	Channel Match	MIRANDA (136T)	G.C. Lampson
		£50		VANDUARA (96T)	J. Clark
23.05.81	2	£100	1st Class Cutters	SAMOENA (90T)	J. Jameson
	11	£30	3rd Class Cutters	BUTTERCUP (10T)	R. Hewett
		£20		LOUISE (20T)	T. Wyan Eyton
08.06.81	10	£50	2nd Class Yachts	GUDRUN (80T)	W. Leask
		£20		CHRISTINE (40T)	G. Burnett
		£10		ARETHUSA (57T)	R. Stuart Lane
23.06.81	3(0)	£100	Channel Match	LATONA (160T)	A.B. Rowley
				SAMOENA (90T)	J. Jameson
				MIRANDA (129T)	G.C. Lampson
13.06.82		Cutter Match abandoned - no entries due to clash of dated with Royal London Yacht Club			
	10	£100	1st Class Schooners	MIRANDA (122T)	G.C. Lampson
	10	£50	2nd Class Yachts	LORINA (85T)	S.H. Morley
		£30		ARETHUSA (54T)	R. Stuart Lane
16.06.82	3(0)	£100	Channel Match	ANNASONA (40T)	J.D Hedderwick
		£50		LORNA (85T)	S.H. Morley
		£50		MIRANDA (122T)	G.C. Lampson
30.05.83		Amateur Handicap Matches			
	12	£20	Yachting not exceeding 13T	MANOLA (5T)	H. Simpson
		£10		VIRAGO (6T)	R. Stone
		£5		MAGGIE (6T)	L. Wheeler
	13	£25	Yachting not exceeding 11T	BUTTERCUP (10T)	R. Hewett
		£15		BONINA (9T)	J. Duncuft
		£10		ULIDIA (10T)	W. Corry
01.06.83		Open to any club yacht exceeding 9 Tons of any rig			
	10	£60		MAY (40T)	N.B. Stewart
		£40		SILVERSTAR (40T)	Foster Conner
		£30		SLEUTHHOUND (40T)	Marquis of Ailsa
		£25		TARA (40T)	F. Taylor
		£15		ULIDIA (10T)	W. Curry
		£10		BUTTERCUP (10T)	R. Hewett
14.06.83		Amateur Handicap Matches			
		Yachts exceeding 13 Tons & not exceeding 35 Tons			
	1	£40		CHALLENGE (20T)	W.B. Webb
		£25		VANESSA (19T)	F. Scovell
		£15		FLEUR DE LYS (33T)	H. Edie
		£10		MAGNOLIA (19T)	G.W. Brown
		£5		TORCH (15T)	W.H. Williams
14.06.83	12	£20	Yachts not exceeding 3 Tons	CHITTYWEE (3T)	Lord F. Cecil
		£10		MASCOTTE (3T)	E.F. Quilter
		£6		SNARLEYYOW (3T)	W. Baden Powell

Date	Course	Prizes		Winning Yachts'	Owners
16.06.83	10	£70	Yachts, any rig, 41 Tons upwards	SAMOENA (88T)	J. Jameson
		£30		MARJORIE (68T)	J. Coats
	10	£40	Yachts, any rig, 22 Tons but not exceeding 41 Tons	MAY (40T)	N.B. Stewart
	10	£30	Yachts, any rig, 9 Tons but not exceeding 22 Tons	FREDA (20T)	H. Salwey
		£15		BUTTERCUP (11T)	R. Hewett
			Handicap Match for vessels 9 Tons and upwards		
	14	£40		MAGNOLIA (19T)	G.W. Brown
		£35		FLEUR-DE-LYS (33T)	H. Edie
		£30		STEPHANOTIS (35T)	C. Arckoll
		£20		POMONA (10T)	C.F. Taylor
		£15		KILMENY (30T)	W. Graham
		£10		IRENE (54T)	H.R. Laing
20.06.83			Channel Match		
	3(0)	£100		MAY (40T)	N.B. Stewart
		£50		MIRANDA (125T)	G.C. Lampson
		£50		LORNA (85T)	S.H. Morley
20.05.84	14	£25	Yachts of 9 Tons not exceeding 22 Tons	ULIDIA (10T)	Corry
		£10		BUTTERCUP (10T)	R. Hewett
04.06.84	10	£70	Yachts, any rig, 41 Tons and upwards	MARJORIE (68T)	J. Coats
		£30		GENESTA (80T)	Sir R. Sutton
	14	£25	Yachts of 9 Tons not exceeding 22 Tons	ULIDIA (10T)	W. Corry
		£10		FREDA (20T)	R. Salwey
04.06.84	14	£40	Handicap Match for yachts of 9 Tons and upwards	ARETHUSA (54T)	R. Stuart Lane
		£25		FLEUR-DE-LYS (33T)	H. Edie
		£15		MAGNOLIA (19T)	G.W. Brown
07.06.84			Channel Match		
	3(0)	£100		GENESTA (80T)	Sir R. Sulton
		£60		LORNA (63T)	S.H. Morley
		£40		MARJORIE (68T)	J. Coats
08.06.85	10	£80	Match for yachts exceeding 38 Tons	TARA (40T)	F. Taylor
		£40		MARJORIE (68T)	J. Coats
	14	£10	Match for yachts 30 ft. on W.L.	CURTSEYH.	W. Forster
12.06.85	3(0)	100gns	Cup presented by Queen Victoria	ULERIN (10T)	E. Vincent
		£50	Channel Match	MARGUERITE (60T)	F. Connor
		£30		TARA (40T)	F. Taylor
22.06.85			Handicap Match for yachts of any rig or tonnage		
	15	£50		BUTTERFLY (20T)	A.W. Watts
		£40		VEGA (36T)	Col. F. J. Smith
		£30		IRENE (54T)	R.H. Laing
		£20		NEPTUNE (46T)	W.G.D. Goff
		£15		STEPHANOTIS (40T)	C. Arcoll
		£10		TERPSICHORE (39T)	J. Duncuft
12.06.86	10	£70	Match for A Class over 39 Tons	IREX (85T)	J. Jameson
	10	£50		MAY (40T)	J. Duncuft
		£35		NEPTUNE (46T)	W.G.D. Goff
		£25	Match for B and C Classes of 39 Tons and under	WENDUR (125T)	H.R. Laing
		£15		ERYCINA (90T)	A. Penn
		£10		ARETHUSA (54T)	R.S. Lane
14.06.86	3(0)	£100	Channel Match	MAY (40T)	J. Duncuft
		£40		ANNASONA (40T)	K. Byrne Jones
		£20		WENDUR (125T)	H.R. Laing

Date	Course	Prizes		Winning Yachts'	Owners
01.06.87	10	£70	Match for yachts of any rig with rating exceeding 18	THISTLE (139T)	J. Bell
		£40		IREX (106T)	J. Jameson
	15	£50	Match for yachts of any rig in classes B and C	NEPTUNE (42T)	W.G.D. Goff
		£20		FOXHOUND (33T)	Capt. C. G. Nottage
04.06.87	3(0)	£100	Channel Match	FOXHOUND (33T)	Capt. C.G. Nottage
		£40		SYBIL (26T)	C.J.G. Still
		£20		NEPTUNE (42T)	W.G.D. Goff
14.06.87 to 27.06.87		£1000	Round Britain Jubilee Race	GENESTA (85T)	Sir Richard Sutton
04.06.88	10	£70	Match for yachts exceeding rating of 60	Results Not Available	
		£30			
	10	£50	Match for yachts with rating between 40 and 60		
		£20			
	15	£20	Match for yachts with rating between 15 and 40		
		£10			
	15	£40	Handicap Match		
		£25			
		£20			
		£15			
		£10			
09.06.88	3(0)	£100	Channel Match	IREX (96T)	J. Jameson
		£50		YARANA (60T)	P.A. Rolli
		£20		MOHAWK (40T)	Col. V. Bagot
24.05.89	10	£70	Match for yachts exceeding rating of 40	VALKYRIE (78T)	Earl of Dunraven
		£40		YARANA (60T)	P.A. Ralli
		£30		IREX (98T)	J. Jameson
	15	£25	Match for yachts with rating between 15 and 40	VREDA (20T)	T.H. Hodgens
		£15		DEERHOUND (40T)	C.G. Nottage
	15	£40	Handicap Match	FOXGLOVE	W.B. Paget
		£25		DECIMA	J. Anabin
		£20		DISS	A.D. Clarke
		£15		MAID MARION	M.B. Kennedy
01.06.89			Channel Matches		
	3(0)	£100		VALKYRIE (77T)	Earl of Dunraven
		£40		DEERHOUND (40T)	C.G. Nottage
		£20		YARANA (60T)	P.A. Ralli
	3(L)	£50	Presented by Lord Brassey for a Handicap Match	VOL-AU-VENT	R. Ingham Clark
29.05.90	10	£50	Match for yachts exceeding rating of 40	Results Not Available	
		£40			
	10	£40	Match for yachts with rating between 20 and 40		
		£20			
	15	£20	Match for yachts with rating between 15 and 20		
		£10			
	15	£40	Handicap Match		
		£30			
		£20			
		£10			

Date	Course	Prizes		Winning Yachts'	Owners
31.05.90			Channel Match		
	3(O)	£100		THISTLE (124T)	J. Bell
		£40		IVERNA (116T)	J. Jameson
		£20		VALKYRIE (76T)	Earl of Dunraven
	3(L)	£35	Presented by Lord Brassey for Handicap Match	MOHAWK (45T)	G.F. Beck
		£15		VANDUARA (99T)	T.H. Hodgens
02.06.91	10	£50	Match for yachts exceeding rating of 40	MAID MARION (72T)	M.B. Kennedy
		£40		VALKYRIE (76T)	Rt. Hon. Lord Dunraven
	10	60gns	Cup presented by M A. Muir Esq.	REVERIE	D.A. Clarke
		£20	Match for yachts with rating between 20 and 40	CREOLE (54T)	Col. V. Bagot
	15	£40	Handicap Match	COLUMBINE (81T)	W.B. Paget
		£20		LETHE (163T)	S.C. Watson
06.06.91			Channel Match		
	3(O)	£100		IVERNA (152T)	J. Jameson
		£40	Silver Jug Goblets Presented by daughters of the late A O Wilkinson	THALIA (59T)	J.A. Inglis
		£20		CREOLE (54T)	Col. V. Bagot
	3(I)	£35	Presented by Lord Brassey for Handicap Match	COLUMBINE (81T)	W.B. Paget
		£15		BLUE ROCK (92T)	J. Sutcliffe
21.05.92	10	£80	Match for yachts exceeding rating of 40	IVERNA (152T)	J. Jameson
		£40		METEOR	H.I.M. the German Emperor
	10	£40	Match for yachts with rating between 20 and 40	QUEEN MAB	T.B.C. West
		£20		CORSAIR	Ad. the Hon V Montague
	5	£40	Handicap Match	COLUMBINE	W.B. Paget
		£30		SIOLA	The Hon. J.S. Montague
11.06.92			Channel Match		
	3(O)	£100		IVERNA (152T)	Jameson
		£40		METEOR	H.I.M. the German Emperor
		£30	Presented by F.W. Popham Esq. for 40 raters	CORSAIR	Ad. the Hon V Montague
	3(I)	£35	Presented by Lord Brassey for Handicap Match	COLUMBINE (81T)	W.B. Paget
		£15		NEAIRA	R. Frost Smith
25.05.93	10	£100	Match for yachts exceeding rating of 40	BRITANNIA (221T)	H.R.H. The Prince of Wales
		£50		IVERNA (152T)	J. Jameson
	10	£50	Match for yachts with rating between 20 and 40	VENDETTA (76T)	Ad. the Hon V Montague
		£20		LAIS	J. Gretton
	10	£40	Handicap Match	CASTANET (64T)	W.R. Cookson
		£30		SIOLA	M.V. Goldsmith
		£20		CREOLE (54T)	Col. V. Bagot
10.06.93			Channel Matches		
	3(O)	100gns	Presented by Col. Peters	VALKYRIE (76T)	Lord Dunraven
		£50		BRITANNIA (221T)	H.R.H. The Prince of Wales
		£25		CALLUNA (258T)	P. Donaldson
	3(I)	£35	Presented by Lord Brassey for Handicap Match	COLUMBINE (81T)	W.B. Paget
		£15		CREOLE (54T)	Col. V. Bagot

Date	Course	Prizes		Winning Yachts'	Owners
31.05.94	10	£80	Match for yachts exceeding rating of 40	BRITANNIA (221T)	H.R.H. The Prince of Wales
	10	£40	Match for yachts with rating between 20 and 40	CARINA (69T)	Ad. the Hon V Montague
	15	£40	Handicap Match	MIMOSA	Col. Clayton
		£20		CREOLE (54T)	Col. V. Bagot
16.06.94			Channel Matches		
	3(O)	£100	Presented by J. Lysaght Esq.	BRITANNIA (221T)	H.R.H. The Prince of Wales
		£35	Presented by Lord Brassey for Handicap Match	CREOLE (54T)	Col. V. Bagot
	3(I)	£15		NAMARA (102T)	W.B. Paget
08.05.95	10	£80	For yachts exceeding rating of 40	BRITANNIA (221T)	H.R.H. The Prince of Wales
	10	£40	For yachts of rating 20 but not exceeding 40	ISOLDE (81T)	P. Donaldson
		£20		CARESS (77T)	Major W.H. Walker
	15	£20	For yachts of rating 15 but not exceeding 20	AUDREY	Earl of Dunraven
		£10		DRAGON	Lord Lonsdale
	15	£40	Handicap Match	NAMARA (102T)	W.B. Paget
08.06.95			Channel Match		
	3(O)	£80		BRITANNIA (221T)	H.R.H. The Prince of Wales
		£40	For yachts of rating 20 but not exceeding 40	CARESS (77T)	Major W.H. Walker
	3(I)	£20	For yachts of rating 15 but not exceeding 20	NIAGARA	H. Gould
		£10		AUDREY	Earl Dunraven
	3(I)	£35	Presented by Lord Brassey for Handicap Match	MAID MARION (92T)	M.B. Kennedy
		£15		CREOLE (54T)	Col. V. Bagot
22.05.96	10	£80	Match for yachts exceeding rating of 65	BRITANNIA (221T)	H.R.H. The Prince of Wales
		£40		SATANITA	C.D. Rose
	10	£40	Match for yachts of rating 52 but not exceeding 65	ISOLDE (81T)	P. Donaldson
	15	£20	Match for yachts of rating 47 but not exceeding 52	NIAGARA	H. Gould
		£10		PENITENT (52T)	C.D. Rose
	10	£40	Handicap Match for yachts exceeding rating of 47	MAID MARION (72T)	M.B. Kennedy
		£30		NAMARA (102T)	W.B. Paget
06.06.96			Channel Match		
	3(O)	£100	For yachts exceeding rating of 65	METEOR	H.I.M. the German Emperor
	3(O)	£40	For yachts of rating 52 but not exceeding 65	ISOLDE (81T)	P. Donaldson
	3(I)	£20	For yachts of rating 47 but not exceeding 52	PENITENT	C.D. Rose
	3(I)	£35	Handicap Match for yachts exceeding rating of 47	MAID MARION	M.B. Kennedy
		£15		NAMARA (102T)	W.B. Paget
26.05.97	10	£70	Match for yachts exceeding rating of 65	CARESS (78T)	H.T. van Lann
	10	£60	Handicap Matches for yachts over 40 Tons	THELMA (41T)	H.T. Michels
		£30		CREOLE (54T)	Col. V. Bagot
	15	£35	Handicap Match for yachts between 9 and 40 Tons	DOREEN (20T)	F. Last
		£15		VANITY (19T)	W.P. Burton
		£10		NORMAN (39T)	Stanley E. Hicks

Date	Course	Prizes		Winning Yachts'	Owners
29.05.97			Channel Matches		
	3(O)	£60	Handicap Match for yachts over 40 Tons	ANEMONE (96T)	J.T. Haggas
		£30		CARESS (78T)	H.T. van Lann
		£15		CREOLE (54T)	Col. V. Bagot
	3(I)	£35	Handicap Match for yachts between 9 and 40 Tons	MERRY MAID (34T)	H. Simpson
02.06.98	10	£100	Match for yachts of rating exceeding 79	BONA (82.1)	Duke d' Abruzzi
	10	£50	Match for yachts with rating between 52 and 65	SENTA (62)	A. Brising
	10	£30	Match for yachts with rating between 47 and 52	PENITENT (51.9)	W.P. Burton
	15	£40	Handicap Match for yachts over 10T	GEISHA (28T)	H.T. Garrett
		£20		CREOLE (54T)	Col. V. Bagot
		£15		MAID MARION (72T)	M.B. Kennedy
11.06.98			Channel Match		
	3(O)	100gns	Cup presented by Col. Peters for yachts over 79	BONA (82.1)	Duke d' Abruzzi
	3(O)	£40	Match for yachts with rating between 52 and 65	ISOLDE (65)	P. Donaldson
	3(I)	£20	Match for yachts with rating between 47 and 52	PENITENT (51.9)	W.P. Burton
	3(O)	£35	Presented by Lord Brassey for a Handicap Match	NAMARA (102T)	W.B. Paget
		£15		GERTRUDE (69T)	J. Flemet
05.06.99	10	£100	Match for yachts exceeding 79 rating	RAINBOW (97.3)	C.L. Orr-Ewing
	10	£100	Match for yachts with rating between 52 and 65	EELIN (65)	Capt. J. Orr-Ewing
		£15		ASTRILD (64.8)	P.U. Inglis
	15	£30	Match for yachts with rating between 47 and 52	SENGA (52)	W.F. Cook
		£15		MORNING STAR (52)	A. Coats
	10	£40	Handicap Match for yachts exceeding 30 Tons	CREOLE (54T)	Col V. Bagot
		£20		MAID MARION (72T)	M.B. Kennedy
		£15		NEIRA (39T)	H.T. Michels
	15	£25	Cup presented by W. Humphrey Ransford for Handicap Match for yachts of 9 Tons to 30 Tons	NAN (29T)	S.M. Mellor
10.06.99			Channel Match		
	3(O)				
	3(I)	Cup	Presented by Queen Victoria for match	CAPRICE (52)	Sir Seymour King
		£50	for yachts of 42 rating and over	TUTTY (64.8)	C.F. von Siemens
		£30		BONA (82.9)	J. Howard Taylor
		£35	Handicap Match for yachts over 10 Tons	CREOLE (54T)	Col. V. Bagot
		£15		MAID MARION (72T)	M.B. Kennedy
07.06.1900	10	£30	Match for yachts of 47 rating not exceeding 52	SENGA (51.9)	Wyndham F. Cook
	10	£50	Handicap Match for yachts over 40 Tons	CREOLE (54T)	Col. V. Bagot
		£25		BRYNHILD (153T)	J.S. Calverley
	15	£25	Handicap Match for yachts between 9 and 40 Tons	CERIGO (23T)	Messrs Knight and Hall
		£15		NORA (27T)	Messrs Giff and Tuff
		£5		NAN (29T)	S.M. Mellor

Date	Course	Prizes		Winning Yachts'	Owners
9.6.1900			Channel Match		
	3(I)	£20	Match for yachts with rating between 47 and 52	PENITENT (51.9T)	W.P. Burton
	3(0)	£50	Handicap Match for yachts over 75 Tons	BRYNHILD (153T)	J.S. Calverley
		£25		NAMARA (102T)	W.B. Paget
	3(I)	£35	Presented by Lord Brassey for Handicap Match	MAID MARION (72T)	M.B. Kennedy
		£15	for yachts between 30 and 75 Tons	CREOLE (54T)	Col. V. Bagot
	3(I)	£20	Handicap Match for yachts between 9 and 30 Tons	NAN (29T)	S.M. Mellor
		£10		GEISHA (30T)	A.E. Sparks
12.06.01	16 (twice)	£40	Match for yachts of 47 rating to 52 rating	MAGDALEN (51.9)	Baron de Forest
	16 (twice)	£50	Handicap Match for yachts over 50 Tons	CREOLE (54T)	Col V. Bagot
		£25		COLUMBINE (81T)	A.F. Fynn
	16 (twice)	£30	Handicap Match for yachts of 20 Tons to 50 Tons	NEBULA (36T)	A.K. Stothert
		£15		NAN (29T)	Messrs Elder and Hall-Say
		£5		MOONBEAM (42T)	C.P. Johnson
	16 (twice)	£15	Handicap Match for yachts of 5 Tons to 20 Tons	VANITY (19T)	J.R. Payne
		£7		ZILLAH (8T)	P.J. Russell
15.06.01			Channel Match		
	3(I)	£30	Match for yachts of 47 rating to 52 ratings	MAGDALEN (51.9)	Baron de Forest
	3(0)	£50	Handicap Match for yachts exceeding 50 Tons	FIONA (80T)	H.M. Rait
		£25		NEREUS (101T)	C.C.S. Guthrie
		£15		COLUMBINE (81T)	A.F. Fynn
	3(I)	£30	Handicap Match for yachts of 15 Tons to 50 Tons	BANBA (19T)	A.H. Royle
		£10		VANITY (19T)	J.R. Payne
06.06.02	16 (twice)	25gns	Cup presented by J.W. Leuchars Esq. for match for yachts of rating 47 to 52	VIERA (51.9)	F. and C. Last
		£5		GAUNTLET (51.9)	A.L. Pierse
	16 (twice)	50gns	Cup presented by A. Barclay Walker for Handicap Match for yachts over 50 Tons	NAMARA (102T)	W.B. Paget
		£20		BRYNHILD (153T)	Sir J. Pender
	16 (twice)	£25	Handicap Match for yachts 20 to 50 Tons	MOONBEAM 941T)	C.P. Johnson
	16 (twice)	£15	Handicap Match for yachts 5 to 20 Tons	DEBONAIR (15T)	J.M. McEwan
		£7		BANBA (19T)	A.H. Royle
07.06.02			Channel Match		
	3(I)	25gns	Melbourne Coronation Cup presented by Alfred Gollin, Commodore RYC of Victoria for yachts of rating 47 to 52	VIERA (51.9)	F. and C. Last
		£15		SENGA (51.9)	G. Terrell
	3(0)	50gns	Presented by A. Barclay Walker for Handicap Match for yachts over 50 Tons	IREX (88T)	H. Marzetti
		£20		NAMARA (102T)	W.B. Paget
		£10		BRYNHILD (152T)	Sir J. Pender
	3(I)	50gns	Cup presented by H.M. Rait Esq. for Handicap Match for yachts 15 to 50 Tons	JAPONICA (30T)	G.H. Ward
		£10		CERIGO (23T)	Messrs Humphreys, Hall and Knight

Date	Course	Prizes		Winning Yachts'	Owners
05.06.03	16 (twice)	£25	Match for yachts rating 47 to 52	MOYANA	J.W. Leuchars
		£10		CAMELLIA (45T)	A. Coats
	16 (twice)	100gns	Cup presented by J.R. Bell Esq. for Handicap Match for yachts over 110 Tons	BRYNHILD (153T)	Sir J. Pender
	16 (twice)	£50	Presented by J. Coats Esq. for Handicap Match for yachts of 50 to 110 Tons	CREOLE (54T)	Col. V. Bagot
		£20		MOONBEAM (41T)	C.P. Johnson
		£10		NAMARA (102T)	D. Eckford
	16 (twice)	£25	Handicap Match for yachts of 25 to 49 Tons	NEBULA (36T)	A.K. Stothert
	16 (twice)	£15	Handicap Match for yachts of 15 to 24 Tons	BINGO (23T)	E.B. Turner
	16 (twice)	£25	Handicap Match for Amateur Helmsmen in yachts of 25 to 50 Tons	NAN (29T)	Messrs Elder and Hall-Say
		£10		GAUNTLET (37T)	J.R. Payne
		£5		VIERA (37T)	F. and C. Last
13.06.03			Channel Match		
	3(I)	£35	Presented by Lord Brassey for yachts of 52 rating	CAMELLIA	A. Coats
		£15		VIOLA	W.B. Paget
	3(O)	100gns	Cup presented by Theodore Pim Esq. for Handicap Match for yachts over 110 Tons	BRYNHILD (153T)	Sir J. Pender
		£25		CLARA (185T)	Max Guilleaume
	3(O)	100gns	Challenge Cup presented by Col. C. Probyn for Handicap Match for yachts of 50-110 Tons	GWYNETH (54T)	H.J. Garrett
		£15		FIONA (80T)	H.M. Rait
		£10		MOONBEAM (65T)	C.P. Johnson
	3(I)	£25	Handicap Match for yachts 20 to 49 Ton	CERIGO (23T)	Messrs Humphreys, Hall and Knight
		£15		JEAN	
		£10		FLAME	
	3(I)	£30	Limited Handicap Match	VIERA (37T)	F. and C. Last
		£20		SENGA (35T)	G. Terrell
		£10		NAN(29T)	Messrs Elder and Say-Hall
15.06.03	6	£70	Handicap Match for yachts over 50 Tons	NAMARA (102T)	D. Eckford
		£25		VALDORA (107T)	D. Kent
		£15		MAIDMARION (72T)	M.B. Kennedy
		£10		CREOLE (54T)	Col. V. Bagot
16.06.03	17	40gns	Cup presented by Almeric Paget Esq. for yachts of 52 rating	VIOLA	W.B. Paget
		£10		CAMELLIA	A. Coats
	17	£30	Limited Handicap Match	SENGA (35T)	G. Terrell
		£20		GAUNTLET (37T)	J.R. Payne
		£10		MORNING STAR (35T)	N.T. Kershaw
	17	£25	Match for South Coast One Design Class	JEAN	
		£10		HEROINE	
27.05.04	16 (twice)	£30	Match for yachts of 52 rating	MAYMON	S. Butler
		£10		CAMELLIA	A. Coats
	16 (twice)	100gns	Cup presented by the Duke of Bedford for Handicap Match for yachts over 100 Tons	CLARA (185T)	Herr Max Guilleaume
		£25		BRYNHILD (153T)	Sir J. Pender
	16 (twice)	50gns	Presented by R. Taylor Esq. for Handicap Match for yachts of 50 to 100 Tons	CREOLE (54T)	Col. V. Bagot
		£20		MOONBEAM (65T)	C.P. Johnson
		£10		ROSAMOND (63T)	A.K. Stothert
	16 (twice)	£25	Handicap Match for yachts of 25 to 50 Tons	NEBULA (36T)	Mrs. G. Turner Farley
		£10		VIERA (36T)	F. and C. Last
		£5		SENGA (35T)	G. Terrell

Date	Course	Prizes		Winning Yachts'	Owners
11.06.04			Channel Match		
	3(I)	35gns	Presented by J.R. Bell Esq. for yachts of 52 rating	MAYMON	S. Butler
		15gns		MOYONA	J.W. Leuchars
	3(0)	100gns	Cup presented by Theodore Pim Esq. for Handicap Match for yachts over 100 Tons	CLARA (185T)	Herr Max Guilleaume
		£25		VALDOR (106T)	J.G. Douglas Kerr
	3(0)	100gns	Probyn Challenge Cup + £35 for Handicap Match for yachts of 50 to 100 Tons	ROSAMOND (63T)	A.K. Stothert
		£15		MOONBEAM (65T)	C.P. Johnson
		£10		CREOLE (54T)	Col. V. Bagot
	3(I)	£25	Handicap Match for yachts of 25 to 50 Tons	NEBULA (36T)	Mr. G. Turner Farley
		£10		SENGA (35T)	G. Terrell
		£5		VIERA (36T)	F. and C. Last
	3(I)	£15	Handicap match for yachts of 9 to 25 Tons (Amateur Helmsmen)	BINGO (23T)	E.B. Turner
		£5		CHULA (18T)	J. Pearce
09.07.04	18		Match for yachts of 25 to 50 Tons	ROSAMOND (63T)	A.K. Stothert
				BRYNHILD (153T)	Sir J. Pender
				MOONBEAM (65T)	C.P. Johnson
	18		Match for yachts over 50 Tons	GAUNTLET (37T)	J.R. Payne
				VIERA (36T)	F. and C. Last
				SLENGA (35T)	G. Terrell
09.06.05	16	100gns	Cup presented by the Duke of Bedford for Handicap Match for yachts over 100 Tons	CLARA (185T)	Herr Max Guilleaume
	16	£50	Presented by M.B. Kennedy Esq. for Handicap Match for yachts of 50 to 100 Tons	ROSAMOND (63T)	A.K. Stothert
		£20		CREOLE (54T)	Col V. Bagot
	16	£30	Presented by Almeric Paget Esq. for yachts of 52	Fleet did not start!	
		£10			
		£5			
	16	£25	Limited Handicap Match for yachts of 25 to 50 Tons	VIERA (35T)	F. and C. Last
	16	£10	Limited Handicap Match for yachts of 9 to 20 Tons	L' AMOUREUSE	Capt. A. Charteris
	(1st Circuit)				
17.06.05			Channel Match		
	3(0)	100gns	Presented by T. Pim Esq. for Handicap Match for yachts over 100 Tons	WHITE HEATHER (132T)	M.B. Kennedy
		£25		BRYNHILD (153T)	Sir J. Pender
	3(0)	100gns	Probyn Challenge Cup for Handicap Match for yachts of 50 to 100 Tons	ROSAMOND (63T)	A.K. Stothert
		£15		MOONBEAM (65T)	C.P. Johnson
	3(I)	£30	Match for yachts of 52 rating	SONYA	Mrs. G. Turner Farley
		£10		MAYMON	S. Butler
	3(I)	£25	Limited Handicap Match for yachts of 25 to 50 Tons	VIERA (35T)	F. and C. Last
		£10		INDUNA (37T)	N.T. Kershaw
		£5		SENGA (35T)	G. Terrell
	3(I)	£15	Limited Handicap Match for yachts of 9 to 25 Tons	EILUN	Messrs Grevile and Fitzgerald
		£5		L' AMOUREUSE	Capt. A. Charteris
19.06.05	18	50gns	Presented by H. Marzetti Esq. for Handicap Match for yachts over 50 Tons	BRYNHILD (153T)	Sir J. Pender
		£25		CREOLE (54T)	Col V. Bagot
		£10		WHITE HEATHER (132T)	M.B. Kennedy
	19	£25	Match for yachts of 52 rating	BRITOMART	W.P. Burton
		£10		MOYONA	J.W. Leuchers
	19	£25	Limited Handicap Match for yachts of 20 to 50 Tons	VIERA (35T)	F. and C. Last
		£10		SENGA (35T)	G Terrell
		£5		INDUNA (37T)	N.T. Kershaw

Date	Course	Prizes		Winning Yachts'	Owners
06.07.06	16	£100	Match for yachts with rating exceeding 79	NYRIA (80.1)	R.W.N. Young
		£25		WHITE HEATHER (83.2)	M.B. Kennedy
	16	£50	Presented by M.B. Kennedy Esq. for Handicap Match for yachts exceeding 50 Tons	ROSAMOND (63T)	A.K. Stothert
		£20		CREOLE (54T)	Col V. Bagot
	16	£40	Match for yachts of 52 rating	SONYA	Mrs. G. Farley Turner
		£10		BRITOMART	W.P. Burton
	16	£25	Handicap Match for yachts not exceeding 50 Tons Amateur Helmsmen	GAUNTLET (37T)	Messrs J R Payne and H Goldie
		£10		CAMELLIA (45t)	G.N.E. Hall-Sey
	16 (1st Circuit)	£10	Handicap Match for yachts of 9 to 25 Tons	CHULA (18T)	J. Pearce
14.07.06			Channel Match		
	3(0)	£100	Presented by T. Pim Esq. for yachts of 79 rating	NYRIA (80.1)	R.W.N. Young
		£25		KARIAD (91.8)	Sir J. Pender
		£50	Presented by A.. Paget Esq. for Handicap Match for yachts exceeding 50 Tons	MERRYMAID (107T)	J.E. Terry
	3(0)	£20		CREOLE (54T)	Col. V. Bagot
		£10		ROSAMOND (63T)	A.K. Stothert
		£40	Match for yachts of 52 rating	SONYA	Mrs. G. Farley Turner
	3(I)	£10		BRITOMART	W.P. Burton
		£25	Handicap Match for yachts of 25 to 50 Tons	GAUNTLET (37T)	J.R. Payne
	3(I)	£10		VIERA (36T)	F & C Last
27.07.06	20		Ocean Match for prizes presented by Neil M. McWharrie	VIERA (36T)	F. and C. Last
				CAMELLIA (45T)	G.N.E. Hall-Sey
				AVEL III (36T)	G.C. Lomer
23.05.07	10	£80	Match for 23 Metre Class	WHITE HEATHER II	M.B. Kennedy
	10	£40	Match for 15 Metre Class	BRITOMART	W.P. Burton
		£15		SHIMMA	W.Yates
		£10		SONYA	Mrs. G. Turner-Farley
	10	£50	Presented by M.B. Kennedy for Handicap Match for yachts exceeding 50 Tons	CREOLE (54T)	Col. V. Bagot
		£25		ROSAMOND (63T)	A.K. Stothert
		£10		MERRYMAID (107T)	J.E. Terry
	10	£25	Presented by G. Terrell Esq. for Handicap Match for yachts of 25 to 50 Tons	CAMELLIA (45T)	G.N.E. Hall-Sey
		£10		NAN (29T)	C.H. Holland
01.06.07			Channel Match		
	3(0)	£50	Presented by A. Paget Esq. for yachts of A Class, schooners and yawls, exceeding 23 Metres	NAVAHOE (86T)	G.W. Watjen
		£20		CLARA (83T)	Herr Max Guilleaume
	3(0)	£100	Presented by T. Pim Esq. for the 23 Metre Class (75.4 rating)	WHITE HEATHER II	M.B. Kennedy
		£25		BRYNHILD	Sir J. Pender
	3(0)	£40	Handicap Match for yachts exceeding 50 Tons	MERRYMAID (107T)	J.E. Terry
		£15		ROSAMOND (63T)	A.K. Stothert
	3(I)	50gns	Presented by Sir George Leach for the 15 Metre. Class (49.2 rating)	SHIMMA	W. Yates
		£15		BRITOMART	W.P. Burton
		£10		MAYMON	G. Terrell
	3(I)	£25	Handicap Match for yachts of 25 to 50 Tons	GAUNTLET (37T)	J.R. Payne
		£10		CAMELLIA (43T)	G.N.E. Hall-Sey

Date	Course	Prizes		Winning Yachts'	Owners
11.06.08	10	Cup	Presented by HM The King for the 23 Metre Class	SHAMROCK	Sir T. Lipton
		£25		NYRIA	R.W.N. Young
	10	£60	Match for A Class Schooners and Yawls	SUSANNE (20.5 metres)	O. Huldschinsky
		£20		CICELY (23.25 metres)	C. Whitaker
	10	£40	Presented by M.B. Kennedy for the 15 Metre Class	BRITOMART	W.P. Burton
		£15		SHIMMA	J.R. Payne and A. Watson
		£25	Handicap Match for yachts of 35 to 55 Tons	MAYMON (46T)	G. Terrell
		£10		SENGA (35T)	Lorne Currie
15.06.08			Channel Match		
	3(0)	£80	Presented by T Pim Esq. for the 23 MetreClass	WHITE HEATHER II	M.B. Kennedy
		£25		BRYNHILD	Sir J. Pender
	3(0)	£70	Match for A Class Schooners	SUSANNE (20.5 metre)	O. Huldschinsky
		£20		CICELY (23.25 metre)	C. Whitaker
	3(I)	£40	Match for the 15 Metre Class	BRITOMART	W.P. Burton
		£5		SHIMMA	J.R. Payne and A. Watson
	3(I)	£25	Presented by A. Barclay Walker Esq. for Handicap Match for yachts of 25 to 55 Tons	CAMELLIA (45T)	G.N.E. Hall-Sey
		£10		MAYMON (46T)	G. Terrell
14.05.09	14	£80	Match for the 23 Metre Class	SHAMROCK	Sir T. Lipton
	14	£40	Presented by M B Kennedy Esq. for the 15 Metre Class	MARISKA	A.K. Stothert
		£20		VANITY	J R Payne, A E Watson and I H Benn
	14	£25	Presented by A. Paget Esq. for a Handicap Match for yachts of 35 to 55 Tons	CAMELLIA (43T)	G.N.E. Hall-Sey
		£10		SONYA (42T)	N.T. Kershaw
		£5		BLOODHOUND (40T)	Marquis of Ailsa
15.05.09	21	£50	Presented by C Arkcoll Esq. for the 23 Metre Class	WHITE HEATHER II	M.B. Kennedy
	21	£30	Match for yachts of the 15 Metre Class	OSTARA	W.P. Burton
		£10		VANITY	Messrs Payne, Watson and Benn
	21	£25	Handicap Match for yachts of 35 to 55 Tons	CAMELLIA (45T)	G.N.E. Hall-Sey
		£10		GAUNTLET (37T)	F. and C. Last
		£5		BLOODHOUND (40T)	Marquis of Ailsa
23.05.09			Channel Match		
	22(0)	£80	Presented by T Pim Esq. for the 23 Metre Class	WHITE HEATHER II	M.B. Kennedy
	22(I)	£35	Rait Memorial Cup for the 15 Metre Class	VANITY	Messrs Payne, Watson and Benn
		£20		OSTARA	W.P. Burton
	22(I)	£25	Presented by A. Paget Esq. Cup presented by Lord Brassey	CAMELLIA (45T)	G.N.E. Hall-Sey
		£10	Handicap Match for yachts of 35 to 55 Tons	BLOODHOUND (40T)	Marquis of Ailsa
		£5		SONYA (42T)	N.T. Kershaw
21.05.10	21	£50	Presented by C Arkcoll Esq. for the 23 Metre Class	SHAMROCK	Sir T. Lipton
		£20	Presented by A Paget Esq.	WHITE HEATHER II	M.B. Kennedy
	21	£40	Presented by Sir J. Pender for the 15 Metre Class	OSTARA	W.P. Burton
		£10		MARISKA	A.K. Stothert
		£5		TRITONIA	G.C. Lomer
		£30	Handicap Match for yachts of 35 to 65 Tons	BLOODHOUND (40T)	Marquis of Ailsa
	21	£10		GAUNTLET (37T)	F. and C. Last

Date	Course	Prizes		Winning Yachts'	Owners
02.06.10	10	£50	Cup presented by A Barclay-Walker Esq. for the 23 Metre Class	WHITE HEATHER II	M.B. Kennedy
	10	£40	Presented by M B Kennedy Esq. for the 15 Metre Class	MA' OONA	A. Paget
		£20		TRITONIA	G.C. Lomer
		£10		MARISKA	A.K. Stothert
	10	£30	Presented by A Paget Esq. for Handicap Match for yachts of 35 to 55 Tons	GAUNTLET (37T)	F. and C. Last
		£10		SONYA (42T)	N.T. Kershaw
04.06.10			Channel Match		
	3(0)	£80	Presented by T Pim Esq. for the 23 Metre Class	SHAMROCK	Sir T. Lipton
	3(I)	£40	For the 15 Metre Class	VANITY	Messrs Payne and Benn
		£20		OSTARA	W.P. Burton
	3I	Cup	Rait Memorial Cup for Handicap Match for yachts of 35 to 55 Tons	SONYA (42T)	N.T. Kershaw
		£10q		GAUNTLET (37T)	F. and C. Last
27.05.11	21	£50	Presented by C Arkcoll Esq. for yacht the 19 MetreClass	MARQUITA	A.K. Stothert
		£20		CORONA	Messrs Payne, Hennessy and Benn
	21	£40	Match for the 15 Metre Class	VANITY	Sir J. H. Campbell
		£10		JEANO	Col V. Bagot
	21	£30	Handicap Match for yachts of 35 to 75 Tons	CREOLE (54T)	A.L Pearse
		£10		CARINA (69T)	
07.06.11	10	£80	Match for the 19 Metre Class	MARIQUITA	A.K. Stothert
		£25		OCTAVIA	W.P. Burton
	10	£40	Match for the 15 Metre Class	VANITY	Messrs Payne and Benn
		£20		JEANO	Sir J. H. Campbell
	10	£30	Handicap Match for yachts of 35 to 70 Tons	BLOODHOUND (40T)	Marquis of Ailsa
		£10		ROSAMOND (63T)	C.C. Allom
		£5		SONYA (42T)	N.T. Kershaw
	14	£20	Handicap Match for yachts of 15 to 34 Tons	BINGO (23T)	J.W. Cook
10.06.11			Channel Match		
	3(0)	£80	Match for 19 Metre Class	NORADA	F. Milburn
		£25		OCTAVIA	W.P. Burton
	3(I)	£40	Match for 15 Metre Class	VANITY	Messrs Payne and Benn
		£20		MARISKA	Capt. The Hon. F.E. Guest
	3(I)	£10	Rait Memorial Cup for Handicap Match	SONYA (42T)	N.T. Kershaw
		£15		ONDA (75T)	Kerr-Smiley
		£5		JOYCE (75T)	S.G.L. Bradley
01.06.12	21	£80	Match for the 23 Metre Class	SHAMROCK	Sir T. Lipton
	21	£65	Match for the 19 Metre Class	NORADA	F. Milburn
		£20		OCTAVIA	W.P. Burton
	21	£40	Match for the15 Metre Class	VANITY	Messrs Payne and Benn
		£15		ISTRIA	C.C. Allom
	21	£30	Match for Handicap yachts of 35-75 Tons	BLOODHOUND (40T)	Marquis of Ailsa
		£10		CARINA (69T)	A.L. Pierse
		£5		CREOLE (54T)	Col. B. Bagot

Date	Course	Prizes		Winning Yachts'	Owners
11.06.12	10	£80	Match for the 23 Metre Class	WHITE HEATHER II	M.B. Kennedy
		£65	Match for the 19 Metre Class	MARQUITA	A.K. Stothert
		£20		CORONA	A. Paget and R. Hennessy
		£40	Match for the 15 Metre Class	VANITY	Messrs Payne and Benn
		£15		OSTARA	F. and C.H. Last
		£35	Handicap Match for yachts of 34 to 75 Tons	BLOODHOUND (40T)	Marquis of Ailsa
		£15		CARINA (69T)	A.L. Pierse
		£10		CREOLE (54T)	Col. V. Bagot
14.06.12			Channel Match		
	3(O)	£80	Match for A and 23 Metre Classes	WHITE HEATHER II	M.B. Kennedy
	3(O)	King's Cup	Match for the 19 Metre Class	MARQUITA	A.K. Stothert
		£25		OCTAVIA	W.P. Burton
	3(I)	Cup	Match for the 15 Metre Class	OSTARA	F. and C.H. Last
		£20		VANITY	Messrs Payne and Benn
	3(I)	Cup	Rait Memorial Cup for Handicap Match for yachts of 35 to 75 Tons	BLOODHOUND (40T)	Marquis of Ailsa
		£10		CARINA (69T)	A.L. Pierse
		£5		WEST WIND (47T)	P. Ashton
31.05.13			Channel Match		
	3(I)	£40	Match for 15 Metre Class	ISTRIA	C.C. Allom
	3(I)	Cup	Rait Memorial Cup Handicap Match for yachts of 35-75 Tons	CARIB (37T)	A.C. Messer
		£10		CARINA (67T)	A.L. Pierse
		£5		CREOLE (54T)	Col. V. Bagot
05.06.13			River Matches - Results not available		
07.06.13	21	£30	Handicap Match for yachts of 35-75 Tons	CARIB (37T)	A.E. Messer
		£10		BLOODHOUND (40T)	Marquis of Ailsa
		£5		CARINA (69T)	A.L. Pierse
01.08.13	23		A Class and Big Cutters Match	MARGHERITA	C. Whitaker
			Match for 15 Metre Class	PAMELA	R.G.L. Bradley
			Match for 12 Metre Class	ALACHIE	G. Coats
			Match for 10 Metre Class	PAMPERO	H. Nordhein
			Handicap Match for 35-75 Ton yachts	MA' OONA	F. and C.H. Last
04.06.14	24	£40	Match for 15 Metre Class	MAUDREY	W.B. Stamp
		£15		ISTRIA	Sir Charles Allom
		£40	Handicap Match for yachts of 35 to 70 Tons	WEST WIND (47T)	P. Ashton
		£15		SONYA (42T)	N.T. Kershaw
		£8		CAMELLIA (45T)	L. Mason
			Handicap Match for yachts of 15 to 35 Tons	EILEEN (19T)	A.C. Adams

Date	Course	Prizes		Winning Yachts'	Owners
06.06.14			Channel Match		
	3(I)	£40	Presented by C. Arkcoll Esq. for Match for 15 Metre Class	ISTRIA	Sir C. Allom
		£20		PAMELA	S.G.L. Bradley
		Cup	Rait Memorial Cup. Handicap Match for yachts of 35 to 70 Tons	MA' OONA	F. and C.H. Last
		£15		WEST WIND (47T)	P. Ashton
		£5		SONYA (42T)	N.T. Kershaw
30.07.14	23		Match for 15 Metre Class (33 miles)	PAMELA	S.G.L. Bradley
				THE LADY ANNE	G. Coats
			Match for 10 Metre Class (22 miles)	IREX	H. Marzetti
		£6	Match for 8 Metre Class	IRENE	I.F. Sharman-Crawford
		£3		VENTANA	A.H.J. Hamilton
	23	£5	Match for 7 Metre Class	STRATHENDRICK	Sir A.E. Orr-Ewing
		£2		PINASTER	Capt. R. Sloane-Stanley
			Match for 6 Metre Class	VANDA	R.T. Dixon
				STELLA	A. Maudsley
			Handicap Match for yachts	LANKA	Mr. Scott
			of 35-70 Tons (33 miles)	MA' OONA	N.T. Kershaw
				SONYA (47T)	Marquis of Ailsa
		£12	Handicap Match for yachts of 10-20 Tons	BLOODHOUND (40T)	W.J.M. Burton
			Match for Redwing Class	JEAN	
				PARAQUET	
			Match for Seaview Mermaid Class	RED GAUNTLET	
				NAOMI	
				VIOLETTA	
31.07.14	23		Handicap Match for yachts over 70 Tons	ZINITA (92T)	M. de Rothschild
				SUMURUM	Lord Sackville
			Handicap Match for yachts of 10 to 30 Tons (33 miles)	JEAN	W.J.M. Burton
					S.G.L. Bradley
			Match for 15 Metre Class	PAMELA	Sir C. Allen
				ISTRIA	G. Coats
			Match for 10 Metre Class	THE LADY ANNE	H.H. Marzetti
			Match for 8 Metre Class	IREX	F.A. Richards
				GARRAVEEN	Sir Ralph Gore
			Match for 7 Metre Class	THE TRUANT	Sir A.E. Orr-Ewing
				STRATHENDRICK	
				ANITRA	Capt. R. Sloane-Stanley
			Match for 6 Metre Class	PINASTER	A. Mandslay
				STELLA	R.T. Dixon
				VANDA	A.D. Grigg
				BUBBLE	

Appendix 8

Circular sent to members concerning Sailing Rules

Royal Thames Yacht Club
Albermarle Street
London

13th December 1881

Sir,

The time is approaching when the Sailing Rules of this Club will undergo the usual revision by the Committee prior to their recommending any alterations to the Annual General Meeting to be held in March 1882.

The Committee still bear in mind the assurance they gave in May last to Racing Owners, to the effect that they would favourably entertain any proposals for amendments in the Laws which would further the convenience and interests of Yacht Owners; and I am now directed to invite you to offer any suggestions you think would be conducive to the further encouragement and promotion of Yacht Racing at the Thames. Any suggestions you may make will be attentively considered, and should reach me not later than 15th January next.

Various influences have been used from time to time to induce the Committee to advise the adoption, in their entirety, of the Rules of the Yacht Racing Association, but it appears to the Committee that several of those Rules are ill adapted for river sailing matches; and moreover the Association are constantly altering their Rules.

The Sailing Laws of the Royal Thames Yacht Club, following, as they have, the progress of yacht building and sailing, are the product of the successful experience of more than half a century; and the Committee, as our Executive body annually appointed, would not themselves be justified in recommending that such laws should be sacrificed to a set of Rules not five years old, and which can hardly be deemed satisfactory, judging from the various alterations in them, which the Association are constantly making, such, for instance, as the Rule of Measurement.

However, if, in response to this circular, it appears to be the wish of the majority of the Club that the Rules of the Yacht Racing Association should be adopted, either partially or in their entirety, the Committee will be prepared, at the Annual General Meeting, to submit a resolution to that effect, and to take the sense of the meeting on the question.

I am, Sir
Your obedient Servant,

H.W. Mellis
Secretary

Appendix 9

List of Measurement Formulae

1. THAMES MEASUREMENT (TONNAGE)
$$\frac{(L - B) \times B^2}{188}$$

2. YRA OF 1880 (TONNAGE)
$$\frac{(L + B)^2 \times B}{1730}$$

3. YRA OF 1887 (TONNAGE)
$$\frac{L \times S}{6000}$$

4. YRA OF 1896 (LINEAR)
$$\frac{L + B + \frac{3}{4}Gs + \frac{1}{2}\sqrt{S}}{2}$$

5. YRA OF 1901 (LINEAR)
$$\frac{L + B + \frac{3}{4}G + 4d + \frac{1}{2}\sqrt{S}}{2.1}$$

6. INTERNATIONAL RULE OF 1906 (LINEAR)
$$\frac{L + B + \frac{3}{4}G + 3d + \frac{1}{3}\sqrt{S} - F}{2}$$

L = Length   B = Beam
G = Chain Girth   Gs = Skin Girth
d = Girth Difference (Gs-G)   F = Freeboard
S = Sail Area

Appendix 10

Ladies elected to membership of the Club 1868-1918

Years Of Membership	Name	Yacht
1874-1877	Baroness Meyer de Rothschild	CZARINA Schooner, 210 Tons
1875-1887	Mrs C M Hamilton (Mrs C M Laurie from 1881)	DIANA Schooner, 84 Tons
1875-1882	Mrs C A Gamble	CECILE Screw Schooner, 278 Tons
1881-1896	Madam de Falbe (Mrs Gerard Leigh from 1883)	THRASHER Screw Schooner, 33 Tons CHASALIE Screw Schooner, 514 Tons
1898-1904	Mrs Edith Deakin	FLEUR DE LYS Screw Lugger, 40 Tons
1900-1912	Mrs Robert Goelet of New York	NAHMA Twin Screw Schooner, 1806 Tons
1905-*	Mrs G Turner Fairley	SONYA Cutter, 35 Tons
1907-*	Miss Marion Kennedy	CASSIOPEIA Screw Schooner, 205 Tons
1907-* 1909-*	Miss Isabel N Napier & Mrs T Valentine Smith	LADY BLANCHE Screw Schooner, 404 Tons
1909-1916	Duchess of Westminster	SORAIS Cutter, 9 Tons
1912-*	Madam Tereschenko of St.Petersburg	IOLANDA Screw Schooner, 1822 Tons
1912-*	Mrs Croft	ORIANA Screw Schooner, 172 Tons
1912-1914	Mrs Frances Francis	BONA Yawl, 123 Tons
1914-*	Lady Alexander Paget	WEGA Screw Schooner, 273 Tons

* These ladies were still members in 1918.

Appendix 11

Notice calling a Special General Meeting on 11 December 1913

Royal Thames Yacht Club
80 Piccadilly, W.
November 30, 1913
Secretary' s Office
Telegrams: 'Amphitrite' , May, London
Telephone No. Gerrard 5913

NOTICE

Whereas Mr. William Tranter, a member of the Royal Thames Yacht Club, took part in the International Regatta held at Kiel, in the month of June, 1912, sailing as the representative of the Royal Thames Yacht Club; And whereas it has been alleged that Mr. William Tranter incurred debts there amounting to the sum of £25 or thereabouts, which he did not then pay and has not since paid: And whereas application has been made to the Royal Thames Yacht Club to discharge such debts:

And whereas at the direction of the Committee written application has been made to Mr. William Tranter to state whether or not the said allegation is true, but such application has been ignored:

Take Notice that a SPECIAL GENERAL MEETING of the members of the Royal Thames Yacht Club will be held on THURSDAY, the 11th day of DECEMBER, 1913, at the Clubhouse, 80, Piccadilly, W., at 4.45 o'clock in the afternoon, when it will be proposed:-
a) That Mr. William Tranter has been guilty of conduct which, in the opinion of this meeting, calls for his expulsion from the Royal Thames Yacht Club, and that he be expelled therefrom;
b) That the said debts incurred by Mr. William Tranter at the Kiel Regatta, in so far as they were incurred when he was representing the Royal Thames Yacht Club, be, for the credit of the Club, paid out of the funds of the Club.

By order,

J.E.H. ORR
Secretary

Appendix 12

Letter to Mr. Joseph Powell - potential Club Manager

Mr. Joseph Powell
Club Master
Caledonian United Services Club
Edinburgh
22nd April, 1870

Sir,
I have this day presented your reply (with Testimonials) to the Advertisement before the Committee of the Royal Thames Yacht Club and I am instructed to inform you that your app-lication will be entertained provided an interview with you could be arranged on Wednesday next 27th inst. At 4.30 p.m.

I may inform you briefly, that the Royal Thames Yacht Club, numbering between 700-800 members, require a Caterer and Manager, who for an allowance of about £100 per month, would be required to find pay-wages and board, and provide (proportionately), with liveries some 25 servants, including 7 or 8 female domestics; the Manager would also have to pay for the gas, coals and washing, and to keep the kitchen utensils and Club furniture in repair; generally to superintend the Establishment, and to cater for the Members in the best possible manner.

He would be entitled to all receipts accruing from dinners and breakfasts, etc. taken in the Coffee Room; wines, minerals, cigars, also billiards, cards and bedrooms of which latter there are seven for the use of Members. These items would be according to the Tariff agreed to by the Committee and which assimilates to others leading Clubs. The foregoing are a few preliminaries, and if you should consider them worth investigating, the Committee will be most happy for you to examine the books, etc.

In conclusion, I may state, that the number of Members and friends daily visiting the Club, range from 100 to 150; and the Dining Members average from 25 to 35, the latter, of course, could considerably increase, provided the cuisine and general management were carried out to the satisfaction of the Members.

Your answer by return of Post, will oblige Sir,
Yours very obediently

P.C. Stuart Grant, Secretary.

Appendix 13

Letter to Members about 6 St. James Square

ROYAL THAMES YACHT CLUB.

7, Albemarle Street, W.
July 15th, 1910.

Sir,

I beg to inform you that a SPECIAL GENERAL MEETING of this Club will be held here on Tuesday, the 26th inst., at 5 p.m., when the following Resolutions will be proposed by the General Committee:-

1. That on account of the increased membership of the Club and the satisfactory condition of its finance, the time has now arrived for the Club to seek new and more suitable premises.

2. That the Trustees of the Club be empowered to accept the terms offered for the surrender of the lease of 7, Albemarle Street, from the 24th June, 1910, and to sign a lease for 21 years for No. 6, St. James's Square, and that the details of the actual agreements be carried out by the Flag Officers and the Chairman of General Committee.

Rent, Rates and Taxes, 7 Albemarle Street
£1,450

Rent, Rates and Taxes, 6 St. James' Square
£2,400

Estimated Income from 3 Bedrooms, 7 Albemarle Street
£160

Estimated Income from 11 Bedrooms, 6 St. James' Square
£660

Estimated reduction of Annual Repairs Bill
£150

Present Balance of Income over Expenditure
£400

Estimated Expense of Moving and of Installation
£317

A guarantee Fund has been provided by certain Members of the Club to meet contingencies.

The committee would welcome the written views of Members who will be unable to attend the Meeting.

Any Member desirous of inspecting No. 6, St. James's Square, can do so by first applying to the Secretary, Royal Thames Yacht Club, who will notify him of the hours during which the house is open for inspection.

Sir,
Yours faithfully,

(Signed) EDWARD HILDER,
Chairman of Committee.

Appendix 14

ROYAL THAMES YACHT CLUB.

81, PICCADILLY, W.
January 19th, 1911

Sir,
I beg to inform you that a Special General Meeting of this Club will be held at 80, Piccadilly, on Tuesday, the 31st of January, at 5 p.m., when the following Resolution will be proposed by the General Committee:-
   'That the Trustees of the Club be empowered to exercise their option to take a lease of Nos. 80 and 81, Piccadilly, for a term of 13 years from the 2nd of January, 1911, at the annual rent of £1,500, upon the terms set out in an Agreement dated the 2nd of January, 1911, made between Mr. W.L.A.B. BURDETT-COUTTS and themselves.'

Plans of the proposed alterations, showing the accommodation which will be available for members if the recommendation of the General Committee are carried out, are appended herewith.

Particulars of the alternative scheme for building on the adjacent site in Stratton Street will be submitted at this Meeting. The Committee do not however recommend this scheme.

I am, Sir,
Yours faithfully,
(Signed) EDWARD HILDER,
Chairman of the General Committee

NOTE. -Members can inspect No. 80, Piccadilly, on any week-day between the hours of 2 and 4 p.m.

Appendix 15

Subject to satisfactory financial investigations and report on both sides recommend:

1. A date to be fixed on which all Admiralty Warrants to wear New Thames colours are to be revoked.

2. All yacht owners belonging to the New Thames and not to the Royal Thames, to have the option of a Certificate of Membership of the Royal Thames as from the above fixed date (these members will pay the higher rate of subscription from the next succeeding 1st January).

3. On the above fixed date the New Thames Club to be legally transferred to the Royal Thames. (It will be called herein the 'Gravesend House' of the Royal Thames).

4. All members of the Royal Thames at the date of transfer are to be entitled to use the Gravesend House on payment of an extra annual subscription of 3 guineas without ballot.

5. All members of the New Thames at the date of transfer can use the London House on payment of the extra current rate of subscription without ballot.

6. After the date of transfer all Candidates will be balloted for at the London House and will have the option of using either or both of the Club Houses by payment of the respective subscriptions, but no yacht owners shall pay less than 5 guineas.

7. After the date of transfer the Gravesend House is to be managed by a Sub Committee of which a fixed proportion must be members of the London House also, and a certain number of the members are to be nominated by the General Committee. The remainder of the Gravesend Sub Committee being elected at the London House and according to its rules.

Appendix 16

ROYAL THAMES YACHT CLUB.

Proposed Agreement between the Royal Thames Yacht Club and the Royal London Yacht Club, submitted by the Flag Officers for the consideration of the Committee.

The RLYC to cease to maintain a Clubhouse in London and to hoist its flag at its house in Cowes, which shall be managed by the Committee of the RLYC and kept open by them at such times as may be determined in agreement with the Committee of the RTYC for the use of members of both Clubs.

At the least 140 fully subscribing members of the RLYC to be nominated for membership of the RTYC and balloted for in the months of April or May, 1909, according to the laws of the RTYC. Members of the RLYC elected to the RTYC at such ballot or ballots to be hereinafter described in this agreement as 'L' Members of the RTYC, and to pay an annual subscription of Seven Guineas each to the RTYC.

Present and future members of the RTYC to have the full use of the Cowes house, and to enjoy the same privileges as members of the RLYC, except those of flying the RLYC colours and voting at its meetings, but to be under no liability in respect of the RLYC or the Cowes house.

Should the RTYC desire to hold races at Cowes, the same to be sailed under the flag of the RTYC, which shall be temporarily hoisted.

The RTYC to allow towards the expenses of the house at Cowes a sum of Three Guineas annually in respect of each 'L' member of the RTYC so long as he remains a fully subscribing member of the RTYC and the Cowes house is kept up, and to allow a similar sum under the same conditions for each future member of the RTYC who may have been proposed for election by an 'L' member, and to pay a sum of Half-a-Guinea per head annually for the same purpose for every other fully subscribing member of the RTYC.

A grant of One Guinea per head for each 'L' member to be forthwith made by the RTYC to the RLYC towards the decoration and furnishing of the house at Cowes.

The Committee of the RLYC to be granted facilities for holding its meetings at the RTYC Clubhouse.

The RTYC to be represented on the Committee of the RLYC by the Chairman of the RTYC Committee and two members selected by the RTYC Committee.

The present Flag Officers of the RLYC to be appointed to the Sailing Committee of the RTYC.

Mr. H H BARTLETT and Mr. C T CAYLEY having been nominated as members of the RTYC to nevertheless be considered as 'L' members under this agreement.

The Chronicles
of the
ROYAL THAMES YACHT CLUB

Volume III

1919-1998

Introduction

This third and final volume covers a period of almost eighty years and is therefore covering a significantly longer period than the previous two. The original intention was to write it as two volumes with the break point taken at the rebuilding of the Knightsbridge Clubhouse which started in 1961. To cover separately the period from 1962 to the present time would have raised two problems. Firstly, it would have been an unnecessarily slim volume and secondly, to try and put 'history' into a time perspective one should view it from a point some twenty or thirty years beyond the events under review. In addition, in a work of this nature, it would not be appropriate to write in detail about those members of the Club who, in the 1960s and 1970s, were officers and committee members and who are still very active in Club affairs. It was these factors that influenced the decision to write a single third volume with the fourth quarter of the twentieth century being covered mainly by key events and in general terms.

This volume starts at the time when those who had fought in what is now recognised as World War I returned to what was hoped would be a 'land fit for heroes'. This illusory bubble soon burst and the streets of our cities were filled with unemployed ex-servicemen busking and begging in an attempt to 'make ends meet'. The general strike of 1926 and the Wall Street 'crash' of 1929 led to the period of high unemployment and economic depression that affected people of all classes. None who came home from war in 1919 would have believed that a second World conflict would have started a mere 20 years later - but it did. When World War II ended in 1945 a further nine years were to pass before 'rationing' of basic commodities ended and the people of this country could look forward to years of relative World peace and freedom from restrictions , though inflation, little experienced in the 1920s and 30s, has at times been a destabilising influence during the past 30 years.

In the fields of technology and medicine the developments have been at an unprecedented pace. Air travel is no longer available to just a privileged few, virtually everyone can enjoy its benefits. Since 1945 the evolution of computers has created a completely new work ethos, while the invention of synthetic material has been equally vital. The ability of the medical profession to control disease and perform life saving 'spare part' surgery has greatly increased life expectancy.

For the Royal Thames these remarkable changes have influenced greatly the affairs of the Club. On the water the Club has based its racing entirely in the Solent and controlled its regattas from Ryde or Cowes. Racing has been provided for all classes of yacht from big handicappers to small keelboats. Over the years the Club's regattas became open to all yachtsmen, not just members. Over the past thirty years the Club has become expert in the management of national and international events and has

been involved in three challenges for the America's Cup. While in the 1920s nearly 100 members owned yachts over 100 tons TM, today's members sail smaller boats built from materials unknown in the earlier years and fitted with navigation and communication equipment based on the latest technology. While the Club has maintained its lifelong involvement in yacht racing, the past 40 years have seen the Club recognise the importance of organised cruises and rallies, initially in the UK, but more recently worldwide.

It was clear in 1919 that the Piccadilly Clubhouse lacked the space and facilities needed if the Club was to develop as was envisaged. In 1923 a new Clubhouse was acquired when a lease was taken on the spacious and elegant Hyde Park House in Knightsbridge, the freehold being acquired shortly afterwards. This move provided members with greatly improved facilities but it also created many financial problems that successive Flag Officers and Committees struggled to solve, such as the spiralling inflation of the 1970s. The much-debated decision to demolish Hyde Park House in 1961 and redevelop the site once again provided improved facilities for members but it coincided with far-reaching cultural changes in society. In spite of these many difficulties the club has been able to survive and maintain its stature in the world of yachting by adapting without discarding sound tradition. Its membership numbers have been kept in the 1300-1500 band, its finances which have reached near crisis point at times, have always recovered and have strength and stability today in spite of the profound effect on members resources caused by depression, recession and losses at Lloyds. Socially, the biggest change has been the gradual and at times much opposed integration of Ladies into the Club membership and into the management of the Club.

Overall it has been Club policy to maintain evolutionary progress rather than a revolutionary change, as it sought to keep pace with the changes in yachting and society over the past two and a quarter centuries. Even so, a potentially radical change was proposed in December 1961 which was that when the Club re-opened in 1963 after redevelopment, it should be re-named the Royal Cumberland Fleet - this was put to the membership as a Resolution at the A.G.M. in the following April and defeated.

In compiling these volumes of chronicles, the debt due to Douglas Phillis-Birt's excellent work in writing 'The Cumberland Fleet' to mark the club's bicentenary, has been acknowledged several times. It is to his credit that he happily accepted to write when others had turned down the opportunity, i.e. E Keble Chatterton and Major B Heckstall Smith (in 1934) and Hugh Somerville (in 1962). It is hoped that these volumes will be found of interest to members, will provide a record of the affairs of the Royal Thames Yacht Club and will be deemed worthy of such a distinguished and important institution.

I
Officers of the Club

Flag Officers

Whereas there were only 10 members who served as Flag Officers during the 50 years covered by the previous volume, no less than 60 members have served in that capacity between 1919 and 1998. The pattern from 1919 until 1945 was little changed from that of earlier years with just seven members being Flag Officers. In the post-war era there were radical changes and many more members became involved. There were two principle reasons for the rapid increase in numbers. Firstly, from 1946, the appointment of members of the Royal Family as Commodores (except for the four years when Elmer Ellsworth-Jones was in office) which led to the appointment of a second Rear Commodore in 1953 in order to have available members to share the Flag Officer duties. Secondly, the term of office for each Flag Officer was no longer determined by death or resignation but was prescribed by the Rules of the Club which provided for three years (and exceptionally four years) for the Vice Commodore and generally two years for the Rear Commodore, although this did vary from between one and three years for short periods. Over the past 20 years it has become the practice to assign one Rear Commodore to oversee Sailing activities and one to House affairs. Even more recently in 1997 the rules were amended to allow for the appointment of a third Rear Commodore. This Officer has been asked to concern himself with membership and finance.

The Club emerged from the first World War with **Theodore Pim** as Commodore. He was coming towards the end of his long years of service as a Flag Officer of the Club and his most important work then was to encourage the members to support the move of the Clubhouse from Piccadilly to Knightsbridge. This was finally approved by the March 1923 AGM. In October of that year he informed the Committee that he wished to resign. He died 6 years later. Information about him and his yacht Rosabelle is given in Appendix 1.

Giving Theodore Pim outstanding support throughout the war was **Lord Queenborough**, the son of Lord Alfred Paget. It was he who chaired the historic AGM in March 1923 and achieved the final agreement to the move to Knightsbridge and it was he who succeeded Theodore Pim as Commodore from March 1924. Like his father, Lord Queenborough was to serve as Flag Officer of the Club for over 40 years. He had already served as Vice Commodore for 13 years when he was elected Commodore - an office he would have held continuously for 32 years but for the decision in 1932 to invite HRH The Prince of Wales to become Commodore and follow in his grandfather's footsteps. Lord Queenborough graciously stood down to enable the Prince of Wales to accept the office of Commodore. A special General Meeting of the Club in June 1932 elected Lord Queenborough Vice Commodore.

The death of King George V in 1935 and the accession (as King Edward VIII) by the Prince of Wales, led to Lord Queenborough once again being elected Commodore in 1936. He was to remain in office for a further 10 years until Earl Mountbatten succeeded him. Even then his service to the Club was not at an end since the members unanimously supported his election to Vice Commodore. Lord Queenborough had given quite exceptional service to the Club but his life was drawing to a close. He died in September 1949. The generosity he had shown throughout his long years of membership of the Club was echoed in his bequests to the Club which included the sum of £5000 as well as several fine marine paintings and silver trophies.

J. Somerville Highfield was elected to membership of the Club in 1907 and at that time he was Engineer in Chief of the Metropolitan Electric Supply Co. and owner of the cutter CLODAGH. His later yachts were the cutter DORINA (from 1923) and the twin screw schooner ANNE from 1935. He was to serve on the General and Sailing Committees and was Chairman of Committees in 1922 and 1923. Elected Rear Commodore in 1924, he was once again elected Chairman of Committees in 1925 - the first flag officer to hold that office - but he was particularly well experienced in the management of the Club; a quality needed to guide the Club successfully into its new Knightsbridge Clubhouse. Like several of his contemporaries he was to give the rest of his life to the service of the Club. He was Rear Commodore through to 1936 when he succeeded Lord Queenborough as Vice Commodore, a post he held until his death in September 1945.

J S Highfield's election to Vice Commodore in 1936 brought into the office of Rear Commodore **Hugh F. Paul** who had become a member of the Club in 1915, at which time he was Rear Commodore of the Royal Harwich Yacht Club. His yachts included the cutter CHIONE (42 Tons) and the yacht SUMURUM (92 Tons), but his best known yacht was the 'J' class Bermudan rigged cutter ASTRA (164 Tons) in which he competed throughout the 1930s. He had completed 10 years service as Rear Commodore when he was re-elected at the AGM on 26 March 1946; sadly, just a week later, the General Committee was informed of his death. He, together with Lord Queenborough and J S Highfield, had served together as the Club's Flag Officers for 10 years. In particular they served throughout the six years of World War II and were unstinting in their devotion to service of the Club, rarely missing a Committee meeting and successfully ensuring that

The One-Ton Cup of the Circle de la Voile de Paris.

the Club survived the many problems that wartime bombing and austerity brought.

In January 1936 there was a proposal that King Edward VIII should be invited to become Admiral of the Club, should the rules of the Club be amended to include that office. Nothing came of this proposal; indeed it was not until the AGM held on 29 October 1969 that a resolution was carried to amend the rules to allow for the election of an Admiral. A year later the first holder of the office of Admiral of the Cumberland Fleet was to be **Earl Mountbatten** who had been Commodore in succession to Lord Queenborough in 1946. Although Earl Mountbatten's diplomatic and naval duties prevented him from having any direct involvement in the management of the Club, he maintained a close and constant contact with the Club and was deeply interested in its affairs. His tragic murder at the hands of IRA bombers in 1979 was felt deeply by everyone.

The number of members who have served as Flag Officers in the past 50 years is considerable and none were in office for a total of more than 6 years (except HRH the Prince of Wales and HRH the Duke of York who, in succession, have been Commodore since 1974). References to the many Flag Officers who have been in office during the past 50 years are made in the appropriate sections of this volume. One unfortunate feature of the early 1960s was that two Rear Commodores died only weeks after their election. Captain R St. A Malleson, AFC RN was elected Rear Commodore in April 1960 and died in July as the result of a car accident while Sir Geoffrey Lowles, who was elected in April 1962, died in June of that year.

Cup Bearers

In 1919 this ancient office was held by **Adrian Hope** but his early death necessitated the election of a new holder of the office at the AGM in March 1920. This was **John Ferguson** who remained in office until 1935 when illness forced him to resign and be succeeded by **Albert Morson** (whose portrait hangs in the Queenborough Room). At the time of his election as Cup Bearer Albert Morson was the senior member of the Club (having been elected in 1884). Following his death in October 1939 **Allan Messer**, who was one of the Club's Trustees, became Cup Bearer in March 1940 but resigned two years later and was succeeded by **Captain Ion Hamilton-**

Benn who, like Albert Morson, was to become the senior member (No 1) of the Club. He served as Cup Bearer for far longer than any other member in the twentieth Century, having been elected in March 1942 and remaining in office until his death in September 1961 at the age of 97. It was in 1957, during his period of office, that the practice of presenting trophies to prize winners at Regattas ceased and was replaced by their presentation at the annual Laying Up Dinner. Ion Hamilton-Benn, who succeeded to a Baronetcy shortly after his election to office, was a distinguished RNVR officer during the first World War and commanded a group of ML's during the operations to block Zeebrugge and Ostend in April-May 1918 (see Appendix 2). His successor as Cup Bearer was **G. Glynn Terrell** who was elected in April 1962 but died 13 months later. Glynn Terrell had been a very active member of the Club and had twice served as Chairman of Committees. He in turn was succeeded by **Sir Malcolm Hilbery** who served only a little longer, dying in September 1965. Since that date the office has been held by senior members of the Club who were also former Flag Officers: **Commodore Colin Campbell** (10 years), **Robert Garnham** (10 years), **F A (Sandy) Haworth** (4 years), **Brigadier John Constant** (4 years) and since 1993 **John Foot**. By 1984 it had long been apparent that combining prize giving (involving many members who were not Club members) with the Laying Up Dinner (which is very much an occasion for members only) was unsatisfactory, especially since the AGM had been changed from April to October in 1968. With this latter change it became the practice to hold the Laying Up Dinner on the night before the AGM in October and it was thus an occasion when the Vice Commodore's speech should be able to include topics specifically for members' ears only. It was decided, therefore, to hold a separate dinner in November each year dedicated solely to prize-giving.

Trustees

The responsibilities of the Trustees have varied little over the years but the Club is always in their debt for the wisdom and experience they bring to bear when major issues are being debated by the Committee, especially matters relating to the property. There appears to be no permanent record of the many officers who have been appointed a Trustee of the Club. This omission is now provided for by the list given in Appendix 3.

Patrons

Throughout the years covered by this volume the Club has been honoured by Royal Patronage. Until his death in 1936 the Patron was **HM King George V** whose love of sailing in his famous yacht **Britannia** is part of yachting history. The March 1936 Annual General Meeting was chaired by Lord Queen-borough. Instead of embarking on the agenda he spoke with great depth of feeling about the recent death of the King, a death coming so soon after the world-wide celebration of his Silver Jubilee. He also spoke with great optimism about the future reign of King Edward VIII, an optimism no one could believe was so soon to be undermined. Lord Queenborough ended his opening remarks to the AGM by recording that *'we have also this year to mourn the loss of Admirals of the Fleet Lord Jellicoe and Lord Beatty, both honorary members of this Club'.*

With the abdication of King Edward VIII, his successor **HM King George VI** became Patron and was to remain so throughout World War II until his death in 1952. The Committee then asked the Commodore, Earl Mountbatten, if he would enquire whether HM Queen Elizabeth II would accept the office of Patron or alternatively whether the Queen and HRH the Duke of Edinburgh might become joint Patrons. In November 1952, the **Duke of Edinburgh** agreed to become Patron of the Club, has remained in office since that date and has maintained a strong link with the Club, not least through his passionate interest in yacht racing at Cowes.

The custom of seeking patronage from other members of the Royal family as well as members of other European Royal families has continued through to the present day. In 1939 the Committee would have been thankful that they did not have the problem faced in 1914 when the Royal list included the Kaiser.

Chairman of Committees

The practice of electing a Chairman and (from 1926) a Deputy Chairman of Committees from the elected members of the General Committee of Management continued through to the 1970s (with certain exceptions). When the office of chairman was first created in 1868, the holder quite literally chaired both the General and Sailing Committees as well as Sub Committees. By the 1920s such a task would have been impossible for one member to undertake and his normal responsibilities, though still considerable, were usually limited to chairmanship of the General Committee and the House and Finance Committee; the Sailing Committee was chaired by a Flag Officer, frequently the Rear Commodore, while Sub Committees appointed a chairman from their members. Continuity in office was important, but the rule requiring one third of the General Committee members to retire each year limited the length of service to a maximum of three years. When possible, continuity was achieved by a member serving for two years as Deputy and one year as Chairman or vice versa.

The exceptions to the custom of electing the Chairman from the members of the General Committee occurred in 1925 and 1939 when J. S. Highfield and H. F. Paul were elected while serving as Vice and Rear Commodore respectively. While these elections took place without comment, those made in December 1970 (when the Vice Commodore and a Rear Commodore were elected as Chairman and Deputy chairman) were challenged as being in contravention of Rule 12. The Committee, however, disagreed and decided that both elected and ex-officio (i.e. Flag Officers) members of the General Committees were eligible for election. In more recent years it has been the custom to elect the Vice Commodore and the senior Rear Commodore as Chairman and Deputy, the concept of Chairman of Committees having been set aside. A full list of members who have served as Chairman and Deputy Chairman is given in Appendix 4.

One member who served both as Chairman and Deputy between 1931 and 1933, Percy T Dean, was the holder of the Victoria Cross; the award being given in recognition of his exceptional gallantry during the operation to block the U Boat base at Zeebrugge in April 1918. An account of Dean's part in the operation is given in Appendix 5. It is based on the record included in John Winton's book 'The Victoria Cross at Sea'.

Treasurer

The office of Treasurer was filled from 1823-63 but then discontinued. A Treasurer was appointed during periods of the 1960s and 1970s when financial problems became extreme. In May 1965 the House and Finance Sub Committee

The Coupe de France Trophy.

recommended *'that Mr J.B.P. Williamson should be appointed experimentally to the post of Treasurer with the duties of keeping an eye on the Club's accounting'* this recommendation was approved by the General Committee but the appointment was not made permanent. Again, in September 1972, the General Committee agreed in principle that a Treasurer should be appointed *'as this would give continuity to the House and Finance Sub Committee since the Treasurer did not have to stand for election every three years as did the other members of the House and Finance Sub Committee'*. Mr P.C.C. Hunter was elected to the General Committee in October 1972 and appointed to the House and Finance Sub Committee in November to monitor financial matters during his three years as a member of that Sub Committee. In October 1976 he was formerly elected to be Treasurer of the Club, a post he held for two further years.

Secretary

In 1919 Captain John Orr was still in office as Secretary and continued his long, successful period of service until the end of 1925 by which time the Club was well established in its new Clubhouse in Knightsbridge. During the next 55 years no less than 14 Secretaries were appointed of which only four served for five years or more - not the best recipe for the continuity of service which is so important for the effective management of the Club. Since the Club Officers and General Committee were particularly thorough in their selection procedures, it would seem that for some Secretaries, either the Club did not suit them or the reverse situation obtained. There were occasions inevitably when ill-health precipitated an early retirement. For most, their departure was in wholly amicable circumstances starting with Captain John Orr whose 17 years as Secretary included active service during World War I. He submitted his resignation in October 1925 but was asked to remain in office until a successor was appointed in April 1926 and was further asked to be available in a consultative capacity for a further 'term'. Richard Warry was another long serving Secretary, completing over 10 years including the whole of World War II, by the time he stood down in July 1945. The next three years became complicated. Captain T B Brunton DSC*, RN followed Richard Warry but ill-health affected his work and he felt obliged to resign only 11 months after his appointment. During that 11 months Mr R G B Brown was appointed Catering Manager of the Club in December 1945. When the Assistant Secretary Mr Mumford died in March 1946, Brown was given that additional post, only to be asked to 'cover' for the office of Secretary for the 5 months following Captain Brunton's premature resignation. In November that year Mr Brown was formally appointed Secretary but it was evident that his extensive responsibilities were affecting his health and he was forced to take a period of rest during 1947. Early in 1948 the Committee decided to appoint two joint Secretaries, Mr Brown being responsible for the 'hotel' services and Air Vice Marshall Sir Douglas Harries for membership, administration and sailing. This somewhat unusual situation lasted for five months only and Mr Brown resigned in July 1948.

Sir Douglas Harries was probably the most respected and most successful of the Secretaries in the post-war period. The terms of his appointment as Joint Secretary (at £1200 p.a. compared with the £600 p.a. salary paid in 1945) were to say the least unusual. The appointment was for a maximum of ten years and there was to be no increase in salary during his appointment! In July 1953 he let it be known that he wished to retire and a Sub Committee was appointed to seek a new Secretary. In the event such an appointment was not made and by January 1954 he had agreed to continue in office *provided his resignation would be accepted without question when he did wish to resign'*. Such an acceptance was forthcoming late in 1957 and Colonel Neville Blair was appointed as his successor in April 1958.

Neville Blair was to be in office for seven and a half years, including the difficult and stressful years covering the redevelopment of 60 Knightsbridge. With his departure at the end of 1965 began a period of over eleven years which saw the appointment of no less than six Secretaries, the first of whom, Major General F H Brooke, was unable to take up his appointment due to ill-health. Group Captain A J Trumble left after two years due to changed personal circumstance. Mr Jack Finch, who had served the Club for many years both in Knightsbridge and at Shore House, was the Assistant Secretary when Group Captain Trumble resigned. He was appointed Secretary in succession but his duties were only administrative; the management of the building, catering, bar and bedrooms being the responsibility of the Club Manager. When appointed Secretary, Mr Finch was already approaching the age for retirement and after only a few months his continuous poor health made it necessary to appoint another Secretary, Air Vice Marshall W F Beckwith. Within a year he had left and Lt. Col. D. W. Browne, who was to stay for over three and a half years, became Secretary. In September 1973, both the Secretary and the Club Manager left the Club and the Committee decided that the next Secretary to be appointed should carry the responsibility of a Chief Executive. Accordingly Captain Keith Stobbs was appointed in February 1974. In the last quarter of 1976 the Catering Manager resigned, the Chief Accountant departed and the Secretary was to leave in March 1977. Faced by these tumultuous circumstances, the Flag Officers and the General Committee turned to Mr E I (Ricky) Hamilton-Parks, a member of the Club

since 1960 who had already been Chief Race Officer since December 1969 and who had been much involved in the 'future policy plans' for the Club and the more cost effective use of the Clubhouse. Mr Hamilton-Parks was appointed Chief Executive of the Club in March 1977 and was asked to remain until the Club's summer closure period at the end of July. By June he had agreed to continue in office for 'an unspecified period'. This proved to be until February 1981, at which time he handed over his duties and left to undergo heart surgery. His contribution, together with that of other key members of the Club, led to the rejuvenation of the Club in the 1980s. A full list of Secretaries of the club is at Appendix 6.

Club Officials

The need for a **Club Medical Officer** was first recognised in 1900 but during the years covered by this volume the sole reference to such an appointment in Club records was in November 1945 when Major A.J. Dix Perkins RAMC, was made 'Club Doctor'. The absolute need for such an appointment lapsed some 20 years ago once the Club staff were no longer accommodated in the Clubhouse.

A new appointment to the Club came in December 1959 with the Committee's decision to make the Vicar of St Paul's Church, Knightsbridge, **Honorary Chaplain** to the Club. The first holder of the post was the Rev. D.B. Harris, a post he held until his retirement 18 years later when he was succeeded by the Rev. A.C.C. Courtauld.

A list of known **Honorary Librarians** is given in Appendix 7. The list almost certainly has gaps in the sequence due either to the absence of a record of a succession or to the absence of a Librarian when interest in such a topic was low in the list of priorities for the Committee. While the Committee made regular, if small, sums available to maintain and enlarge the Library its location has varied frequently when space was sought for other functions. Access to the Club's Library has always been difficult in more recent years as the room it occupied has generally been available for meetings.

It was at the 1935 AGM that the Vice Commodore, Lord Queenborough explained that the Committee proposed to build up a Half Model Collection. In the limited space available it was proposed to display models by class. He said that *'the collection will be not only historic, but practically interesting… and although it will not in any sense compete with the wonderful collection in the New York Yacht Club, it will be of most amazing interest to yachtsmen'*. The appointment of **Curator of Half Models** is not well recorded but it is known that the post was held by Col. J D K Restler in 1947, for many years by S H (Stewart) Morris in the 1950s and 60s, by J Glover Wyllie in 1971 and C J H Thornhill in 1977. Stewart Morris's contribution was considerable as has been that of the present incumbent, A Charles Chapman, who has done much to complete, expand and display what is now a formidable historic collection.

A meeting of members interested in playing in a Golf competition was held in January 1934 and appears to be the first reference to such activity by Club members. The appointment of a **Captain of Golf** is a much more recent practice but interest in the sport has been reasonably continuous. In 1936 the Berkhampstead Golf Club offered the Royal Thames members use of their course while in 1959 the New Zealand Golf Club offered terms for the use of their course - an arrangement that still stands today.

II
Club Affairs on the Water

Introduction

When peace descended on Europe in November 1918 the Royal Thames could once again start planning for a new racing season in 1919. During the four years void of yacht racing, the number of yachts owned by members had dropped from 499 to 246, their tonnage had fallen from 97,523 to 47,211 and the number of yachts over 100 tons had changed from 143 to 70. Over the next 80 years the number of yachts would increase considerably but their size would reduce further. The real changes, however, would be in the materials used for hulls, spars and sails while their design would, as always, be influenced by measurement formulae.

The Royal Thames has always been recognised as the club which led the development of yacht racing from the Club's inception in 1775 and through much of the nineteenth century until the founding of National (RYA) and International (IYRU) bodies to create common regulations for the sport. Many members of the Club had also distinguished themselves in the field of Cruising but any lead given by the Club was taken over by the Royal Cruising Club after its foundation in 1880. The concept of 'Ocean Racing' was still relatively new in 1919 and the Royal Thames involvement had been limited. Six years later that form of racing was to be dominated by a club formed to be dedicated solely to Ocean Racing - the Ocean Racing Club, which became the Royal Ocean Racing Club in 1931.

When it came to regattas, many members in 1919 expected to see a continuation of Royal Thames matches held in the Thames Estuary and the long-standing Nore to Dover race. The former simply did not happen and the latter soon faded, both to be replaced by Solent-based regattas. Other changes were the increase in racing by class as well as the earlier racing by handicap, all being open to members of many clubs other than the Royal Thames; also, in the post 1945 years, the club established itself as a leader in the organisation of National and International Regattas; but the most controversial involvement by the club in yacht racing was its decision to challenge for the America's Cup over three decades from 1960.

When the club moved into the realm of organising top level regattas there were those who felt that too much effort was going into providing racing for the elite among racing yachtsmen and too little was being done for the average member of the Royal Thames and that this in turn discouraged young yachtsmen from joining the club; this was particularly true when coupled to a relatively high annual subscription (when compared with most other senior yacht clubs) - clubs which are not London based. Happily the Club's continued determination to maintain high standards in yacht racing - whether it be in club regattas or solely as an organising authority - has allayed these fears, while the move over the past 15 years to develop to the highest level the special skills required in team racing can only add to the attractions of the club for aspiring yachtsmen.

Club Racing 1919-1939

The Club's racing base at Stokes Bay was still under Admiralty requisition in 1919 but the Club had been able to lease the pavilion on Ryde Pier to replace the facilities at Stokes Bay. Their first full racing season was 1920 and the programme had changed little from the immediate pre-war era, including as it did a day for River Matches in the Thames starting from Southend Pier, the Southend to Harwich Race and the Nore to Dover 'Channel' Race. It also included two days racing at Ryde. In August the club successfully defended the One Ton Cup against yachts representing France, Holland and Spain.

In the following season, 1921, it was decided to suspend the River Matches to the dismay of many members; in fact such matches, starting in the river, were never again to be included in the racing programme. The other traditional event, the Nore to Dover race survived until 1925. An attempt to revive it in 1935 was frustrated by bad weather, but it was held for the last time in 1936. 1921 also saw the introduction of racing for Solent classes on two separate days in July, the second day being coupled with the two days at Ryde which were to become the annual Royal Thames Regatta. Finally, in August, the One Ton Cup was again retained by Lord Queenborough's *CORDELLA* sailed by H G Sabiston.

While the gradual demise of Royal Thames racing on the Thames and in the Estuary was regretted by many members, the migration to the Solent was probably inevitable, not least because many members of the Royal Thames were also members of Solent based clubs, particularly the Royal Yacht Squadron and the Royal London Yacht Club. Add to this the Club's increasing involvement in International events such as the One Ton Cup and the Coupe de France, racing based on the Solent had many benefits for a London based club that wished to organise International events on suitable waters. This was well-illustrated in 1920 when American yachtsmen suggested that three British boats should cross to America to sail a team race against a like number of Americans, and that the Americans should return the visit in the following year. It was suggested that the boats might be International 18 footers. In October 1920 the Royal Thames nominated

Start of a race for the British-American Cup (1923).

Algernon Maudslay and Sir Ralph Gore as delegates to a committee to be formed from four clubs, the RYS, the Royal London, the Royal Victoria and the Royal Thames to consider the American proposals. In the event the contest was to be for four-boats-a-side in International 6 metres and in British waters. In July 1921 fourteen boats entered the elimination trials from which the four to race in the British team were chosen together with a reserve (Agernon Maudslay's *FREESIA*). The match comprised six races, the first being held on 29 July at Ryde. The trophy, the British-American Cup, was paid for by both countries and was a copy of the Ashburnham Cup, made in 1739 by Paul de Lamerie and presented to Clare Hall, Cambridge, by the Earl of Ashburnham.

The British team were successful in 1921 but lost the return match at Oyster Bay by a small margin. They were successful again at Ryde in 1923, while in 1924 they won only after a successful protest eliminated the American winner of the deciding race. The British team had won the cup outright, having achieved three victories. The Cup, which is held by the Royal Thames, was made available to the 6 metre Association for their National Championship in the 1980s. The Royal Thames was well represented in both the 1922, 1923 and 1924 British teams. In 1923 the team included two Fife designed boats *REG* (owned by Norman Clark Neill and sailed by RT Dixon) and which had been in the 1922 team, and *SUZETTE* (owned by ET Peel and sailed by Sir Ralph Gore), while in 1924 the team included *ZENITH* owned by J Lauriston Lewis and *THISTLE* owned by Lady Baird.

The One Ton Cup continued to be held at Ryde and run by the Royal Thames. While a contemporary report in 1922 states that the Spanish boat *DON JUAN* won the cup that year, with, in second place, Lord Queenborough's *CORDELIA*, a report on the 1924 races states that the Royal Thames had held the Cup since 1913! Certainly *CORDELIA*, now owned by Noel Exshaw, a Royal Thames member, was successful in 1923

while in 1924, it is also certain that the Dutch boat *HOLLANDS HOPE* was victorious at the expense of the RTYC's *ROSE* (FA Richards) as well as the French and Swedish entries. The fact that the One Ton Cup was handed back to the Circle de la Voile, Paris in August 1922 supports the contemporary report of a Spanish victory.

In August 1922 the Vice Commodore, Lord Queenborough, offered the Club a Cup to be competed for by, perhaps, boats of the International Six metre class. A copy of the regulations dated August 1924 is at Appendix 8. The first regatta for the Cup (in 1925) was competed for by yachts from the Royal Italian Yacht Club, the Yacht Club de France and Sir Ernest Roney's *EMILY* from the Royal Thames. Regrettably it is not certain whether the Italian or French boat won the series - the Royal Thames certainly did not win that year; but it is equally certain that they were successful in 1926 with Sir Arthur Pagets' *SIRIS*. The club presented the crew of *SIRIS* with commemorative medals and a house dinner was held in their honour on 7 December to celebrate the Club winning both the Cumberland Cup and, through J Lauriston Lewis's *ZENITH*, the One Ton Cup.

While *SIRIS* and *ZENITH* individually brought honours to the Royal Thames in 1926, it was *SIRIS II* that took the honours in 1927 winning both the Coupe de France and the Cumberland Cup (but the One Ton Cup went to the French). By 1927 the annual Southend to Harwich race (inherited from the New Thames Yacht Club) was no longer run but the club was now giving a day's racing in the annual Southend Yachting Week. This week was inaugurated in 1920 with the aim of promoting yacht racing for the local classes and to encourage juniors to take part in the sport. Those who forecast that little interest would be shown in this venture were proved wrong and the week progressed from one success to another each year. The presence of the Royal Thames encouraged the big yachts such as *BRITANNIA* to take part and this ensured

British-American Cup Teams on the lawn of the Royal Yacht Squadron (1923).

that Southend itself benefited from the publicity attracted by the Yachting Week. The Royal Thames involvement was to continue for over 20 years.

Southend at this time was frequently the opening event for the Royal Thames racing season and was followed in June by one or two regattas for International and Solent Classes. These included the 12, 8 and 6 metre classes as well as the West Solent Restricted Class, Solent Sunbeams, Redwings and Seaview Mermaids. At the end of July or early in August the club organised racing for the Handicap Classes as well as the International and Solent classes. In 1927 the handicap classes were: between 10 and 35 Tons TM, between 35 and 110 Ton TM and over 110 Tons. This latter regatta was held at the beginning of Ryde Week and in 1927 started with a Round the Island race for four handicap classes, the 35-110 ton class being split at 70 tons. It was inevitable that the greatest spectator interest centred on the 'big' boats which that year comprised the King's cutter *BRITANNIA* (with King George V on board, closely followed, therefore, by HMS Tiverton) together with the *SHAMROCK, WHITE HEATHER, LULWORTH* and *WESTWARD* (all but the latter being owned by the Royal Thames members). On this occasion it was to be a victory for *WHITE HEATHER* which completed the 54 mile course in 3 hours, 33 minutes and 57 seconds. It was a busy time for the Royal Thames race officers. Having started the four handi-cap classes they then started the 12 metre class and, before starting the 8 and 6 metre class, they started the concluding races for the Cumberland and One Ton Cups and followed the 6 metre class by the four Solent classes. - by which time the 'big' class were already racing up the east side of the island! Almost as busy as the race officers were those members of the press who, having seen the starts of the Solent classes, motored across the island in the expectation of watching the big class pass. As was recorded in The Yachtsman *'they arrived only in time to see the topsails disappearing round the Point, and such was the speed of these big yachts with*

a following wind and a strong tide that it was not until Ventnor that the car hurrying along the winding road came abreast of them'.

A number of interesting yachting-related matters arose in the 1920s. In October 1922 the Club actively opposed the insertion of German yachts in Lloyd's Register. In March 1925 the Club once again supported the Royal Yacht Squadron in a protest to the Board of Trade against proposed restrictions in the use of the Solent due to the activities of the Army Range at Browndown. In May 1926 the only recorded effect on the Club of the general strike was that it made for difficulty in getting the Race Programme posters printed; while in May 1927 a letter received from the Admiralty gave permission for the Blue Ensign to be flown from launches and boats belonging to yachts holding a warrant. Lastly, in September 1929 (and 1931), the Club Pavilion at Ryde was used by the Royal Aero Club officials for the Schneider Trophy International Seaplane Race. It is not without interest to note that the first race for this trophy in 1919 was won at an average speed of 45.75 mph but such was the pace of development of aircraft design that in the last race for the trophy in 1931 that average speed had been lifted to 340.08 mph by the Supermarine company and from which plane emerged the renowned 'Spitfire' fighter aircraft that played a major part in the Battle of Britain nine years later.

In November 1928 the Sailing Committee gratefully accepted the offer of a Cup from Club member, J J Morgan, which was to be put up for a race for Cruising yachts from Ryde to the Cherbourg breakwater and back. The first race for the Morgan Cup took place on 20 July 1929 and was won by *FLAME* owned and sailed by Charles E Nicholson. On only a few occasions since then have there been sailing seasons that did not include a Morgan Cup race organised by the Royal Thames, alone initially, but later shared with the Royal Ocean Racing Club and, in time, competed for by handicap class

Cumberland Cup Match (1930) NONA versus L'AILE VI.

racing yachts. The first race attracted thirteen entries ranging in size from the schooner *LAMORNA (263 Tons)* to the 23 Ton cutter *NEITH,* the handicap being from scratch to over five and a half hours. The race started at 9.30 am in a very light N W breeze and it was well into the afternoon before the Needles was reached. Once clear of the Isle of Wight there was a little more wind and the leading yacht, Mr Charles Nicholson's Bermudan cutter *FLAME (33 Tons)* rounded the Cherbourg breakwater shortly before 8.00 am the following day. The return journey was blessed with a freshening wind but made hazardous by a thick fog. *FLAME* was able to maintain her lead and found the Nab Tower through haze, crossing the finishing line at Ryde at 8.32 pm, some 35 hours after starting, and four hours ahead of the next boat *NEITH* - the second of only six boats that completed the race. A vivid description of an electrical storm experienced during the race is given in Douglas Phillips-Birt's book 'The Cumberland Fleet' as recounted by Charles Nicholson's son John who was a member of the crew on board *FLAME* . A copy of that description is given in the Appendix 9.

Another long-standing Challenge Cup donated by a club member of that period is the Cory Cup, given in February 1931 by Mr R W Cory. It was not until November of that year that a Sub Committee was established to write the rules for this Cup which was to competed for by a representatives of various clubs sailing in boats of the West Solent Restricted Class. The first race for the Cory Cup was held on 26 July 1932 within the two day programme for the Royal Thames Regatta at Ryde. Twelve boats, representing Solent based clubs and other clubs outside that area came to the start in strong winds. The race was stopped at the end of the first round of the $10^1/_2$ mile course, the winner being *SQUIRREL* representing the Royal Southern Yacht Club, and sailed by F A Richards (he was also a member of the RTYC) - also on board was K H Preston, another RTYC member who later became Vice Commodore of the Club. Second was the representative of the Royal Burnham YC *PERSEPHONE* and they lodged a protest against *SQUIRREL*and *NIOLA* (third). The Royal Thames race

committee were unable to reach a decision on the day, in fact it took several meetings of the Sailing Committee before it was decided in late October that the protest should be rejected. In that first race the Royal Thames boat finished fifth of the twelve competitors, but in later years the Club were successful in winning the cup. In more recent years the race has been competed for in boats of the Daring class.

In the period 1923-33 a number of interesting matters arose including an approach by the Royal Thames to the Ministry of Works as regards the possibility of sailing on the Serpentine - but nothing positive emerged at that time. A worrying factor at the time was the number of members who discontinued sailing due to the effects of recession. This in turn had a serious effect on the livelihood of the (paid) crews whose only other source of income was largely fishing outside the sailing season. This must surely have been one of the factors that persuaded the Sailing Committee when they met in October 1932 to plan the programme for 1933 to include a day at Brixham. The Club, assisted by local officers, provided racing and prizes for the first day of the Brixham Regatta in August. The Club's presence was welcomed with great enthusiasm and not least because the racing included two races for trawlers (ketch rigged and under/over 40 tons registered tonnage). It was reported that some of the larger trawlers carried as many as forty visitors in addition to the working crew. Each trawler was set to sail three times round a rectangular shaped course within Torbay. This enabled the large crowd of visitors lining the cliffs and headlands to see the trawlers during the whole race. The Club continued to support Brixham until 1948. Two small silver cups awarded by the Club in the 1930s at Brixham were returned to the Royal Thames in 1988 by a Mrs Wallace. (See Section VII under 'Other Silver Trophies').

The General Committee met in September 1932 and set up a Sub Committee to consider whether the lease of the Ryde Pavilion should be renewed or whether an alternative yachting headquarters should be acquired. By the end of October the

Sub Committee was authorised to take an option on the 880 Tons TM steam yacht *VEGA* which was lying in JS White's yard at Southampton and which offered possibilities as a floating headquarters for the Club's yachting activities. In December the General Committees called a Special General Meeting of the Club to consider a resolution authorising the Committee to take up forty £25 shares in a syndicate of members for the purpose of purchasing (subject to satisfactory survey) the *SY VEGA*, the Committee guaranteeing 4% p.a. on the £8000 needed for the capital cost of the *VEGA* plus the running expenses of the Syndicate for three years. The 131 members attending the SGM eventually agreed by a large majority that the scheme was financially unsound and voted against the purchase in spite of its many other attractions, not least that it might provide a facility attractive to young members. Consequently, a further lease on Ryde Pavilion was sought in spite of its shortcomings: poor anchorage offshore, interference from ferries and a starting box of very limited capacity. Once again, Douglas Phillips-Birt gave a comprehensive account of the Sub Committee's report in his Bicentenary book and part of this is recorded in Appendix 10. The project remained alive until 1934 when it was clear that no suitable vessel could be found and in any case the cost of operating and maintaining a vessel of a suitable size was prohibitive. For all that, it was an imaginative project if difficult to put into practice, while the criticism levelled at the prospect of having waterside premises could be said to be prophetic.

On the water the Club's representatives in the annual Coupe de France and Cumberland Cup faired particularly well, defeating their French challenger in almost every year from 1928 to 1936. Especially notable was the achievement of Mr R B Worth who won the Coup de France six times in his 8 metre yachts *SEVERN* and *SEVERN II*, while in 1932 he also won the Cumberland Cup. In the Cumberland Cup races, the successful owners were Lord Forster with three wins in his 8 metre yachts *UNITY* and *NONA* and Col. E T. Peel who also achieved three victories with *SUZETTE II* and *REALITY*. The French challenger in the late 1920s and early 1930s was Madame Virginie Heriot with her series of yachts named *L'AILE*. A trophy bearing her name was competed for at a later date.

The Club's standing in yacht racing in the 1930s was as high as at any time in its history and is well illustrated by the opening remarks in a report on the Club's Jubilee Regatta held from 31 July to 2 August 1935: '*The Royal Thames Yacht Club, which does more to foster yacht racing than any other club in country*'. That regatta included, on the first day, a race round the Isle of Wight for the specially presented Prince of Wales Jubilee Cup. This was intended originally to be awarded to the winner of the Nore to Dover race, but when that was postponed due to severe weather the Cup was transferred to the Club's Jubilee race round the Island. This was a handicap race for J Class and 12 metre yachts. It attracted seven entries from each class including *YANKEE*, owned by the visiting American yachtsman Gerard Lambert. On the third day of the regatta the Club staged a schooner race for a 100 guinea cup presented by Allan E Messer, a Club member. It was many years since the Solent had witnessed Schooner racing and the hoped-for spectacle was not fully achieved because of the light winds prevailing when the five competitors (of the seven entered) crossed the line for an east about course round the Isle of Wight. The *WESTWARD (323 Tons TM)* owned by Club member Mr T B F Davis), the scratch boat, proved to be best suited to the light conditions and was an easy winner.

A full programme of races was provided by the Royal Thames in every year up to 1939; it extended the number of Solent classes offered racing to include the Q class, the Dragon Class and the Teal and X One Design classes, while in 1938 the Club gave a day's racing at Weymouth and in 1939 had planned a day at Dartmouth on 28 August! Another landmark in 1939 was the presentation of a small silver Challenge Cup to the Ranelagh Sailing Club for the 12ft dinghy class to commemorate their fiftieth anniversary. The Club would also provide six silver and six bronze medals each year. The Royal Thames has maintained a close relationship with Ranelagh for the past 60 years. Lastly, in the immediate pre-war years it is noteworthy that the Club supported the Thames Barge Races by offering Cups and prize money. As the 1939 season ended few, if any, realised it would be seven years before the next race season came about or that the 'Big Class' would virtually disappear from the programme.

Racing and Cruising 1945-80

When the Sailing Committee met on 29 June 1939 the impending hostilities were already casting a shadow over the season's racing. The Honorary Sailing Secretary, Mr B T Rumble, reported his discussion with the King's Harbour Master at Portsmouth on prohibited areas and not only those caused by the Browdown Firing Range. The racing season was in full swing, courses were planned, race officers identified and trophies allocated. Negotiations were in hand to persuade either the Southern Railway Company or Ryde Borough council to erect a new starting box on Ryde Pier and charge the Club an annual rental. Those race officers starting the Fastnet Race on 5 August were granted permission to use the starting box and its gear. All this activity merely hid the fact that the next meeting of the Sailing Committee would not be held until 13 October 1942. The meetings in those mid-war years concerned themselves principally with two topics. Firstly, the classification of yachting and non-yachting candidates for election by the General Committee and which was now the Sailing Committee's responsibility and, secondly, the question of yachting headquarters for the Club when racing resumed after the war. As far as the latter was concerned the Committee were unanimous in their belief that headquarters should be on the Hamble River (where many members kept their yachts). It was also agreed that the lease on Ryde Pavilion should be allowed to lapse since it was little used by members (and in any case it was commandeered by the Military Authorities in 1942) but the starting box should be retained. In 1943 Ranelagh S.C. informed the Club that racing for the RTYC Trophy could take place. The Club then discovered that a government order prohibited the production of medals (for leisure activities) and had to find alternative commemorative items to present to Ranelagh. In July 1944 the Club itself participated in a dinghy racing match against Oxford University. At this post-D Day period an end to war suddenly seemed nearer and optimism for the future was rising. When, in July 1945, the Admiralty restored the Club's warrant allowing members to fly the Blue Ensign, the Club was ready to start planning for the 1946 season. Meanwhile the Club decided to renew the lease of the Ryde pavilion until the end of 1946. In February 1946, the Chairman of Committees, Mr G Glynn Terrell, reported that he had been to see Shore House at Warsash and recommended its purchase, for about £6,500, as the Club's yachting headquarters, a recommendation that was accepted and then implemented by the end of May. Within a year the Club had started the process of acquiring moorings near Shore House.

The 1946 season's programme looked very little different from the pre-war pattern, with the Club giving a day's racing at Southend and Brixham as well as racing for Handicap and Solent classes at Ryde - and of course, the Morgan Cup race.

The Sailing Committee met in April 1947 and one of their tasks was to appoint an Honorary Sailing Secretary. With a view to the future they decided to make a joint appointment by re-appointing B.T. Rumble (now Sir Bertram) and also appointing G.G. Dudley Head. The latter took over the duties in his own right in March 1948 while the death of the former was reported in January 1949, so ending a long and distinguished service to the Sailing Committee.

When the race programme for 1948 was being discussed, the Sailing Committee, while agreeing to a programme similar in content to that of 1947, decided that racing for Solent Classes should be from a line in the vicinity of Warsash (with today's traffic on the Hamble it is hard to realise that such a decision could be implemented in practice). They were also informed that Ryde Pier was no longer a suitable place from which to hold regattas. It was decided, therefore, that the club would still hold their regatta at Ryde but would conduct it from a committee boat. Later on, the Club was invited to nominate an entrant for the Virginie Heriot Cup in Dragons at Cherbourg - but no suitable member could be found. Fortunately G G Dudley Head did agree to represent the club in his Dragon *JEAN* in the race for the Cory Cup.

Changes to the race programme were in the air and in October 1948 the Sailing Committee recommended that the regattas at Brixham and Southend should be discontinued. In fact, the Club was to retain patronage of Southend Week for many years to come but it no longer provided a day's racing. It was also agreed that the Club's regatta at Ryde should be discontinued and transferred to the 'Warsash Area'. This led to agreement with the RAF Yacht Club for the Club to use a starting line at Calshot, a practice that was to continue for the next four seasons.

The Club was always looking for new ways of attracting younger yachtsmen into membership, and not least encouraging them to join as Cadets. In November 1949 Lt Col. Cecil N.C. Howard presented a Challenge Cup for competition by the sons and daughters of members who were aged under 18. The first race for the Howard Junior Cup took place on 19 August 1950 in Star class dinghy borrowed from the RAF YC. Interest in the annual Junior Cup races was further stimulated in June 1951 by Mrs P.B. Neal who presented two cups to the Club, one of which was to go to the yacht in second place in Junior races. This event was to continue in various dinghy classes and at different venues including Ranelagh SC, Emsworth SC and Tamesis until 1963 after which date lack of interest led to its being discontinued. Another initiative to attract younger members was the proposal that the Club should have it own dinghy/keelboat class based on an existing design and located at Warsash. The initial suggestion was to use the Redwing class but with blue sails and called the Cumberland Fleet class, but this proved to be unacceptable to the Redwing Class. Alternatives considered were National 12s based at Ranelagh and Flying Fifteens, but none of these ideas bore fruit.

Throughout the 1950s the core of the Club's race programme changed little, being based on racing for Solent Classes and Handicap Classes from starting lines initially at Calshot. When it became apparent that use of Calshot was likely to be banned due to the ever-increasing traffic in Southampton Water, the Club moved the starts to the East Bramble buoy and then to Hillhead, but by 1959 the Solent Classes were being started from a Committee Boat, a procedure that was to become very popular with yachtsmen and at which the Royal Thames excelled. The race for the Morgan Cup continued each year, but as the decade proceeded the involvement of the Royal Ocean Racing Club in this race increased even though the Royal Thames provided the handsome permanent cups for the class winners.

Around these core regattas the Club was involved in a range of other events. In 1950 there was a passage race to Weymouth and back, while from 1954 the club organised a week-end passage race from Warsash or Cowes to Poole and back, an event that continued annually through to 1971 and was often co-ordinated with a Rally at Poole for cruising members. In 1956 the club ran a race from the Hamble to the Nab Tower and back to Cowes and took part in a match in Dragons at the Royal Norfolk and Suffolk Yacht Club. That year was also the fourth year that the Club held its regatta on the first Sunday of Cowes Week. Having started by sharing the day with the Island Sailing Club in 1953, the Club, from 1954, held a separate regatta. In short, the Club was maintaining a full and varied programme for the full spectrum of yachts from the big handicap class to the smallest keelboat - as well as continuing to support racing by Ranelagh SC and London Corinthian SC; providing patronage of Southend Week and, in the mid fifties, the Thames Barge Races. In addition, from 1953 the club held regular matches with Seaview Yacht Club in their Mermaid class, a practice continued intermittently through to the 1980s, and, for some years, a match with Brading Haven YC. Such a programme as this on this had met at least some of the recommendations of a 1952 Sub Committee formed to report on the club's yachting activities for the future. Under the chairmanship of the Honorary Sailing Secretary G G Dudley Head, the Sub Committee recommended: that Shore House was an excellent yachting base; that consideration should be given to establishing a starting box on piles between Baldhead Buoy and the entrance to the Hamble River in conjunction with other clubs (to replace the Calshot line), that a club one design class should be adopted and operated from Warsash at weekends and that four small Sub Committees should be established to deal with Class racing in the Solent, Cruising, Offshore Racing and Centreboard boats (in conjunction with Ranelagh SC) with a view to the Club running one of the national dinghy championships each year. When it is realised that Shore House continued to be the Club's yachting base for a further 28 years (in spite of the problems that arose) and that support of racing in the Solent, Offshore Racing, Dinghy Racing and Cruising Rallies is still strong today, the Sub Committee can be said to have had a clear view for the future of yachting within the Club. The starting box proposal was simply not supported while a one design class for the Club has remained no more than an aspiration over the past forty years.

In spite of all this activity on the water by the Club the most adventurous decision came about when the Sailing Committee, chaired by the Vice Commodore, Kenneth Preston, met on 20 May 1954. He informed the Committee that the British American Cup Committee had issued a challenge to the USA to bring four 6 metre yachts to this country in 1955. It had been suggested that new boats for the British team should be built by syndicates. Mr F G Mitchell had supported this idea and had said *'that the Royal Corinthian Y C would produce one boat if the RTYC would do the same'.*

The Royal Thames decided to go ahead with this proposal, the concept being that the members, not the club, should be invited to put up the money needed. By November over £5000 had been subscribed or promised by members and the yacht was ordered at Woodnut's Yard on the Island to a design by David Boyd. At this time the 6 metre class was in decline in popularity - in this country the few remaining boats were in the Solent and on the Clyde - but as Douglas Phillips-Birt remarked '*in 1955 they were the most expensive yachts in the world per ton but the brilliant performance of these most thoroughbred of inshore racing craft had held the loyalty of the few*'. When the yacht was launched in May 1955 it was appropriately named *ROYAL THAMES*.

The racing performance of *ROYAL THAMES* was, perhaps, predictable. In this country against modest opposition she was very successful but against the Americans (with their superior sail material) her performance was mostly less than moderate. In 1955 she went to Sweden for the Royal Swedish YC's 125th anniversary regatta and faired poorly. In 1956 in UK waters she achieved 22 firsts and 2 seconds in 26 starts! Even this latter performance did not encourage other clubs to form syndicates to build 6 metres. Even so in 1957 the *ROYAL THAMES* was shipped to Norway and raced at Hankö and Marstrand with only very limited success finishing fourth in the One Ton Cup series at Hankö when sailed by one of her several skippers Michael Crean. At Marstrand, sailed by J Howden Hume she managed only a fifth position and a sixth (out of eight). It was already clear that, irrespective of performance, the 6 metre class showed no signs of revival and the cost of running *ROYAL THAMES* was proving to be more than the funds subscribed. During Cowes Week in 1958, with Michael Crean again handling her, she took six flags before being shipped to Le Havre for the One Ton Cup. With Colonel R S G Perry at the helm she proceeded to win the Cup and so justified her purpose. The following year she defended the Cup at Poole against 'the best in the world' but a first and four thirds were not enough and the Swedish entry was to win. Whatever the outcome at Poole it had already been decided to sell *ROYAL THAMES*. The eventual purchaser was Dr Peirre Blendeau of Lorient who named the yacht *HATSHEPSIT*. Later on the yacht again changed hands, but when the General Committee met on 3 September 1964, Major Peter Snowdon was able to report that he had sighted the yacht, still in good order, in Brittany.

Throughout the 33 years that the Club had its yachting base at Shore House, the property was perceived either as an essential Club facility or as the item at the top of the list of options available to reduce Club expenditure and therefore improve the Club's financial position. Whichever view members of the General and Sailing Committees might take there was always a determined effort to make Shore House a going concern and ideally, self-supporting and more attractive to members. To this end the facilities were extended and improved. By 1954 a new jetty was built. From 1 January 1955 the Household Brigade Yacht Club were made Honorary members of Shore House for an annual fee of £350 (which was subject to annual review). In 1961 and again in 1966 the possibility of developing a Marina at Warsash was pursued but came to nothing. 'Small' boat regattas were organised from Warsash including the Jollyboat championship which was held there in July 1960 and it was used as a base for the selection trials for the British Olympics Team. It was also used as a location for Cocktail Parties in conjunction with rallies on the Beaulieu River. In spite of these and many other initiatives, Shore House could not pay its way; could not attract sufficient usage; was used

only during the sailing season and it proved almost impossible to attract staff of a suitable quality and ones prepared to stay long enough to develop sound management practices.

The dominant feature of club racing in the 1960s was the Club's challenge for the America's Cup which eventually materialised in1964. The build-up to that challenge will be recorded later in this section. The big J Class yachts that had competed for the America's Cup until 1938 were replaced by yachts of the smaller International 12 metre class when the competition was resuscitated in 1958. At the Royal Thames, interest in a challenge by the Club was first voiced in 1958. This in turn stimulated interest in the 12 metre class and when the Sailing Committee met in June 1960 they proposed that the Queen's Cup won by *FIONA* in 1868, and recently donated to the Club by Chairman of Committee, A W Munns, should be raced for in match races between the two 12 metre yachts gaining the most points in Cowes Week. The trophy was competed for throughout the decade, the first winner being the 1958 America's Cup challenger *SCEPTRE* from *FLICA II* (J A Boyden).

The importance of encouraging match racing was also stimulated by the interest in the America's Cup and the subject was raised at a meeting of the Sailing Committee in November 1960 by Lt Col T H Trevor who proposed that match racing in selected classes take place after regattas - a small Sub Committee was set up to consider the proposal. It was decided that the Club should not be expected to organise match racing for the selected classes but the load should be spread to other clubs. Accordingly, in January 1961, a letter was sent to clubs at locations where regatta 'weeks' were held: Burnham, Clyde, Cowes, Falmouth and Firth to seek their views. Supportive replies were received from four of the five centres by May, but within in a month insurmountable difficulties arose and the whole project was abandoned. In July a disillusioned Lt. Col. Trevor resigned from the Club.

Handicapping had always been very much a Club or area affair and standardisation was either unwelcome, irrelevant or impracticable. For the Royal Thames the policy was to keep up to date and as they became more involved with offshore racing it was no surprise that in 1962 they adopted the classes used by the Royal Ocean Racing Club, the previous year namely: Class 1 over 30 feet; Class II 24 to 30 feet; Class III 19 to 24 feet; Class IV 15 to 19 feet. This decision lowered the bottom end of Class I and the top ends of Classes II and III with the object of providing stronger opposition for boats regularly winning Classes II and III handicap races.

There had been several unsuccessful attempts to streamline the organisation of Cowes week. In 1963 it was hoped to introduce a combined programme for all clubs participating in the week's races and a standard entry procedure. It was also proposed that the Combined Cowes Club Committee should be extended to include all clubs racing at Cowes. The Royal Thames Sailing Committee agreed and nominated Mr Jonathan Janson as their representative. For 1964 the Island Sailing Club proposed that there should be one permanent race committee for the whole of Cowes Week but there was no support for the proposal - and it is not hard to imagine that such a committee would probably be in a state of exhaustion by the end of the week.

While the Knightsbridge Clubhouse was being re-built the Sailing Committee agreed in November 1961 to start to explore the possibility of marking the opening of the new

Robin Aisher and his 5.5 metre YEOMAN VII at the 1960 Olympics in Naples.

clubhouse by a regatta to be sailed on the Serpentine in the autumn of 1963. Approval to hold the regatta was eventually obtained from the Ministry of Public Buildings and Works. It took place on 4 January 1964 (very close to the achieved re-opening date). The competing clubs were the Royal Thames and Ranelagh SC, London Corinthian SC and Tamesis. The match was between teams of two from each club in each of four classes of dinghy: International 14, National Merlin Rocket, National 12 and National Firefly. This first match was won by Tamesis, the Royal Thames being fourth - it was to be some years before the club improved its position in this very

popular match. Certainly the first match and the cocktail party in the new clubhouse were considered to be a great success. The approval given by MPBW to use the Serpentine was on the basis that it did not become a permanent fixture and they later said that the event must be an open regatta, with the result that Tamesis hosted the match at Twickenham when the Serpentine was not made available, or as in 1966, when the Serpentine was frozen over. Another dinghy racing match held annually for three years from 1966 was against St George's Hospital SC. These matches were held at the Welsh Harp in Fireflies.

The question of which starting line to use in Royal Thames' regattas was rarely off the agenda of the Sailing Committee in the 1960s. The Royal Yacht Squadron line or the Royal London line were most used as well as the much favoured committee boat starts. A new possibility arose in January 1965 when it was reported that an excellent starting line could be made from the old tower at Castle Point, East Cowes. The owner of the surrounding ground was prepared to sell a ten and a half acre plot, including access, for £4,500. It was soon learned that the owner of Norris Castle was prepared to buy the plot and to lease to the Club a small area round the Old Castle. This offer was taken up for the Solent Classes regatta in June 1965 (at no rent). While the competitors reportedly favourably on the line, the race officers found it difficult to operate as they had had to land their equipment by launch. Consideration was given to use the Castle Point start line as an alternative to the Squadron line during Cowes Week but the proposal received little support from other clubs.

The Club's racing activities during the 1960s included other innovations such as providing racing for contenders for selection to the 1965 British Admiral's Cup team - a practice that was to be maintained for the years ahead. At the end of August 1968 the Club organised a race from Cowes to Cherbourg and back, the winner to receive the Lochan Cup. Regrettably, of the seven entries only three boats took part. In spite of the poor support the event was repeated in the next two years but the destination was Alderney rather than Cherbourg. 1969 also saw the start of a period of liaison with the Junior Offshore Group. The club agreed to run their return race from Le Harve in June when they would compete for a trophy given by Rear Commodore John Savage and to be known as the Royal Thames Yacht Club Challenge Cup for Offshore Racing. In the summer of 1969 five Royal Thames members including the future Vice Commodore, John Maddocks, made up the amateur crew of the Duke of Edinburgh's yacht *BLOODHOUND* for a cruise to Norway to coincide with a state visit to that country by H M The Queen and the Duke of Edinburgh. Lastly, when the Sailing Committee met in December 1969 two important matters were resolved which were to have a long term influence on the Club's racing and race programme. Commander F A C Behenna felt it was time for him to stand down as Chief Race Officer and it was decided to appoint Mr E I Hamilton-Parks to that office. It was also agreed to support a proposal from the Commodore of the Royal Southern Yacht Club that a Points Championship for Handicap Classes in the Solent be instituted in the 1970 season - an event that the Club has supported since that season.

The history of the **America's Cup** is synonymous with questionable interpretations of the variable rules and the consequent grounds for disagreement between defender and challenger. When the Royal Thames embarked on what was to become their 1964 challenge, they would have been familiar with that history but, even so, the reality of the problems that would arise as the challenge unfolded, must have been far in excess of anything they could have foreseen.

It was noted earlier that in January 1958 a proposal was made that the Royal Thames should consider forming a syndicate to challenge for the America's Cup in 1962. When the Sailing Committee met under the chairmanship of Rear Commodore Eric Marshall they were informed that discussions between the Flag Officer and Lord Craigmyle, a member, had considered a challenge. In a letter from Lord Craigmyle, the committee heard that he was chairman of the Red Duster syndicate which

proposed to carry out research and then build a 12 metre yacht. If necessary, he would finance the whole venture himself and he asked whether the club would be prepared to issue a challenge to the New York Yacht Club on behalf of his syndicate. It was pointed out that the NYYC would not accept a challenge unless at least two yachts were being built to take part in elimination trials (this was later refuted by the NYYC and under the Deed of Challenge the NYYC had no authority to require prior elimination trials). The Committee also learned that other potential challengers, including Mr Owen Aisher, were active - but might not wish to challenge through the Royal Thames. The Committee agreed to recommend acceptance of Lord Craigmyle's offer and set down the conditions they would seek to safeguard the Club's position and to ensure that the club could control all aspects of the challenge. It was also noted that Australia was considering placing a challenge. Lastly, it was made clear that ten months must elapse between the date of acceptance of a challenge and the start of the races.

In February 1960 the Vice Commodore, Major Charles Ball, informed the General Committee that he had attended a luncheon given by the Commodore, Earl Mountbatten; also present were the Vice Commodore of the Royal Yacht Squadron and HRH the Duke of Edinburgh. Prince Philip had told them that there were likely to be two challengers from Australia and perhaps two from Canada and he therefore favoured a 'Commonwealth' challenge, should the NYYC agree, by the best yacht among the Commonwealth challenges. It was decided to establish a co-ordinating committee with Prince Philip as chairman. In view of this the letter informing the NYYC of the Red Duster challenge through the RTYC was not sent.

The co-ordinating Committee's letter dated 19 April, which was sent to all potential challengers in the Commonwealth inviting them to be represented on the committee, was received in the Royal Thames on 20 April. On the same day a press announcement appeared saying that Australia had placed a challenge with the NYYC (i.e. before they could have received the letter). By this time not only had Lord Craigmyle become a challenger but so too had another member Mr J A Boyden (owner of *FLICA*). The Club was therefore in a position to lodge a challenge following elimination trials between at least two yachts. A cable, stating the Club's interest to challenge, was sent on 21 April as was a copy of the letter of 19 April under cover of a letter explaining why the club had delayed sending the letter prepared in February. The America's Cup Board of Trustees was due to meet on 28 April to consider the Australian challenge. Two days before that meeting Captain John Illingworth went to America to represent Lord Craigmyle and Mr Boyden. He was asked, in addition, to represent the Club and to explain the reasons for the delay in forwarding the Club's letter of intent to challenge which had been dated 18 February. In addition the Rear Commodore, Mr Eric Marshall, offered to go to New York at this time to represent the club and to ensure no discord arose between Australia and the UK.

On 3 May Mr Eric Marshall reported to the General Committee the outcome of the meetings in New York during his visit. The NYYC were interested in the idea of a Commonwealth challenge and recommended that such a challenge should be put in writing. The Board of Trustees however made it clear that under the rules they were bound to accept the Royal Sydney Yacht Squadron's challenge because it has been the first to be received. They also agreed that should the

RSYS accept the requirement for elimination trials between Commonwealth yachts, then they would allow the challenge to shift to the club under whose burgee the winning yacht was sailing. During his meeting with the Trustees, Mr Marshall had asked that should the NYYC defend successfully in 1962, when would they accept the next challenge and how could the RTYC preserve its claim to be the next challenger?

By February 1961 the NYYC had accepted that, provided they won the 1962 match, the RTYC would have first claim to be the challenger in 1963/64. It soon became apparent that the Royal Sydney Yacht Club wished to proceed with its accepted challenge and the Royal Thames made it equally apparent that they would do nothing to undermine the challenge. What was regrettable was that inadequate communication had failed to alert the Royal Thames to the fact that the Australian challenge was imminent even though they had been alerted to a possible challenge months earlier.

The Club was now in a position to concentrate its thinking on the 1963/64 challenge. Accordingly, when the Sailing Committee met in November 1961 it was agreed to set up a Race Committee which would run the elimination trials and report to a Selection Committee which would choose the yachts to sail against each other and make the final choice of yacht to sail the challenge. The Race Committee would be chaired by Major Ball and the Selection Committee by Sir Kenneth Preston. The meeting was also made aware that the well-established Red Duster Syndicate would wish to see the challenge races set not later than September 1963 even though other potential challengers might not be ready by that time. The Club was alive to the need to involve 12 metre owners and decided to do this through the 12 Metre Association, who in turn responded by asking the Royal Thames to run weekend racing for the class in July 1962 in Poole Bay.

In April the Club learned that Lord Craigmyle had withdrawn from the Red Duster Syndicate and by June the syndicate was wound up as alternative finance had not been found. The better news for the Club was that Mr Boyden had placed an order for a new yacht and would sail under the Club's burgee. There were still others who were considering the possibility of building a yacht but were awaiting the outcome of the Australian challenge; these still included Mr Owen Aisher and also a possible consortium of 12 Metre owners. By early September the General Committee had agreed, provided the NYYC won the 1962 challenge, to issue the Royal Thames challenge for 1963 immediately after the races against the Australians. If the latter won, the challenge action would be delayed for further consideration. Although the Vice Commodore went to America to see the races and place the challenge, in the event he had to leave before a clear victory was achieved but was assured by the NYYC Flag Officers that there was no immediate need to issue the challenge provided it was received within a month i.e. by 25 October. By now it was emerging that the New York Yacht Club were not keen to sail a challenge in 1963 but would prefer 1964. There was also concern that as soon as the Club's right to challenge expired on 25 October, the Royal Sydney Yacht Club would challenge for 1964.

Meanwhile it was now understood that the 12 Metre Association would place an order for a yacht to be built to another Boyd design once a challenge for 1963 was issued. Both Mr Boyden and the Association were keen to challenge in 1963 which they believed would give them a design advantage over the Americans and keep the cost of the challenge within tolerable limits. It was thought that both boats would be sailing by April 1963 and be ready to challenge in September. A special meeting of the General and Sailing Committee on 16 October agreed to issue the challenge and ask the Commodore to approve their decision the following day. Regrettably, the committee decision was leaked to the BBC after the meeting and the NYYC heard of it that evening. On 17 October the Commodore endorsed the dispatch of the challenge cable to the NYYC and a covering letter explaining why the Club wished to keep to the originally agreed date for the challenge in 1963. On the 18th the National newspapers published the New York Yacht Club's rejection of the challenge for 1963 and the RTYC received a cable from the NYYC that same day. In twenty four hours of hectic activity it was established that Mr Tony Boyden would challenge in 1964 but the 12 Metre Association could not commit themselves. By 20 October the Club had decided to send a further challenge cable for 1964 unless the NYYC would review their rejection of 1963. Three days later the Club's challenge was accepted and the match was to be sailed in September 1964. While the Club was anxious to ensure that there was at least a two-boat challenge, a press report of a challenge by the Isle of Man YC caused some surprise - but not for long as the report proved to be bogus! Meanwhile, Mr Boyden had told the Club that his yacht would now be launched in July 1963 and would initially stay on the Clyde and race against Erik Maxwell's *SCEPTRE*.

As the weeks passed in the early part of 1963 the prospects of building a second boat were fading and at the April AGM Tony Boyden was asked to talk to members present and to not only encourage them that his challenge was well founded but also to persuade them to help with funds for a second boat. The summer months passed and the prospect of launching a second boat in 1963 disappeared. Tony Boyden's David Boyd designed yacht, which was named SOVEREIGN, was launched on 6 July 1963 at a time when much of the Committees' energies were devoted to the problems associated with the completion of the new Clubhouse. Such a diversion did not prevent the Vice Commodore and Sir Kenneth Preston from seeking to find a suitable second boat to compete with *SOVEREIGN*. On 5 September, they were able to report to the General Committee that they had arranged with Mr John and Mr Frank Livingston (who had considered making an Australian Challenge in 1963 through the Royal Victoria Yacht Club) that they would order a second 12 metre yacht to be called *KURREWA V* and built on the Clyde to another of David Boyd's designs and which would be launched on 31 March 1964. Mr Owen Aisher had agreed to manage the boat for the Club and to finance her fitting out, her sailing in the UK and the elimination trials in USA. At that meeting the Vice Commodore also made it known that, on health grounds, he would not be available for re-election in April 1964. In view of this the Committee proposed that Mr Kenneth Poland should be nominated as his successor and take over Major Ball's duties for the America's Cup challenge.

At last the Club had available the wherewithal for an effective two boat challenge and could start the detailed planning of races in the UK and in USA waters as well as all the administrative arrangements for America and the support facilities needed over there. Tuning up trials were planned to take place off the Nab Tower during May 1964 and from Weymouth in June before the yachts were shipped to America on about 1 July. Final selection trials would commence off Newport RI around 20 August and the Challenger would be named by 8 September. Meanwhile, Sir Kenneth Preston had been able to arrange for a 30 knot launch to be available to the Club at Newport at no charge.

Early in 1964 members were invited to subscribe to an America's Cup fund which would contribute towards the cost of running the elimination trials. At the AGM in April certain members made it clear that the general funds of the club should not be used to support the challenge - all cost should be down to the owners! Some saw this as a niggardly attitude by members of a yacht club while others, rightly, sought confirmation that the Club's assets were properly protected. The appeal was to raise less than £3,500 towards the forecast expenditure of £10,000.

The trials in the UK were somewhat inconclusive with *SOVEREIGN* winning 9 races and *KURREWA* winning 10 times but it was noted that when *SOVEREIGN* won it was by a larger margin. It was now known that *KURREWA* would not be ready to go to the States until three weeks after *SOVEREIGN* but two other yachts, *SCEPTRE* and *NORSAGE*, would probably be available to race against *SOVEREIGN* until *KURREWA* arrived. By the beginning of July *SOVEREIGN* had been shipped out and Peter Scott had been nominated as helmsman with Bruce Banks as relief helmsman; *KURREWA* was to leave on 17 July. The final selection trials quickly came and went and *SOVEREIGN* was selected to be the challenger. While both yachts' performance had improved markedly during the elimination trials, when it came to the match, *SOVEREIGN* simply was not up to the standard of the defending yacht *CONSTELLATION*, who won easily with four straight wins.

In spite of this comprehensive defeat and the inevitable sense of disappointment there was still a feeling that the Club should challenge again - not necessarily in 1967 but in 1970. The Sailing Committee decided that before any further challenge was considered a Sub Committee should be set up to report on the conditions which should be met before another challenge was made. The Sub Committee was established in December and comprised Mr Kenneth Poland, Mr Elmer Ellsworth Jones, Mr Jonathan Janson, Sir Gordon Smith, Sir Kenneth Preston and Mr Ian Butler - a powerful and experienced team of whom four were to be Vice Commodore of the Club. Mr J V Mackinnon later joined the Sub Committee. Their report was completed in December 1966 and presented to the General Committee in February 1967. A copy of the recommendations is at Appendix 11.

Perhaps the most interesting postscript to the 1964 challenge came a year later when Mr Walter Gubelmann of the New York Yacht Club was entertained to a luncheon at which he presented a half model of *CONSTELLATION* and made these points about the challenge:

a) There was little to choose between the helmsmanship and crewing of CONSTELLATION and SOVEREIGN

b) That America had made very great efforts to improve sail material and design, and the sails of CONSTELLATION were consequently far superior to those of SOVEREIGN

c) That the industrial potential of America was enlisted to experiment and provide the optimum in equipment

d) That, with thirty-one members in the syndicate, financial backing was virtually unlimited.

To say that the odds were stacked against SOVEREIGN would be a gross understatement. Mr Gubelmann's observation served to underline the shortcomings and strengths of the 1964 challenge. Whilst this country was clearly capable of developing the technology needed to improve the performance of potential challengers, perhaps the biggest obstacle to overcome was the reluctance of commerce and industry to back a challenge, which in turn delayed preparation for a challenge and left it to the challenging owner to provide his own finance. In addition, the difficulty of establishing two or more modern 12 metre yachts to compete against each other (and raise the standard of performance to match the Americans), made successful challenging particularly difficult. In spite of everything, by May 1965 Mr Owen Aisher and Mr Tony Boyden were reported to be interested in a 1970 challenge should their plans come to fruition. The Royal Thames, also maintained an interest, and Mr John Maddocks was invited to witness the 1967 Americas Cup races when the Australians were challenging once again.

The General Committee meeting in December 1970 were informed that a syndicate had been formed who were willing to challenge in 1973. The syndicate were said to be willing and able to finance the challenge at no cost to the Club. On these terms the General Committee was prepared to accept a challenge through the Royal Thames. The Sailing Committee met three weeks later under the chairmanship of the Rear Commodore Mr John Foot and took a more cautious view. In particular they questioned whether the General Committee had considered the conditions for a challenge set down in the report of the post-1964 challenge Sub Committee. In order to ensure that the conditions of that report were met and that the Club retained control of the challenge without incurring financial liability it was decided to establish a further Sub Committee to satisfy themselves that the challenge should proceed. It was to comprise the Flag Officers together with Sir Gordon Smith, Mr Jonathan Janson, Mr Ian Butler and Brigadier John Constant. The Sub Committee was satisfied that the syndicate met the spirit of the conditions of the 1966 report and that they were financially sound. The immediate problem centred on the running and location of elimination trials among the seven challengers. After a range of discussions and exchanged telegrams the Royal Thames agreed to conduct the trials at Newport RI in April 1974. As late on as March 1972 the head of the syndicate, Mr Tony Boyden, was hopeful that a successful challenge would be launched. Three months later at a special joint meeting of the General and Sailing Committees chaired by the Commodore, Mr Elmer Ellsworth-Jones, it was reported that the costs of the challenge might be far more than had been anticipated by the syndicate and that no other syndicate was forthcoming to provide the all-essential second boat for the Royal Thames challenge. Under these circumstances it was agreed that the Club should withdraw from the 1974 series but would continue to run the elimination races, the cost of which would be borne by Mr Boyden's syndicate.

Although just Australia and France were now challenging, the commitment undertaken by Mr 'Ricky' Hamilton Parks and his race committee was considerable, calling for the setting up of an office complex, renting mark boats, transporting the paraphernalia of race equipment and above all, ensuring that there was rigorous adherence to the rules for the series. The successful conduct of the elimination races not only brought great credit to the Royal Thames, it also established standards of race management, a field in which the Royal Thames was and is pre-eminent.

The club was to have no further involvement in the America's

**Stewart Morris (with David Bond) in SWIFT wins
a Gold Medal in the Swallow Class in the 1948
Olympics in Torbay.**

Cup for another 30 years but the experience gained in the
unsuccessful attempts in 1964 and 1974 was well recorded so
that it would be available at the time of any future challenge.

Throughout its long history the Royal Thames Yacht Club has
always been prepared to make bold decisions in respect of its
promotion and support of yacht racing. As the Club moved
from the seventh to the eighth decade of the twentieth century it was decided to move into the realm of international and
national championships starting in 1970 with the running of
the World Soling Championships at Poole in June in conjunction with the Poole Bay Olympic Sailing Association, while
many of the facilities needed were made available by the Royal
Motor Yacht Club. Mr John Savage, who had recently stood
down as Rear Commodore of the Royal Thames presented
a handsome gold trophy to be won outright at the championship. Another feature of this successful championship was
the acceptability of receiving discreet commercial financial
support for a major event. On this occasion sponsorship was
provided by Simpsons of Piccadilly.

The Club was keen to support not only Olympic classes such
as the Solings, but also the popular level rating classes and
their associated international championships. In 1970 the
Royal Thames decided to follow the lead of other senior
clubs and adopt the International Offshore Rule for the
1971 season, when in conjunction with the Junior Offshore
Group, they ran the International Half Ton Cup Championship
using HMS Vernon at Portsmouth as their base. These 'Ton'

championships based on fixed ratings under the IOR Rule
were now being run at five levels from Quarter Ton to Two
Ton. Perhaps the most unusual feature of the 1971 championship was that the Royal Navy made available to the race
committee the fast patrol boat *HMS TENACITY* which was
capable of speeds up to 50 knots. It is doubtful whether any
other race committee had been able to relocate itself at such
speed! 1971 also saw the Club provide training races for
Olympic Classes at the request of the RYA - these were
based on Shore House - and included Solings, Finns, Flying
Dutchmen and Tempests.

In February 1971 Mr John Savage asked the Sailing Committee
to consider sponsoring a series of four races in 1972 to be
run on the lines of the Admiral's Cup. He suggested that the
series might be called the Mountbatten Cup - but nothing
came of his proposal. Lastly, another topic raised at the AGM
in October 1971 was that the Club should consider seeking
approval to fly once again a deface White Ensign. While those
present were in favour of the proposal it was not followed up.
It must have been very unlikely that approval full of change
would have been forthcoming from the Ministry of Defence.

In 1972 Shore House was once again used as a base for racing.
This was for the Wayfarer National Championships which
were sailed in the Hill Head area on Olympic courses.
This was yet another busy year for the Race Committee;
in addition to their usual regattas and racing with JOG, the
Club ran the National Championship for the two-man 470
class. For many years the Club had been encouraging members who entered races in the RORC championship series to
do so under the Royal Thames burgee. At long last in 1972
their encouragement was rewarded and the Club won the
championship for the first time.

The Club's commitment to level rating racing continued
throughout the decade. In 1973 they were to run the
International Quarter Ton Championship at Weymouth,
an event that attracted entries from seven nations though
predictably the bulk of the 38 competitors were from the UK.
Three years later the race committee went to Plymouth to
organise the International Three-Quarter Ton Championship,
grateful to be supported by sponsorship from Coca Cola who,
together with the Daily Telegraph, gave further sponsorship
in 1978 of the International Half Ton Cup which was run out
of Poole as was the Two Ton Cup in the following year.

Many yachting organisations and clubs in the UK were acutely
aware of the rising popularity of level rating racing and sensed
the need to form a British Level Rating Association.
The Royal Thames was closely associated with this objective.
With encouragement from Bruce Banks they included a regatta
for Level Rating Classes in their 1974 race programme as well
as a race from Cowes to Deauville. Two years later the Club
ran the BLRA National Championship as well as an earlier
weekend regatta. This pattern continued to the end of the
decade with the National Championship held at Lymington
and sponsored by Dunhills. In 1979 it was very successfully
held at Harwich with sponsorship by Chloride Industrial
Batteries Ltd - who were also the sponsor in 1978. The big
entry for this championship in the 1970s continued into the
next decade, but by 1980 the cost of building and racing level
rating yachts (which tended to be outdated in a season or two)
was becoming prohibitive and yachtsmen were turning to the
increasingly popular range of one design classes which
retained their effectiveness for many seasons and could be
used in reasonable comfort for family cruising.

Once racing had settled down in the post war years a succession of proposals was made by the Clubs involved to standardise aspects and procedures followed during Cowes Week. These were rejected on a regular basis in the 1960s but the pressure for change remained. For the 1970s season agreement was reached to establish a panel of course setters to operate throughout the week with the expectation that this would develop expertise in this difficult and ever-criticised task. In 1973 the Royal Thames and the Royal London decided to work together and operate through a combined team of race officers for their two days of Cowes Week. Four years later the Royal Southampton Yacht Club was added to the Thames and London combined team to form a triumvirate to control the first three days of Cowes Week, the three clubs taking it in turn to provide the Principal Race Officer and to organise the team of Race Officers. In 1975, the Bicentenary year, the Club held a match against the Seanwanhaka Corinthian Yacht Club in August, the match being sailed in *DARING* class yachts. There was some concern that the RTYC team contained only two Club members and although the English Speaking Union Trophy competed for in that match had been set up for the Bicentenary year only, a second match in the USA was agreed for 1977 when, with help from the Daring Class, the club fielded a more representative team led by John Godfrey.

1977 was the year of HM The Queen's Silver Jubilee. To recognise this anniversary the Royal Thames organised a Silver Jubilee Race which embraced yacht clubs from all around the British Isles. Invitations to participate were sent to the Royal Channel Islands, Royal Corinthian, Royal Cornwall, Royal Dee, Royal Forth, Royal Northern, Royal Harwich, Royal Ulster and the Royal Western (of England) Yacht Clubs. Each club organised its own race, the object being to sail the greatest nautical mileage around listed marks within a 24 hour period. These races took place during the weekend 4 - 6 June in very unpleasant weather conditions with winds varying between Force 6 and Force 9! This meant that of the 118 entries only 71 started and in the Royal Ulster race none of the five starters finished.

The prize for the overall winner on corrected time was the Cup presented by the Prince of Wales to mark the Silver Jubilee of HM King George V in 1935 (and then won by the 12 metre yacht *VANITY* owned by W R Westhead). On this occasion the winner was *ANDROMEDA* owned by A L Stead of the Royal Dee YC.

Honorary Sailing Secretary

When Mr John Maddocks was appointed to this office in 1970 in succession to Mr Jonathan Janson, the appointment coincided with the Club's decision to widen its activities into the realms of national and international championships. This inevitably brought with it a considerable increase in secretarial work. To meet this demand it was agreed to appoint a full time, paid, Assistant Secretary (Sailing) - who in turn evolved into today's holders of the post of Sailing Secretary.

Prior to 1935 all sailing was managed by the Sailing Committee and the Ryde Committee also provided assistance. The first Honorary Sailing Secretary was Mr B T Rumble who held the office until Mr G G Dudley Head took over in 1948. He in turn was succeeded by Major Peter Snowden in 1955, the succession sequence being completed by Mr Jonathan Janson in 1961. These distinguished members of the Club undertook onerous and time-consuming duties. In addition, although

answerable to the Sailing Committee, it was their individual abilities that ensured that the Club was properly represented in many important yachting circles and committees.

Motor Yachts and Cruising

There have always been many Royal Thames Yacht Club members who have owned yachts equipped with a combination of sail and either steam, petrol or diesel engines. These gentlemen's sailing interests were with cruising rather than racing but it was not until 1952 that the Royal Thames took measures to give these yachting members organised activities.

In January 1952 Mr Glynn Terrell wrote to the Sailing committee with the suggestion that a Sub Committee should be elected and known as 'The Motor Yacht Sub Committee' and that its terms of reference should be:

i) To look after the interests of members owning motor yachts

ii) To organise cruises in company to and from various ports both foreign and at home.

The Sailing Committee considered that the activities of motor yachts must be co-ordinated by them and not by a separate Sub Committee, but they did agree to ask Commander Colin Campbell to form a small Sub Committee to draw up proposals for motor yachts. That Sub Committee reinforced the opinion that the Sailing Committee must co-ordinate motor yacht activities. They also recommended that a joint Honorary Sailing Secretary should be appointed for power craft. Lastly they proposed a cruise to Deauville in August 1952 and another in the Solent to Yarmouth at Whitsun; they made the point *'that although these proposals were mainly intended for power craft owners, there might be a number of members who own sailing craft who would also like to take part'.*

The Sailing Committee endorsed these recommendations and appointed Mr P E G Matthey as Joint Honorary Sailing Secretary and decided that craft should rendezvous at Deauville and Trouville immediately prior to the Le Harve regatta so that both the power and sailing craft would be there at the same time. Both these cruises/rallies were very successful and established a pattern for the future. In the following year a fitting out cruise (and dinner) to Cowes was added to the programme as was a cruise to Bembridge. During the remainder of the 1950s cruises to Seaview attracted members as did the rally at Poole in conjunction with the Cowes-Poole passage race. This period also saw the start of rallies on the Beaulieu River and in 1958 a cruise to Cherbourg. In 1956 Mr Peter Matthey asked to stand down as Cruising Secretary, his place being taken by Lt. Col. John I D Home who in turn was succeeded by Mr G C Ray Marshall in 1957 who held the post until January 1962 when Commander Colin Campbell became Honorary Cruising Secretary, ten years after his Sub Committee had recommended the creation of that post. He stayed in office for three years when Mr John B S Savage took over responsibility for cruising.

In December 1974 the Club appointed Major General A O G Mills as a full time Sailing Secretary and immediately concluded that an Honorary Cruising Secretary was no longer required, although a Cruising Sub Committee was retained within the Sailing Committee until the end of 1980 when it was decided that it would be more logical to transfer cruising to the Social

Model of the Folkboat JESTER owned by Michael Richey.

Committee (a decision which has recently been reversed).

During the 1970s the list of venues for cruising and rallies changed little although Lymington was added to that list and proved very popular. While cruising activities were kept within the control of the Sailing Committee it was perhaps inevitable that they took second place after racing, the management of which was the Sailing Committee's principle responsibility. Once the transfer to the Social Committee came about, a far more ambitious programme was to evolve over the next decade but, as the passage of time had shown, the logic changed with the appointment of a Chief Sailing Officer.

Some Successful Royal Thames Yachtsmen

There is a high risk factor associated with identifying successful or outstanding yachtsmen. It is inevitable, therefore, that some of those who are identified in the next few paragraphs will be representative of the many. On the other hand the achievements of some are unique and would be included by most in their list of outstanding yachtsmen.

In the 'between war' years many of the successful Royal Thames yachtsmen have been mentioned already and not least those who sailed in the national and international events raced in 8 metre and 6 metre yachts for the Coupe de France, the Cumberland Cup and the British American Series. In these events some of the most successful were **Sir Ralph Gore**, **Roland B Worth** and **Colonel E T Peel**. In the later 1920s and throughout the 1930s much of the glamour of yacht racing centred on the 'Big Class' yachts including the J Class. In this class the names that come to mind most readily are **Tom Sopwith** (*ENDEAVOUR*), **Hugh Paul** (*ASTRA*) and **Herman Andreae** (*CANDIDA*). The spectacle of this class competing in crisp sailing conditions brought excitement of a high order to any regatta - and it must never be forgotten that most of the Big Class were designed by **Charles E Nicholson**, who was also a member of the Royal Thames, and built at Camper and Nicholsons's yard. *ENDEAVOUR's* challenge for the Americas' Cup must surely be one of the most poignant 'almost successful' occasions in yachting history. While neither *ASTRA* nor *CANDIDA* challenged for the America's Cup, their success is well illustrated by their achievements in their early years - ASTRA took 26 flags from 49 starts in the 1928-30 seasons while *CANDIDA* took 43 from 69 starts in 1929-30 alone.

In the post-war years many Royal Thames yachtsmen were selected to represent their country in the Olympic Games. The first and arguably the most successful was **Stewart H Morris** who won a Gold Medal in 1948 in the Swallow Class in his boat *SWIFT*. Others might say that Stewart Morris's success was better demonstrated by his achievements with the many boats he owned in the International 14 class and in particular by winning the Prince of Wales Cup for that class on more than a dozen occasions. The cup was presented by the Prince of Wales (later Edward VIII) in 1927 to encourage racing in 'open' boats - he could not have envisaged the huge class that would grow from his encouragement. Stewart Morris who died in 1991, was Yachtsman of the Year in 1961 and had been President of the RYA 1980-83. He bequeathed to the Royal Thames a number of his silver trophies and a collection of half models of his successful boats. These are all displayed in the Royal Thames Library.

In the 1956 Olympics **Lt. Col. R S G Perry** (who had also represented Great Britain in the 1952 Olympics) won the

Silver Medal in the 5.5 metre class with his yacht *VISION* and was one of the successful helmsman of the Club Syndicate's 6 metre yacht *ROYAL THAMES*. In the 1960 Olympics no fewer than five members were selected: **William L Davies** - who presented to the club a half model of his Flying Dutchman - **Robin A Aisher** in the 5.5 metre class, **J R Roy Mitchell** in the Star Class, **Vernon G L Stratton** in the Finn Class and **Jonathan Janson** who crewed in the Dragon Class. The Team Captain for the British entry in 1960 was **Sir Kenneth Preston**, who had taken part in the 1936 Olympics (in the 8 metre class) and again in 1952 (in the 6 metre class).

There were some Royal Thames yachtsmen who had one particular year of special success. Among those are **Simon Tait** who, in 1965, won the European Dragon Class Championship and the Edinburgh Cup; **David Macaulay** whose feats in 1968 are referred to under 'Models' in Section VI. Voted Yachtsman of the Year in 1975, **Robin Aisher** had captained the successful British team in the Admiral's Cup in his yacht *YEOMAN XX* (also in the team was Rear Commodore **John Prentice** in *BATTLECRY* and who was later to take a leading part in the revival of the 6 metre class in the 1980s). Robin Aisher's successes are too numerous to list here but they include representing Great Britain in the 5.5. metre class in the Olympic Games of 1960, 1964 and 1968 (when he won a Bronze medal) and winning the Coupe de France in 1967. The British Admiral's Cup teams have included many other Royal Thames members such as **David May** and **Donald Parr** or more recently **Graham Walker**, all of whom have met success in other events. The 1968 Olympic Games also saw another yachtsman (who was to become a member of the Royal Thames in 1969) win a gold medal - **Iain Macdonald-Smith** crewed for Rodney Pattison in the Flying Dutchman class.

Success of a different kind was achieved by **Michael W Richey** in his modified folkboat *JESTER*. The boat was built by Harry Feltham at Portsmouth 1953 for Colonel H G 'Blondie' Hasler (whose wartime exploits were made into the film 'The Cockleshell Heroes'). It was Hasler who, dissatisfied with the racing scene 'which went nowhere', conceived the notion of a Single Handed Transatlantic Race (OSTAR) and who with three others (including Sir Francis Chichester) competed in the first race in 1960. It was also Hasler who decided to fit out *JESTER*, prior to the race, with a Chinese Lugsail, a self-steering gear of his own design and who brought all 'controls' to a single point in the cockpit. When Michael Richey bought *JESTER* in 1964 she had already completed four Atlantic crossings and he was to complete (nearly!) a further ten crossings. On the return crossing to this country in 1986 *JESTER* met a violent storm in the middle of the night some 300 miles west of Ushant. The boat made two 360⁰ rolls and Richey seriously injured his back but was able to call for aid - which came from a nearby Geest banana boat that rescued both Richey and *JESTER*. Two years later he was not so fortunate when the boat was overwhelmed in a storm 470 miles south east of Nova Scotia. This time Richey was rescued but, very reluctantly, he had to abandon *JESTER*.

To mention only successful racing yachtsmen would be to ignore the many who have embarked on long and adventurous cruises ever since Earl Brassey's famous voyages in *SUNBEAM* a hundred years ago. In modern times **John Foot** cruised extensively in the Mediterranean in his yachts *WATER MUSIC* and experienced the extremes of weather that that sea can provide. Even more recently **Bernard Fison** in *OD I* completed a remarkable and fascinating circumnavigation of the World and sent back to the club his description of his experiences in his own unique style. **Christopher Robinson** in *RISING STAR* has cruised the length and breadth of the Pacific Ocean. Cruising, a vital element in the life of the Royal Thames finds its members ever ready to challenge the oceans of the world.

Throughout its long history the Royal Thames Yacht Club has done much to encourage yacht racing through its generous award of prizes and trophies to members of the Club and to other yachtsmen who are not members. For today's members the most prestigious trophy to be awarded by the Club is the **Docker Cup**. This elegant cup was presented to the Club in 1952 by the then Vice Commodore, Sir Bernard Docker. It was agreed that the cup would be awarded to the member of the Club who had achieved the outstanding performance in yachting during the year - provided the Sailing Committee considered that there was a member whose achievements justified the award.

A list of the winners of this trophy is given in Appendix 12 from which it will be seen that the first winner in 1952 was Myles Wyatt who crossed the Atlantic to take part in the Newport – Bermuda Race and came 2nd in Class A of that race. The most recent winner in 1998, Bob Miller, broke the record for the fastest crossing of the Atlantic in a monohull. During the years in between these two winners most of the

members featured above as 'successful yachtsmen' as well as members referred to elsewhere in this book, are also past winners of the Docker Cup.

Among the winners whose achievements have not been recorded are Sir Gordon Smith, Dragon World Champion in 1961 and Derek Boyer who, in 1963, won the Fastnet Race and was an Admiral's Cup team member. Two members were awarded the cup when they were octogenarians - Sir Owen Aisher for his outstanding performance with Yeoman XXI in 1981 and Lord Harvington in 1985 for his many years of devoted service as a Race Officer. A very different basis for the award occurred in 1993 when Pat Dyas's exceptional endeavour led to the resurrection of the Royal Corinthian Yacht Club at Cowes. Another 'resurrection' to be recognised was the restoration of the *ENDEAVOUR* in 1989 by Frank Murdoch, a member of Tom Sopwith's afterguard in the 1934 America's Cup Challenge with *ENDEAVOUR*. Peter Snowden's years of untiring devotion and service as Secretary of the Cowes Combined Clubs Committee and the SCRA earned him the cup in 1990. As is evident, the Club over the years, deemed it appropriate to widen the field from which winners were selected to include not only racing members but also race officers such as Ricky Hamilton-Parks, David Arnold, Ralph James and George Shillitoe, while in 1991 David Diehl's drive that produced the Inter Club One Design Class, the Sigma 38, was recognised.

III

Administration

Committee Structure

Throughout the 'between war' years the Committee structure varied little. The General and Sailing Committees continued to be the major executive committees with considerable support from the House and Finance Committee and the Wine and Cigar Committee. In addition there were smaller committees for Cards and Billiards (these two were combined in 1938), a Garage Committee, a Ladies Room Committee (from 1925) and a Ryde Committee (from 1927).

The problems that beset the Club in wartime were manifest in March 1940 when the General Committee resolved *'that for the duration of the war, unless circumstance should necessitate otherwise, the General Committee would function as the House and Finance Committee'*. In practice this situation lasted only until April 1943 when a separate House and Finance Committee was restored into office.

The General Committee in 1919 comprised 21 elected members of whom one third were required to retire at each AGM, retiring members being ineligible for re-election for a further year. This rule is unchanged today. What has changed over the years is the number of members forming the Committee and the qualifications of those members. At the AGM in 1935 a strongly debated resolution was eventually carried which altered the Rules to require that of the 21 members at least 12 should be 'yachting' members. This may seem a strange and even unnecessary regulation in a yacht club. In fact it simply reflects the number of non-yachting members who had been attracted by the Club's social facilities. In 1951 it was agreed that a more slimline committee might operate more easily and the size was reduced from 21 to 15 members of whom not less than 9 must be yachting members. A further reduction was approved in 1971 when the number of members of the committee changed from 15 to 12 of whom not less than 7 must be yachting members.

The General Committee of Management is by definition the ultimate arbiter on important matters of overall Club policy and, when appropriate, on individual matters recommended by Sub Committees. A typical example of the latter arose in July 1966. The House and Finance Committee set up a review of the operation of the Clubhouse. The report included a recommendation to increase the bar prices. This they referred to the Wine and Cigar Committee for approval, but, the General Committee disagreed and decreed that the formula for arriving at bar prices must rest with the House and Finance Committee and be subject to General Committee approval. It might be thought that this was a heavy handed

procedure but at that time in particular, when the finances of the Club were in a delicate state, the Committee were only too well aware of the need to achieve the right price - if it was set too low the inadequate profit margin would aggravate the deficit; set it too high and members would not only complain but resign and so further aggravate the deficit!

In spite of what might be concluded from the above, the General Committee were prepared to delegate authority. In March 1967 they decided that they would meet once every other month (instead of every month) and in order to allow financial expenditure to be incurred they delegated to the House and Finance Sub Committee authority for the expenditure of up to £100 on any one item with a total expenditure of £500 between any two meetings of the General Committee.

Changes to the Committee structure were by no means a rare occurrence even though most of them had the same objective - to improve the control of the Club's financial affairs. Not all the changes were productive, some were short-lived and others were decidedly unpopular. In July 1969 it was decided to use the services of a wine consultant to advise on a purchasing policy for wines. Although members were elected to the Wine and Cigar Sub Committee in November 1969 they would seem to have been kept in a state of animated suspension. It was not until September 1970 that a member put down a resolution for the October AGM wishing to dispose of the wine adviser and reconstitute the Wine and Cigar Sub Committee. The General Committee agreed before the AGM took place and the resolution was withdrawn.

In December 1969 more Committee structure changes were agreed, the more important of which were that the General Committee would meet monthly, the Secretary would take on much of the work of the House and Finance Sub Committee and the latter would be convened only if and when considered necessary by the General Committee.

It had always been the responsibility of the House and Finance Sub Committee to plan for and arrange social affairs in the Club's calendar. In May 1975 it was agreed to appoint a Social Sub Committee. This Sub Committee's responsibilities were expanded in 1981 when the Cruising Sub Committee (of the Sailing Committee) was transferred to them and they subsequently were called the Social and Cruising Committee. A far more radical change was decided upon in August 1977 with the formation of the Membership Sub Committee to whom the General Committee delegated the authority to elect members of the Club, thus replacing the historic procedure of election by ballot at meetings of the General Committee.

Perhaps the most far-reaching change took place at the October 1979 AGM when it was agreed that the General Committee could vary annual subscriptions instead of relying on the acceptance of a resolution by a General Meeting of the members. This decision gave the General Committee the authority they needed if they were to manage effectively and not be frustrated by those members who chose to attend General Meetings and were not persuaded by the Flag Officer or a Committee member who presented a resolution to vary subscription rates.

The Flag Officers and the members of the General Committee all too often found themselves and their decisions to be the subject for complaint and criticism when the Club's affairs were not running smoothly. The critics would do well to recognise that these are the only members of the Club who are elected to their office by a General Meeting and that by attending the Annual General Meeting every member has the opportunity to vote for the most able of the nominated candidates. It would be naive to suggest that this represented a truly democratic process since less than 5% of members attend an AGM (though when critical topics are on the agenda 10-15% have attended). Even so it is a practice accepted over the decades. A proposal to introduce postal voting was made in 1952 and rejected. Later, at the 1973 AGM, a resolution to introduce postal voting was put forward but once again the resolution was not carried, albeit by a small majority.

The Royal Thames has been fortunate in that the vast majority of its Flag Officers and Committee members have been able and hard working in the interests of the Club. It might even be said that there have been occasions when they have gone too far in trying to meet members' wishes.

Perhaps one of the best illustrations of the lot of the Committee member is reflected in the remarks by the Commodore at the April 1971 Special General Meeting when introducing yet another resolution to increase subscriptions. He said to the 84 members present *'I would ask you to remember that the Committee members are also members of the Club and sometimes the things they have to do are just as distasteful to them as to any other members. It is not a pleasant duty'.*

What is certain is that the Royal Thames members of the General Committees over the years do not in any way resemble the figures portrayed by Richard Hawkness in his cynical comment written in the New York Herald Tribune on 15 June 1960 when he asked *'what is a Committee?'* and replied *'it is a group of the unwilling picked from the unfit to do the unnecessary!'*

Membership Categories

In 1919 the membership of the Club was limited to 1250 members, that number excluding Honorary Members, Supernumerary Members and Ordinary or Service Members permanently resident abroad. There were no variations in the category of membership - everyone was an 'ordinary' member of Club. There were, however, variations and concessions when it came to the subscription payable. A member's subscription varied depending upon the year of election (and the subscription payable at that time), whether or not he owned a yacht of not less than 9 ton TM and whether he had served in the armed forces or were still on active service. By 1939 little had changed except the general level of subscription payable. In 1928 there were a series of amendments

to the rules agreed at the AGM and for the first time a rule was included in the Members' Book specifying the limitations to the privileges enjoyed by Lady Members. Two years later the Members' Book listed Lady Members separately. In fact, the only change made in the 20 years period to 1939 was the introduction of Cadet Membership in 1931 for *'Gentlemen over the age of 18 years, but under the age of 25 years, who, in the opinion of the Committee are bona fide yachtsmen'.* Cadets were not required to pay an entrance fee on election and, like Lady Members, their privileges were restricted.

In 1940 a member suggested that a subscription concession should be made for members living outside London. This was not pursued at the time but 'Country' membership was introduced shortly after the war. In 1949 it was agreed that members *'domiciled outside a radius of 50 miles from Hyde Park Corner and having no place of residence or business within that area'* shall pay a reduced subscription - a concession that was to remain in force for nearly 50 years.

As in the 1914-18 war, a special subscription concession was made *'as a mark of honour to yachtsmen who have served their country'.* This was limited to 50 bona fide yachtsmen.

The AGM in March 1949 was not only a protracted meeting for the 131 members present, it was also one that had to address the Club's pressing problems of shortage of income, increasing costs and falling membership (at the time of the meeting numbers were just below 1000). After lengthy discussion, increased subscription levels were approved; the membership limit was raised to 2000 and more concessions were approved to encourage young yachtsmen to apply for membership. Two 'Younger Member' categories were agreed: 21 - 28 years of age and 27 - 32 years - they would pay subscriptions of one third and two thirds that paid by ordinary members. The upper age limit for Cadet members was adjusted down to 'under 22'. In 1980 the lower age for Cadets (male or female) was reduced to 16 years.

By the end of 1949 it was clear that the actions agreed in March were insufficient to stem the Club's operating loss. Accordingly a Special General Meeting was called in December, the principal resolution for the meeting being a proposal to introduce two categories of associate member. The first category was for wives of ordinary members; and the second was for *'any member of a selected Yacht Club, provided that he is a bona fide amateur yachtsman'.* The reasoning behind the proposal for the latter category was that it was felt that many yachtsmen, members of other yacht clubs, work in London and would welcome the opportunity to use a London yacht club during the week. Once again this meeting provoked intense discussion from the 170 members present but eventually the proposal for two categories of Associate members was agreed in principal only and the Committee were asked to review the conditions for membership before implementing the resolution. The committee quickly decided to proceed with election of Associate Lady Member and 20 were elected in January 1950 (the limit being 50). They were elected for one year only but could be re-elected each year. A resolution concerning the introduction of Associate Yachtsmen came before the March 1950 AGM but was withdrawn at the meeting; it then reappeared at the SGM in October 1950 and the voting was 62 in favour with 46 against, the vote not achieving the two thirds majority required by the Club Rules. The Committee abandoned the Associate Yachtsmen proposal, changed the title of Associate Lady Members to Lady Associate Members and increased their limit from 50 to 75. It was further increased in 1954 to120. The maximum numbers for Lady Members was also to be increased in 1957 from 25 to 50 in recognition of the wish of the Committee and the members to increase the use of the Club by Ladies even though the facilities available for them in Hyde Park House were quite inadequate.

The Associate Members scheme reared its head again in a resolution to the April 1971 SGM under the title 'Nominated Members'. Once again it was not supported. It finally emerged in 1974 as the Controlled Membership Scheme for visiting yachtsmen but did little to enhance usage of the Club's facilities.

The April 1959 AGM introduced further subscription concessions with the aim of encouraging new members and retaining the older members. The resolution allowed *'Senior or Aged members who have retired from active business to apply to the Committee for a reduced subscription'* and allowed all members to pay their subscriptions quarterly or half-yearly *'for an addition of half a guinea with each payment'.* The rule concerning older members' subscription was put on a more regular basis in 1967 when it was changed to provide that members aged 65 or over whose age plus years of membership totalled 85 would pay half the ordinary members subscription. This AGM also introduced the requirement for candidates for election to have not only a proposer and seconder but also five supporters. The latter requirement proved to be somewhat 'two-edged' - it gave assurance as to the suitability of the candidate but it also had the potential to discourage candidature. The Committee recognised this latter problem and on occasions were prepared to assist candidates to find supporters.

The number of members rose rapidly from 1949 so that by 1964 it was fast approaching 1600 and the Committee became concerned that the facilities of the new Clubhouse might become overloaded. In consequence they introduced restrictions on the number of candidates to be elected each month. The plan was to elect not more than 10 per month of whom only one could be a non-yachting member. The remainder, who had already been classified by the Sailing Committee, would be placed on a waiting list. This precautionary action proved to be unnecessary and two years later the limit was removed but the election of only one non-yachting member in ten was retained.

Over the past 30 years changes to the membership structure has been relatively small. Reference has already been made to the dropping of the Country category of membership in 1987. The categories for Younger Members have been changed from two to three levels and in this age of 'political correctness' the Lady Associate Member category has been renamed Associate Member to enable a spouse of a member (male or female) to be admitted to that category. At the same time in 1992 no more Ladies were admitted to the category of Lady Member. Those ladies already elected and who so wished could now apply for Ordinary Membership under the same terms as men.

Long before the term 'political correctness' was coined, two matters that might have come under that heading arose. In June 1928 a proposal was made that the Royal Thames should form a Club Masonic Lodge to be called ' The Cumberland Fleet Lodge'. The Committee rejected the proposal. Six years later the question of electing to membership people of Jewish faith arose. The Committee resolved *'that Jews should come up for election in the ordinary way*

and that they should not be rejected on racial grounds'. In spite of this unequivocal position taken by the Club at that time and since, the rumour has persisted that the Royal Thames Yacht Club is opposed to the admission to membership of the Jewish faith. This misrepresentation has continued to rear its head from time to time and has always been absolutely rejected.

The other category of membership that has been introduced in the past 20 years is the 'Knightsbridge Member'. This came about as part of the agreement with the Anglo Belgian Club when they moved to 60 Knightsbridge at the beginning of 1980. The object was to create a Royal Thames category separate from existing categories that could equate to the Anglo Belgian 'Town' member in terms of both privileges and subscription level.

From the earliest days of the Club, the Members' Book has contained, among other important information, the rules concerning membership and the subscription to be paid by the different categories. Once the responsibility for setting subscription levels was transferred from the AGM to the General Committee there was no need to include the subscription to be paid in the Rules and it was omitted from 1982. Today members are accustomed to the loose leaf Members Book produced from the Club's computerised records. What may not be known is that a proposal to computerise membership records was made as early as September 1965 and another proposal for a loose leaf Members Book was made in January 1970. Unfortunately such innovations involved increased expenditure and could not have been justified in those times of financial stress.

Membership Numbers

Throughout the years covered by this Volume the number of members of the Club has varied considerably from just under 1000 to just over 1600. Since the income from member's subscriptions forms a significant part of the Club's annual income, this has made life particularly difficult for those members responsible for the management of the Club.

During the years 1914-18, and in spite of the war, membership held up at around 1080 but, by 1923, the years of uncertainty - both nationally and within the Club (while a decision was made to move to a new Clubhouse) - reduced numbers by 12%. Once established in Hyde Park House, the Club prospered and by 1930 the membership had increased by 48% over seven years and stood at over 1400. The years of national economic depression in the early 1930s took their toll on many Club members (in 1931 alone some 150 members resigned) and by 1934 there had been a loss of 14% of the membership.

The outbreak of war in September 1939 saw the immediate resignation of 50 members (the Club not being prepared to offer them reduced subscriptions for the duration of the war but accepting their resignation and hoping they would rejoin at a later date). Even so, numbers were maintained at around 1200 through to 1945. In the post war years numbers increased steadily until 1964 when they had reached 1600 - which was just as well since other sources of income were not doing well and rising costs and wages were bearing down on the Club's ability to 'break-even'. The numbers were kept at around 1500 for the next ten years but by the end of the 1970s they could barely maintain a figure of 1300, with 192 resignations in 1974 alone.

For the past 20 years a level of 1400-1500 has been maintained for much of the time although the problems caused for some of the members who were 'names' at Lloyds at the time of their heavy losses did have an effect on membership.

Over the years many strategies have been agreed by the Committee with the aim of increasing membership, which in turn, would increase usage of the Club's facilities. Apart from making concessions on subscription or withdrawing the requirement to pay an entrance fee, the principal tactics were either to attract suitable members from London Clubs that were closing down or to consider amalgamation with Clubs that were struggling to continue. In 1931 and 1934 respectively, former members of the Junior Athenaeum Club and the Wellington Club were offered membership of the Royal Thames. In the post war years, two schemes for amalgamation were considered. The first was with the Thatched House Club in 1949 (a club that had often opened their facilities to Royal Thames members when the Clubhouse was closed for maintenance work) but nothing came of the proposal. Later, in 1951, there appeared to be a much better chance of success with the Oriental Club but eventually that scheme also came to nought. Yet another option considered early in 1977 was amalgamation with the Junior Carlton Club but this too failed to materialise. It was not until 1980 that a successful joint usage of the Clubhouse was achieved and this led to the arrival of the Anglo Belgium Club.

Membership for Ladies

The acceptance into membership of the Club of ladies who are yacht owners has never been a contentious issue, but once the social aspects of ladies' membership arose, the privileges of membership for them were strictly limited. The Royal Thames Yacht Club was seen as being no different from all the other Gentlemen's Clubs in London and ladies did not feature in the social life of these male bastions.

In 1919 there were only five Lady Members of the Club but by 1930 the number had increased to 14 and to 17 by 1939, the maximum number permitted being 25. The number of Lady Members was only 15 at the time when Lady Associate Members were accepted in 1951.

In spite of the presence of ladies in the Club membership, their rooms in Hyde Park House were quite separate - and quite inadequate. Even after the redevelopment and building of the present Clubhouse the ladies had from 1964 a separate lounge and a separate staircase leading to a separate dining room. There were several plans to modify or extend Hyde Park House in the post war years with a view to providing improved facilities for the Ladies (but none came to fruition) and both the Committee and the members at large recognised the need to encourage ladies to become members. Even so ladies were not permitted to make use of the public rooms except on special occasions such as a Coronation Day. On the other hand gentlemen could dine with the ladies in the latter's dining room and when the numbers in there became too great (in the present Clubhouse) it was agreed that the folding partitions may be opened - not least when the 'gentlemen's dining room' was much under occupied. Use of all public rooms by ladies eventually was accepted by 1980 except that the Cumberland Bar was to remain in use for gentlemen only at lunch time.

There were many occasions when the subject of privileges for ladies in the Clubhouse appeared on the agenda of meetings of the General Committee - some of these are recalled in the paragraphs that follow.

In the years following the cessation of hostilities in 1918 the Clubhouse was open throughout the public holidays. When the Committee met in December 1921 a letter written on behalf of several members was considered. It requested approval to bring ladies into the Clubhouse for dinner on Christmas Eve, Christmas Day and Boxing Day. After considerable deliberation the Committee decided that they could not grant the request. On the other hand in February 1922 members were allowed to bring one or two ladies into the Clubhouse to watch a (Royal) Wedding procession (there was a charge of 2/6 per lady).

In 1926 a bye law was introduced requiring members and their male guests to wear evening dress when using the ladies dining room after 7.30pm (accompanied by ladies). This did not please all members and was relaxed, for Sunday evenings only, in 1932. The bye law was suspended during the 1939-45 war years and withdrawn altogether shortly after the war. In December 1927 the Committee received a particularly strongly worded letter from a member expressing disapproval of *'those members who introduced ladies into Public Rooms on Armistice night'*. Many years later in February 1965 a very different form of complaint was received and this concerned a member who had taken his lady guest into the Ladies Room when she was wearing trousers. The Committee decided that *'it would be difficult for the Hall Porter to draw the attention of a member to the fact that his lady guest was unsuitably dressed'* and therefore introducing a bye law to that effect would be inappropriate. Instead it was decided that members should report such matters to the Secretary who would then ask the Chairman to write to the members concerned. More than a decade was to pass before 'trouser suits' were deemed to be suitable attire for ladies.

In December 1965 the Sailing Committee were required to make a difficult decision involving discrimination against ladies. This concerned the presentation of the Club's Challenge Cups at the annual Laying Up Dinner. They decided, after some considerable discussion, that the status quo should be maintained and that *'should a lady win one of the Club's Cups she should be asked to nominate a male person to attend the dinner to receive the cup on her behalf'*. The question arose because this ruling had been challenged by a lady who won a cup in 1965. The details of this 'challenge' are recorded later in this volume in Section VIII. A related topic arose 14 months later and concerned the Fitting Out Dinner due to be held in March 1967. A letter signed by 10 members deplored the Committee's decision to allow ladies to be present a the Fitting Out Dinner. The Chairman informed the signatories that 43 members had signified a wish to attend the Dinner with their ladies! This was yet another occasion when the Committee were to find themselves criticised no matter what their decision might be. In the event, this particular dinner was cancelled because the principal guests were unable to attend.

The integration of ladies into the privileges of membership that were available to gentlemen was a long and, by some, a resisted process. Most members recognised that it was both necessary and important. In 1967 it was agreed that Lady Members may reserve bedrooms and the ceiling on Lady Members was raised to 100. In 1976 ladies were permitted to attend the Laying Up Dinner and by 1978 ladies were to serve on Sub Committees. In 1980 Lady Members privileges were extended and before long they were to be elected to the General Committee. This would seem to leave just one further step to be taken - for the Club to elect their first lady as a Flag Officer.

Distinguished Members

To attempt to identify who should be included under such a heading is an invidious task dependent on highly subjective criteria and, inevitably, personal choice. As has already been said in the Flag Officers section only a few can be chosen if the subject is to be kept within reasonable bounds and many worthy members will regrettably be omitted.

In February 1926 the Committee elected to membership of the Club a gentleman listed as 'Member of Lloyds'. His name was Malcom Campbell and no one at that time would have foreseen his future achievement of holding speed records on both land and water. At the March 1931 AGM the Commodore, Lord Queenborough, included in his remarks the words: *'Occasionally we have something which is out of the ordinary here in this Club, and I have in mind a very successful dinner which we gave to a very gallant man two or three nights ago'.* This referred, of course, to **Sir Malcolm Campbell**'s attempt on the World Land Speed Record and his further successful attempts. In November 1946 it was the Sailing Committee who discussed a letter from him seeking approval to fly the Club's Burgee during his attempt to obtain the World Water Speed Record. The Committee's reply was that *'should his attempt on the record be of a sporting and pleasure nature and not be of a commercial character, there could naturally be no objection to his flying the Club Burgee'.* He was to die 2 years later.

A month after Malcolm Campbell's election to membership another gentlemen was elected who was to reach the pinnacle of a racing yachtsman's endeavour. **Thomas O M Sopwith** was a very experienced yachtsmen by the time he bought *SHAMROCK V* from Sir Thomas Lipton in 1932. His experience with this unsuccessful challenger for the America's Cup encouraged him to build his own J Class challenger *ENDEAVOUR* for the 1934 races (and later to build *ENDEAVOUR II* for the 1937 challenge). Many consider that *ENDEAVOUR* came closer than any other British challenge to wresting the trophy from the Americans. Although Tom Sopwith's challenge was through the Royal Yacht Squadron, the Royal Thames chose to recognise his outstanding performance by giving a dinner in his honour in November 1934.

Another courageous member of the Club who knew what is was to push himself far beyond what most people can achieve was **Sir Douglas Mawson**. His intrepid journey into and out of Antarctica was recorded in Volume 2. In May 1929, as he was preparing for another expedition into Antarctica, the Sailing Committee agreed that it would be appropriate for him to fly the Royal Thames Burgee and Ensign once again in his boat *DISCOVERY*.

F A (Sandy) Haworth was elected to the Club in October 1935. After war service in the Royal Navy he was to distinguish himself as a racing yachtsman with the Lloyds YC's *LUTINE* of which he was a regular and successful skipper including achieving victory in the 1953 Fastnet Race. Although he became Admiral of Lloyds Y.C., his loyalty and service to the Royal Thames was outstanding. Between 1956 and 1964 he was three times Chairman of Committees and twice Deputy Chairman. He was then to serve as Rear Commodore

Sir Tom Sopwith - Owner of ENDEAVOUR (1934).

(1965-67) and yet a further year as Deputy Chairman (1973-74). Sandy Haworth was liked and respected by all who met him. Any newly elected member could be assured of a welcome from Sandy when making his first tentative steps on to the Quarterdeck and towards the Cumberland Bar. He was an outstanding character in Club life in post-war years and, not least, his gourmet meals were a delight to all whether they were given at his home or on board the Committee Boat when he was serving as a race officer.

In March 1939 the Committee noted the passing of one of the Club's most senior members **Sir Arthur Underhill** (elected 1887). He had founded the Royal Cruising Club in 1880 and was its Commodore from 1885. Two other distinguished members of the Club died a few years later in March 1944 - **William Fife** (elected 1903), one of the great yacht designers of all time and **E Keble Chatterton** (elected 1914) the yachtsman and author.

Three other members should be included in these paragraphs. Firstly the remarkable **Miss Isobel Napier** (elected 1907) who celebrated her 100th birthday in 1970 and became the senior member of the Club, secondly, **Elmer Ellsworth Jones** who was elected Commodore in 1970 (when Earl Mountbatten became Admiral of the Cumberland Fleet) and was thus the only 'commoner' to hold that office in the post war years. Lastly, **Major Charles J.P. Ball** (elected 1935) was to have the onerous task of being Vice Commodore before, throughout, and after the completion of the redevelopment of the Clubhouse. He had already served as Deputy Chairman and Chairman of Committees and as Rear Commodore, when he was elected to office in 1959. Over the next five years he was at the centre of the problems associated with persuading

the membership that redevelopment was the way ahead.
He then provided the leadership to see it implemented and
to keep the Club together and alive during those years without a Clubhouse that were spent at the Army and Navy Club
in Piccadilly.

Distinguished Honorary Members

Honorary Membership was, by custom, offered to distinguished visitors to London. Three such instances are noted
here. In May 1921 the visiting **Australian Cricket XI** were
made Honorary Members - an interesting if surprising gesture
(cricket buffs may not wish to be reminded that Australia won
the series 3-0). It was always the practise to offer Honorary
Membership to selected foreign Ambassadors in London. In
October 1932 the Committee decided that sufficient time had
passed since 1918 to enable them to include the **German
Ambassador**. Little did the Committee know that they would
once again withdraw that Honorary Membership less than
seven years later in September 1939. By far the most popular
award of Honorary Membership in the 1930s went to the
American **Gerard B.Lambert**, owner of the big cutter
YANKEE (228 Tons TM), in 1935. She was the first of her
kind to sail across the Atlantic and compete since *VIGILANT*
in 1894. Yankee raced throughout the 1935 season with other
big yachts from the J class, the 23 metre class and Britannia.

Gerard B Lambert - owner of YANKEE (1935).

Review of Yachts in the Solent to celebrate the 90th birthday of HRH Queen Elizabeth, The Queen Mother, 1990.

The Sail Past of the Cumberland Fleet to mark the Bicentenary of the founding of the Cumberland Fleet, 1975.

(Above) WHITE CRUSADER
off Freemantle during
1986-1987 America's
Cup series.

(Right) E I (Ricky)
Hamilton-Parks in his
office at Freemantle, 1986.

WHITE CRUSADER and C2 during trials off Freemantle, 1986.

(Above) Racing on
the Serpentine.

(Right) Team racing
in Sigma 33s for the
Mum's Bucket Trophy.

(Below) The Royal Thames'
RIB in action.

Racing for the Serpentine Cup

(Left) The Royal Thames'
'Flag Officers' team, Peter
Hunter, Paul Archer and
John Bassett (1992).

(Below) Laser racing
in 1995.

(Left) David Arnold fitted into an Illusion (1984).

(Below) Optimists racing in 1992.

RTYC Committee Boats

(Top) FRESHWATER BAY
(David Arnold).

(Above) STROMVARDIE
(Bill Pugh).

(Right) PETER PAN
(Royal Parks).

(Above) 6 metre class racing off Falmouth (1988) in the European Championship.

(Left) 6 metre class yachts alongside in Falmouth (1988).

(Right) The RTYC 'fire-fighters' in action during 6 metre World Champion-ship in Torbay (1991).

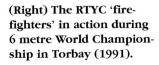

Medina Rally 1992 - What was in the watering can?

Osborne Bay Rally 1992.

(Above) Medina Rally 1990.

(Left) St Vaast Rally 1989.

Sigma 33 racing at RTYC Regatta 1992.

Contessa Class racing at RTYC regatta 1992.

Handicap Class at RTYC Regatta 1987.

Sigma 38 Class racing at National Championship 1989.

(Above) Graham Walker's
INDULGENCE racing
in 1990.

(Right) ENDEAVOUR -
Painting by Frank Mason.

BRITANNIA - Painting by Norman Wilkinson.

The RNLI's 'ROYAL THAMES' at the naming ceremony at Eastbourne 1993.

**(Right) Match Racing in
Seaview Mermaids.**

**(Below) Golf at the
New Zealand Golf Club:
Charles Liddell,
His Royal Highness
The Duke of York and
Peter Hunter (1997).**

(Above) Etchells Class National Championship
in Christchurch Bay 1997.

(Left) Boats of the Etchells fleet under tow to Poole Bay
for their National Championship in 1991.

(Below) Etchells Class European Championship
held out of Yarmouth, Isle of Wight in 1990.

(Left) 50' World
Championship off
Hayling Island in 1993.

(Below) Scandanavian
Gold Cup for 5.5 metre
class 1998.

(Bottom) 5.5 metre British
Open Championship 1998.

IV

The Clubhouse

Piccadilly to Hyde Park House

There were only 40 members present for Annual General Meeting held on 27 March 1919, but they were to hear a statement by the Vice Commodore, Lord Queenborough which was to have a profound effect on the future life of the Club. The key point made in his statement was that *'the Committee was trying indefatigably to find a house more suited to the increasing membership and was glad to say that the Club was strong enough financially to take a larger house and to pay more rent'*. At this stage it would seem that there were no intentions of acquiring the freehold of a property.

In March 1921 a small Sub Committee was appointed to consider the acquisition of Vernon House in Park Place but they found it unsuitable and unable to meet the Club's needs. It was not until April 1922 that they were able to present to the General Committee a positive report containing these salient points:

> *The Club's lease of its Piccadilly premises terminates 1 January 1924.*
> *60 Piccadilly and No 1 Stratton Street are owned by Burdett-Coutts who are seeking a purchaser. Such a purchaser could terminate the Club's lease 1 January 1923 provided they gave six months notice and a payment of £2000.*
> *81 Piccadilly and No 1 Bolton Street will revert to the Sutton estate when the tenancy terminated. In order to secure the Club's future the Sub Committee have inspected several premises but it is proposed that the Club acquire Hyde Park House in Knightsbridge which has more accommodation than 80/81 Piccadilly and some 24 bedrooms as well as staff quarters. It could also provide two rooms for Lady Members and for entertaining ladies and, if desired, it could also provide two squash-courts. This Cubitt built house owned by the Naylor-Leyland family and which could be purchased for £80,000 is in first class repair. There would need to be an increase of 200 in membership to cover the higher expenses involved in operating the house.*

Over the next few months the Committee developed the option to acquire Hyde Park House. The deeper they delved into the financial implications the clearer it became that, in the first instance, a lease should be taken rather than outright purchase. By the end of the year they were ready to put this proposal to the membership and a Special General Meeting,

to be held at Hyde Park House, was called for 24 January 1923. At this meeting the 208 members present were informed by the Vice Commodore that any scheme to redevelop their present Clubhouse on the Piccadilly site would be far too expensive and the Committee therefore recommended taking a 21 year lease on Hyde Park House at £3,500 p.a. This was judged to be the best option the Club could afford and it did include an option for a reasonable purchase of the freehold. During the protracted discussion which followed, the supporters of the scheme were matched all the way by the critics whose principal objections were that the financial estimates drawn up were at best inaccurate; that the Club would sink into financial ruin; that Knightsbridge was far too distant and inaccessible for the many members who worked in the City and that the Club would be swamped by non-yachtsmen. When the resolution to acquire Hyde Park House was put to the vote it was carried by a large majority but no doubt the critics were able at a later date, to remind the Committee that some aspects of their gloomy views came to fruition. Financial ruin was not one of them - though finances were to become stretched.

The tenancy of Hyde Park House commenced on 24 June 1923 and occupation was possible from 1 July. With the move from Piccadilly to Knightsbridge complete, the Club held two celebratory functions. On 27 September a Ball was held at the new Clubhouse - tickets 30 shillings each. Sadly, no detailed account of the evening has been found but no doubt it would have been a splendid occasion held in the magnificent Smoking Room - a room as sumptuous as any Ballroom. The second celebration took place on 1 November when a dinner was held at which the Commodore, Theodore Pim, was a guest - he had just announced his intention to stand down from office at the AGM in March 1924. An article in the December 1923 issue of Yachting Monthly reports the occasion saying *'On 1 November, the first-house dinner was held by members since the Club's removal from their old headquarters at 80 Piccadilly'*. At this dinner a telegram was read which had been received from Lord Stamfordham, Private Secretary to the King. It said: *'I am commanded to thank the Flag Officers and Members of the Royal Thames YC for their kind greetings on the occasion of the first club dinner in their new clubhouse. His majesty congratulates them upon the acquisition of these fine quarters and wishes all possible prosperity, both to the club and to the sport of yacht racing and sailing, with which for the last century and a half it has been so closely identified'*.

When the General Committee met just one week later on 8 November, a Sub Committee was set up to consider a scheme for the purchase of Hyde Park House. The Sub Committee included J.S. Highfield who was Chairman of Committees (and shortly to be elected Rear Commodore) and Allan E Messer who was to succeed him as Chairman and who was re-elected to the General Committee for an extra year to provide continuity with the negotiations. A resolution was put to the March 1924 AGM that the Club purchase the freehold of Hyde Park House and, in order to provide the money needed for the purchase price, a sum not exceeding £70,000 to be raised by the issue of 3500, 5% redeemable mortgage bonds at £20 each. The resolution was carried unanimously. A Special General Meeting had to be called in November 1924 to amend the Club Rules to cover the legal requirements for borrowing money and the provision of security for any sum borrowed. It was also necessary to table a further resolution modifying the one carried in March. This provided that the 3,500 Bonds at £20 each should be 'A' Bonds at 5% redeemable at £21 or 'B' Bonds at $2^{1}/_{2}$% redeemable at £30, the Committee to decide the respective numbers of 'A' and 'B' Bonds, with the whole secured by a Deed of Trust on the property. Messrs Highfield and Messer were able to inform a meeting of the General Committee on 15 January 1925 that the purchase of the freehold had been completed on 8 January. They were rightly well pleased with their achievement, one which today's members would also applaud. Such was the state of elation that the Committee agreed to hold a celebratory dinner (at a date convenient to the Commodore, Lord Queenborough) and to hold a reception at a later date as well as directing the Sailing Committee to arrange special races round the Isle of Wight. The club was now well and truly established for the twentieth century and would be able to grapple with all the many trials and tribulations that were to arise.

The Between-War Years

The first sixteen years of the Club's tenure of Hyde Park House saw a period of relative calm and stability. In April 1924 the Committee agreed to the expenditure of £525 on the building of a squash court, one of the very few alterations made to the property. The membership grew rapidly from 1923 reaching a total of over 1400 by 1930 (swamped by non-yachtsmen?!). This increase in number brought with it increased usage of the Clubhouse facilities, enabling the Club, by 1930, to operate without the burden of a large overdraft. Even so, in 1925 it was necessary to seek the bank's approval to increase the overdraft limit in order to pay Bondholders their dividend. The following year saw the first redemption of Bonds when 33 'A' Bonds and 23 'B' Bonds were drawn by lot. Perhaps the most encouraging feature of the Bond issue was that at the 1928 AGM the Commodore could report that all 3500 Bonds had been taken up.

The General Strike of 1926 barely caused a ripple to Club life except that it created great difficulty in getting out the Race Programme posters. The same could not be said of the repercussions in the UK from the 'Wall Street Crash' of 1929. The membership of the club dropped sharply (151 members resigned in 1931) as did the usage of the dining and bar facilities. Fortunately both were to increase gradually as the 1930s passed. Similarly, the recession limited sailing activities; paid hands were laid off or at best had their wages reduced by 10%.

The discussion at annual meetings of the Club at this time tended to centre on a plea by members for a reduction in charges for meals, wines and spirits, especially if the Club had made a 'profit' in the previous year. At the same time the officers of the Club were appealing to members to make bigger donations to the Regatta Fund and thus avoid the necessity for the all-important sailing programme to be subsidised by the Club's General Fund. Over the past 50 years inflation, at widely ranging levels, has become an accepted factor by those responsible for managing the Club's finances and it is easy to forget that it hardly existed in the between-war years. This is well illustrated by the standard subscription: from 1920 this was thirteen guineas (eleven guineas for yachtsmen, owner of a yacht of not less than nine Tons TM, later reduced to five Tons TM) and this remained unchanged until 1943. If members wanted cheaper meals and the Committee wished to meet their requests then savings had to be achieved either by reducing staff (or even reducing their wages, which already were low) or by foregoing the cost of maintenance of the Clubhouse, neither of which was in any way attractive. Happily, for the majority of the members life proceeded smoothly, the successful ball of 1923 was repeated on 27 September 1924. On 28 January 1928, HRH the Prince of Wales (who had become a member in 1926) attended a House Dinner; members regularly took advantage of the invitation from the Naval and Military Club to use their tent at Ascot and occasionally at Lords.

The annual ball, now moved to the New Year period, remained popular through much of the 1920s and into the next decade. In October 1936 the Ball Sub Committee reported that 190 double and 9 single tickets had been sold already; they also noted that the ladies attending would be given a powder puff case carrying a club burgee and that entertainment at the Ball would be provided by the Roosters Concert Party. Two years later a very different situation existed. On 13 October 1938, the Committee decided that there would be a Staff Ball on 6 January 1939 but there would be no Ball for members. This latter decision was not well received and consequently, seven members invoked the terms of Rule 47 which allows them to call a Special General Meeting. This was almost certainly the first occasion that the rule had been made use of in order to raise a contentious matter. The Vice Commodore J S Highfield chaired the meeting on 19 December, a meeting attended by 57 members, and described it as an Historic Meeting. The Vice Commodore reminded the members of the long history of the Club Balls since 1775. The Vice Commodore also reminded the meeting that in order to make the Ball financially viable 300 tickets needed to be sold and in the past five years that number had been reached only once. In January 1938 only 188 tickets had been sold and that factor combined with the Munich Crisis (and seemingly, impending hostilities) persuaded the Committee that they were not prepared to risk failure through poor support for a Ball. The other factor that influenced the Committee was the large number of complaints received each year from members deprived of the use of the clubhouse on the day of the ball. The protracted discussion opened amiably enough with those seeking to have the Ball reinstated reminding those present that there was precedent for holding a Ball at a time of crisis - the Ball held on the eve of the Battle of Waterloo! As the meeting progressed the amiable attitudes evaporated and acrimony crept in; further, the discussion moved away from the cancellation of the Ball and centred on the variance between the case made by the seven members calling the SGM (to re-open the matter for further consideration) and the statement sent to members calling the meeting (to consider the action of the Committee). Eventually the Vice Commodore persuaded the meeting to vote on a resolution *That a Ball will be held in 1939 on a date to be determined'*. The resolution was carried by 30 votes to 24. By April it was agreed to hold a Ball on 31 May.

The Annual Ball may have been the most elegant event in the social calendar but the regular House Dinners were prestigious occasions held to honour members' achievements or to welcome distinguished guests. On 7 December 1926 a dinner was held to mark the winning of both the Cumberland Cup and the One Ton Cup by the Royal Thames. Mention has already been made of the dinners for the Prince of Wales and Sir Malcolm Campbell. Many other dinners of note were held in the 1930s including one on 5 July 1933 to coincide with the International Regatta, the guests included the French Ambassador, French Naval Attaché and the First Sea Lord. In October 1936 it was agreed to give a dinner at which the guests were Charles W.A. Scott and L. Rome Guthrie, members who had won the Portsmouth to Johannesburg Air Race while on 5 July 1937 the principal guest at a House dinner was HRH the Crown Prince of Norway.

Cocktail Parties, which are a feature in today's calendar, did not appear in the 1930s programme but occasional receptions were held to mark important anniversaries. One such was held on 23 May 1935 to mark the 160th anniversary of the foundation of the Club - the reception was from 9pm to midnight, tickets 5/-.

During the years 1935-37 the Club was much affected by the affairs of the Monarch. In 1935 it was the Silver Jubilee of HM King George V, in 1936, the death of the King and the all too brief reign of King Edward VIII, while 1937 saw the coronation of King George VI. To mark the Silver Jubilee the Club sent to the King (Patron of the Club) a Loyal Address, a coloured copy of which is today hanging on the Quarterdeck of the Clubhouse. Members of the Club also witnessed the Naval Review held to mark the jubilee. Mr Harry Vandervell, a member of the committee, chartered a steamer for the RNVR so that they could watch the Review and offered 100 seats to members of the RTYC at £1 per person. (Many members also attended in their own yachts). At the same time a member of the Committee, Col. J D K Restler, was representing the Club on the committee organising a motor boat pageant to be held on the River Thames on 10 May 1935. In 1937 the Club took the initiative to view the Naval Review by chartering the *SS. BALMORAL* (at a cost of £625) and offering 350 seats to RTYC members and 250 seats to the RNVR Club (each ticket cost 28/-). In addition a special train, having available 400 first class seats, was arranged to leave for Southampton from Waterloo (£15 return fare). For those travelling to Southampton by road, cars could be garaged near to the boat in the Southern Railway 'sheds'.

While members' interest was centred on the events celebrating the Silver Jubilee during March 1935, another event was also drawing members to the Clubhouse. This was the General Election which brought Stanley Baldwin into the National government as Prime Minister in place of Ramsay Macdonald. The arrangement made for members included a license extension until 0300 light refreshments in the Committee Room for members and their male guests and in the Ladies Dining Room for members and their lady guests; there was a transmission of results by amplifier to the Smoking Room and Ladies Dining Room as well as a 'State of the Parties' display in those rooms.

Apart from use of the squash court, recreation in the Clubhouse was mainly devoted to the card room and the billiards table. Each recreation had its own Sub Committee to monitor the rules for play (including permitted level of stakes) and use of the rooms, though in 1938 the Cards and Billiards Sub Committees were merged into one Sub Committee. Interest in the card room was no doubt bolstered by Sir Guy Domville (elected 1927), a bridge player of considerable standing (he was also the last member to be a permanent resident in the club). Such was the interest in cards that in May 1935 the club authorised the purchase of 3000 packs of cards (carrying the club burgee) at £9 per gross. These were to be sold at 3/- per pack (gilt edged) or 2/6 (without), while used packs were available at 9d. A simple calculation suggests that this was a highly profitable deal for the club. Other forms of entertainment for members were available. In November 1933 Sir Harry Vandervell offered to show 'Cinema Pictures' in the smoking room (the records do not relate whether they were silent or sound pictures). It was not just the members for whom entertainment was provided. The large 'living-in' staff were also helped to set up entertainment for themselves. A good example of this was the approval in 1927 of a donation to the staff of £15 to enable them to play cricket.

The between-war years were successful and stable years for the Club, but there were occasional 'behind the scenes' problems. In November 1934 the expenditure of 15 guineas was necessary to place a one year contract with the National Scientific Institute and requiring the Institute to exterminate vermin in the basement of the Hyde Park House. In July 1936 a member of the Committee, Captain FR Harrold RN, felt obliged to place before the Committee a lengthy letter in which he drew their attention to *'the unbelievably dirty and unhygienic condition of the culinary department of the Club (with the exception of the Still Room) and the uncomfortable and inadequately furnished state of the staff quarters'.* He ended his letter with a number of positive proposals to deal with the criticisms he had set down. His letter was well received and the problems acknowledged. The Club had already agreed that a fee of £120 should be paid to Mr S. Phillips Dales, Consulting Architect, to undertake a complete and full survey of the Clubhouse including the possibility of developing the extreme west of the Club to provide improved rooms for ladies and a full sized squash court. Time, cost and World War II prevented the latter from happening, while the sum of £1000 allocated to undertake the repairs needed in order to meet Captain Harrold's criticisms was found to be inadequate. Further money was provided and Captain Harrold received a vote of thanks from the Committee on completion of the improvements. The somewhat antiquated kitchen was always liable to cause problems but improved equipment was made available when needed including the installation of an ice-cream machine in 1938, the year which brought international tension between Britain and Germany to the brink of war, a war that was in fact delayed by only a year, in spite of Neville Chamberlain returning from Munich and standing triumphantly at the airport waving the document signed by Hitler and proclaiming *'Peace in our time'.* At least it provided breathing space for this country to speed preparations for war should it come. Meanwhile Westminster Council had already written to the Club on the subject of 'Air Raid Precautions' indicating the action that should be taken by the Club. A quite different item, but one which illustrates how different life at the Royal Thames was in the 'pre-war' years is that, in July 1939, the Committee agreed that Sir Eastman Bell (one of the permanent residents) could install a bath and lavatory in his bedroom at his own expense. Both would become Club property when his tenancy of the room ended.

Hyde Park House, RTYC Clubhouse (1923 - 1961).

Use of the Clubhouse by other Yachting Organisations

Today, members are well accustomed to seeing members of other yacht clubs and institutions using the meeting rooms in the Clubhouse or even having a permanent base at the Royal Thames. A look at a current set of accounts shows that such activities provide a useful contribution to Club income, a contribution which is achieved at minimum inconvenience to Royal Thames Members. This practice has almost entirely been built up since 1945 but there were exceptions at early dates. In January 1921 the Council of the YRA accepted an invitation to hold their meetings at the Royal Thames, a practice that is still followed. In 1923, the Royal Cruising Club became tenants in the newly-acquired Hyde Park House at an annual rental of £150. They were to stay there for 10 years, terminating their lease in 1933 - it was to be nearly 60 years before they returned to Knightsbridge in 1992.

The War Years 1939-45

Perhaps the biggest difference between the effect of a World War on the Club in the years 1939-45 and the years 1914-18, was the much greater degree of activity in the Clubhouse between September 1939 and August 1945. The Club's successful survival of those six years of war and the privations it caused, was in no small part due to the service in office throughout the war years of the three Flag Officers, Lord Queenborough, J S Highfield and Hugh F Paul, combined with the tireless work undertaken by the Chairman of the Committee Colonel Herbert N Clark for four years (1940-43) and his Deputy, Dr Clifford C Chance for over three and a half years. They ensured that the problems of reduced membership, shortage of staff and the need to economise in spite of material shortages, did not undermine to any serious extent the club's finances. Operating losses were kept to a minimum and many members made voluntary contributions that helped cash flow difficulties.

When the Committee first met after the declaration of war on 3 September 1939 they immediately withdrew Honorary Membership for the German Ambassador and alien members were struck off - provided Home Office approval had been obtained. A large number of members resigned (79 before the end of the year) since the Club did not find itself able to offer them reduced subscriptions but, rather, they hoped they would re-join after the war. Coal was soon difficult to obtain and the cost of peat and oak logs was investigated as a means of eking out the coal ration. To compensate for the loss of members, six months Honorary Membership was offered to members of H M Forces based in London provided they were certified by a proposer and seconder.

There were no Club regattas throughout the war and the Sailing Committee did not meet between June 1939 and October 1942. Even so Ranelagh SC was able to continue its races for the RTYC trophies on the River Thames at Putney. When they did meet, they immediately proposed that the Club should not renew the lease on Ryde Pavilion and should seek to acquire a yachting headquarters on the Hamble River. They also recommended that the Sailing Committee should identify which candidates for election should be classified as 'Yachtsmen' before their names went to the General Committee to ballot for election to membership - this was put into practice from 9 March 1943.

Not all the problems that members had to accept in wartime

CHARLOTTE H returns from Dunkirk (1940) - Owned by Captain The Hon Michael Henderson.

were of the same importance and even those who played cards had to accept that when the stock of new packs expired they would have to play with used cards. 'Used' periodicals were still of value and were sent to RNVR Depots at Harwich and Thurso. Inevitably there were problems associated with food rationing but, for some, the shortages of wines and spirits were of greater concern. By the end of 1941 the stock of sherry was exhausted; port and spirits were served in small measures only. By May 1943 it was necessary to ration the bottles of port, whisky and gin available each day in the Coffee Room, Ladies Room and Smoking Room, while by January 1944 it was forecast that the stocks of port would last only until September and those of whisky and gin until June 1945 - even stricter rationing was imposed. Happily V-E Day in May 1945 came just in time. Even so the General Committee meeting in May and discussing wine stocks, decided that *'purchases could not be made on the 'Black Market' but any member of the Committee who could influence supplies should get in touch with the Secretary'.*

Economies were necessary in all aspects of Club life, not only due to shortages. In order to increase income, members voluntarily made a 'War Contribution to Club Funds'. The annual redemption of Bonds was suspended in 1940 to reduce expenditure.

The Club was particularly fortunate in one aspect - it suffered only relatively minor bomb damage and it was not until the summer of 1944 that the Club had to close for two months to make good the damage. Consequently it was able to offer hospitality to members of the Arts Club when their building was bombed. As a precaution, the Club established a reciprocal arrangement with the Carlton Club in case either suffered serious damage. Suprisingly it was not until June 1941 that a small Sub Committee was established to decide which paintings and trophies should be removed from the Clubhouse to the relative safety of selected members homes - but the Committee directed that *'the Club was not to be left with bare walls'*.

Generous acts in wartime were not uncommon and one that involved the Royal Thames was the decision by an American yachtsman to donate to the Club a mobile kitchen for use in badly bombed areas of London. The kitchen defied the U-Boats and was safely shipped across the Atlantic in June 1941 and handed over to the Commodore, Lord Queenborough, by Mr R W Cotten, representing the International Commodores' Association of the United States. Lord Queenborough was then able to present it to Sir Henry McMahon, Chairman of the YMCA, for it to be used in the Millwall Docks area of the East-End.

The shortage of suitable staff became acute so that by 1942 waiters were almost unobtainable - even an attempt to recruit former railway staff proved fruitless. By 1943 licensing hours were reduced because of staff shortages (and to economise on the use of lighting).

In May 1942 Ryde Pavilion and Starting Station were requisitioned from the Club by the Military Authorities and occupied by a Royal Artillery Troop. The War Office paid an annual rental for the building but it did not fully cover the annual cost of the lease so the Club considered terminating the lease. In the end the Club decided to retain the lease until December 1946.

Inevitably, several members of the Club were to lose their lives while on active service and it was the sombre task of Lord Queenborough to announce their deaths in his opening remarks at each wartime AGM. In 1941 he referred to Lieutenant Vernon McAndrew, a well known yachtsman both with the Royal Thames and in the West Country. He also mentioned Lt. Col. Claude Beddington who was killed while manning a Lewis Gun in his own boat *CACHALOT* at Dunkirk and R B Redfern a young member. In 1944 he informed the AGM of four more members who had been killed while serving in the RNVR. The list was added to in 1944-45, a year which also saw the death (as mentioned earlier) of William Fife and E. Keble Chatterton as well as a famous Honorary Member, Sir Arthur Quiller-Couch, that renowned man of letters universally known as 'Q'.

In April 1943 the General Committee set up a Sub Committee to investigate irregularities in the management and operation of the catering in the Club. Resulting from their report, the House and Finance Sub Committee was immediately reinstated, but it was not until May 1944, following complaints about the food (even allowing for the consequences of rationing) that it was decided to implement all the recommendations in the report and in particular the appointment of a competent, qualified caterer. Even then it was May 1945 before the position was filled by Mrs Hobbs Fernie. Not only was she appointed as Catering Manager but she was also to be Staff Manager, Dietician and Storekeeper. When she first attended a meeting of the House and Finance Sub Committee she asked that staff quarters be improved which, if done, would enable her to recruit suitable staff which in time would improve the food served to members.

Although the Committee supported her requests, she resigned six months later and was succeeded by Mr R G M Brown (who was to become Assistant Secretary in March 1946 and Joint Secretary of the Club in February 1948). While the irregularities were readily put right the problems with food were far more difficult to resolve in the prevailing circumstances.

It would seem that troubles never came singly for, in July 1945, the Wine and Cigar Sub Committee were informed by Mr Vennor (the wine stock auditor, originally appointed in June 1939 and whose firm still perform that function) that *'his checks show the (wine) accounts to be in an appalling state'*. Fortunately he was able to add *'this cast no suspicion on the cellarman and was probably caused by the combination of the recent death of the Assistant Secretary, Mr Mumford and the resignation of the ledgers clerk'*. New appointments soon rectified this unfortunate situation.

Following the Allied Landing in Normandy in June 1944, Paris was recaptured less than three months later and France was soon to be released from German domination. In February 1945 the Sailing Committee were informed that a letter dated 16 December 1944 had been received bearing greetings from the Yacht Club de France - the first contact between the two clubs for over five years. Victory in Europe was to follow in May 1945 and to mark the occasion the Club staff were awarded two days extra pay. By July the Admiralty had restored the Club's warrant to fly the Blue Ensign. The dropping of the Atomic Bombs on Hiroshima and Nagasaki brought to an end the war against Japan and the Club could give thanks that it had survived the six years of war, relatively unscathed both materially and financially. The Club now had to face up to several years of austerity, plan for its future both in London and on the Solent and fight its way through a series of financially testing times; but above all it could now look forward to re-establishing itself as a major influence in yacht racing, starting from the new season in 1946. In the short term, one of the post-war decisions made was to hold a Victory Ball on New Year's Eve and to offer Winston Churchill Honorary Life Membership of the Club.

The Years leading to Redevelopment (1946-63)

The Annual General Meeting of March 1946 made two decisions that were to have an important bearing on the Club's affairs for 30 years and more. The first was to elect Admiral Lord Louis Mountbatten to the office of Commodore. The other was to endorse the Sailing Committee's recommendation to purchase Shore House at Warsash as the Club's yachting base in place of Ryde Pavilion.

The Committee agreed to extend a formal welcome to Lord Mountbatten after his election to office through a Reception and Dinner on 4 July - a dinner at which it was hoped Winston Churchill would be a guest; but he was unable to attend. A remarkable feature of the dinner, that reflected the problems posed by post-war austerity, was that the Committee decided that *'the dinner should be cold to facilitate service'*.

In December 1945 the Sailing Committee decided to extend the lease on Ryde Pavilion for a further year and review the situation in September 1946. Two months later the Chairman of Committee, Glynn Terrell, recommended to the Sailing Committee the purchase of Shore House for £6,500 and, if possible, to purchase the adjacent land as a car park. Once AGM approval was given a draft contract for the purchase of Shore House was available in April; completion was achieved in May, and the new base was ready for use shortly afterwards. The adjacent land was acquired by a member (believed to be Mr Eric Marshall, a member of the Shore House Sub Committee). He generously donated it to the Club in 1954 for use as a car and boat park. The first Club mooring was acquired in July. The Club was established at Warsash.

As early as April 1945 the Committee were concerned at the cost of paying dividends to Bond Holders and the cost of redeeming them. A suggestion was made that the Club should take out a mortgage on the property to meet these costs. No immediate action was taken but at the AGM in March 1947 the Committee put down a resolution to increase subscription levels based on the Ordinary Member whose subscription would rise from 15 to 20 guineas. The proposals received only qualified support and the meeting agreed to set up an ad hoc Committee *'to examine the Club's requirements and report, the report to be circulated to members and a Special General Meeting called to meet within 30 days'*. The Chairman of Committees, Henry J Davis, chaired the ad hoc Committee and by the end of April they had identified the root cause of the unsatisfactory state of the financial operation of the Club as being the general increase in cost of all purchases, the loss of income (due to shortage of spirits), the need to spend at least £25,000 on deferred repairs to the Clubhouse (provided a permit could be obtained to undertake the work which included re-wiring of the Clubhouse and replacement of the passenger lift) and the need to reduce the high level of overdraft. Their proposals were fourfold: to take a mortgage on the freehold of £66,000; to pay off Bonds at a cost of over £52,000; to use the £13,000 balance to undertake urgent repairs, and to increase subscriptions by up to five guineas. At the SGM on 24 June the first proposal was modified to seek approval to take a mortgage of up to £80,000. To put it mildly, the resolution was debated thoroughly but eventually received almost unanimous support. By the end of 1947 the Club had obtained an £80,000 mortgage at 3$\frac{1}{2}$% for 10 years. It was also agreed to establish a so-called Sinking Fund, later renamed as a Mortgage Redemption Fund, in order to reduce the sum needed when the capital was repaid at the end of the 10 years.

While these actions helped to halt the downward course of the Club's finances they were not sufficient to ensure long term improvement and they certainly did not and could not address other problems such as the quality of food in the Coffee Room. Even though the Club was prepared to pay for unrationed supplies to put variety into the fare offered, in 1948 such supplies were very difficult to obtain. Similarly the Club needed to replenish its stock of household linen and had to appeal to members to offer their clothing coupons so that the purchases could be made. Food rationing was to continue until 1954, but the battle to get the most out of the rations never flagged. In May 1951 it was noted that although the butter ration was one-seventh of an ounce per member per meal, the Club was able to provide 104 pats of butter out of every pound - nearly a tenth more per pat than the ration! While the Committee struggled with these problems, the Auditor recommended that all charges should be increased and that the Club should further improve its financial position by foregoing the services of a Catering Manager. Ironically, later in the year when the Committee decided that they did need a Catering Manager, the selected candidate was too ill to take up the post.

If it seems that the General Committee and the House and Finance Committee spent all their time wrestling with a never-ending string of proposals to increase the Club's income and reduce expenditure, this is not far from the truth. The next phase of the struggle to stabilise and improve the Club's financial position came early in 1949 when the Finance Sub Committee recommended a string of proposals: the disposal of Shore House (the Club to amalgamate at Warsash with the Household Division Yacht Club whose lease ran until 1952); the sale of 60 Knightsbridge to a commercial organisation with the aim of re-building on site and including floors for the RTYC; reduce staff and staff wages; introduce new categories for younger members with the aim of attracting young people and increasing use of the Clubhouse and, with the same objective, suspension of the entrance fee. There was vigorous opposition to the sale of Shore House which was considered to be an essential element within the range of facilities available to members. A decision on 60 Knightsbridge was deferred. The remaining proposals were agreed and endorsed by the AGM in March. Whatever financial gain was achieved through these proposals, control of expenditure was not helped when the medical officer of health issued, in June 1949, an adverse report on the state of the kitchen, a report that could not be ignored.

The Committee was acutely aware of the need to establish a strategic plan for the Club in conjunction with schemes to improve the financial position. To this end a Long Term Policy Committee was established in 1949. By July of that year they described the financial position as *'becoming precarious'* and suggested that the Club should: sell 60 Knightsbridge; amalgamate with another London club (even though an attempt to amalgamate with the Thatched House Club had just come to nought) and increase Lady Membership and improve facilities for ladies. By October the position was described as *'desperate'* and additional proposals were made to seek 18 guineas from each ordinary member (or 12 guineas) and to sell Shore House in order to boost cash flow. Additionally they recommended trying to defer the annual provision for mortgage redemption for three years. Later in October the Rear Commodore, Sir Bernard Docker, delivered a rallying call to the General Committee encouraging them to let the Club ride out the financial difficulties, stay at 60 Knightsbridge, increase subscription for Town members, reduce those for Country members and improve the facilities for ladies. (It had already been appreciated that limitations imposed by the 1947 Town and Country Planning Act might in any case make the sale of 60 Knightsbridge difficult). Consequently, that consideration together with professional advice from a member persuaded the General Committee to reject an enticing offer from the Brazilian Embassy for the purchase of 60 Knightsbridge.

The death in September 1949 of the Vice Commodore, Lord Queenborough, not only brought an end to his family's long connection as Flag Officers of the Club, but it also necessitated the calling of a special General Meeting of the club on 8 December to elect a successor. The opportunity was taken to extend the agenda for the meeting (attended by 170 members) to include a statement on the Club's financial position and to put down resolutions that could lead to an improvement in that position. After respects had been paid to the late Lord Queenborough, the meeting elected Sir Bernard Docker to be his successor. Sir Wallace Akers, Chairman of Committees, made a long statement about financial matters and the losses being incurred. In his statement he included the words *'clubs are not run to make a profit; they are run for the benefit of the members and perhaps to make a little extra money to*

Lt Col R S G Perry (1956 Olympics in 5.5 metre class) and his yacht VISION.

put away against a rainy day'. While his words included much to be commended, experience suggests that rainy days call for far more than 'a little extra money'. The meeting ended by supporting the General Committee and rejecting the resolution proposing the sale of 60 Knightsbridge to the Brazilian Embassy and by supporting the concept of Associate Membership (recorded in the Administration Section of this volume).

While the Committee were inevitably much concerned by the financial situation of the Club, it should not be thought that this cast a long dark shadow over activities. A full programme of yacht racing was conducted each season, while in the Clubhouse the regular house dinners were popular and the annual ball was highly successful and profitable. The heart of the financial problem was the need to increase usage of the Clubhouse and to improve its facilities, both of which would enhance the Club's income, while at the same time keeping a tight control on expenditure at a time when wages were increasing and the first modest pressure from post-war inflation was being experienced.

The search for a possible amalgamation with another club continued and two very different possibilities were considered during the year 1950-51. In April 1950 a suggestion was made that the Club could share premises with the Royal London Yacht Club at Cowes, this to be achieved by selling Shore House and purchasing the Royal London premises. Both clubs took a serious look at this suggestion and each prepared proposals for implementing it. Eager as each club was to find common ground for a merger, each found (once again) aspects of the other club's proposals unacceptable and the concept was abandoned by June 1951. In February 1951 it was revealed that the Oriental Club might be closing and a possible amalgamation was investigated. Such an amalgamation would have necessitated the purchase and conversion of No 2 Albert Gate, adjacent to Hyde Park House, using the funds available from the sale of the Oriental Club. It soon became clear that it could take 'years' to obtain a licence to undertake the conversion and any possible deal with the Oriental Club was abandoned by September 1951.

While the five post-war years had seen the club operating with significant financial deficits, the following five years saw modest surpluses (only to be followed by another five years of deficit). One element in achieving an improvement from 1951 stemmed from the approval given by the 118 members present at a Special General Meeting chaired by the Commodore, Lord Mountbatten and held on 12 October 1950, to a resolution to raise a sum of money not exceeding £150,000 by the issue to members of unsecured bonds. These were to be in two forms; the 'A' Bonds issued in units of 10 carried an interest of 1% per annum while the 'B' Bonds also at £10 carried no interest but entitled the holder to an abatement of his subscription of one guinea per annum for every £100 of 'B' Bonds held by him. Following a circular sent to members, it became clear that members were unlikely to take up more than £50,000 of Bonds. This, at least, made it possible for part repayment of the mortgage, reducing it from £80,000 to £30,000. Although the balance would attract a higher rate of interest, the annual payment into the Mortgage Redemption Fund was reduced and the total annual cost to the Club was reduced - except for the cost of interest on 'A' Bonds and the loss of subscription on 'B' Bonds.

As the 1950s progressed there was increasing pressure from members for the Club to provide facilities to enable them to hold mixed parties. While there was general support for the Sub Committee formed to look into this proposal, members of the General Committee were reminded, when they met in September 1953, that 'any re-arrangement of rooms should not affect male comfort!' Much has already been said about the obstacles that had to be overcome to integrate ladies into the Club and yet the Royal Thames had never been opposed to membership for ladies who were bona fide yachtsmen. To the younger members today it may seem strange that London clubland was almost entirely for the benefit of men in the 1950s. When the Vice Commodore, Kenneth Preston, addressed the 1954 AGM he once again stressed the urgent need to increase membership; increase usage of the Clubhouse and to provide improved facilities for ladies. But he also reminded those present that 'this is a men's club and (tongue in cheek) a lot of us come here to get-away from our wives!' The ladies may have been the subject of gentle jokes but the Committee were earnest in their endeavour to make the Clubhouse more attractive for ladies. In truth their wishes were not to be realised until another ten years had passed.

The modest improvement in the club's finances following the Bond issue persuaded the Committee that, seven years after the recommendation had been made, they should appoint a catering manager. In spite of a gradually increasing membership, the number of meals taken by members was dropping each year as were the bar sales. The catering profit margin

was unacceptable even when compared with the very modest target set and pilfering of food was causing concern. The quality of food was at best indifferent and even the impending end of food rationing did little to help. In the end it would take more than the hard work by the Committee and the appointment of a catering manager to rectify these problems. Meanwhile, down at Warsash the operation of Shore House was just as difficult, not least because of the difficulty of finding and retaining a satisfactory Steward.

In the midst of all these problems there was still much for members to enjoy: successful winter and summer balls; a dinner for the new Patron, HRH the Duke of Edinburgh, on 21 December 1954 or even a snooker match between members and the staff on 2 February 1955. Down at Shore House, the new jetty had been completed.

In October 1955 it was clear that the temporary improvement in the financial state of the Club was coming to an end - unavoidable expenses were increasing faster than income and would overtake income during 1956. A special meeting of the General Committee was called for 6 October 1955 with the Chairman of Committees, Eric G Marshall, in the chair. He emphasised to those present that he believed it was not possible to provide 'a really first class service to club members under existing conditions with the uneconomical design, layout and fittings of the present Clubhouse'. He added that 'in his view, the only real solution would be to pull down the whole building and to start again. He believed this could be achieved and financed'. After considerable discussion the Committee agreed unanimously to a resolution to: 'Set up an ad hoc Committee consisting of seven members of the Club (not necessarily members of the General Committee) to investigate the possibility of redeveloping the club at Knightsbridge and, if thought fit, the purchase of adjoining premises or to obtain other premises on terms that would achieve a similar object'.

The detailed account that follows, of the progress towards redevelopment of the Clubhouse, is given in such detail to ensure that proper tribute is given to the small group of members who gave so much of their time to produce the best possible outcome for their fellow members.

By October 1956 the ad hoc Committee were able to report that a scheme to rebuild the Clubhouse had been put together. The new building would also incorporate the adjacent land occupied by the Westminster Bank and possibly that occupied by the Bank's sub-tenant, the Danish Club. The Westminster Bank's landlord would have to be bought out and the Bank accommodated in the new building, in which the Club would occupy three floors, the remainder being leased to Legal and General for office accommodation. The scheme would cost six or seven hundred thousand pounds and would be financed by Legal and General. The negotiations with L&G had been undertaken by Mr Benjamin Allsop and Mr David Pollock and all parties involved had been very interested and willing to progress the scheme. After careful consideration of the financial aspects of the scheme the Club decided it would be too expensive to implement.

In January 1957 the Committee were temporarily diverted from this concentration on development schemes at Knightsbridge by an enquiry from the Royal Victoria Yacht Club at Ryde as to whether the Royal Thames would consider selling Shore House and take over their clubhouse. Once again, nothing came of this proposal, it receiving no support from the Sailing Committee. The ad hoc Committee now put forward an alternative scheme for redevelopment at Knightsbridge which added to the previous scheme an extension to be occupied by the Hyde Park Hotel, so increasing the ground rent that would be due to the Club. The Club decided to seek planning permission for this scheme from the London County Council, a procedure which was likely to involve prolonged negotiations. In view of this it was decided to seek agreement with the Royal Exchange Assurance Company to extend the term for repayment of the residual mortgage of £30,000 (due at the end of 1957). By November, Royal Exchange offered a period of 15 years from 1 January 1958 at 6%. The Club accepted their offer. When the General Committee met in September 1957 they decided unequivocally that provided the problems with planning permission were resolved satisfactorily (LCC had already required a reduction in height of the new building by 2 floors from the scheme put forward and they required the exclusion of the 'lawn' at the rear of the Clubhouse), then redevelopment was the preferred option rather than amalgamation with another club or relocation. The wait for planning permission continued and gave the Committee breathing space in which to decide that the April 1958 AGM should be asked to increase the Town Members subscription from 20 guineas (set in 1948) to 30 guineas if the Club was to 'balance the books'. Although a majority of the 117 members present supported the increase in Town Members' subscription that majority just failed to reach the necessary two thirds and the resolution was, therefore, defeated and subscriptions were unchanged for another three years.

In May 1958 Eric Marshall, Chairman of the ad hoc Committee was able to report to the General Committee that the LCC had given planning approval for the redevelopment of the site occupied by the Club and the Westminster Bank. The redeveloped site would be divided (by floor area) with the club having 20,518 sq ft while 25,830 sq. ft. would be for offices and 4764 sq ft for flats. The estimated cost of the redevelopment was £600,000 to be financed by a 125 year lease to a developer or by agreement with the contractor to defer payment until six months after completion by which time leases could be arranged. The latter arrangement was financially attractive but would have placed the Club in what amounted to a 'commercial status' and involved the Club in considerable administrative work and at some risk if tenants were not readily found. The report also envisaged that the planning work could attain a target date for its completion of September 1958. Finally, Mr Marshall listed nine Sub Committees to be co-ordinated by him. These addressed every aspect of the redevelopment and involved a dozen members of the Club who had specialist knowledge appropriate to the field covered by each Sub Committee. Among these dozen members were Messrs Allsop and Pollock, who were mentioned earlier, and two others who were to become much involved, Mr Guy Morgan in the Sub Committee for architectural work and Mr Brian Colquohon as Engineering Consultant to the Architectural Sub Committee.

While the Sub Committees worked hard at their particular specialist commitments, the sailing and social activities of the Club continued successfully but the General Committee and most particularly , the House and Finance Committee, struggled to limit the operating losses each year. Entrance Fees were now channelled into the Bond Redemption Account, which helped the General Fund, but annual wage increases had to be accepted. Attempts to save money by bringing in contract cleaners failed because (at that time)

suitable contractors could not be found; urgent renewal of equipment and repairs could not be ignored. Meanwhile investigation showed that Royal Thames prices for meals and charges for drinks and bedrooms were low compared with other London clubs and accordingly they were increased. In the light of these factors it is not surprising that the Committee rejected a request to install a deep freeze, describing it as being 'a pleasant luxury'!

In spite of unforeseen difficulties in completing the redevelopment plan, such a plan was available to a special meeting of the General Committee in November 1958, a meeting called to consider how to present their proposals to a General Meeting of the Club. Among those present at the meeting were Guy Morgan and his partner Mr John Taylor, but it was the Chairman of the ad hoc Committee who presented the report on redevelopment. The General Committee supported the ad hoc Committee's report but made the point that they must present to an AGM alternative schemes such as modernising the present building or selling it and moving to another site. There was once again a case made for deferring an increase in subscription since it was possible that a redeveloped Clubhouse (and the financial terms that might accompany redevelopment) could exclude the need to make increases in subscriptions. The meeting ended by authorising Eric Marshall to approach potential developers for a general reaction, without disclosing the terms the Club might seek. A further point made was that Bondholders must be assured of the security of their Bonds under any scheme.

A further special meeting of the General Committee was held in March 1959, seven weeks before the AGM. Earlier, the Committee had already learned two facts - firstly, that the majority of Bondholders were content with the redevelopment proposals and that the price being sought by the landlords of the Westminster Bank was unacceptably high. In addition, the Hyde Park Hotel had lost interest in the scheme. Under these circumstances, the ad hoc Committee had plans developed based only on the present Clubhouse site which gave the Club, on three floors, 23,578 sq ft with 28,000 sq ft for five floors of offices and 11,200 sq ft for two floors of flats. This scheme had been presented for planning permission in February. It was estimated that it would cost in the order of £500,000 and provide the Club with a gross income of £44,000, while the financial prospects for a developer were attractive and the Club could therefore seek a substantial premium from a developer.

With the exclusion of the Bank and the Hotel from the scheme, the questions of 'lights' at the western end would limit the height of the building at that end. The alternative options of modernising the existing building presented by Mr Norman Houghton included ways of raising the considerable finance needed and the fact that it might be possible for members to continue using the Clubhouse during the estimated year it would take to complete the modernisation. The main features of the two modernisation schemes presented (one being more extensive and costly than the other) were to include provision for improved facilities for ladies, updating of the kitchen, the heating arrangements and the bedrooms. In July the Committee felt they would be able to make an effective presentation to a General Meeting by November. They had already decided against employing an independent architect to monitor the redevelopment; they had received twenty two bids to undertake the redevelopment and they had now agreed that subscription increases would be necessary whether redevelopment, modernisation or status quo was agreed at the SGM. These three options would increase the Town Member's 20 guineas subscription to 25, 45 and 40 guineas respectively.

The SGM was held on 11 November 1959 under the chairmanship of the Commodore, Earl Mountbatten, and attended by no less than 320 members. The timetable for the meeting, which started at 2.30pm, showed that it was expected to last for four hours including a break for tea. A long and encouraging introduction by the Commodore was followed by a much longer statement by Mr Eric Marshall explaining how the ad hoc Committee had reached the redevelopment plan placed before the meeting. Mr Norman Houghton then explained the other options based on modernisation of the existing building or removal to a new location. Finally, Mr Ben Allsop reported on the offers received for redevelopment and the financial benefits related to those offers. In particular he informed the meeting that the top offer was for the Club to retain the freehold, the developer to take a 150 year lease on the site and to lease-back the three floors for the Clubhouse to the RTYC at a peppercorn rent. In addition the developer offered the Club a premium of £215,000 and £1,000 p.a. ground rent. He strongly recommended this scheme as the one most beneficial to the Club as it would provide the Club with funds to pay off the mortgage and to furnish the new Clubhouse as well as providing 23,000 sq ft of space rent free. Another benefit of the offer was that the developer would maintain the structure and pay for the maintenance of central heating and hot water (but the Club must maintain the interior decoration).

Mr Guy Morgan explained to members who wanted the Club to be located at the top of the new building that once the Westminster Bank and Hyde Park Hotel opted out of the scheme, the question of the Hotel's rights to 'light and air' arose. This necessitated limiting use of the full site area to two floors and the high part of the new building had to be furthest away from the hotel in order to preserve those rights. Location of the Club at the top would not provide the space needed. In responding to a question asking *'why not take a fourth floor?'* Mr Eric Marshall explained that this would lead to considerable reduction in the premium offered by the developer.

Sometime after the tea break the resolutions were put to the vote. Of the 315 recorded votes, 300 were in favour of redevelopment of the Club on the present site. The meeting also carried unanimously the resolution to increase subscriptions from 1 January 1960. In one general meeting the Club had made a stride forward to raise money and create a Clubhouse for the next century.

When the General committee met five days later they re-affirmed the decision not to seek a fourth floor for the Club as it was not needed and would have involved the loss of £30,000 premium. They also dissolved the ad hoc Committee (which had completed its task) and set up a small Buildings Sub Committee comprising the Chairman, Deputy Chairman, Major Green, Mr Allsop (Surveyor), Club Trustees and Messrs R O Bond and R H A Squire (both architects and with whom Guy Morgan, as the Architect for the Development Project, felt able to work). At a special meeting ten days later the General Committee were informed that an Investment Company who had acquired the freehold of the Westminster Bank and the leasehold of No2 Albert Gate had offered £250,000 for the freehold of the Club site in order that they, in conjunction with a construction company, could build a skyscraper hotel in which the Club would have first class premises on the top floor. The Committee, recognising that retaining the freehold was of vital long term importance and that in any case it could easily be five years before such a project obtained planning permission, unanimously rejected the offer.

The Committee could now concentrate on the detailed plans for the new Clubhouse and set a provisional date of 30 September 1960 for demolition. There was still uncertainty in some Committee members' minds as to whether three floors would provide the facilities needed or whether more space was required. The case for a fourth floor was re-examined and alternative designs for the west end of the new building were evaluated. Meanwhile the offer by the Naval and Military Club in Piccadilly to use rooms in their clubhouse during the rebuilding was accepted in principle. A later offer from the Caledonian Club was not accepted but several members did make their temporary 'home' there and formed the basis for a close relationship between the Royal Thames and the Caledonian. This is maintained today through joint dinners by a group of members from each club and which was well and truly cemented through a cocktail party for members of the Caledonian Club held at the club in May 1964 by some 40 members who had been temporary members of the Caledonian during the rebuilding years. The accommodation offered by the Naval and Military Club was a Bar, Sitting Room and Writing Room for exclusive use by the Royal Thames members. The Royal Thames would pay a block subscription of £9,000 p.a.. Up to 30 members of the Royal Thames staff being retained would move to temporary accommodation.

As the months of 1960 passed by, agreement for a layout of the Club was not achieved and it was evident that the contract with the developer might not be signed in time for demolition to start on 1 October. Fortunately, by the end of July the Building Sub Committee reported that the latest scheme for the west wing now met all the Club's requirements and the contract could now be signed in time for demolition to start on 1 October, but two matters were now causing ripples in the otherwise smooth progress. Firstly, concern was expressed that a member of the Club, Guy Morgan, was acting both as advisor to the Club and working with the developer as their architect. This concern was to prove to be well-founded. The other problem was that the LCC were unable to approve the redevelopment until the Ministry of Transport decided which solution to the traffic problem in Knightsbridge they would select - the choice being either to extend the Hyde Park Corner underpass as far as Knightsbridge Barracks or to widen Knightsbridge to provide for 8 lanes of traffic. As is manifestly apparent today, neither scheme was pursued; the LCC planning permission was received in November 1960 and the drilling of test bore holes started.

When the General Committee met on 7 December they learned that the Hyde Park Hotel had offered up to £650,000 for the freehold of the club site, that another offer had been received which would provide a 150 year lease and no ground rent, with a premium of £200,000. These offers could not be considered until after a meeting on 14 December between the Buildings Sub Committee and the proposed developer. The General Committee met again on 22 December under the chairmanship of the Vice Commodore, Major Charles Ball and received the report on 14 December meeting which informed them that the proposed developer, Mr Donovan Drewery, was unable to provide satisfactory financial guarantees and that the Building Sub Committee recommended that the club terminate the negotiations. The Committee then decided to

RYTC Clubhouse, 60 Knightsbridge (1963 -).

review the original list of tenders. A revised and improved offer from one tender, Bernard Sunley Investment Trust (Management) Ltd had been received on 3 November and the Buildings Sub Committee had instructed Mr Ben Allsop to investigate this new offer. Mr Allsop reported that he adjudged the total value of Mr Sunley's offer to be £717,180 compared with £650,000 from Mr Drewery and £650,000 form the Hyde Park Hotel (for the freehold). Mr Sunley's offer had to be accepted or rejected that day and after some discussion the Committee conceded that it was a good offer and that they might not get a better one. Mr Sunley sought one major change to the terms of the contract. Viz the right, within the 150 years lease, to demolish the building to be erected after 60 years, and to build another, provided the Club was accommodated in premises of equal size and all reasonable expenses incurred during the rebuilding were paid. This was accepted and later that evening contracts were exchanged between the Club's Trustees and Bernard Sunley.

It was soon agreed that the Club would close on 27 April 1961 with a cocktail party (which was attended by 640 people) to be held on that day. The developer would take possession of the site on 22 June. Before that date the first of what were to be a number of contentious issues was raised when the Buildings Sub Committee were asked to consider whether the new building should be air-conditioned. (The development scheme provided for a hot water central heating system with the developer bearing heating and hot water costs). In March the Sub Committee recommended the provision of double glazing and air-conditioning for the whole building but the General Committee ruled that the latter should be confined to public rooms only and not to bedrooms. At the General Committee meeting in June the question of air-conditioning was debated in depth. Those present were reminded that this

issue had originated from considerations of reducing noise by fitting double glazing which itself led to the need to provide air conditioning for the 'sealed' building. Guy Morgan and Ben Allsop attended the meeting and the former advised that the installation of full air-conditioning would cost nearly £36,000 and would involve an annual running cost of some £700 - both of which must be borne by the Club. The views of the Committee members and the four advisers present ranged from 'wholly in favour' to 'totally unnecessary'. Before a vote was taken the Chairman, Arnold Munns advised that the Club's future financial commitments included £75,000 for furnishing, £30,000 for mortgage repayment, repayment of bonds and payment of professional fees. If air-conditioning was installed *'there would not be a great deal left of the developer's premium of £250,000'*. When the vote was taken only one committee member was in favour of air-conditioning and seven, including the Vice Commodore, were against (as were Messrs Morgan and Allsop). The only other topic discussed at that meeting was the selection of an interior decorator, a topic that had been considered in the previous year, opinions at that time varying on whether or not an independent interior designer should be appointed. This meeting decided 'not' and appointed Messrs Maples, whose schemes and costings would be vetted by a Decoration Sub Committee comprising Raglan Squire, R O Bond, John Hunter, Norman Houghton and Guy Morgan.

In spite of the decisions taken at that June 1961 meeting the two contentious issues did not go away. By September the Committee instructed Guy Morgan to obtain tenders for a revised scheme for air-conditioning the public rooms. By December the General Committee *'unanimously agreed that air conditioning should be installed and left it to Mr Bond and Mr Morgan to plan the details to give the Club the best installation in the circumstances'.* In February 1962 the Decoration Sub Committee expressed their dissatisfaction with Maples designs and the General Committee decided to reverse their decision of the previous June and appointed an independent designer, Mr Brian O'Rourke, (who had already been considered for the task a year earlier). By now there was concern that the installation of air-conditioning would delay completion of the new building by up to three months and that this might make the Club liable for loss of rents from the offices and flats, but Sunleys gave an assurance that this would not be so. It was expected, in April 1962, that structural work on the new building would be completed by the end of June.

It was in April 1962 that an unfortunate dispute arose between the Club and the Architect, Guy Morgan, over the fees claimed by the latter. Initially, the Club disputed that they were liable for most of the fees claimed. Later the Club offered to pay certain items. Their offers were rejected and by July 1964 Guy Morgan issued a writ against the Club to recover his fees. Fortunately, by the end of 1965 an out of court settlement was agreed and a final agreement was achieved in February 1966. The details of this dispute are not appropriate for recording here with the benefit of hindsight, but it does seem that this aspect of the redevelopment would have benefited from an early agreement between the club and the developer as to who was liable for the payment of fees.

It is greatly to the credit of those Flag Officers and members of committees that, while they were wrestling with the problems arising from the rebuilding they were also able to *'hold the Club together'* during those difficult years. After a short period of settling in at the Naval and Military Club and reaching final agreement on the use of rooms there and the related annual fee, membership of the Royal Thames was not only maintained but increased. Annual dinners were held and a winter ball was held late in 1961 at the Hyde Park Hotel - the ticket price of five guineas was subsidised by the Club. A proposal to rename the Club the Royal Cumberland Fleet was defeated at the 1962 AGM.

There was much discussion during 1962 as to whether to appoint a General Manger to oversee the staff and the catering in the new building. The House and Finance Sub Committee were not in favour of such an appointment as they felt it would overlap the duties of the Secretary while the General Committee felt that there must be a 'hotel-trained manager' in place to control the 'hotel' functions of the Club. This issue was left unresolved.

At the end of 1962 there was a report that the Club would be given first refusal to take over the Royal Corinthian Yacht Club clubhouse at Cowes and a Sub Committee was set up to consider it. Their report was that members saw no need for a clubhouse at Cowes provided access to the Royal London Yacht Club continued to be available: they also confirmed that Shore House *'was the place to be'.* Important, but less serious matters resolved at that time were that the address of the new Clubhouse should be '60 Knightsbridge', while that of the offices and flats should be 'Hyde Park House' at 60A Knightsbridge and that the private dining room incorporated into the new building was to be called the Edinburgh Room.

By August 1963 confidence was hardening that the new Clubhouse would open by the end of the year and a New Year's Ball was planned accordingly; tickets at six guineas were limited to 420 members and guests. The confidence felt in August was maintained and the Cumberland Bar was to open on 9 December on which day the Club burgee and ensign were first hoisted. The coffee room and ladies' rooms were opened on 19 December and the bedrooms on 30 December - the Royal Thames was back in residence at Knightsbridge and the Club had successfully passed yet another important milestone in its long history.

The Years Leading to Radical Changes (1964-80)

In 1963-64 the Committee were not only absorbed by the new Clubhouse, they were also immersed in the preparation of a Royal Thames challenge for the America's Cup. It was truly a time of hectic activity for the Committee and before the end of 1963 they had authorised the Trustees to enter into an agreement with the developer (through Beaufort Investments Ltd) for the 150 years lease (this was signed on 5 March 1964) and to execute an encroachment license for the crown land behind the Clubhouse and, finally, to complete an agreement to allow Hyde Park Hotel to have a fire escape over part of the new building.

There were always requests received for the Club to support charitable bodies. When this was deemed appropriate the Club made donations on a selective basis, but when it came to the RNLI the Club rightly maintained an annual donation. In March 1964 this was increased to 100 guineas. This coincided with a particularly generous donation by a member, George J F Jackson, of £10,000 which paid in part for a new lifeboat at Caistor which was given the name 'Royal Thames' at a naming ceremony in July.

Management of the new Clubhouse inevitably raised new problems. Early in 1964 there were potentially conflicting opinions including those varying from *'we must control the intake of new members to avoid overloading the facilities'* to *'since the budget for 1964 predicts an operating deficit we must increase subscriptions from 25 to 30 guineas'.* At the AGM in April members were informed that not more than 10 candidates would be elected at each monthly ballot in order to limit numbers. A proposal to increase subscriptions was not agreed, but the Committee were asked to review the financial position in October and increase subscriptions only if necessary - an option they did not hesitate to implement. In May the first dark cloud cast its shadow over the new building when it became apparent that the air-conditioning appeared to be inadequate. This was just the first occasion when the air-conditioning failed to meet the reasonable expectations of the members and the Committee; there were to be many more over the next two decades!

The much-improved accommodation of the new Clubhouse encouraged the Committee to develop the Club as a national centre for yachting. It was already the practice for the RYA to hold their Council meetings at the Royal Thames and for the IYRU to hold their annual meeting there. It was now agreed that the Billiards Room would be used for meetings to provide an extra room over and above the Committee Room (and possibly the Edinburgh Room for Club committees). These changes were the first of a number taken over the years and represented the realisation that a worthwhile income could be acquired by allowing selected clubs, institutions and individuals to hold meetings and private functions in the Clubhouse. The committee even considered leasing either a floor of offices or a penthouse from the head lessee for this purpose but the cost was prohibitive.

There were soon complaints that the Knightsbridge side bedrooms were too noisy; the card room was too small; there was a need for a chart room; the catering was not profitable and the hot water system was inadequate. The latter problem proved to be the most difficult to rectify on a permanent basis while a further three years passed before secondary glazing was installed to reduce noise in the Knightsbridge bedrooms.

The catering continued to be a problem both in terms of quality, profitability and the reducing numbers of meals served. When the Club manger left without notice in June 1965 Mr Norris Coultous, who had been a member of staff since 1938, was appointed House Manager while the members of the House and Finance committee assumed responsibility for Catering and Mr JBP Williamson was appointed Honorary Treasurer (though he was unable to take up the post until April 1966). These appointments 'steadied the ship' for a while but greater disturbing forces were to appear, not least rising inflation. Mr Coultous, along with Edward Merchant the barman in the Cumberland Bar, gave a total of over 100 years service to the Club between them and provided the continuity of service so much appreciated by members. Mr Coultous's management of private functions became a by-word in the Club.

As one problem was resolved another arose and this time it was the question of responsibility for the payment of those elements of the electricity accounts relating to underfloor heating and hot water. The Club and Sunley's could not agree and the matter was left to their solicitors. By July 1965 Sunley's made their position clear - they had agreed to pay £1000 pa for oil fired central heating and domestic hot water. When the Club elected to change to underfloor heating and air-conditioning, Sunley's were to pay only up to £1000 pa and the Club must pay the balance. A further four years were to pass before agreement was reached and Sunley's finally settled for paying £1100 pa. Satisfactory completion of this agreement was deemed by the Club to be an absolute requirement before they were prepared to agree to a final settlement of Sunley's redevelopment account. That agreement was finally reached in January 1969 - five years after the re-opening of the Club.

As has been the case throughout the Club's history, problems were never allowed to stop the progress of the Club and the year 1966 was no exception. In March the Club entertained the Lord Mayor of London, Sir Michael Denny, to lunch - a practice still repeated from time to time. October saw a number of interesting decisions made by the Committee; it was decided that the 1967 Fitting Out Dinner should be held at Knightsbridge (in the past it was usually held at Cowes) and that the two newly elected Honorary Members, HRH the Duke of Kent and HRH Prince William of Gloucester, be invited to attend. Mr Norman Houghton proposed that a wreath be laid on the grave of the Club's founder, the Duke of Cumberland, as an annual event on the anniversary of his death. He had died on 18 September 1790 but had not been buried in Westminster Abbey until 27 October 1790. In 1966, Sunday 18 September happened to be the day for the annual commemoration of the Battle of Britain. The wreath laying was therefore delayed until 27 October. On that day the Cup Bearer, Commander Colin Campbell, who was to lay the wreath, joined the Dean of Westminster, who was assisted by the Club chaplain, at his private entrance and together with Flag Officers and officials, they moved in procession to the tomb in the Henry VII chapel at noon. This ceremony was not carried out annually as envisaged but consideration should always be given to it being undertaken from time to time as

part of any special Club celebrations. Also in October, the Chairman of the Development Sub Committee Mr A J M Miller sought guidance from the General Committee on future plans for the Club. Notwithstanding the view agreed in July 1963 the General Committee considered there was a need for a clubhouse and line at Cowes and instructed the Rear Commodore to examine any possible future plans on the basis of this requirement. Finally, in October, a member proposed that the Club should issue a regular newsletter but the Committee decided it would be too expensive - a few months later in June 1967 the first newsletter was produced!

In November Rear Commodore Alan Miller was able to report back to the General Committee about the possibility of establishing a clubhouse at Cowes. He said that he had learned that the Grantham Hotel could be bought at a price which he understood to be in the region of £40,000. He also understood that, in principle, the Household Brigade Yacht Club were interested in taking over Shore House and would allow the Royal Thames similar reciprocal arrangements to those which HBYC enjoyed at that time. Lastly he reported that he had investigated the possibility of taking over the Corinthian YC at Cowes but had concluded it would take too large a sum of money to refurbish it. Although the Rear Commodore and his Sub Committee were authorised to obtain all the figures needed if purchase of the Grantham Hotel was to be considered, by June 1967 it was decided that no further action should be taken.

Many other matters arose in 1967 that are worthy of being recorded. Early in the year it was agreed that the time had come when the Club needed to start considering the form that celebrations might take to mark the Club's Bicentenary in 1975. Accordingly a Sub Committee, chaired by Lt. Cdr. F A C Behenna, was set up to start on that project. While considering celebrations in general it was realised that the New Year's Ball for 1967 would fall on a Sunday so a suitable alternative was sought - conveniently, 1968 was leap year and the ball was held on 29 February. As the date for the 1967 AGM approached the Committee identified two important matters which must be raised. Firstly, a large drop in operating surplus for 1966 was expected to be followed by a significant deficit in 1967 and a subscription increase from 30 to 50 guineas was proposed. Secondly, there was a case to be made for changing the Club's financial year from 1 January - 31 December to 1 July - 30 June. At the AGM it was explained that the reason for the change was mainly that it would make subscriptions due for payment in July, a time of the year when members were subject to fewer demands on their resources than in January. It would also ensure that Flag Officers were elected at a time when they could be shown in Lloyds Register from the date of its issue. The resolution to change the date of the AGM was carried but that for the increase in subscriptions was once again defeated and an amendment carried to review the position is six month's time. This latter decision did nothing to boost the Club's finances but it was not entirely inconvenient. The next AGM was not now until October 1968 and it was decided, therefore, to hold an Extraordinary General Meeting in October 1967 to elect Flag Officers. This would also provide an opportunity to present alternative proposals for subscription increases.

In July the General Committee decided that a small ad hoc Committee, comprising the Flag Officers, the Chairman and Deputy Chairman, should be established and given a broad brief to examine subscription rates, the utilisation of the Club premises and methods of increasing membership.

They recommended that the Town Member subscription should be increased from 30 to 40 guineas and other categories by a proportional amount except Lady Associates, whose subscription was to be reduced from 15 to 5 guineas (and their ceiling numbers raised to 100). This latter proposal was part of a series of changes made to encourage ladies to become members. The EGM in November approved the subscription changes (and voted against an alternative resolution based on a Town Subscription of 50 guineas). There was, however, a strong feeling that income should be improved through increased membership rather than subscription increases, especially increases which would lead to an operating profit of a level that, as a Committee member observed, 'might be frittered away by a future Committee on lavish expenditure'. The EGM also voted against converting the card room into a cocktail bar (aimed at attracting younger members).

In March 1968 yet another ad hoc Committee was set up to consider primarily the financial side of affairs and also the wine purchasing policy as well as all matters relating to the heating and air-conditioning of the Club (no mean brief). The committee was to comprise the chairman (Mr Donald Campbell), the Deputy (Mr Donald Leggett), Mr Ian Butler and Mr E I Hamilton-Parks. In early July their report, together with reports from a catering consultant and a management consultant, were considered by the General Committee and a number of actions agreed. When the General Committee met again just two weeks later, several of the agreed decisions were reversed. The chairman, Mr Donald Campbell, informed the Committee at the end of that second meeting that 'he was very disturbed at the way the Committee was working...and he could no longer act in his capacity as chairman and was resigning forthwith'. A week later, at a special meeting of the General Committee, the Vice Commodore took the chair with the object of 'clearing the decks and making a new start'. The final result of these three meetings was agreement to resuscitate the office of Honorary Treasurer; to change the House and Finance Sub Committee into an Executive Committee; to increase Staff Wages immediately at a cost of £3,500 pa with the aim of facilitating recruitment and retaining staff of suitable quality; to appoint a Sub Committee to review the need for a younger members' bar; to set higher targets for profits on catering, wines and spirits; to increase bedroom charges and, yet again, to seek an experienced club manager to have direct control of the 'hotel' functions. In practice only some of those decision were effectively implemented and even then complaints continued in respect of the quality of the catering, while in financial terms the club had an operating deficit every year from 1968 to 1979 (with just two exceptions in 1971-72, after the next subscription increase, and 1972-73). The size of the deficits in the later years was of potentially crippling proportions. Many actions taken by the committee such as folding back the partitions between the Coffee Room and Ladies Dining Room in the evenings were very successful but in spite of the many schemes that increased the income from the 'hotel' functions, the increase in expenditure, against a background of ever increasing inflation, blighted most of the Committee's never ending endeavours to at least 'balance the books' each year.

In September 1970 a new Sub Committee under the guidance of Mr Jason Borthwick and Mr E I Hamilton-Parks was directed to write a report on 'The Future Development of the Club'. The report was formally considered at a special meeting of the General Committee chaired by the Commodore, Mr Elmer Ellsworth James, on 30 December. It must be said that several of the proposals in the report were radical - too radical for some members of the Committee and some of the membership to accept in 1970. It was inevitable, therefore, that many proposals were not proceeded with in 1971 - but, many of them were ultimately implemented in the next two decades, which must surely allow it to be said that it was a far-sighted report. A précis of its introduction and main proposals is set down in Appendix 13.

In 1971 it was necessary to hold two General Meetings of the Club. The extraordinary meeting in April accepted increases in subscription based on a Town Member's subscription changing from 40 guineas to £60. The potential financial benefits from these increases were somewhat diluted as they precipitated one hundred resignations. Overall the proposals in the Borthwick report were rejected except for the introduction of credit trading (while credit trading was introduced with enthusiasm, it was to be withdrawn in February 1975). Additionally it was agreed that the Committee should investigate further the conversion of bedrooms for use as double rooms and the possible conversion of staff quarters into members' bedrooms. Although one bedroom was immediately changed to a double room, another ten years were to pass before the conversion was completed in all rooms where it was a practical option. The conversion of staff quarters was undertaken in 1979-80. The annual meeting in October agreed to the establishment of a Bicentenary Fund to help offset the costs of the celebrations planned for 1975, each member to contribute £3 per year for 5 years from 1 July 1972. It also agreed that the Cumberland Bar should be for men only, and that possibly it should be closed in the evenings since the Committee had already agreed to try having a temporary mixed Bar in the Smoking Room in the evenings. Finally, in November, Mr Peter Hunter was appointed to the House and Finance Committee where he would provide the continuity needed on financial matters.

Happily, in the midst of the struggle to achieve financial stability, there continued to be a succession of memorable social occasions including the dinner held on 16 November 1971 when the Club's Patron, HRH The Duke of Edinburgh presented the newly-designed Admiral's pendant to The Earl Mountbatten - the office to which he had been elected in October 1970. There was also the Halloween Ball on 31 October 1972 attended by HRH The Princess Anne.

The increase in subscriptions in July 1971 did bring a period of relief from the years of operating deficits but the SGM in June 1973 was to be advised that the Club would soon see a reversion to an operating deficit due principally to heavy losses on catering. The Committee decided to implement the long-standing agreement to appoint a professional Caterer as General Manager to be in charge of the 'hotel' services. The Committee selected Mr Peter Wilson and again appointed Mr Norris Coultous as House Manager. The 119 members present were much divided in their support for the appointment of a General Manager and in the selection of Mr Wilson, but a resolution to endorse the Committees action was carried by a modest majority. Three months later Mr Wilson was dismissed!

As the Club entered 1974, Eagle Star Life Assurance took over the lease of the property from Bernard Sunley and the International Yacht Racing Union moved into the offices formerly occupied by the Secretariat on 8 March, having agreed to pay a rental of £3,500 pa - a welcome boost to the Club's income; even so, such a bonus was not going to solve the Club's financial problems, the causes of which have been well recorded in earlier pages. It was already apparent that some unwelcome and radical decisions would have to be made. Where these changes should be implemented was not an easy decision for the Committee to make as the Club entered the years of rapidly escalating and economically damaging inflation. Perhaps the most difficult and controversial topic was centred on the future of Shore House.

There was still the view among Committee members and the membership at large that a sailing base on the Solent was an essential part of the Club facilities which, if necessary should be operated at a loss and therefore accepted as an inevitable 'expenditure' in the Club's accounts. For all that, the Committee was in a situation when they were striving to reduce expenditure and the problems associated with Shore House could not be ignored. Ever since it had been acquired it had proved exceptionally difficult to recruit and retain efficient and reliable stewards; the Committee found it difficult to decide whether to oversee the Steward through a local Secretary, a local Sub Committee or directly from Knightsbridge; the original property needed improvements and expansion including the provision of a berthing jetty; the maintenance costs, especially for the jetty, were significant; the place was used far too little and even that was for only some seven months of the year. Although the Club had considered several alternative sites none were either suitable or affordable. By 1974 it seemed that there were three options to consider: Keep Shore House and accept that it must be subsidised; keep Shore House and find the means of making it self-financing, or sell it. All three options were to be closely examined in the next few years before a final decision was made and none of them would find universal support.

Before examining the events which led to the radical decisions taken in 1977-78, a breathing space is merited to record in outline the celebrations of the Club's Bicentenary in 1975. Many of these are recorded in some detail by Douglas Phillips-Birt in his book 'The Cumberland Fleet - 200 years of yachting' - a book which was commissioned to mark the Bicentenary. It had taken nearly eight years to evolve the plans for 1975, at first under the leadership of Lt Cdr Behenna and later under Mr John Savage and finally Mr Sandy Haworth. Nearly all their plans were brought to fruition in the splendid style expected of the Royal Thames. The one exception was the planned race from the Nore to Greenwich which attracted little support and was abandoned.

The celebrations started in the best possible fashion with the New Year's Eve Ball at Knightsbridge on 31 December 1974 and continued on 7 February with a ceremony in the Henry VII chapel of Westminster Abbey to lay a wreath over the tomb of the Duke of Cumberland - as had been done before in 1966. On this occasion the wreath was laid by the Admiral of the Cumberland Fleet, Earl Mountbatten in the presence of the recently elected Commodore, HRH The Prince of Wales as well as other flag officers and members. As they left the ceremony members saw the club burgee flying over the Abbey - a unique experience. The Commodore then made his first visit to the Clubhouse to unveil the bronze bust, created by Vasco Lazzolo, of his father, the Club's Patron , HRH The Duke of Edinburgh. This was the occasion for his much reported remarks *'accustomed…er, unaccustomed as I am to unveiling busts…'.*

On 29 June the New York Yacht Club started a Transatlantic Race from Newport, R .I. Twelve yachts from six countries took part ranging in size from the 79ft American ketch *KIALOA* to the 40ft sloop *ROBIN* - also American. The fleet were only some 200 miles out when they ran into 65 knot winds due to hurricane Amy. Three yachts were forced to retire and one had to return for repairs before continuing. The race finished at the Nab Tower nearly 15 days after leaving Newport, first across the line being *KIALOA* who won the Emmett Cup, recently presented to the Club, but the winner on corrected time was *ROBIN* who received the Cumberland Cup, presented to the NYYC by Earl Mountbatten in 1970 to mark the hundredth Anniversary of the first America's Cup races.

A few days later on 25 July there took place what was perhaps the most complex of the celebration ceremonies - the parade and sail past of some two hundred yachts of the Royal Thames in Osborne Bay. The salute was taken by the Admiral, Earl Mountbatten, from the Training Ship *ROYALIST*, which was manned by Cadets. The Commodore, The Prince of Wales and Princess Anne were aboard *EXCITE*, the motor yacht of the Vice Commodore, Mr John Maddocks, who led the sail past in ideal weather conditions. For those members not on board yachts, the Club chartered two steamers from which they could view this splendid occasion. That evening the Club held the Warsash Ball in the spacious rooms of the School of Navigation. The seven hundred members and guests were received by the Commodore and danced to music provided by a band of the Royal Marines. Also, during the Ball, the Commodore presented Cups to the winners of the Transatlantic Race. Once again the Commodore made an unforgettable remark concerning the ex-Commodore of the New York YC, Donald Kipp when he referred to him as *'Kimmodore Kopp…!'*

During the next two days the Club held its Bicentenary Regatta at Cowes and had a special commemorative medal struck and given to competing yachts. The final celebration took place on 4 November when the Club held a banquet at the Guildhall, London. This glittering occasion was again attended by the Admiral, the Commodore and Princess Anne as well as other distinguished guests.

The joyous celebrations of 1975 must have been welcomed by the Flag Officers and Committee both for what they were and represented, as well as providing a relief and diversion for them from the financial stress in the Club's affairs. They had entered into 1974 in the knowledge that the Club's assets had fallen by nearly half since 1963; that the Club was maintaining too large a bank overdraft and that their hope of obtaining some relief by acquiring exemption from VAT on subscriptions was remote. Accordingly they called a Special General Meeting on 17 June at which were tabled three options for subscription increase. The most favoured option, by 64 to 43 votes, was for a 75% increase i.e. Town subscription from £60 to £105, which would provide for each member a £50 voucher. This, it was hoped would encourage members to use the Clubhouse rather more. Within 24 hours it was realised that the vote had achieved only 60% support, not the required two thirds majority called for by Rule 71. This realisation persuaded a majority of the Committee to look for an alternative resolution on subscription rates and they decided that they could not wait until the October AGM as increases were needed from 1 July. They therefore proposed a further SGM. Four senior members present tabled their resignations, but an SGM was held on 27 June and the proposal for a simple 75% increase to all subscriptions was approved. In September it was reported that 192 resignations had been received and six months later a large number of subscriptions were still unpaid, all of which did little to increase subscription income. When the General Committee met in April 1975 it was considered that, after the Bicentenary Celebrations, the Club might have to sell 60 Knightsbridge or bring in another club. It had become clear that major subscription increases were counter-productive to the search for financial security. Meanwhile hopes of expanding the facilities of Shore House by constructing a dock had been thwarted by refusal of planning permission.

Catering continued to be an endless source of difficulties, the epithet used in September 1976 was a *'disaster'* and the contract catering group, Gardner Merchant were invited to investigate and report. For all their efforts little serious improvement emerged and their services were dispensed with by April 1977. On a happier note the Bicentenary Fund had been used to enable a permanent bar to be created in the Smoking Room. At first it was called the Bicentenary Bar but in February 1976 this was changed to Britannia Bar. Later in 1976, and clearly sensing the doubts about the Club's future location, Bernard Sunley made several (increasing) offers for the freehold of 60 Knightsbridge, but the Committee were not prepared to consider them unless departure from 60 Knightsbridge proved inevitable. The October 1976 AGM once again approved a further increase in subscription as a result of which Town members would pay £135 from 1 July 1977.

As 1976 drew to a close the situation continued to deteriorate, the Catering Manager resigned, the Club Accountant was dismissed and the Secretary was to leave by the end of March 1977. Hopes that the Junior Carlton Club would amalgamate with the Royal Thames did not come to fruition, the overdraft was even higher and the latest description of the food was *'diabolical'*.

When Captain Stobbs, the Secretary left, Mr E I Hamilton-Parks was appointed Chief Executive in his place. The Special General Meeting held on 30 June 1977 (at which only 60 members were present) was told of the disquieting options facing the Club including selling both 60 Knightsbridge and Shore House; abandoning catering and having a simple 'pub lunch' or the need to raise £120,000 in order to retain 60 Knightsbridge and convert it to a financially sound operation.

Following the October 1977 AGM, at which Mr Robin Aisher was elected Vice Commodore, the first meeting of the new

General Committee under his chairmanship spelt out their future policy for the club and defined a new range of options. Those options were firstly, to convert the ground floor into offices for letting (planning permission for this conversion was obtained by February 1978 and a Special General Meeting held in March 1978 endorsed this proposal); secondly, to convert the first floor into a public restaurant which members could use at a discount; thirdly, to bring in a catering company to manage and operate the hotel functions i.e. catering, bars and bedrooms (Sutcliffe Catering were given a contract in December and started operating in June 1968); fourthly, to convert the staff accommodation into bedrooms for members and, fifthly, to sell Shore House.

In the midst of all this hectic activity a successful Spring Ball was held and another bright spot was a request by the IRYU to extend their offices (with an appropriate increase in rental). By June 1978 contractors had been identified who would convert the staff accommodation and at Warsash consideration was given to selling Shore House and acquiring land alongside the Royal Southern Yacht Club, but it was soon decided that funds from the sale of Shore House must be used to develop 60 Knightsbridge.

In September it was learned that the Anglo Belgian Club, whose lease in Belgrave Square was soon to terminate, were interested in moving into 60 Knightsbridge on the ground floor. These rapid developments were now presented to the AGM in October and resolutions to sell Shore House and to complete an agreement with the Anglo Belgian Club were carried, the agreement being completed in December. It was also agreed to raise £50,000 through the issue of loan notes. In fact, the latter was not successful, only £15,000 being taken up by members, but the sale of Shore House to Warsash Sailing Club was agreed by March 1979. The Club now had the funds needed to carry out the planned conversion of the staff quarters, which would provide two floors of small cabins for members' use (and offices for the Secretariat on the top floor of the west wing). The October 1979 AGM also gave conditional authority for the General Committee to set subscription levels - which they did, and set the Town Subscription at £145 from 1 July 1980. By June 1980 the somewhat austere new cabins were available for members' use at modest charge. The radical changes needed were now a reality and the Club, looking somewhat different, had a sound platform from which it could move forward with guarded optimism.

V

Towards the Millennium

These chronicles have traced the affairs of the Royal Thames Yacht Club for over two hundred years up to 1980. Throughout these years the Club has never wavered from its prime purpose - to bring together people with a common interest in yachting, to promote the sport and to provide yacht racing, cruising and social events to meet all tastes. The management of the Clubhouse and the control of the Club finances has proved to be a much more difficult aspect of the Club's life - it might be thought of as a 'rollercoaster' journey with its succession of ups and downs as the years went by.

Perhaps the most difficult period was the years after the Second World War culminating in the serious financial worries of the 1970s. Happily, the Club's long record of successfully overcoming such problems was once again demonstrated by the time that decade ended. Eighteen years later it can be affirmed that it has been possible to establish a sound financial base from which to operate all aspects of Club activities and to provide the not inconsiderable demands for capital expenditure during those eighteen years. As we move inexorably towards the Millennium it will be as well to review briefly what has transpired since 1980.

The death of Earl Mountbatten, Admiral of the Cumberland Fleet, at the hands of IRA terrorists in August 1979 was a tragedy felt deeply by Royal Thames members. It was, therefore, deemed to be appropriate to create a memorial to Earl Mountbatten in the form of a 'garden' to be sited in Hyde Park, beyond the carriageway at the rear of the Clubhouse. It had been noticed that the existing copse at that location was a somewhat rundown area of the park and it was hoped that the park authorities would welcome the opportunity to make worthwhile improvements. When the Vice Commodore, John Foot, opened negotiations he felt confident of a successful outcome once he learned that the Superintendent of Hyde Park was Mr Legge! His confidence proved to be well-founded. It was agreed that the copse would be landscaped and space provided for the planting of six flowering trees. In the meantime arrangements were made for the Commodore, HRH The Prince of Wales and the Princess of Wales to perform the planting ceremony and take lunch with the Flag Officers and members after the ceremony on 19 November 1987.

The weather during the period when the landscaping was undertaken was abominable but the work was completed with the minimum of time to spare. Matting was put down to ensure that the Prince and Princess did not sink through the newly-laid turf and on the day the sun shone from a watery sky and the public turned up in large numbers to see the newly-married couple perform the ceremony. Some eighteen months later a commemorative stone, created by the sculptor John Skelton (who had earlier been commissioned to do work at Broadlands, the Mountbatten home) was placed in the copse carrying a suitable inscription. A further act of commemoration took place on 20 January 1982 when Countess Mountbatten attended a lunch given by the Flag Officers and members of the General Committee, at which she unveiled a bronze bust of Earl Mountbatten (sculpted by Mr Pitt-Roche) in the first floor rooms, since named the Mountbatten Suite.

The office of Admiral of the Cumberland Fleet was to remain unfilled for seven years after the death of Earl Mountbatten. In 1986 HRH The Duke of York succeeded his elder brother as Commodore of the Royal Thames Yacht Club and this allowed HRH The Prince of Wales to accept his appointment as Admiral. This was formally acknowledged in March 1987 by a dinner at Knightsbridge during which the Patron, HRH The Duke of Edinburgh presented his son with an Admiral's pendant - a ceremony he had performed seventeen years earlier when Earl Mountbatten took the office of Admiral. Later that year the Club was able to entertain the new Commodore and the Duchess of York at the Laying Up Dinner held in the Clubhouse in October.

If these occasions represent some of the most important high points in the Club's social life during the 1980s there have been many more including the America's Cup Ball held at the Grosvenor House Hotel in September 1986 and attended by the Prince and Princess of Wales. This was a glittering and memorable evening, which also raised a significant sum of money to support the British Challenge. A very different and waterborne occasion arose in November 1987 when the incoming Lord Mayor of London led a procession down the Thames from Westminster to the City and invited the Royal Thames to form part of the procession. The Club was represented by David Arnold's motor yacht *FRESHWATER BAY* from which the Vice Commodore, Ian Butler, flew his flag.

The successful progress of the Club through the 1980s brought with it the desire and enthusiasm to reinstate an annual club ball, the first one being held at the Hyde Park Hotel in May 1988 while later on the balls were held in the Clubhouse, as were evenings specifically intended for the younger members of the Club such as the popular Valentine Disco - and some who attended could hardly be described as 'younger members'! The Fitting Out Dinner, the Laying Up Dinner and the Prizewinner's Dinner, regular 'Dine-Ins' and lecture evenings together with the Cowes Week Cocktail Party (held at the Royal London Yacht Club) provided a very full social programme.

Another important feature established in 1990 is a liaison with the frigate HMS Cumberland as a tribute to the Club's founder. Time at sea for Club members and dinners for the Commanding Officers and Wardroom Officers at Knightsbridge have been manifestations of that liaison. Finally, another aspect of the Club's social life that has gained momentum has been the support for golf matches, encouraged in recent years by the presence of the Commodore, HRH The Duke of York. All this has been possible due largely to the enthusiasm of the Captains of Golf including Gordon Pugsley, Charles Liddell and Peter Hunter and the (not always straightforward) arrangement that enables RTYC members to use the facilities of the New Zealand Golf Club. Perhaps the most ambitious concept has been the successful weekend matches with the Anglo Belgian Club played in Belgium in September 1996 and April 1998.

The cruises and rallies for members have proved very successful and increasingly ambitious, not least due to the lead given by the Captain of Rallies, Charles Liddell. While the West Country is still the most popular venue 'at home', the Channel Islands and northern France have been equally well supported locations. More ambitious still have been the rallies held in Majorca, Corsica, Turkey, New Zealand and St Lucia. The cruising element of the Club's calendar is stronger now than it has ever been (which is important since it helps to ensure that the three major elements of Club life - racing, cruising and social activities - are well represented).

Throughout the 1980s and 1990s the Club has maintained a strong race management team led by the Chief Race Officer (and recently by the Chief Sailing Officer). As has already been indicated, what has changed over the past 18 years is the move by yachtsmen from the Level Rating Classes to the One Design Classes, while within the Club emphasis has been given to providing more racing for members through team racing events.

The Race Committee's ability to organise successfully the complexities of world, european and national championships has been demonstrated annually and has received recognition from both yachting authorities and competitors. Support for the running of these championships by Club members has always been forthcoming (eventually!) whether it is given through the provision of their yachts as committee boats or by serving as race officers and in other supporting duties. Even the problem of finding financial support through reasonably discreet commercial sponsorship has generally been overcome, not least due to the development of high technology media opportunities for a sponsor. The decade from 1980 opened with the World Half-Ton Championship at Poole sponsored by Gordon's Gin and attracted a big entry. Although the Club was to organise other 'Ton' championships during the decade, the entry numbers were in decline. In 1988, when once again the Club ran the Half-Ton Championship out of Poole, sponsored by Rank Xerox, they also ran the European and National Championships at Falmouth for the re-emerging Six Metre Class and the National Championship for the new Sigma 38 class - a season which really stretched the race committee. Although the Club was selected to run the Three-quarter Ton World Championship out of Torbay in 1992, the event was cancelled due to lack of entrants. By that time the Club had continued its support for the Six Metre Class and taken on the European and National

championships for the Etchells Class.

Much has already been recorded of the contribution made to the development of high quality race management by the Royal Thames, not least due to the leadership of E.I. (Ricky) Hamilton-Parks after his appointment in 1970 as Chief Race Officer. When he was forced to stand down for health reasons Major Ralph James took over and maintained those standards until he too was beset by health problems in 1986. At that time the Club decided that a full-time, paid CRO was needed and they appointed a former Flag Officer, David Arnold who had just completed two years as Chief Executive of the British America's Cup Challenge. In making this appointment the Committee were aware that not only were they acquiring an experienced race officer but also that the Club would acquire a permanently available principal committee boat in David Arnold's well equipped FRESHWATER BAY, built in Belgium for another member of the Club, Frank Murdoch. While this inevitably led to an increase in the cost to the Club of maintaining a full race programme, the General Committee did require the Sailing Committee to offset the cost through sponsorship. David Arnold's nine year service as CRO ended in 1996 when he was succeeded by Iain MacDonald-Smith who led the Race Committee in 1996 and 1997 before handing over to Malcolm McKeag, the first Chief Sailing Officer whose responsibilities embrace both racing and cruising.

With the virtual demise of the World 'Ton' Championships the Race Committee turned to the running of one design class championships for the J24, Sigma 38 and Etchells and, in 1998, to the International 5.5 metre class in conjunction with the Royal Corinthian YC and the British-American Cup with the Royal Yacht Squadron. Although the Club has continued to be associated with the SCRA Classes, to provide practice/ selection races for Admiral's Cup and Commodore's Cup competitions as well as the first triumvirate in Cowes Week, the move over the past decade has been more and more towards team racing.

Team racing in dinghies for the Serpentine Cup has been maintained and since 1995 extended beyond the original four clubs. The match in 1991 had to be abandoned due to the freezing over of the Serpentine, while 1993 saw the Royal Thames the winners after too many years of coming fourth; the victory was repeated in 1998. The Serpentine was also the venue from 1983-87 for a November regatta in Illusions, the mini 12 metre boats. Some members of a larger build found they almost needed a shoe-horn to ease themselves into the boats. In the years 1986-89 the Club was invited to participate in the Viyella Cup series with some success, Iain MacDonald-Smith steering the Royal Thames entry to first place in 1987. The not insignificant prize money was required to be used to promote sailing opportunities for young people. The Club decided to purchase a number of Optimist dinghies to support the RYA youth scheme and in return asked that the recipients, with others, to come to the Serpentine each November for a day of team racing. The 'Oppie' regatta still continues today.

When the Royal Thames went to the United States in 1983 for a team racing match against the New York Yacht Club based on the American Yacht Club at Rye they achieved two things. Firstly, the match further cemented the relationship with that illustrious club and secondly, the defeat showed up the lack of team racing skills and tactical understanding by the Royal Thames team. That match has continued every two years or so ever since 1983 both in the USA and in the UK. The Club has raised its team racing skills to a high standard and has consequently been able to win the George Nicholls Trophy, donated by the NYYC for the match, in 1989 and 1995. This significant improvement has been achieved through the team racing experience gained from matches in Seaview Mermaids and the Mum's Bucket matches with the Sigma 33 Association, as well as developing experience from inter-club matches with the Royal Bermuda Yacht Club (for the General Sir Thomas Astley Cubitt Cup), the Royal St George Yacht Club, the Royal Hong Kong Yacht Club and the Royal Burnham Yacht Club.

ENDEAVOUR (1993) after being re-built for RTYC member Elizabeth Meyer, racing against VILLE DE PARIS.

The Club is now able to carry through a very full annual programme of ten or more events for handicap classes, keelboat classes and team racing matches as well as major championships and the Club's own regattas - a tribute to the enthusiasm of the Sailing Committee, the skill of the Race Committee and the support by members for the much wider range of racing opportunities now available to them in the Club's sailing programme.

In the two previous volumes, an appendix has been included giving details of each sailing match, the prizes awarded and the names of the prize winners and their yachts. Since 1919 the racing organised by the Royal Thames Yacht Club has largely been open to all yachtsmen. In view of this and the consequence that race winners could belong to clubs other than the Royal Thames (and therefore of less interest to Royal Thames members) the corresponding appendix in this volume (Appendix 14) has been limited to a listing of regattas, championships and, in the later years, cruises and rallies. The lists are not completely comprehensive, due primarily to the lack of detail in the records available.

While the Club has become a force in team racing, brief mention must also be made of some of the individual successes in the last few years. 1996 saw **Shirley Robertson's** successful selection for the British Olympic team in Savannah and saw **Adam Gosling** winning the World Etchells Championship at Cowes. A year later **Mary Falk** won her class in the Europe One Star Transatlantic Race, **Bruce Owen** won the World International 6 metre championships in Cannes and **Charles Stanley** the World International 14 Championship. With such successes the Club's future in yacht racing is well assured.

Before ending this selective review of the Club's sailing activities during the years 1981-98 three very special occasions must be mentioned. In the Summer of 1990, the Club was called upon in the planning of the arrangements for a Review of Yachts in the Solent from the Royal Yacht *BRITANNIA* to mark the ninetieth birthday of HM Queen Elizabeth, the Queen Mother. The review took place on 30 July 1990 just a few days before Her Majesty's birthday and is recorded in a painting hanging outside the Queenborough Room in the present Clubhouse. Four years later, in July 1994, the Royal Thames was one of the small number of Clubs around the world to be invited by the New York Yacht Club to participate in their sesquicentennial celebrations comprising racing by day and social functions in the evening - the privilege extended to the Club was yet again a reflection of the bond between the Royal Thames and the New York Yacht Club that extends back to the nineteenth Century when the Royal Thames invited members of the New York Yacht Club to participate in Royal Thames sailing matches. The third and perhaps the most testing occasion was the Royal Thames challenge for the America's Cup at Fremantle in 1996-97.

Over its long history the **America's Cup** has been synonymous with controversy, volatile regulations and a multitude of pressures that at times resulted in litigation or the threat of it. When in 1993 the Australians became the first country to wrest the trophy from the Americans, they let it be known that any club wishing to challenge must place that challenge and deposit the specified sum of money by midnight on 30 April 1994. It appeared that there would be no UK challenge until a few days before the deadline, when the Vice Commodore of the Royal Thames, John Foot, received calls indicating that it was unthinkable that there should be no UK challenge and that there were those around who wished to

ensure that a challenge was made. The deadline in Britain was, of course, earlier at 17.00 on Monday 30 April and late in the morning of that day the Vice Commodore was able to bring together a small group including the Rear Commodore, W P Andreae Jones, who was Chairman of the Sailing Committee and Philip Tolhurst (who had been associated with the 1993 challenge by Peter De Savary through the Royal Burnham Yacht Club). After some five hours of discussion weighing the conflicting factors it was agreed that a conditional challenge should be lodged. A few days later a meeting of the General and Sailing Committees met to endorse the action taken and to accept the case for a challenge made by Admiral Sir Ian Easton in preference to that presented by a member of the Royal Thames, Mr C C (Kit) Hobday.

Admiral Easton had already been approached by a designer, Warwick Collins, with a revolutionary design for a 12 metre yacht but in the end nothing came of it nor did the hoped-for sponsorship from the first company approached - British Aerospace. Meanwhile, he had asked one of the country's leading exponents of match racing, Harold Cudmore, to be in charge of the sailing programme and was seeking a suitable person to be chairman of the challenge - a position he himself did not wish to hold. David Hollam took over the design of the radical boat and Ian Howlett, vastly experienced in twelve metre design, was asked to produce a conventional boat. The ideal would be to produce a third boat based on experience of racing the other two - but this was not to be possible. By the end of 1984, Admiral Easton had persuaded a member of the Royal Thames, Mr Graham Walker, to be chairman of the challenge, Phil Crebbin had been appointed as Technical Director and Angus Melrose as sailmaker.

At a press conference in January 1985 the Club confirmed that the challenge would go ahead in their name and that the challenge would be run by a company which ultimately was called British America's Cup Challenge (BACC). The challenge had now brought together some of the best technical and sailing ability in Britain but the elusive sponsorship to finance the five million pound programme was not forthcoming from the commercial world in spite of the efforts of professional fundraisers. This created a serious problem for the Royal Thames. The Deed of Gift from the America's Cup required it to be between Yacht Clubs irrespective of how the challenge is mounted. The Royal Thames is a private members' Club and should BACC at any time fail to meet legitimate demands by their creditors, the Club's assets and members could be expected to meet those demands. This uncomfortable situation and the continuing absence of financial support strained relationships between the Club and BACC. In April 1985 the Club asked BACC to agree to a number of conditions if the challenge was to continue, bearing in mind the lessons learned from the unsuccessful challenge by the Royal Thames in 1964 and the aborted challenge in 1970. The three main conditions were that Graham Walker should underwrite a large proportion of the budgeted cost of the challenge; that BACC should indemnify the Club against claims on BACC and that either the Club or BACC could terminate the challenge but neither could act unilaterally. A large legal document was drawn up to give the Club the protection it sought in a financial environment where the sums involved were so large.

It did not help the challenge, already a late-starter, that the construction of the two boats was delayed, in part due to the problems already mentioned and also because the planned builder went into receivership, but start it did in May 1985, seventeen months before the elimination races were due to commence in the waters off Fremantle. The launch of the conventional boat took place on 4 December 1985, the ceremony being performed by the Princess of Wales, the boat being kept under wraps and named *CRUSADER* (a name chosen to relate to a potential sponsor). In January 1986 *CRUSADER* appeared at the London Boat Show in the hope that it might attract a sponsor. A few weeks later it was shipped to Australia, followed four weeks later by the radical boat now known as C2. An advance party under Andrew Spedding were already in Australia and had set up a base for the challenge and had acquired accommodation for the crews and support team.

In April 1986 the Club had appointed Ricky Hamilton-Parks and Mrs Eileen Caulcutt to represent the Club on the Race Committee for the elimination series for the competing boats from the USA, Canada, France, Italy and New Zealand. The Club had also agreed to invite members to make donations towards the cost of the challenge and arrangements had already been made to hold an America's Cup Ball in September to be attended by the Prince and Princess of Wales and 800 guests. Though both raised worthwhile sums the burden of financing the challenge was still largely borne by Graham Walker, and a late sponsorship deal with White Horse Whisky relieved him of only a modest part of the cost. It also led to the conventional boat being re-named *WHITE CRUSADER*.

Trials off Fremantle showed that although C2 was fast on certain points of sailing, *WHITE CRUSADER* was the better all-round performer in the exciting waters where the race courses were set and where the wind in the afternoons was always likely to be around Force 6. The performance of *WHITE CRUSADER* and her highly trained crew under Harold Cudmore brought praise from many quarters at Fremantle as well as the belief that she would reach at least the semi-finals of the elimination series. In spite of early successes, races were lost that might have been won and a place in the semi-finals proved to be just beyond her grasp. Inevitably there was great disappointment that the boat had not quite attained its full potential and critics would rehearse the well worn phrase 'too little and too late' but it should be recognised that much was achieved and once again many lessons were learned - some might say re-learned.

As in 1964 the Club set up a Sub Committee (chaired this time by Peter Nicholson) to review the challenge and consider the position of the Club in respect of any future challenge. Perhaps the most significant conclusion drawn by the Sub Committee was that in view of the vast cost of mounting a modern challenge, it should be made through a club set up specifically for the purpose and with whom the Royal Thames could co-operate without being exposed to a potentially overwhelming financial burden.

During the 1980s the Club was able to build up the much-needed financial reserves and thus was able to keep on top of the maintenance required for the Clubhouse as well as undertaking limited updating of the cabins and the reception area. Modern equipment for the administration of the Club was acquired, the first word processor arriving in 1981 followed by computerisation of financial controls and the hotel functions. In spite of these actions the Clubhouse was starting to look a little shabby and dated by 1989 - twenty five years after the rebuilding. A refurbishment Sub Committee was set up in July under the chairmanship of the 'House' Rear Commodore, Robert Dean, to make recommendations for a complete refurbishment of the building and a review of

the catering operation. From the outset it was clear that such an undertaking would cost well in excess of half a million pounds over a period of at least three years. It was also agreed that an independent professional review should be made. A report from the latter was available by the end of 1990.

The General Committee now had available the information it needed to launch a **refurbishment programme** which they proposed to finance from three sources: the Club's general funds (supplemented by over-inflation increases in subscriptions); an issue of £250,000 of debentures to members and by the sale of a modest proportion of the Club's investment portfolio. They also agreed to seek tenders for the renewal of the catering contract and, most important of all, for a design consultant to undertake the design and management of the refurbishment. In March 1991 Mr Robin Moore-Ede was selected as the Design Consultant and, in June, Sutcliffe Catering were chosen for the renewal of the catering contract.

Just when the way ahead for planning the programme for refurbishment seemed clear, the Head Lessee, Mountleigh Ltd (who had taken over from Chelsfield), produced plans to redevelop 60 Knightsbridge and No.2 Albert Gate as an hotel which would include two floors for the Royal Thames Yacht Club. These plans were given serious consideration but in the end they did not materialise, not least because Mountleigh went into receivership in 1992. A further complication was the future plans of the International Yacht Racing Union who in May 1990 indicated that they would not renew the lease on their accommodation in the Clubhouse when it fell due at the end of the year. In the event they decided to delay their departure until April 1992 by which time the Royal Cruising Club had agreed to take part of the area occupied by the IYRU.

The first stage of the refurbishment programme was completed in the Summer of 1991 and comprised the 'park' side of the ground floor. Out of this was created the Paget and Queenborough committee rooms and the development of the model room to enable it to be used as a chart room, a reference library, a quiet room and, if all other facilities were in use, as a room for small meetings. The second stage, undertaken in 1992, included the cabins in the west wing, the ground floor cloakrooms and the conversion of the IYRU offices to provide an area to meet the RCC's requirements; a further meeting room which would also house the remainder of the Club's library and an office for the General Manager.

It was already clear that, if the refurbishment was to continue without requiring the Clubhouse to be shut down for an extended period, the programme would need to be extended beyond the original period of three years. If this extension was seen as an inconvenience by members, it paled into insignificance with that experienced when the Kuwait government (who in 1992 had purchased No.2 Albert Gate and the head lease of 60 Knightsbridge as their Embassy) modernised the offices above the Clubhouse and refurbished No.2 Albert Gate. The extension to the refurbishment programme was greater than was expected due in part to the need to upgrade the kitchen (once again) if the Club was to meet the standards required in order that the Club's operating licence could be renewed in 1995. The completion of the Coffee Room and, in particular, the ceiling, was not achieved until 1997 due mainly to the need to identify the source of the intermittent water leaks which had regularly damaged the ceiling over many years (not least in the late 1980s when water started emerging from the ceiling on the morning of the Prizewinners Dinner and had to be caught in strategically placed large drums, suitably disguised!).

If the 1984-87 America's Cup was the major feature in the Club's sailing affairs during this period, the refurbishment of the Clubhouse (1991-97) was not only a major feature of house affairs but also a highly successful one that produced a modern, attractive Clubhouse ready to face the twenty first century.

Another major venture by the Club started in April 1989 when the Vice Commodore, Ian Butler, proposed that the members be invited to contribute in the region of £200,000 in order that the Club's name could continue to be associated with a new lifeboat for the RNLI since the existing boat was being taken out of service. The Club's support of the RNLI goes back to 1856 in the form of financial support or the funding of lifeboats in whole or part. The Vice Commodore and his wife Anne had long been associated with the RNLI and their lead was enthusiastically supported by the membership and the sum needed was realised within two years. Initially the new boat was allocated to south-east Ireland but in June 1992 it was learned that a vacancy would occur at Eastbourne - close enough to Knightsbridge to enable the Club to maintain an effective liaison with the crew and its supporters. Club Officers and members were present in Eastbourne to attend the naming ceremony performed by HRH Princess Michael of Kent on 6 September 1993.

Before closing this selective review of the affairs of the Royal Thames Yacht Club since 1980 there are other topics which should be included. Mention has already been made of the Cup known as Mum's Bucket and presented by Mr Pat Kelly in 1988 and the painting of the Review of Yachts on the occasion of The Queen Mother's ninetieth birthday in 1991. To these must be added the purchase by the Club in 1985 of the full model of the (now paid off) Royal Yacht *BRITANNIA* flying the flag of the Patron, HRH The Duke of Edinburgh. This model was made by Mr H D Turner who worked in the Royal Navy's Hydrographer's Department as an engraver of the copper plates from which charts were produced before computers took over. Model making for shipping lines was his hobby but the *BRITANNIA* model had become a long-term project because he was always having to modify the model to keep it up to date! Turner was also responsible for making the model of *JESTER*. This model, situated in the Coffee Room, was commissioned as a tribute to the owners and the yacht's remarkable achievements. Lastly, three paintings should be mentioned. In 1991 the Club was able to purchase another of the paintings of their former Marine Artist, N.M. Condy. This 1845 painting depicted the cutters *PHANTOM*, owned by A O Wilkinson of the RTYC and *BELVIDERE* owned by Lord Alfred Paget. It now hangs in the Edinburgh Room as does a second painting purchased in the same year and depicting the cutter *VICTORINE*, owned by Henry G Lord of the RTYC. The yacht is shown off Ostend; the artist being Louis Verboeckhoven. When Edward Sparke-Davies, a Jersey based member died in 1990, he bequeathed to the Club a sum of money. With his widow's agreement it was decided to use the money to commission a painting of Sparke-Davies' 12 metre yacht *GAEL-NA-MARA* sailing off St Helier. That painting by Rex Phillips now hangs outside the Queenborough Room, a very welcome addition the Club's collection of treasures.

'Treasures' may not be quite the appropriate description of Edward Merchant, Norris Coultous and Tony Farr, but these three members of the staff at Knightsbridge gave quite exceptional service to the Club and its members. All of them have retired in the last few years but each had made a significant contribution to the history of the Club over the past 67 years. Edward, as barman in the Cumberland Bar knew every member and could provide 'chapter and verse' on past members from his 'reference books' kept behind the bar. The respect in which members held him was well-illustrated in 1981 when they came in large numbers to a lunchtime celebration held to mark his fifty years of service to the Club. The same was true of Norris Coultous in 1988 when he too completed 50 years of service broken only by wartime service as a radio operator in Bomber Command. His outstanding ability to manage Club functions and private parties has already been referred to, but he also had a considerable knowledge of and interest in the Club's silver collection. Tony Farr's length of service was considerably shorter, a mere 18 years, but his courteous and efficient service in the Britannia Bar was greatly appreciated by members of both the Royal Thames Yacht Club and the Anglo Belgian Club. Long-serving members of staff provide a continuity that is greatly appreciated by members and at present Billy O'Driscoll (the cellar man and wine waiter) and Joseph Grexhammer (for a long period the Head Waiter in the Coffee Room but more recently the successor to Norris Coultous) are well on the way to continuing the tradition of long service as is Carol Turp (originally the cashier and nowadays the Front of House Manager). In these days when people change their employment frequently, the tradition of long-service at the Royal Thames is all the more welcome.

Once Shore House was sold in 1979 the search for alternate waterside premises has rarely been off the agenda of the General Committee. In 1983, a Sub Committee concluded that no suitable and affordable premises could be found - not least because it had been decreed that such premises must be self financing. Early in 1988 consideration was given to using 800 square feet of space available at Moody's Yard at Bursledon but it was not suitable. Ten years later and the search continues. Most agree that a waterside facility on the Solent is a highly desirable adjunct to the Knightsbridge Clubhouse but many also have an acute awareness of the financial and administrative problems that the Club had experienced when running Shore House. The alternative of combining with a Solent-based club has been examined many times in the past century but in spite of much good will on both sides a basis for a final agreement has never been achieved. It would seem that different options need to become available for examination, especially when the desire to acquire waterside premises is coupled with the wish to have available a permanent vessel for use by the Race Committee - perhaps a new century will bring a realisation of these ambitions.

Whatever the new century brings it cannot alter the fact that the Royal Thames Yacht Club is today as soundly based as it has ever been in its long history and can look forward to a successful future as it makes preparations to celebrate the Millennium.

VI
Club Treasures

The Club has been particularly fortunate to be the recipient of large numbers of portraits, marine paintings and prints as well as silver trophies. To that list can be added books, models, half models and a range of memorabilia. The flow of these artefacts into the club continued throughout the years covered by this volume and will be described later in this section.

The practice of appointing **MARINE ARTISTS** for the Club goes back to 1843 when N M Condy was nominated for the office. When this volume opens in 1919 the last artist appointed was Louis Nevill in 1911. He was to be followed in 1920 by the distinguished painter **Norman Wilkinson** who is remembered by Royal Thames' members through his wonderful painting of King George V's famous yacht *BRITANNIA*. That painting was bought by the Club in January 1933 for 350 guineas. The club also bought 200 prints of the painting, each being signed by the artist. These were sold on to members at three guineas each. Norman Wilkinson's successor in 1927 was another well known marine painter **William L Wylie**. Following the death of Mr Wylie, the Annual General Meeting (on 14 March 193) was invited to appoint **Mr Cecil King** as the Club's Marine Artist. Two of Cecil King's paintings are still to be seen in the Clubhouse. The proposal to make this appointment came from Commander P T Dean, who a few days later would be appointed Chairman of Committees; it was seconded by Vice Admiral T. K. Loring, a former Chairman. While Commander Dean confined his support for Cecil King to '*I know Cecil King personally, both as a yachtsman and a good fellow, and as a very clever Marine Artist...*', Admiral Loring was vastly more expansive and fulsome in his praise of Cecil King - or was his lengthy peroration merely a reflection of the more leisurely pace of life in the 1930s? - a copy of Admiral Loring's remarks is at Appendix 15.

Two further appointments as Marine Artist to the Club have been made since that of Cecil King. In March 1944 **Lt. Cdr. Peter Scott**, the son of the Antarctic explorer Robert Falcon Scott, who was well known to the Club as a yachtsman and who had been an Olympic medallist in 1936 (and was later to be helmsman of the RTYC America's Cup Challenge in 1964) was appointed. Renowned in more recent times for his Wildlife Trust at Slimbridge and earlier for his exploits in World War II with coastal forces, he was already a well-established marine artist. Ten years later **Bernard Adams** was appointed Honorary Artist to the Club. He will be known by today's members through his portrait of HRH The Duke of Edinburgh which hangs in the entrance hall. During the re-building of the Clubhouse at Knightsbridge, it was Bernard Adams who advised on the restoration of paintings, the selection of those to be retained and the decision to reduce

the length of the large portraits of past Officers from three-quarter to half-length. It has often been suggested that the artist Frank H. Mason was appointed Marine Artist to the Club but there is no evidence to support this suggestion. He was elected to membership of the Club in 1945; he was consulted by the Committee on matters relating to marine paintings and many of his works still hang in today's Clubhouse - but that appears to be the extent of his connections with the Club. In more recent years, there have been at least two proposals to appoint a Marine Artist to the Club but no appointment was made. A complete list of Marine Artists is given in Appendix 16.

Paintings of Club Officers

Between the years 1920 and 1955 the Club acquired a further five portraits of officers of the Club.

HRH The Duke of Cumberland - a portrait of the Duke who gave his name to The Cumberland Fleet in 1775 hangs on the quarterdeck today. In 1919 this oil painting is recorded as having been presented to the Club by William Yates but on what date is not stated. A note that the Club purchased 'a picture' of the Duke of Cumberland for twelve guineas in May 1920 clearly refers to one of the prints in the Club's possession.

Sir James Pender - a Flag Officer in the years 1904-1910, his portrait by I. M. Heaton was presented to the Club in June 1933 by a Mrs Bragge. The Committee had received a letter from a former Club Secretary, Captain Orr, informing them that the painting was on offer and they gratefully accepted it. When this painting, along with all other oil paintings of Officers of the Club, was sent away to be cleaned in the 1980s, it was quickly realised that it was not, as had been assumed, another oil painting - the first pass with a 'cleaning cloth' removed Sir James Pender's face! Happily all that was needed to restore it was available.

J. S. Highfield - the oil painting of this gentleman who gave over 20 years of service to the Club as Chairman of Committees and as a Flag Officer, is by Fredrick Whiting. It was acquired by the Club in 1944. At a meeting of the General Committee on 14 September of that year, it was recorded that '*the Chairman (B. T. Rumble) informed the Committee that he had been informed that a portrait of the Vice Commodore would be presented to the Club if*

Lt Norman Wilkinson RNVR (1917) - Marine Artist to the RTYC (1920 - 1927).

the Committee would accept it' - which they agreed to do. Mr Highfield, the Vice Commodore, was present at that meeting and although it was not recorded, it can reasonably be assumed that he was presenting the portrait which today hangs in the Paget Room - as does the portrait of Sir James Pender.

Earl Mountbatten - In April 1953 it was suggested that a portrait of the Commodore (Earl Mountbatten) might be acquired from a Maltese artist, William Apap, who had already created a full-length portrait with a Maltese background. By the end of July it was agreed to ask the artist to produce a similar portrait but of only three-quarter length - to match the other portraits in the Clubhouse at that time. Today that portrait hangs in the east corridor on the ground floor.

HRH The Duke of Edinburgh - On the day in July 1953 when the General Committee decided to proceed with the portrait of the Commodore they also heard from a Committee Member (Sir John Cordingley) *'that a portrait painter of repute, Mr Bernard Adams, had offered to paint a portrait of our patron. Arrangements for his sittings would be made by another artist who was already in contact with the Royal Family - Simon Elwes. He believed that the artist would accept a fee of one hundred guineas'.* Although the Committee agreed to proceed with the portrait, it was February 1955 before sittings could take place. It had been suggested that the patron should unveil the portrait but this was not in accord with precedence and the Commodore, Earl Mountbatten, agreed to unveil the portrait at the Laying Up Dinner of 24 November 1955.

Paintings by Nicholas Matthew Condy

Any member who has attended a meeting or social function in the Edinburgh Room of the present Clubhouse will almost certainly have admired the fine collection of paintings by N M Condy. The Club's archives do not reveal how the Club came to possess this collection but the following may give an indication of their source: firstly there is evidence that the paintings were not in the Club's possession in 1939; secondly, part of the bequest to the Club in November 1949 from the estate of Lord Queenborough was 'a collection of pictures' which the Committee decided to keep together and hang in the Committee Room of the original Knightsbridge Clubhouse; thirdly if, as is suspected, that collection was the set of Condy paintings, that suspicion is reinforced by the fact that the majority of the paintings include the yacht *MYSTERY* owned by Lord Alfred Paget, the father of Lord Queenborough.

Silver trophies

From the historical rather than the financial viewpoint, the most important cups in the Club's impressive collection are the **Cumberland Cups** and the **Vauxhall Cups** which were referred to in the section on the Provenance of the Club. They were all raced for on the Thames by members of the Cumberland Fleet in the late 18th and early 19th centuries. Today the Club has in its collection five of the Cumberland Cups and four of the Vauxhall Cups. The route by which these cups came back to the Club is not known with absolute certainty in every case but the following facts are known and provide moderately conclusive evidence: in December 1955 Mr Freeman-Taylor, a great, great grandson of Commodore Taylor, Commodore of the Cumberland Fleet (1780-1816) loaned to the Club three silver cups won by Commodore Taylor in 1776, 1780 and 1781; the 1777 cup was discovered in Buckingham Palace by Earl Mountbatten in 1975 and presented to the Club; the 1782 Cup was bequeathed to the Club by Mr J. H. Hughes of Marion, Massachusetts in 1986; in April 1928 Mrs G. A. Tonge (widow of a member) presented to the Club the 1792 Vauxhall Cup; the 1794 Vauxhall Cup was presented to the Club in February 1956 by a member, Major B. C. Windelar; in June 1933 it is recorded that a subscription list was posted (subscriptions limited to 2 guineas) to enable the Club to purchase Cups given by the Proprietors of Vauxhall Gardens, while in July 1933 it is recorded *'D & J Wellby to be paid for the Vauxhall Cups, £65'.* It is probable that this latter reference is to the Vauxhall Cups of 1802 and 1806. (Whether D & J Wellby were related to Club member A. S. Wellby is not mentioned, but it is known that D & J Wellby were silversmiths (who for example manufactured the 1921 British American Cup).

During the period covered by this volume well over forty silver cups have been presented to the Club; over three quarters of them are still in the Club's collection today and the majority are still competed for each year. The winners are awarded their trophy at the Annual Prizewinners Dinner but security demands that only rarely are they permitted to take them away from the Clubhouse - as compensation the Club gives each winner a keeper prize.

Those cups acquired since 1919 are listed below.

Queenborough Cumberland Cup - this trophy was presented by Lord Queenborough in August 1922 as an International
Cup for the 6 metre class and, as has been recorded earlier,
it was regularly competed for in the 1920s and 30s but only
occasionally since that period.

Morgan Cup - was presented in February 1929 by John Julius
Morgan, a member of the Royal Thames and also of the New
York Y.C. and the Circle de la Voile, Paris. The first race for the
trophy took place on 20 July 1929 the course being: Ryde -
Needles - Cherbourg - Nab Tower - Ryde and was won by
FLAME (Charles E. Nicholson). The Cup has been competed
for almost every year since 1929.

Cory Cup - was presented in February 1931 by a Royal
Thames member R.W. Cory. It was first competed for on 26
July 1932 in an inter-club race in yachts of the West Solent
One Design class and more recently in yachts of the Daring
class. This George II trophy was made by James Dixon and
Sons of Sheffield in 1905.

Prince of Wales Cup - has been mentioned earlier as having
been presented by HRH The Prince of Wales in 1935 to mark
the Silver Jubilee of HRH King George V (and again in 1977
for the Jubilee Race on the occasion Queen Elizabeth II's Silver
Jubilee). In 1935 it was won by *VANITY* (W.R. Westhead).
In modern times it is presented to the winner of the International J 24 class race on Royal Thames day in Cowes Week.

Sandbach Cup - came into the Club's possession in
November 1937 from the executor of the late Mr J.C. H.
Sandbach (member) together with £150 to be an annual prize
at the Royal Thames Regatta. In 1946 it was awarded to the
winner of the 6 metre class and, in 1957, to the International
One Design Class. More recently, in the 1980s, it was a prize
at the BLRA Championships.

Glazebrook Challenge Cup was the subject of another
bequest by an RTYC member, Harter K. Glazebrook.
This bequest comprised £100 of which half purchased from
Wellbys the 1843 Cup by the Barnards and half went to the
Regatta Fund. Throughout the years that cup has been awarded
at Cowes Week to the winner of Class 1 or its equivalent.

Albert Morson Cup. Albert Morson died in October 1939.
The cup was made in London in 1938 by A & F Parsons
but there is no direct evidence to show that Albert Morson
presented the cup before his death. What is certain is that
the RTYC 12 metre class races in June 1939 were won by
VIM owned by Harold S. Vanderbilt and that his prize was
probably the Albert Morson Cup. This assumption is based
on the record in May 1940 that *'under the Deed of Title, the
Albert Morson Cup should be returned to the Clubhouse by
1 May 1940. The Cup is at present in America in the custody
of the winner - Mr Harold Vanderbilt and under the present
(wartime) circumstances it might by safer to leave it in
America'*. It was suggested that it be handed over to the New
York Yacht Club for the time being; to be returned to the
Royal Thames Yacht Club when conditions became normal
again. In fact it is subsequently recorded in July 1940 that the
Cup had been returned from America and Lord Queenborough
had interviewed the donor of the Cup, Mr J. F. Melling (elected
RTYC 1917), which rather blurs its provenance. Suffice it to
say, the Cup is still awarded today at Cowes Week. When Mr
Melling died, it is noted by the Sailing committee in November

1948 that *'The Trust Deed between the late Mr J. F. Melling
and the Royal Thames Yacht Club instituting the Albert
Morson Cup was brought to the notice of the Committee'*.
The Deed was to be consulted and its conditions to be put
into effect. It must be assumed that the conditions gave
ownership of the Cup to the Royal Thames.

Howard Junior Challenge Cup. This small cup was made in
Sheffield in 1918 and presented to the Club in November 1949
by Lt. Col. C.N.C. Howard, a member of the Club. Initially the
Cup was competed for by members' sons and daughters who
were under 18 years: this was changed to 21 years of age in
1954. As noted in the sailing section of this volume these
junior races were abandoned in 1964 due to lack of support.

Festival of Britain Challenge Cup was made in Sheffield
in 1903. It was presented to the Club by A. D. Ambrumenil,
a member, in January 1951 (the year of the Festival of Britain)
and was awarded to the yacht that gained most points in the
4 - 10 Ton Handicap Class in RTYC races each year.

The Neal Cups - In June 1951, Mrs P. B. Neal (wife of Mr B.H.
Neal; they were both RTYC members) presented two cups to
the Club. One trophy - the Neal Junior Challenge Cup was
made in Birmingham in 1922 and was awarded to the second
placed yacht in the Junior Races in which the winner received
the Howard Junior Challenge Cup. Today it is awarded in
Cowes Week to the winner of the *SONATA* class. The second
trophy - the Neal Challenge Cup, made in Birmingham in
1908, was awarded to the *DRAGON* class winner in the 1951
RTYC regatta. Today it is awarded to the winner of the Sigma
33 class in the Solent Clubs Championship. Mrs Neal also presented other cups in 1952 (for the 5.5 metre class) and 1953
(for the 8 metre class) but both these were won outright in
1953 so are not in the Club's present collection of trophies.

The Docker Cup - This cup was made in 1846 by Robert
Garrard and was presented in 1952 by Sir Bernard Docker
while he was Vice Commodore of the Club. The trophy was
to be presented to that member of the Club who had made
an outstanding achievement as a yachtsman.

The Duncan-Mitchell Trophy takes the form of a Victorian
centrepiece and was made in London in 1860. The centrepiece comprises a Nautilus mounted on an elaborate base.
It was presented to the Club in February 1953 by Mrs V.H.
Mitchell in memory of Mr Andrew Duncan, an RTYC member
1857-97.

Theodore Pim Cup was part of the bequest made to the
Club by the late Commodore Theodore Pim, in November
1930. Initially it was competed for by yachts of the 12 metre
class but by 1953 it was allocated to the 5.5 metre class.

Tom Thorneycroft Cups were donated in February 1953 by
the then Rear Commodore, Tom Thorneycroft. These three
cups were all made in London. The first one is dated 1923 and
was initially allocated to the 5.5 metre class in Cowes Week for
the Royal Thames day on 2 August 1953; for over 30 years
since then it has been awarded to the winner of the Daring
Class in Cowes Week. The other two cups, both dated 1924,
have always been awarded at Cowes Week for the winners
of the Redwing and National Swallow classes respectively.

Michael Brady Cup was presented in 1954 in memory
of RTYC member Michael Brady. This 1928 Mappin and
Webb Trophy was awarded for the Cowes-Nab Tower race

initially, but in 1958 was re-allocated to the winner of the return race in the Cowes - Poole passage races. In more recent years it had been awarded to a handicap class in Solent Clubs Championship.

Carmela Cup - This trophy made in London in 1935 was competed for from that year in the RTYC regatta, but its origin is obscure. How it came by that name and who presented it to the Club is not recorded.

The Victory Trophy was presented in 1946 by RTYC member Sir Frank Spencer Spriggs to commemorate the end of World War II. This trophy, made in Birmingham in 1930, was first competed for by the 6 metre class at Cowes on 1 August 1947. In 1962 the donor agreed to transfer it to the Class IV Handicap yachts on the Royal Thames day in Cowes Week - it is still awarded to a similar class today.

Colin Campbell Challenge Cup was made in Dublin in 1909 and presented to the Club in September 1959 by Commodore Colin Campbell shortly after he stood down as Vice Commodore. It was allocated as a prize to the winner of Class II in the Morgan Cup in 1960 and has been a class prize in that event ever since that date.

Queen's Cup - In June 1868 that redoubtable cutter *FIONA* (E. Boutcher) won a Royal Thames match from Gravesend to the Mouse Light and back. The prize that day for the winner was a cup presented by Queen Victoria. A year earlier in 1867 *FIONA* had won another Queen's Cup at a regatta given by the Royal Western Yacht Club at Queenstown, Ireland.

In January 1960 Lt. Col. T.H. Trevor, a member of the Club reported that he had seen these two cups for sale in a London shop priced £85.00 and £68.00 respectively. The Committee decided to offer 100 guineas for the two cups and to open a subscription list. A month later Mr Arnold Munns, Chairman of Committee and former Rear Commodore purchased the 1868 Cup for the Club and, with the permission of H.M. Queen Elizabeth II, the cup was rededicated as The Queen's Cup. At the same meeting in February Mr Glynn Blaxter informed the Committee that he and other members had purchased the 1867 Cup. The 1868 trophy was competed for by yachts of the 12 metre class throughout the 1960s but there is no record of the 1867 cup being competed for since it was bought for the club. Unfortunately there is a considerable doubt about the provenance of the Queen's Cup rededicated in 1960. While the Club's record specifically states that both cups were won by *FIONA* (and *FIONA* did win Queen's Cups in those years) and both were presented by Queen Victoria, the assay marks on both the cup and the lid of the 1868 cup show that it was manufactured in 1892! The only inscription on the cup is 'Queen's Cup 1960'. If this was the 1868 Cup presented by Queen Victoria it would almost certainly have had an inscription that said so (as does the 1867 Cup won at Queenstown). There is also no evidence to show that it was won by *FIONA* at a date later than 1868. It does seem therefore that this is not the 1868 cup.

Glynn Terrell Tray. This silver tray was made in 1909 and was presented to the Club in July 1963 by Mrs Glynn Terrell in memory of her late husband George Glynn Terrell who had been a Rear Commodore of the Club in 1953 and chairman of Committees 1945-46.

Harold Edwards Cups. In September 1966 Harold. F. Edwards, a Club Committee member, donated two cups to

be awarded to the first RTYC yacht in the two classes of the Island Sailing Club's 'Round the Island' race. One cup was made in London in 1900, the other in Birmingham in 1908. The former is still awarded for the same purpose while the second is with the Sigma 38 Association by Deed of Gift. Harold Edwards died in 1971 and in May 1972 his daughter, Mrs Alec Foucard, donated two further cups in his memory to be competed for by yachts of the Soling and Mermaid Classes in Cowes Week. Both cups were made in Sheffield in 1914. The cup for the Mermaid class is still awarded today.

RTYC Offshore Challenge Cup. In June 1969, while he was serving as Rear Commodore of the Club, Mr John Savage presented this cup (made in London in 1926) for the winner of the race from Le Havre to Southsea.

Warsash and Knightsbridge Cups. In May 1969 the Sailing Committtee took an unusual step; it is recorded that *'two cups (unspecified) chosen by the Sailing Committee from the Club's silver had been renamed the Warsash Cup and the Knightsbridge Cup and they were engraved accordingly'.* The Warsash Cup is a Mappin and Webb silver bowl made in Sheffield in 1902 while the Knightsbridge Cup was made in London in 1897. Currently they are awarded to class winners in the Morgan Cup race.

The Solent Trophy was presented in July 1972 by Mrs Eileen Caulcutt, who was the Assistant Sailing Secretary of the Club. It was allocated to the winner of the Dragon Class in Cowes Week and has continued to be so awarded since 1972.

Commodore's Salver was presented in January 1974 by the then Commodore of the Club, Mr Elmer Ellsworth-Jones. Made by Francis Howard in Sheffield in 1973, it was awarded to the RTYC member who gained the highest number of points in the RORC Championship.

John Burt Cup - made in London in 1928, this cup was presented to the Club in June 1971 for the winner of the Handicap Class V race at Cowes by Mr John Burt, a committee member and one of the most experienced Race Officers. Today it is still allocated to the winner of a handicap class at Cowes.

Spirit Cup - was presented to the Club in January 1973 by Mr F.A. Haworth, a renowned member of the Club and a former Rear Commodore. This tiny antique, Danish silver beaker (7.5 cm high) was described by 'Sandy' Haworth as the smallest trophy to be competed for by the biggest yachts. Certainly Mr Haworth's intentions were that the trophy should be competed for in an International Level Rating Match for yachts with a rating of 30 feet I.O.R but this seems to have happened rarely. The only record of it being competed for comes in 1982 when it is noted that it was won by *KIALOA* owned by the American, Mr Jim Kilroy.

Other Silver trophies. The Club has, over the years, been presented with many other trophies that are no longer in the Club's possession. In recent times these included the **Lochan Cup** presented by Mr Frank Douglas in 1967 for the winner of the Cowes-Cherbourg-Cowes passage race; the **250 Trophy** presented in 1973 by Mr John Maddocks and awarded to the winner of the Quarter Ton Class in the BLRA Championship and the **Saida Cup** presented in 1974 by Mr John Burt for the Three-Quarter Ton class.

The custom of presenting silver trophies to the Club has

virtually stopped in the past 25 years. Two exceptions are the gift in 1987 of **Mum's Bucket** by Mr Patrick Kelly to be competed for by teams racing boats of the Sigma 33 class and the Silver Neff presented by Mr David Diehl when Rear Commodore, and competed for by the Sigma 38 class in their National Championship.

Lastly, in 1988 , two small silver cups were presented to the Club by a Mrs. D.C. Wallace of Budleigh Salterton in Devon, a friend of the MacAndrew family of Dartmouth. Vernon MacAndrew, a distinguished member of the Royal Thames lost his life in his boat *CAMPEADOR* which was sunk in the English Channel in 1940. His daughter, Miss Mary MacAndrew (later Mrs Baker) won these two cups in the ladies race in the **Brixham Regattas** of 1933 and 1934.

Books

Today's Club library, split between the present 'Library/Meeting Room' and the Model Room, comprises a wide range of books on yachting and related subjects as well as works of reference. Most of the collection has been acquired by the generosity of members who presented the books. A few of the books are worthy of special mention including **Charnock's 'History of Marine Architecture'** donated by Sir George Metcalfe in October 1930; a copy of the beautifully illustrated **'Yachts and Yachtsmen'** given by Mr J.B. Saunders in February 1935; **'The Americas Cup - its origins and history'** which came from Mr C M Cockerel in July 1947 and **'British Sports and Sportsmen'** which came from Mr C. Fortescue-Webb in July 1947. By far the most valuable book in the collection is the **'Liber Nauticus'** which today is located in a display cabinet on the quarterdeck. In 1965, when the Club's finances were somewhat stretched, a proposal was made to sell this historic volume but happily the proposal was rejected.

Models

Thanks to the meticulous and unstinting work of the Curators of Half Models, the historic collection in today's Model Room is well recorded on the label by each half model and does not require any further information within these chronicles. The fully-rigged model of Sir James Pender's **Lamorna** has already been referred to in the previous volume and will be familiar to all members who sit alongside it at the circular member's table in the Coffee Room.

When the General Committee met in September 1934, the Rear Commodore, J S Highfield, informed them that *'Mrs Smithers (sisters of the late Mr H. E. France) had presented a model of Theodore Pim's steam yacht* **Rosabelle***'.* That model is now displayed in the Mountbatten Suite and the yacht's lively history is recorded in Appendix 1.

The close and friendly relationship between the Royal Thames Yacht Club and the New York Yacht Club was further cemented in 1965. At the Annual General Meeting held in April 1965 the Chairman (Vice Commodore Kenneth Poland) announced that among those present was Mr R.C. (Dick) Eames, a member of both the RTYC and the NYYC. He and a number of friends at the NYYC, including Commodore Vanderbilt,

presented to the Club a bone model of the **Royal George** made by French prisoners of war from the Napoleonic Wars. Mr Eames explained that this was not an official presentation by the New York Yacht Club but an expression of gratitude by a number of members of that illustrious club for the warm hospitality shown by the Royal Thames. The model, which stands in its case on the quarterdeck, is considered by many to be one of the finest examples of the skills of French prisoners.

The silver models of **Candida** and **Longbow** are today in their cases in the reception hall and on the landing of the main stairs respectively. The former model of the famous J class yacht built by Camper and Nicolson in 1929 for Herman A Andreae was presented to the Club by his son H.K. Andreae in June 1967 while the latter was presented by Deed of Gift by the owner Mr J.D. (David) Macualay in 1984. In 1968 Longbow had had a quite outstanding season winning a great many trophies, including a number given by the Royal Thames. In 1969 a burglary at David Macaulay's home saw the theft of some of those trophies. To compensate for this unfortunate occurrence, David Macaulay decided to present the silver model to the Club.

The model of MGB501 was given to the Club by a member, Frank Murdoch, in 1992 and is located in the Model Room. Frank Murdoch, who had been in the afterguard of *ENDEAVOUR* in the 1934 Americas's Cup Challenge, was an engineering consultant to Camper Nicholson who built MGB501 in 1942. This boat had a place in history as it was used as a test bed for the first seaborne installed Gas Trubine.

Memorabilia

One of the most interesting artefacts in the Clubhouse is the pair of **stone lions** which are located outside the Britannia lounge. For many years there has been uncertainty as to their origin. Fortunately, tenacious research by the Club librarian, Nick Greville, has shown that the lions were a part of Hyde Park House when it was acquired by the Club from the Naylor-Leyland family in 1923. The Naylor-Leylands had acquired the lions which are copies of the lions sculptured by Tanova in 1790 and which are placed at the tomb of Pope Clement XIII in St Peter's, Rome. It is interesting to note that an earlier copy of the lions was acquired by the 6th Duke of Devonshire for Chatsworth House.

In the previous volume reference was made to the tiller from the cutter *FIONA* that hangs on the wall of the main stairs. In March 1921 Mr Charles J. Morris, member of the Club, presented the second **tiller** displayed on the stairs. The tiller came from Captain Clarkson's Schooner *CYLTIE*.

The **chronometer** which can be seen in the large display case in the cross passage on the ground floor was presented by Mr J.H. Clutton in April 1922, while the Ship's Bell from **HMS Thames** which hangs in the reception area of the Clubhouse was donated by another member, Mr H E Fenner, in June 1925. Forty years later in April 1965 a Mrs Tucker presented the framed lines of HMS Thames in memory of her father, W H Livens, a former member of the Club; at the same time the Club decided to purchase a picture of HMS Thames for 50 guineas so completing the present collection of HMS Thames memorabilia.

The slightly decrepit lines of the famous yacht **America** which hang on the wall of the stairs leading to the Secretariat have often been the subject of envy by members of the New York Yacht Club. These were presented to the Club in April 1936 by Mr Algernon Maudslay. One of the smallest items on display today is the silver **Boatswain's Call** or whistle which was the gift of yet another member, Rear Admiral Charles P.R. Coode in January 1937. Members will be familiar with the telescope, displayed in the first floor cross passage, which had belonged to **Admiral Lord Nelson** and had been presented by Lord Alfred Paget; what is surprising is that a glass case for the telescope was provided only in 1938! Another piece of Nelson memorabilia was given to the Club by a Colonel Ballantyne in December 1963. This was a copy of an unpublished letter written by Lord Nelson from Naples on 10 December 1798 - it hangs close to the telescope on the first floor.

It is fully recorded elsewhere that King George V's highly successful cutter **Britannia** was, after his death, sunk off the Isle of Wight in compliance with His Majesty's instructions. In July 1936 Lord Queenborough, the Commodore, informed the General Committee that *'His Majesty the King (Edward VIII) and Her Majesty Queen Mary have graciously present-ed to the Club one Racing Flag and two RTYC Burgess which were flown on HM Yacht Britannia'* - the racing flag was ordered to be framed and hung in the Club. Another artefact from Britannia was presented to the Club by Lord Powerscourt in June 1947 - this was a **Main Block** and was located in Shore House; today it is at Knightsbridge on the Quarterdeck,

Mr R S Brooke-Hitching, a member, made a gift to the Club of **three Guns** in October 1955, while Mrs Brooke-Hitching presented two **Signal Guns** in December 1963 in memory of her husband. These are located on the quarterdeck.

In November 1962, Mrs Eileen Caulcutt (who was to become Assistant Sailing Secretary) informed the Club that her mother, the widow of Club member G.C. Hans-Hamilton wished to present to the Club a **Parliamentary Clock**. This offer was gratefully accepted and this fine old clock was hung on the wall of the 'Ladies Stairs' - the staircase near to the ladies cloakroom and which used to give them access to their first floor dining room (it is now on the ground floor opposite the main display case). Another item of interest, but on a very much smaller scale, is the **Tie Ring** displayed in one of the reception area showcases. This was the gift of a member, Mr J H Coste, in June 1969. The ring which had an RTYC burgee on it was believed to have been made in 1875.

Today the Club maintains an active liaison with the Type 22 Frigate **HMS Cumberland**. The previous warship to bear that name was a 1930s cruiser that ended its days as a test bed for naval missiles. The Bell from that cruiser was presented to the Club in July 1975 by the father of a current member of the Club, Christopher Thornhill.

As was mentioned in the previous volume, the Club's archives contain many documents of historic interest which in the main relate to Club affairs, though some are of national and interna-tional interest. The regularity with which these documents have been retained is probably directly related to the interest in such matters shown by the succession of Club Secretaries! The retention is certainly very patchy, with the period form 1920 to 1939 being one of the best. Many of the documents kept are telegrams between the Club and members of the Royal Family offering honorary membership of the Club or, in the case of the Prince of Wales, inviting him to become

Commodore of the Club. This form of correspondence is generally made through the various Private Secretaries at Buckingham Palace, an exception being an acknowledgement, by the late Duke of Kent, of a present sent to him by the Club on the occasion of his marriage in 1934 - he himself 'topped and tailed' the letter of acknowledgement in his own hand.

Earlier in this volume in Section III reference was made to **Sir Malcolm Campbell** and his attempts on the world land and water speed records. His handwritten letter dated 20 March 1931 and addressed to the Commodore, Lord Queen-borough, is among the archives. In it he expressed his gratitude for having been a guest of honour at 'last night's banquet'. Members may be familiar with the framed **Loyal Address** sent by the Club to HM King George V on the occasion of his Silver Jubilee in 1935 (it is hanging in the west passage). Somewhat unusually, acknowledgement of this gift did not come from Buckingham Palace but from the Home Office - even more strange is that the Loyal Address was sent to 'The Secretary of State for Foreign Affairs, Home Office, London SW1'.

As well as letters of historic interest, the Club's archives include cuttings from newspapers that have an important place in yachting history. At the Club's AGM in March 1933 the then Vice Commodore, Lord Queenborough, recalled distinguished members who had died in the previous twelve months starting with Madame Virginie Heriot, a member of the Royal Thames since 1922. He described her as *'the most distinguished yachtswoman of her day who invariably com-peted in practically all our regattas over here and, I think, won far more prizes and medals that any yachtswoman had done in her lifetime'*. A press cutting reveals that shortly after her death, which was announced in The Times on 29 August 1932, Lord Queenborough wrote a tribute to her. A copy of his tribute to this remarkable lady is at Appendix 17. His reference to 'small boat racing' needs to be put into the context of the early 1930s since the boats concerned were of the international six metre and eight metre classes.

In the issue of The Daily Telegraph dated 23 June 1932, an article entitled 'What Royal Support has done for Yachting' was included. It had been written by Major B Heckstall-Smith (an honorary member of the Royal Thames while he was Secretary of the Yacht Racing Association) who later was to compile the 'Catalogue of Prints, Portraits and Oil Paintings in the Clubhouse of the Royal Thames Yacht Club' in 1938 (copies of which are still available to members). An extract from his article is at Appendix 18. The main thrust of the arti-cle is evident from its heading, but it makes special reference to HMY Britannia which it is concluded, revived 'big class' sailing when it was built in 1893 and again after World War I. The article was published just six days before the Royal Thames formally elected HRH The Prince of Wales as Commodore. The concluding paragraphs of the article include a brief history of the Royal Thames.

Perhaps even more interesting is a letter from 'Yachtsman, Westcliffe-on-Sea' published in 25 June 1932 issue of The Daily Telegraph and referring to Heckstall-Smith's article. The letter said: *Allow me as a yachtsman to compliment you on your very interesting article on the RTYC. It had always been a matter of surprise to yachtsmen that this Club, which stands head and shoulders above all other British Clubs, has not been granted the privilege of wearing the White Ensign. As long ago as 1853 it had both the largest mem-bership and also the largest number of yachts on its register.*

I believe it has held that record ever since. In the interest of the yachting industry it seems to me that the exclusive right to wear the Naval Ensign should be given to the Club that renders the greatest service to the sport of yachting, and not from the social point of view'. Many of today's members might well agree with the sentiment expressed in the letter but it must also be true that many more members of other establishments would strongly challenge the justification for such an aspiration.

There are far too many 'items of interest' in the archives to include them all in this compilation. Just two further have been selected. The first is a page from the 1879 issue of 'Dickens Guide to the Thames' which lists the Royal Thames Yacht Club in Albermarle Street and says that the object of this Club *'is the encouragement of yacht building and sailing on the River Thames and the funds are appropriated, after payment of necessary current expenses, to the purchase of prizes to be sailed for'.* No doubt today's Flag Officers and Committee would find their duties much less stressful if their objectives were that simple - and members would be encouraged by the then annual subscription of seven guineas! The second item is a letter to the Club written in French by a Monsieur Fernando Rey from Dijon and dated 2 October 1938. In the letter he recalls how well he was received by the Royal Thames Yacht Club when he was at Ryde in his 8 metre yacht *FRANCE* to compete in the Coupe de France races. He then goes on to praise the efforts of Mr Neville Chamberlain in securing peace in Europe. The Club sent a copy of the letter to the Prime Minister which had been written as an expression of gratitude from a French family. None expected that peace to be torn asunder in less than twelve months.

VII

Anecdotes

Each of the two previous volumes of these chronicles has ended with a section of anecdotes that reflected the attitudes of the day or exceptional occurrences in sailing or in the Clubhouse. Anecdotes are perhaps most interesting when viewed with an historic perspective. Consequently, this volume with its contemporary content is less suitable for recording such events. In spite of that a few are described here.

8 July 1920
The Chairman of Committees, Mr H H Underhill, was addressing the General Committee and when the last item on the agenda was reached he pointed out 'that the stock of Vintage Port in the Club was perilously low'. The committee's response was to resolve that the Chairman should be given power to purchase from time to time any parcels of Vintage Port for the Club, should opportunity occur. They also empowered him to pay cash for them and if necessary to obtain an overdraft from the Bank to enable him to acquire any parcels.

Comment: Life was certainly difficult twenty months after the 1914-18 War, but what this really illustrates is the 'hand to mouth' operation of the Club in those not too distant days.

19 September 1935
The Secretary, Mr R A Warry, informed the House and Finance Committee of two deaths of staff members. Firstly he reported the death of William Knowles, late steward of the Club, and added that a letter of condolence had been sent to his widow and that the Club's Bankers had been instructed to cease payment of his pension. Secondly, he reported the death of a chambermaid, Mary Peart - she had fallen from a window on the fourth floor. The Secretary was required to arrange for the inspection of windows and to consider the advisability of fitting bars to them.

Comment: Is this just terse reporting or were people really like this 63 years ago?

16 June 1938
Sir Francis Dent, the Chairman, reported to the House and Finance Committee that the Squash Marker had been charged with stealing money from members'wallets in the squash court and that he had been sent to a remand home for a fortnight. He also instructed the Secretary to post a notice in the squash court requesting members not to leave money and valuables in their garments.

Comment: No further reports of theft in the squash court are recorded.

13 July 1939
Reference has been made already in this volume to this particular anecdote but its uniqueness warrants inclusion here. On this day the House and Finance Committee learned that Sir Eastman Bell requested permission to have a bath and lavatory fitted in Bedroom No.16 at his own expense; both to become the property of the Club when his tenancy of the room ceased. This request was agreed to subject to the architect, Mr Sydney Tatchell approving the plan of installation as satisfactory.

Comment: Who needs a refurbishment programme when benefactors such as Sir Eastman Bell are around?

11 July 1940
The General Committee found themselves discussing the continued employment of an Italian as Chef when taking into consideration the political situation. It was pointed out that the Chef had been in this country for 26 years (i.e. since before the 1914-18 war) and had come to the RTYC from Buck's Club ten years earlier. He had worked well, been very loyal to the Club and helped it considerably in the difficult wartime conditions. Since the Home Secretary had given permission for him to stay in the UK under the most favourable terms, it was finally decided that the Chef should continue in his appointment.

Comment: The ambivalent loyalties of the Italian government in two World Wars were clearly having no influence on the Chef.

17 May 1945
When the General Committee met a few days after VE Day they considered a recommendation by the Wine and Cigar Committee that in order to conserve dwindling stocks, only small gins and small whiskies be served - unless a member particularly ordered a double. This was agreed and it was also decided that purchases could not be made on the Black Market, but any member of the Committee who could influence supplies, either at wholesale or retail rates, should get in touch with the Secretary who was instructed to buy all he could obtain in order to build up club stocks.

Comment: The inference from the recommendation is that prior to this decision members would be served with doubles unless they particularly ordered a small one. As regards the ways and means to be taken to restore the Club's cellar stocks the ethical stand of the General Committee would seem to have been sorely tested.

25 November 1947

The range of problems to be dealt with by the Club's Committees seem to be unlimited in variety. On this day the Chairman, Mr H.J. Davis, informed the House and Finance Committee that the sauce cook, Mr Hudspith, had been arrested for obstructing the police in their duties, while acting as a picket for strikers from the Savoy Hotel. The Committee were of the opinion that it was not in the interests of the Club that he should continue to be employed by the Club, yet on the other hand a legitimate reason must be found for dispensing with his services, in order that there would be no question of victimisation.

Comment: Regrettably, the records do not reveal what form the 'legitimate reason' took.

28 January 1952

On this occasion the Chairman of the House and Finance Committee, Major Charles Ball, informed them that on 29 December a man had broken into the beer store in the early morning but had been captured by the night porter, Mr Heminway (on the last night of his service with the Club). The burglar had now received a sentence of eighteen months imprisonment. As an expression of their gratitude for Mr Heminway's good work, the Committee authorised the payment of one week's wages (or not less than five pounds) to him.

Comment: Well done Mr Heminway; perhaps the Club should have tried to retain his services and so ensure the security of other valuable stores.

1 July 1959

Whilst not wishing to make these anecdotes into *'a felons guide to an easy living'* it is remarkable to realise that the Club has been subject to the deeds of so many different unscrupulous people. This time a person purporting to be a member of the Club, telephoned the hall porter late one night and asked him to pay £10 to a friend, Mr Edmonds, who would shortly call at the Club. The person promised to send the hall porter a cheque the following day. The hall porter assumed that the caller would be Mr J.H.Edmonds, a member of the Club, but the person who arrived was a complete stranger. Eventually the £10 was handed over and, needless to say, no cheque was received. Equally predictable, the purported member who telephoned was contacted and denied all knowledge of the affair. The confidence trickster was £10 better off, while the Club wrote off £10 and informed the Association of London Clubs (and the police) so that other Clubs could be made aware of the presence of this trickster.

Comment: Sadly, such tricksters can succeed.

23 October 1965

The requirement that ladies that win Royal Thames' cups should nominate a male person to receive the cup at the Laying Up Dinner was mentioned earlier in this volume. In 1965 the winner of the Holt Cup, awarded to the Flying Fifteen Class on the Royal Thames' Day in Cowes Week, was a lady who happened to be the daughter of a Royal Thames' member. She felt aggrieved that she could not collect her cup in person during the presentation ceremony that, at that time, took place as part of the Laying Up Dinner evening. She decided to contact a national newspaper in order to air her grievance. The article in the newspaper came to the attention of the Chairman of Committees, Mr Ian Butler, shortly before the date of the dinner. His dilemma was compounded by the Commodore, Earl Mountbatten, who had also become aware of the existence of the newspaper article and informed the Chairman that *'the girl must attend!'*. Mr Butler knew that all seats available for the dinner had been allocated and that all speeches had been prepared for an all male attendance. The dinner was now only 24 hours away but fortunately Mr Butler knew the lady's father and was able to contact him and offer him a solution to the problem whereby she would arrive at the Clubhouse at the time when the prize giving would commence; she would then be asked to take a seat in the Coffee Room behind the Chairman; in due course she would receive her cup - and depart. This solution was offered on condition that the lady would make no further contact with the media nor would she gloat over her achieving a breach of the Club's custom - and this was agreed. Sadly she chose not to honour the undertaking and the following morning she was to be heard on a BBC radio programme 'claiming a victory'.

Comment: A story of mixed and confusing moral standards.

19 November 1981

The tree planting ceremony in Hyde Park as a memorial to Earl Mountbatten has already been described in an earlier section of the volume. Everything proceeded smoothly as planned until the ceremony was complete and the Prince and Princess of Wales were scheduled to return to the Clubhouse by car via the Edinburgh Gate. However, the large crowd and the sunny day intervened and persuaded their Royal Highnesses to talk to people in the crowd and to return to the Clubhouse separately and on foot accompanied respectively by the Vice Commodore and his wife, Mrs Nikki Foot. The Prince was first to arrive in the reception area of the Clubhouse where he was introduced to Club Officers and long serving members of staff including Mr Norris Coultous. While these introductions were being made the Princess arrived at the Clubhouse and, as planned, was immediately taken by Mrs Foot to the cabin on the second floor that had been specially prepared and cleared by a Palace security officer. To her dismay, Mrs Foot found that the cabin was securely locked! Where was the key? It was securely located in Mr Coultous's pocket! Happily, Mrs Foot found another cabin that was unlocked, unoccupied, clean and tidy, so all was well. The security officer was not amused.

Comment: The best-laid plans do go awry.

Appendix 1

Theodore Pim and "Rosabelle"

Recent correspondence with the Maryvale Pastoral Centre at Bramley in Surrey reminded the Club that for the 22 years (until his death in 1929), it was the home of Theodore Pim, Commodore RTYC 1905-23.

It was noted in Volume 2 that Theodore Pim owned several yachts names ROSABELLE; a model of the second of these is still displayed in the Clubhouse. This was a yacht of 614 Tons TM and bought by him in 1901. In January 1915 she was hired for war service as an Auxiliary Patrol Vessel and armed with a 3 inch gun and two 6 pounders. She served until March 1919 and spent until August 1916 patrolling the Falmouth area and the rest of the war in Orkneys. Throughout her service she engaged many U-boats but was unable to destroy one. Her end came during World War II when she was sunk in the Straits of Gibraltar by U374.

Theodore Pim cruised extensively in *ROSABELLE* but in 1929 he fell heavily in the billiard room of his home, Snowdenham Hall, and died shortly afterwards. His funeral cortege was headed by the Captain and 26 members of the crew of *ROSABELLE*, each carrying a wreath.

Appendix 2

Sir Ion Hamilton-Benn. Cup Bearer 1942-61

Many members of the Royal Thames served with distinction in World War I including this distinguished member who took the opportunity at the AGM held on 26 April 1956 (in his 94th year) to recount to the members present some of his experiences during the years 1914-18. An extract from his remarks, made after his re-election as Cup Bearer, is set out below.

When the first war broke out in 1914 I was in the House of Commons and I saw a good deal of the fun going on. Among other things I heard that Winston Churchill, who was then First Lord of the Admiralty, was raising a Corps to go to the relief of Antwerp. It seemed to me that was something in which I might take a hand, so I went to see him at the Admiralty. He looked at me and said 'You know, I don't think it's quite the thing for you' and I replied 'Well I was 8 years in the Artists Rifles and I am now Honorary Colonel of the 10th London, so I know something about the job'. He said 'What age are you?' and I said 'I am 51'. He said 'This is a young man's job. I could only give you a command which would put you under men much younger than yourself and I do not think it is quite appropriate. But what is wrong with your steam yacht?' I said 'Nothing, except that she is under charter at the present moment bringing wounded from St Nazaire'. He said 'Get her back; lend her to the Admiralty and I will give you a commission to command her. F.E. Smith has told me of his sea-going expeditions already and he has also told me that you won the Kaiser's Cup many years ago (This refers to one of the Heligoland Cups listed in Volume 2). I think it is quite an appropriate thing to send her into Portsmouth and I will give you a commission to command her'. So I did and he gave me a commission as Lieutenant Commander RNR. She was fitted out with a couple of guns and extra crew. Concurrently another member of Parliament was fitting out his yacht. When the Captain at Portsmouth asked the Admiralty where the two yachts should be sent the reply came back 'send the MP's as far away as possible!' We were sent to the south coast of Ireland.

By the end of the year I said I was out of my métier and I was sent back to Portsmouth to take over fast motor launches which were coming over from Canada and the United States. I took them to be based at Dover and for three years I enjoyed the most interesting time of my life, living in a motor launch, and among other operations we took an active part in the blocking of Zeebrugge and Ostend.

Well, the result of that affair was that three of my young fellows who were in command of ML's got VC's. I was promoted Captain and got a CB.

Note: This casually-recounted description of Ion Hamilton Benn's involvement in the first World War does not mention that one of the young fellows awarded a VC was Lieutenant Percy Dean, also a member of the Royal Thames. An account of how he earned the award is given in Appendix 5.

Appendix 3

Appendix 4

Chairmen and Deputy Chairmen of Committees

Year	Chairman	Deputy Chairman	Year	Chairman	Deputy Chairman
1868	C. Smart		1936	A.E. Messer	Lt. Col. R.T. Harper
1869-70	S.N. Driver		1937	C.J. Ritchie	C.H. Burne
1871-75	W.F. Moore		1938	Sir Francis Dent	C.H. Burne
1876-83	W.F. Stutfield		1939	H.F. Paul	C.C. Chance
1884-85	E.R. Hancock		1940	Colonel H.N. Clark	D.C. Arnell
1886	G. Wadham		1941-42	Colonel H.N. Clark	C.C. Chance
1887	W.H. Palmer		1943	Colonel H.N. Clark	H.L. Thornhill
1888-90	E.R. Handcock		1944	B.T. Rumble	Sir Francis Dent
1891	T. Breen		1945	G. Glynn Terrell	Sir Francis Dent
1892-94	E.R. Handcock		1946	G. Glynn Terrell	H.J. Davis
1895	A. Manning		1947	H.J. Davis	H.J.E. Smith
1896-98	E.R. Handcock		1948	Sir Wallace A. Akers	H.J.E. Smith
1899	T. Breen		1949	Sir Wallace A. Akers	Major C.J.P. Ball
1900-01	J. McN. Miller		1950-51	Major C.J.P. Ball	Major E.S. Harston
1902	J.W. Domoney		1952	Major E.S. Harston	K.G. Poland
1903	J. McN. Miller		1953	K.G. Poland	G.G. Dudley Head
1904	J.W. Domoney		1954	G.G. Dudley Head	E.G. Marshall
1905	J. McN. Miller		1955	E.G. Marshall	Cdr. C. Campbell
1906	J.W. Domoney		1956	F.A. Haworth	J. Stuart Bennett
1907-08	J. McN. Miller		1957	F.A. Haworth	D.L. Pollock
1909	H. Samuelson		1958-59	J.E. Mellor	R.J. Clutton
1910	E. Hilder		1960-61	A.W. Munns	J. Stuart Bennett
1911-14	W.H. Matthews		1962-63	J. Stuart Bennett	F.A. Haworth
1915	J. Temperley		1964	F.A. Haworth	I.G. Butler
1916	C.A. Hill		1965	I.G. Butler	F.G.C. Jackson
1917-18	H.H. Underhill		1966	F.G.C. Jackson	N. Houghton
1919	N. Craig		1967	D.A. Campbell	D.M. Leggett
1920-21	H.H. Underhill		1968-69 *	E. Ellsworth Jones	D.M. Leggett
1922-23	J.S. Highfield		1969-1970	A. Wallace Barr	
1924	A.E. Messer		1970-71	R. Garnham	J.C. Foot
1925	J.S. Highfield		1971-73	J.B.S. Savage	A.P.de B. Tapping
1926	Vice Admiral E.K. Loring	C.J. Ritchie	1973-74	D.O. May	F.A. Haworth
1927	C.J. Ritchie	H.H. Underhill	1974-77	J.L. Maddocks	R.A. Aisher
1928	C.R. Graham	T.S. Manning	1977-79	R.A. Aisher	J.C. Foot
1929	A.E. Messer	H.H. Underhill	1979-80	R.A. Aisher	S.L. James
1930	C.H. Burne	C.J. Ritchie	1980-81	J.C. Foot	P.C. Nicholson
1931	C.J. Ritchie	P.T. Dean			
1932-33	P.T. Dean	C.H. Burne			
1934	C.H. Burne	C.R. Fairey			
1935	C.J. Ritchie	Lt. Col. R.T. Harper			

From this date onwards the Vice Commodore was elected Chairman and the senior Rear Commodore was elected Deputy Chairman.

* AGM changed from April to October

Appendix 5

Lieutenant P T Dean, RNVR

Percy Thompson Dean was born in Blackburn in 1877 and became their Member of Parliament from 1919-22. He died in March 1939. A keen yachtsman, he joined the RTYC in 1919. This is a brief account of his involvement in the Zeebrugge Operation.

The object of the operation was to block the entrance to the canal which ran from Zeebrugge Harbour to the U Boat base at Bruges. Lieutenant Dean was the Commanding Officer of the Motor Launch 282 and his task was to follow the block-ships through the deep channel inside the long mole at Zeebrugge. Once the blockships were scuttled he had to embark their crews. He was under constant and deadly fire at point blank range from heavy and machine guns located on the banks of the canal and from the mole. Dean handled his ML *'as calmly as if engaged in a practice manoeuvre'* and took off more than 100 officers and ratings. As he started to leave the harbour three men at his side were killed but he used the six revolvers available on the bridge to keep the German gunners occupied. At the same time the ML's steering gear broke down and he had to manoeuvre his ML on the engines. Once clear of the canal entrance he learned that an officer was in the water. He immediately stopped and turned back to rescue him. Although ML282 was hit many times she managed to get away and transfer those on board to the destroyer HMS Warwick.

For his exploits at Zeebrugge Lieutenant Dean was awarded the VC (one of eight awarded for the operation) and promoted to Lieutenant Commander RNVR.

Appendix 6

Secretaries of the Club

Year	Name	Year	Name
1823	Mr. J. Tomkins	1934	R.A. Warry
*1830	Mr. W. Norris	1944	Major W.H. Thatcher-Gale
*1832	Mr. Murray	1945	Captain T.B. Brunton R.N.
1838	Mr. J. Covington	1946	R.M.G. Brown
1839	Captain F.H. Durand	1948	Air Vice Marshall Sir Douglas Harries
1853	Paymaster J.C. Aldridge R.N.	1958	Colonel N. Blair
1854	Captain P.C.S. Grant	1966	Group Captain A.J. Trimble
1872	H.W. Mellis	1968	J. Finch
1882	E. Grimston	1969	Air Vice Marshall W.F. Beckwith
1885	Captain Thornton Scovell	1970	Lt. Col. D.W. Browne
1900	Lt. Col. G.C.B. Dick	1974	Captain K. Stobbs
1904	Lieutenant F.W. Chaine R.N.	1977	E.J. Hamilton-Parks (Chief Executive)
1909	Captain J.E.H. Orr	1981	Captain A.R. Ward R.N.
1926	Major C.M.B. Hamilton	1993	Captain D. Goldson R.N.
1929	Major H.R. Crailsham		

* Date of taking up office is uncertain.

Appendix 7

Appendix 8

THE CUMBERLAND CUP
of the
ROYAL THAMES YACHT CLUB

Regulations

Article I

This cup, hereafter to be known in perpetuity as 'The Cumberland Cup of the Royal Thames Yacht Club', was given by the Vice Commodore Lord Queenborough to the Club as an International Prize which may be challenged for by recognised Yacht Clubs of
1. Britain Overseas
2. United States of America
3. All nations in the IYRU
or by the Royal Thames Yacht Club
to be sailed at present by yachts of the International Eight Metre Class. The challenge of one Yacht Club only will be accepted from each country and of one yacht only from that club.

Article II

The Cup shall remain the property of the Royal Thames Yacht Club until it shall have been won by another Club three years in succession, when it shall become the property of that Club, which will guarantee to provide a Cup of similar value for the continuance of this Contest, failing which it shall be given back to the Royal Thames Yacht Club.

Article III

The yachts may be designed and built in any of the above countries.

Article IV

The crew shall be amateur yachtsmen of the nationality of the challenging Club and shall belong to a recognised Yacht Club of that nationality, with the exception of one paid hand.

Article V

The races for the Cup shall be sailed under IYRU rules, except as modified in these regulations, and shall be under the management of a Special Committee consisting of one member of each Club competing. The member of the defending Club shall preside. No appeal shall be made from the decisions of this committee; three to form a quorum; the President to have a casting vote. Should there be only one challenging Club, the challenging and defending Clubs shall each name two members to serve on this Committee.

Article VI

The races shall be held at the place and date chosen by the defending Club in their national coastal waters.
This condition shall not apply to Canada or Switzerland.

Article VII

The date of the first race (not earlier than July 1st) shall be fixed by the defending Club and shall be notified to the challenging Club on or before the 15th of April. The challenging Clubs must furnish 14 days before the first race :-
1. Name of yacht
2. Certificate of rating
3. Name of owner
4. Copy of racing flag
5. An undertaking signed by a Flag Officer of the Club and the Owner of the Yacht to abide by the decisions of the Special Committee without appeal.

Article VIII

On receipt of this information the defending Club will furnish all challenging Clubs with the same information regarding the defending yacht.

Article IX

The course shall be 20 to 24 nautical miles. The mean speed of the winner shall be not less than four nautical miles per hour. The yacht which first wins three races shall be declared the winner. After at least three races or as many races as there are competitors a yacht not having won a race shall not compete further.

Article X

The special committee shall judge of the necessity of postponing races owing to weather, and may at its discretion permit a substitute to sail in case of illness or unavoidable absence of a member of a crew during the races.

Article XI

Challenges shall be delivered to the defending Club not later than the 1st of March in the year for which the challenge is intended.

Article XII

The competing yachts must be placed at the disposal of the Special Committee 96 hours before the date of the commencement of the races in case the Special Committee shall desire to verify the rating.

Article XIII

The Royal Thames Yacht Club reserves the right before the 1st of September in any year to vary the International class in which the Cup shall be competed for the following year, or to modify the above rules.

August 1924

Appendix 9

The first race for the Morgan Cup 20th July 1929

An account of the race by John Nicholson, a crew member on board the winning yacht Flame

At the Needles the larger craft were ahead in a southerly wind, very light conditions. At teatime, about six miles south of the Island, all amateurs were below when the skipper, Jack Grist, called 'Quick gentlemen, all hands on deck'. We tumbled up the companion and about a mile ahead we saw a long black and white horizontal line east and west. SUSANNE (154 Tons) was about a mile ahead of us on our weather bow. The owner quickly said 'Let go all sheets'. Within minutes the heavy electrical storm hit us and the flapping of canvas and the sheets of spray (no sea in such a sudden squall) continued for some ten minutes and then passed to the north.

We went below to finish our tea. As we were doing so the schooner SUZANNE was abeam of us and we sailed past her deck chairs, lifebuoys etc. for she had been wiped over

to her skylights in this dangerous phenomenon. NEITH, our particular rival, was astern at the time and could not be seen after the incident. The Sunday papers cashed in on this unusual squall. The coast from Eastbourne to Portland Bill saw minor domestic calamities with children and nursemaids.

As evening approached the wind was cutting and we had a council of war. The owner rightly advised that we should hang up to windward, miles to the east of Cherbourg as at dawn a strong ebb tide would soak us down to the west.

At daybreak we just fetched the east end of the breakwater; by breakfast time we trickled round the west end to see the whole fleet kedged and waiting for an air to take them to the east. We saw many rich owners attired in lush bedwear enjoying the early calm. We all conversed, and then in FLAME we shaped a course for Dunnose, getting our gun off Ryde shortly before dinner that day.

Appendix 10

Extracts from the report of Sub Committee on Yachting Headquarters. December 1932

The Sub Committee neatly summarised their objections to a waterside premises: It is obvious that at all suitable places around the coast, particularly those accessible to London, a local club is already in possession and thereby absorbs the local membership, and any establishment set up by the Royal Thames Yacht Club would be in direct competition with existing clubs......It could only be fully occupied during the times of the local regattas...... and for the greater part of the year it would be of no great advantage to the Royal Thames members than would be membership of the other clubs.

As regards a floating headquarters the Sub Committee reported: The obvious and attractive alternative to having a fixed establishment is the possibility of the Club owning a vessel suitable to act as a floating headquarters. It is essential that such a vessel should provide accommodation for at least a limited number of members and preferably, deck accommodation on which to carry small one-designed or other sailing boats. It should be suitable for use as headquarters for the club with office and social accommodation.

This method would have the advantage that the Club headquarters through the season would move from one regatta to another; in fact, the Club would have an establishment wherever yachting was established for the time being. It would be available for members and a useful meeting place for all yachtsmen, and would solve for a number of them the difficulty of obtaining accommodation when towns were temporarily crowded at regatta times.

It is further possible that such a scheme would produce an annual supply of cadet members, a proportion of whom would graduate to full membership which would not only assist the scheme to become self-supporting but by attracting and assisting the younger generation in their apprenticeship to yachting would be a fulfilment of one of the avowed objects of the Club.

During the winter months it is suggested that such floating headquarters could be moored at a suitable place accessible to London. It would be open to cadet members and others during weekends, or at other times when sailing matches for the smaller classes could be arranged, and would provide a centre of social attractions for all members who choose to avail themselves of its facilities.

Appendix 11

In accordance with the decision of the General Committee at their meeting on 5 November 1964, a Sub Committee was formed under the Chairmanship of Sir Gordon Smith, with Mr Ian G. Butler, Mr PV MacKinnon and Mr Jonathan Janson as members.

The Sub Committee was instructed to examine the conditions which the Royal Thames Yacht Club should lay down before agreeing that a Challenge for the America's Cup should be made in the name of the Club.

Before preparing this Report the Sub Committee studied a number of articles concerning the last British Challenge and sought the views of a number of persons who were intimately connected with this Challenge.

The following are the recommendations of the Sub Committee:

1. Any applicant or applicants who wish to challenge through the Royal Thames Yacht Club should satisfy a Sub Committee consisting of the Flag Officers and four members of the Club, to be nominated by the Sailing Committee, that he or they are in a position to fulfil all the subsequent conditions.

2. No short-term challenge should be considered by the Club. The Sub Committee hold that two years preparation by owners are needed before a challenge is submitted to the defending Club and think that it would be preferable if these preparations were made in consultation with the RTYC.

3. The Challenger should be in a position to back the project for the five year period prior to the Challenge Cup races in the sum of at least £500,000. It is further recommended that the Challenger should be prepared to pay the RTYC the sum of £5000 as a contribution to the Club expenses. This should cover inter alia the organisation of trial races in the USA before the actual Challenge races.

4. The Challenger should make every effort to buy or charter a recently successful America's Cup boat or boats.

5. The Challenger should be prepared to embark on a properly-conducted Hull development programme.

6. Similarly, the Challenger should be prepared to arrange a properly-conducted programme of Sail and Rig development.

7. In consultation with the RTYC the Challenger should be prepared to take part in an intensive regatta programme with particular emphasis on races with American boats.

8. The Challenger should be required to arrange a training programme for helmsmen and crew, bearing in mind that the races will take place in an unnaturally confused sea owing to the pressure of a large number of spectator boats.

9. The Club should reserve the right to withdraw the Challenge if insufficient regard is being paid to the Conditions laid down by the Club, bearing in mind that, once the defenders have embarked on a building programme, one is probably committed to going ahead with the Challenge.

The Sub Committee further recommended that, in the event of the Club deciding to Challenge on behalf of an individual or a syndicate, a committee consisting of a Flag Officer and two members of the Club shall be responsible for directing the conduct of all aspects of the Challenge thereafter.

The Sub Committee wish to emphasise in the strongest terms that the adherence to these Conditions which are regarded as minimal must be accepted by the Club as a requirement if the Club is not again to be placed in an invidious position.

Appendix 12

Winners of the Docker Cup

1952	Myles Wyatt	1977	E I Hamilton-Parks
1955	K H Preston & J Raymond	1978	D O May
1956	F A Haworth	1981	Sir Owen Aisher
1957	S H Morris	1983	Peter de Savary
1958	Lt Col R S G Perry	1984	Michael Richey
1960	S H Morris	1985	Lord Harvington
1961	Sir Gordon Smith	1986	Graham Walker
1963	Derek Boyer	1987	Major Ralph James
1964	Brig P D G Wakeham	1988	John Prentice
1965	Simon Tait	1989	Frank Murdoch
1967	Robin Aisher	1990	Peter Snowden
1970	T O M Sopwith & I S MacDonald-Smith	1991	David Diehl
1971	John Foot	1993	Pat Dyas
1972	Arthur Slater	1994	George Shillitoe
1973	Robin Aisher	1995	David Arnold
1974	E I Hamilton-Parks	1996	Mary Falk
1975	Robin Aisher	1998	Bob Miller

Appendix 13

Introduction

1. The Sub Committee consider that the dual objectives of maintaining a high class West End Club and continuing to increase the stature of the Royal Thames as a Yacht Club are perfectly compatible. However, the first objective must be made viable to provide a base for the second.

2. The way to combat rising costs is to increase revenues from services which will automatically increase in proportion to inflation.

3. The object of this report, therefore, is to outline a series of major proposals which would keep the Club finances on a break-even basis, at least until 1976, and also create a reserve to replace capital which will have to be used before the effect of the (proposed) increased subscriptions and new savings or sources of revenue can be felt.

4. The Club is using too much floor area per member.

5. The efforts of the Committee must follow three courses. The first is to increase the revenue from revenue-producing areas, the second to reduce the extent of non-revenue areas and the third is to tighten administration and control.

6. Of the usable space 55% is revenue-earning ie. Coffee Room, Bars etc. 13% is low-revenue earning i.e. Smoking Room, Billiards Room and 32% is non-revenue earning. The latter breaks down into 20% for normal and essential use by members and 12% is used by living-in staff.

7. Proposals for use of the low-revenue and non-revenue areas and on which the Committee are invited to make recommendations/decisions are set out in three categories:

Section A - proposals requiring changes to Club rules:

1. Introduction of Nominating Members to increase membership and make optimum use of non-revenue areas

2. Introduction of Credit Trading i.e members deposit (say not more than 25% of subscription) as prepayment for meals etc.

Section B - proposals to increase revenue for revenue-earning areas

1. Installation of double beds in present single bedrooms where possible.

2. Installation of a new bar to the west of the Smoking Room door.

3. The Billiard Table receipts do not warrant its retention. The Model room could be converted into a comfortable men-only reading room and Model room.

4. Allow Wedding Receptions to be held on Saturday afternoons.

Section C - proposals which might bring short term financial benefits:

1. Introduce a simple Sunday lunch during the winter e.g. a curry or smorgasbord.

2. Operate a (legal)winter sweepstake.

3. Increase use of Club for more Club functions and private functions.

Appendix 14

<table>
<tr><td>

**Sailing
Matches/Regattas/Championships(1920-98)
and Rallies/Cruises (1952-98)**

</td></tr>
</table>

Year	Date	Event

1920

28th May
    River Matches starting from Southend Pier
29th May
    Southend to Harwich Race
12th June
    Nore to Dover Channel Race
29th-30th August
    Ryde Regatta. RTYC Days for Handicap classes
17th-20th August
    One Ton Cup

1921 *20th June*
    Nore to Dover Channel Race
29th-30th July
    Ryde Regatta. RTYC Days for Handicap classes
15th July
28th July
29th July
    RTYC racing for SCRA classes
    British American Cup in the Solent
    in 6 metre class
12th August
    One Ton Cup

1922 *8th July*
14th July
    RTYC racing for SCRA classes
15th July
    One Ton Cup at Ryde
9th-10th August
    Ryde Week. RTYC Days for Handicap classes

1923 *9th July*
13th July
    RTYC racing for SCRA classes
26th July
    Nore to Dover Channel Race
1st-9th August
    British American Cup in the Solent
15th-16th August
    Ryde Week. RTYC Days for Handicap classes

1924 *14th June*
    Southend to Harwich Race
21st June
    Nore to Dover Channel Race
14th-16th July
    Ryde Week. RTYC Days for Handicap classes,
    6 & 12 metre classes
12th-13th August
    RTYC racing for SCRA classes
15th August
    One Ton Cup at Ryde
6th September
    British American Cup at Oyster Bay, USA

1925 *6th June*
    Nore to Dover Channel Race
21st-22nd July
    RTYC racing for 6 metre and SCRA classes
24th July
    Cumberland Cup at Ryde in 8 metre class
12th-13th August
    Ryde week. RTYC Days for Handicap
    and 6, 8 & 12 metre classes

1926 *12th June*
    RTYC racing at Ryde for all classes
7th-8th July
    RTYC racing at Ryde for 6 & 8 metre
    and SCRA classes
7th 9th July
    RTYC racing at Ryde for 6, 8 & 12 metre
    and Handicap classes

1927 *4th-6th June*
    RTYC racing in Southend Yachting Week
18th-19th July
    RTYC racing at Ryde for 6 & 8 metre
    and SCRA classes
20th-23rd July
    Coupe de France races at Le Harve
4th-10th August
    One Ton Cup at Ryde
    Cumberland Cup at Ryde
8th-9th August
    RTYC racing at Ryde for Handicap
    & SCRA classes

Year	Date	Event
1928	*29th May-1st June*	Cumberland Cup at Ryde
	14th-16th June	RTYC racing in Southend Yachting Week
	28th May,	
	14th, 16th & 17th July	RTYC racing at Ryde for 6 & 8 metre and SCRA classes
	13th & 14th August	RTYC racing in Ryde Week for Handicap, 12 & 6 metre & SCRA classes
1929	*30th May*	RTYC racing in Southend Yachting Week
	15th & 17th June	RTYC racing at Ryde for 12 & 8 metre and SCRA classes
	20th July	Morgan Cup - Ryde to Cherbourg and back
	22nd & 23rd July	RTYC racing at Ryde for 8 & 6 metre and SCRA classes
	24th-27th July	Cumberland Cup at Ryde
	1st-5th August	Coupe de France at Ryde
	12th & 13th August	RTYC racing in Ryde Week for Handicap & SCRA classes
1930	*22nd May*	RTYC racing in Southend Yachting Week
	28th May	RTYC racing at Ryde for Handicap, 12, 8 & 6 metre and SCRA classes
	19th July	Morgan Cup Race
	19th-22nd July	Cumberland Cup at Ryde
	28th-29th July	RTYC Regatta at Ryde
1931	*28th May*	RTYC racing in Southend Yachting Week
	15th June	RTYC racing at Ryde for Big Class, 12 & 8 metre and SCRA classes
	17th-20th July	Cumberland Cup at Ryde
	18th July	Morgan Cup Race
	21st July	Coupe de France at Ryde
	25th-28th July	RTYC Regatta at Ryde for Handicap, 12, 8 & 6 metre & SCRA classes
1932	*25th-29th June*	Cumberland Cup at Ryde
	1st-4th July	Coupe de France at Ryde
	11th July	RTYC racing at Southend Yachting Week

Year	Date	Event
1932	*15th-20th July*	British-American Cup at Ryde
	25th & 26th July	RTYC racing at Ryde Week for Big Class, 12, 8 & 6 metre & SCRA
	26th July	Cory Cup at Ryde in West Solent Restricted class
1933	*1st June*	RTYC racing at Southend Yachting Week
	3rd July	RTYC racing for International and SCRA classes
	3rd-7th July	Cumberland Cup at Ryde
	8th & 9th July	Coupe de France at Ryde
	27th & 28th July	RTYC regatta at Ryde for 'J', 12, 8 & 6 metre & SCRA classes
	15th August	RTYC racing in Brixham Regatta
1934	*8th June*	RTYC racing at Southend Yachting Week
	12th June	Match for ENDEAVOUR and VELSHEDA
	1st-3rd August	RTYC Regatta at Ryde for 'J', 12, 8 metre & SCRA classes
	24th August	RTYC racing in Brixham Regatta
1935	*6th June*	RTYC racing at Southend Yachting Week
	22nd June	RTYC Jubilee Regatta in West Solent
	27th July	Morgan Cup race
	31st July-2nd August	RTYC Regatta at Ryde including Schooner Race round the Isle of Wight on 2nd August
	22nd August	RTYC racing in Brixham Regatta
1936	*11th June*	RTYC racing at Southend Yachting Week
	13th June	Nore to Dover Channel Race
	11th July	Morgan Cup race
	13th-16th July	Coupe de France at Ryde
	17th July	RTYC Regatta at Yarmouth of 'J', 12 metre & Handicap classes
	18th-24th July	Cumberland Cup
	28th & 29th July	RTYC Regatta at Ryde for 'J', 12 metre, Handicap & SCRA classes
	21st August	RTYC racing in Brixham Regatta

Year	Date	Event
1937	*25th June*	Coronation Regatta at Torbay including day in Brixham Regatta
	24th July	Morgan Cup race
	23rd-27th July	RTYC racing in Ryde Week for Handicap, 12, 8 & 6 metre and SCRA classes
	24th August	RTYC racing at Southend
1938	*9th June*	RTYC racing at Southend Yachting Week
	23rd & 25th July	RTYC racing in Ryde Week for Handicap, 12, 8 & 6 metre & SCRA classes
	8th August	RTYC racing for SCRA classes
	19th August	RTYC racing in Brixham Regatta
	31st August	RTYC racing in Weymouth Regattas
1939	*16th June*	RTYC racing in Southend Yachting Week
	15th July	Morgan Cup race from Ryde to Le Havre and back
	26th-28th July	RTYC racing in Ryde Week
	18th August	RTYC racing in Brixham Regatta
	28th August	RTYC racing at Dartmouth
1946	*13th July*	RTYC racing in Southend Yachting Week
	22nd July	Morgan Cup Race
	31st July-2nd August	RTYC regatta at Ryde for all classes
	23rd August	RTYC racing in Brixham Regatta
1947	*23rd-26th May*	
	21st & 23rd June	
	30th August	RTYC racing for Solent classes based on Warsash
	12th July	RTYC racing in Southend Week
	30th July-1st August	RTYC Regatta at Ryde for all classes
	22nd August	RTYC racing in Brixham Regatta

Year	Date	Event
1948	*15th & 17th May*	
	19th-21st August	
	12th & 13th August	RTYC racing for Solent classes based on Warsash
	26th June	Morgan Cup race
	10th July	RTYC racing in Southend Week
	28th-30th July	RTYC Regatta at Ryde for all classes
	20th August	RTYC racing in Brixham Regatta
1949	*4th-6th June*	
	2nd & 3rd July	
	10th-12th August	RTYC racing for Solent classes starting at Calshot
	26th June	Morgan Cup race
	July	British-American Cup at Cowes
	26th & 28th July	RTYC Regatta for all classes starting at Calshot
1950	*27th & 29th May*	RTYC racing for Solent classes starting at Calshot
	8th July	Morgan Cup Race
	7th-9th August	RTYC Regatta for all classes starting at Calshot
	19th August	Howard Junior Challenge Cup race in STAR class dinghies
	August	Passage Race Warsash to Weymouth
1951	*June*	RTYC team win Trent Challenge Cup
	9th June	
	2nd & 3rd August	RTYC racing from Calshot for Handicap classes
	10th June	RTYC racing from Calshot for Solent classes
	21st-22nd July	RTYC regatta for all classes from Calshot
	21st July	Morgan Cup race
1952	*20th April*	Howard Junior Challenge Cup at Ranelagh
	30th & 31st May	RTYC racing at Calshot for Solent classes
	June	RTYC team win Trent Challenge Cup
	3rd June	Cumberland Cup in 6 metre yachts
	30th July	Morgan Cup race
	30th-31st July	*RTYC racing at Calshot for all classes*
	7th June	Cruise to Yarmouth, Isle of Wight
	24th August	Cruise to Deauville

Year	Date	Event
1953	*25th April*	
		Trent Challenge Cup at London Corinthian SC
	May	
		RTYC racing at Calshot for Solent classes
	6th June	
		Morgan Cup race
	24th June	
		RTYC racing for Handicap classes from Bald Head
	8th-10th July	
		Oxford versus Cambridge match at Calshot
	1st & 2nd August	
		RTYC Regatta for all classes from RLYC line.
	22nd August	
		Team racing versus Seaview Yacht Club
	25th April	
		Fitting Out Cruise to Cowes
	23rd May	
		Cruise to Cherbourg
	20th June	
		Rally at Yarmouth, Isle of Wight
	18th July	
		Rally at Bembridge
	16th August	
		Cruise to Ouistreham
1954	*2nd May*	
		Howard Junior Challenge Cup at Ranelagh
	29th-30th May	
		Passage Race/Rally Hamble to Poole & back
	5th-7th June	
		RTYC racing for Solent class
	24th June	
		RTYC Cup for Thames Barge Race
	17th July	
		Morgan Cup Race (cancelled due to bad weather)
	24th & 25th July	
	1st August	
		RTYC races for Handicap & International classes in Cowes Week
	4th September	
		Team racing versus Seaview Yacht Club
	5th September	
		Team racing versus Brading Haven Yacht Club
	1st May	
		Fitting Out Cruise to Cowes
	27th June	
		Cruise to Cherbourg
	19th June	
		Cruise to Yarmouth, Isle of Wight
	24th July	
		Rally at Warsash
	15th August	
		Cruise to Deauville
	4th September	
		Cruise to Bembridge

Year	Date	Event
1955	*17th April*	
		Howard Junior Challenge Cup at Ranelagh (Cancelled due to lack of entry)
	21st & 22nd May	
		Passage Race/Rally to Poole
	21st & 22nd May	
		RTYC races for Solent classes from East Bramble
	June	
		Morgan Cup Race
	10th & 23rd July	
		RTYC race for Handicap & Solent classes from East Bramble
	31st July	
		RTYC races for Cowes Week
	May	
		Fitting Out Cruise to Cowes
	11th June	
		Passage Race/Rally to Yarmouth, Isle of Wight
	23rd June	
		Cruise to Bembridge
	3rd September	
		Cruise to Seaview
1956	*28th April*	
		RTYC race, Hamble-Nab Tower-Cowes
	19th-21st May	
		RTYC race for Solent classes
	26th & 27th May	
		Passage Race to Poole, Rally at RMYC
	8th June	
		Morgan Cup Race
	21st & 22nd July	
		RTYC race for handicap classes from Hillhead
	5th August	
		RTYC races in Cowes Week
	27th August	
		Howard Junior Cup at Emsworth Sailing Club
	1st September	
		Team racing versus Seaview (Cancelled due to bad weather)
	2nd September	
		Team racing versus Brading Haven Yacht Club
	23rd June	
		Passage Race & Rally to Yarmouth, Isle of Wight
	24th August	
		Cruise to Deauville
	1st September	
		Rally at Seaview
	8th September	
		Rally on Beaulieu River
1957	*4th May*	
		RTYC race to Nab Tower & back
	18th & 19th May	
	1st & 2nd June	
		RTYC races for Solent classes from Royal London line
	21st June	
		Morgan Cup Race
	27th & 28th June	
		RTYC races for Handicap classes from Hillhead
	4th August	
		RTYC races in Cowes Week

Year	Date	Event

1957   *7th September*
      Team racing versus Seaview YC
    9th September
      Howard Junior Challenge Cup at
      Emsworth Sailing Club

    29th June
      Passage Race/Rally to Yarmouth, Isle of Wight
    17th August
      Cruise to Deauville
    31st August
      Rally on Beaulieu River
    7th September
      Rally at Seaview

1958   *17th & 18th May*
      Passage Race to Poole & back
    24th-26th May
      RTYC races for Solent classes
    6th June
      Morgan Cup Race
    27th July
      RTYC races for Handicap and Solent classes
    3rd August
      RTYC races for Handicap and Solent
      classes in Cowes Week
    September
      RTYC win One Ton Cup at Le Havre
    1st September
      Howard Junior Challenge Cup at
      Emsworth Sailing Club
    6th September
      Team racing versus Seaview and Rally
    7th September
      Team racing versus Brading Haven Yacht Club

    3rd May
      Fitting out Cruise to Cowes
    24th May
      Cruise to Cherbourg
    28th June
      Cruise to Yarmouth, Isle of Wight
    16th August
      Cruise to Deauville
    30th August
      Rally on Beaulieu River

1959   *12th April*
      Howard Junior Challenge Cup at
      Ranelagh Sailing club
    17th May
      Cowes to Lisbon Race for Vasco de Gama Cup
    29th May
      Morgan Cup Race
    30th & 31st May
      Passage Race to Poole and return
    30th-31st May
    14th June
      RTYC races for Solent classes
      (from Committee Boat)
    19th July
      RTYC races for Handicap and Solent classes
    2nd August
      RTYC races for Handicap and Solent classes
      in Cowes Week

1959   *12th August*
      One Ton Cup at Poole
    5th September
      Team racing versus Seaview Yacht Club
      (and Rally)
    6th September
      Team racing versus Brading Haven Yacht Club

    2nd May
      Fitting Out Cruise to Cowes
    13th June
      Motor Cruiser Race Cowes to Poole
    18th July
      Rally at Yarmouth , Isle of Wight
    29th August
      Rally on Beaulieu River

1960   *10th April*
      Howard Junior Challenge Cup at Tamesis
      Sailing club
    14th & 15th May
    4th-6th June
      RTYC races for Solent classes
      (from Committee Boat)
    17th June
      Morgan Cup Race
    18th & 19th June
      Passage Race (and Rally) to Poole and return
    11th-15th July
      Jollyboat championship from Warsash
    23rd & 24th July
      RTYC regatta for Handicap and Solent classes
    1st August
      RTYC races in Cowes Week
    8th August
      RTYC races in 12 metre class for Queen's Cup
    3rd September
      Team racing versus Seaview Yacht Club

    14th May
      Fitting Out Rally at Cowes
    4th June
      Rally at Yarmouth, Isle of Wight
    18th June
      Cruise to Cherbourg
    23rd July
      Motor Cruiser Race to Poole
    27th August
      Rally on Beaulieu River

1961   *9th April*
      Howard Junior Challenge Cup at Tamesis SC
    27th & 28th May
    17th & 18th June
      RTYC races for Solent classes
    9th June
      Morgan Cup Race
    24th & 25th June
      Passage race (and Rally) to Poole and return.
    23rd July
      RTYC races for Handicap & Solent classes
    30th July
      RTYC races in Cowes Week
    27th August
      RTYC races in 12 metre class for Queen's Cup

Year	Date	Event

1961 *2nd September*
Team racing versus Seaview Yacht Club

13th May
Fitting Out Cruise to Cowes
17th June
Cruise to Yarmouth, Isle of Wight
24th June
Motor Cruises Race, Cowes to Poole
26th August
Rally on Beaulieu River

1962 *8th April*
Howard Junior Challenge Cup at Tamesis SC
26th & 27th May
9th-11th June
RTYC races for Solent classes
6th July
Morgan Cup Race
29th July
Regatta for Handicap and Solent classes
5th August
RTYC races in Cowes Week
25th & 26th August
Passage Race (& Rally) to Poole and return
18th & 19th August
25th & 26th August
1st & 2nd September
RTYC race for 12 metre class
2nd September
RTYC race in 12 metre class for Queen's Cup

5th May
Fitting Out Cruise to Cowes
9th June
Cruise to Cherbourg
30th June
Rally at Yarmouth, Isle of Wight
July Motor Cruiser Race Cowes to Poole
24th August
Cruise to Deauville
8th-9th September
Rally at Warsash and on to Beaulieu River

1963 *14th June*
Morgan Cup Race
15th & 16th June
RTYC races for Solent classes
28th July
RTYC races for Handicap & Solent classes
4th August
RTYC races in Cowes Week
31st August
Team racing versus Seaview Yacht Club
31st August & 1st September
Passage Race (and Rally) to Poole & return
Howard Junior Challenge Cup at Tamesis
(cancelled, no entries)

27th April
Fitting Out Rally at Cowes
29th June
Rally at Yarmouth, Isle of Wight
14th September
Motor Cruiser Race to Poole

1964 *4th January*
Team racing on Serpentine versus Ranelagh SC,
London Corinthian SC and Tamesis SC
16th-18th May
13th-14th June
RTYC races for Solent classes
20th June
Passage Race (and Rally) to Poole & return
26th June
Morgan Cup Race
May and June
RTYC run America's Cup trials off the Nab
and at Weymouth
26th July
RTYC regatta for Handicap & Solent classes
2nd August
RTYC races in Cowes Week
8th November
Team racing at Tamesis for Serpentine Cup

25th April
Fitting Out Rally at Cowes
16th May
Cruise to Cherbourg
30th May
Rally at Yarmouth, Isle of Wight
20th June
Motor Cruiser Race to Poole
19th&20th September
Rally at Warsash and on to Beaulieu River

1965 *4th January*
Team racing on Serpentine versus Ranelagh SC,
London Corinthian SC and Tamesis SC
22nd & 23rd May
12th 13th June
RTYC races for Solent classes using Old Castle
Point line on 22nd & 23rd May
12th & 13th June
Passage Race (and Rally) to Poole and return

18th June
Morgan Cup Race
1st August
RTYC regatta for Handicap & Solent classes
and Admiral's Cup contenders.
14th November
Team racing at Tamesis SC for Serpentine Cup

1st May
Fitting Out Rally at Cowes
29th May
Rally at Yarmouth, Isle of Wight
19th&20th September
Rally at Warsash and on to Beaulieu River

1966 *15th January*
Team racing for Serpentine Cup on Serpentine
(had to be transferred to Teddington with
Tamesis SC - Serpentine frozen)
28th & 30th May
11th & 12th June
RTYC races for Solent classes
10th June
Morgan Cup Race

Year	Date	Event
1966	*18th & 19th June*	
		Passage Race (and Rally) to Poole and return
	24th July	
		RTYC regatta for Handicap and Solent classes
	27th July	
		Team racing versus St. George's Hospital SC
		at Welsh Harp
	31st July	
		RTYC races on Cowes Week
	5th November	
		Team racing for Serpentine Cup at Tamesis SC
	3rd December	
		Team racing on Serpentine
	14th May	
		Rally to Yarmouth, Isle of Wight
	28th May	
		Cruise to Deauville
	16th&17th September	
		Rally at Warsash and on to Beaulieu River
1967	*13th & 14th May*	
	10th & 11th June	
		RTYC race for Solent classes
	17th & 18th July	
		Passage Race to Poole and return
	23rd July	
		RTYC regatta for Handicap and Solent classes
	26th July	
		Team racing versus St George's Hospital SC
		at Welsh Harp
	30th July	
		RTYC races in Cowes Week
	11th November	
		Team racing for Serpentine Cup at Tamesis SC.
		RTYC win Coupe de France at Le Havre
	12th & 13th May	
		Rally at Warsash & Fitting Out Cruise to Cowes
	17th July	
		Rally to Yarmouth, Isle of Wight
	22nd July	
		Motor Cruisr race to Poole for Twining Shield
	13th &14th September	
		Rally to Warsash and on to Beaulieu River
1968	*11th & 12th May*	
	1st-3rd June	
		RTYC races for Solent classes
	12th June	
		Team racing versus St George's Hospital SC
		at Welsh Harp
	21st June	
		Morgan Cup Race
	22nd-30th June	
		Coupe de France at Poole
		(cancelled due to lack of entries)
	28th July	
		RTYC Regatta for Handicap and Solent classes
	4th August	
		RTYC races in Cowes Week
	31st August	
		Cowes to Cherbourg Race and return
		for Lochan Cup

Year	Date	Event
1968	*10th & 11th May*	
		Rally at Warsash and Fitting Out Cruise to Cowes
	30th May	
		Cruise to Deauville
	13th July	
		Rally at Yarmouth, Isle of Wight
	20th July	
		Motor Cruiser Race for Twining Shield
	13th&14th September	
		Rally at Warsash and on to Beaulieu River
1969	*10th & 11th May*	
	31st May & 1st June	
		RTYC races for Solent classes
	25th May	
		RTYC run Le Havre to Southend race for J.O.G.
	7th & 8th June	
		Passage Race to Poole and return
	20th June	
		Morgan Cup Race
	27th July	
		RTYC regatta for Handicap and Solent classes
	3rd August	
		RTYC races in Cowes Week
	30th August	
	7th May	
		Fitting Out Rally at Cowes
	7th June	
		Motor Cruiser Race to Poole for Twining Shield
	28th June	
		Rally at Yarmouth, Isle of Wight
	31st May	
	27th July	
		Predicted Log races round Isle of Wight
	20th September	
		Rally at Lymington
1970	*23rd-25th May*	
	7th June	
		RTYC races for Solent classes
	9th-15th June	
		World Soling Championships at Poole
		with Parkstone YC
	13th-14th June	
		Passage race to Poole and return.
		Race on 13th June to be for SPC
	19th June	
		Morgan Cup Race
	26th July	
		RTYC regatta for Handicap and Solent classes
	2nd August	
		RTYC races in Cowes Week
	28th August	
		Hamble to Alderney and return for Lochan Cup
	1st & 2nd May	
		Rally at Warsash and Fitting Out Rally at Cowes
	23rd May	
		Cruise to Deauville
	6th June	
		Rally at Yarmouth
	13th June	
		Motor Cruiser Race to Poole
	18th & 19th Sept	
		Rally at Warsash and on to Lymington

Year	Date	Event

1971 *22nd & 23rd May*
12th & 13th June
RTYC races for Solent classes
- Committee Boat Starts
22nd May
RTYC race in SPC
5th & 6th June
Passage Race to Poole and return
11th June
Morgan Cup race
3rd & 4th July
Training races for Olympic classes from Warsash
23rd-30th July
Hamble - Le Havre race and return for J.O.G.
20th July
Half Ton Cup for J.O.G.
25th July
RTYC regatta for Handicap and Solent classes
1st August
RTYC races in Cowes Week

30th April & 1st May
Rally at Warsash and Fitting Out Rally at Cowes
28th May
Cruise to Deauville
27th June
Rally at Yarmouth
September
Rally at Warsash and on to Lymington

1972 *3rd & 4th June*
Races for $^{1}/_{4}$ and $^{1}/_{2}$ Ton classes for J.O.G.
9th June
Passage race for $^{1}/_{4}$ and $^{1}/_{2}$ Ton classes for J.O.G
10th & 11th June
RTYC races for Solent classes
16th June
Morgan Cup Race
23rd July
RTYC regatta for Handicap and Solent classes
30th July
RTYC races in Cowes Week
20th-28th August
Wayfarer National Championship out of Warsash
1sr September
RTYC Offshore Challenge Cup Race for J.O.G.
23rd September
RTYC race for S.P.C.

1973 *2nd June*
RTYC race for SPC
2nd & 3rd June
30th June & 1st July
RTYC races for Solent classes from
Committee Boat start at Hill head
22nd June
Morgan Cup Race
23rd & 24th June
RTYC races for J.O.G
24th July
RTYC regatta for Handicap and Solent classes
31st July
RTYC races in Cowes Week
17th & 26th August
$^{1}/_{4}$ Ton Cup at Weymouth

1974 *11th May*
RTYC race for SPC
11th & 12th May
22nd & 23rd June
RTYC races for Solent classes
12th May
23rd & 24th May
RTYC race for Level Rating classes
1st & 2nd June
15th & 16th June
RTYC races for 1 Ton Cup contenders
21st June
Morgan Cup Race
28th July
RTYC regatta for Handicap and Solent classes
4th August
RTYC races in Cowes Week

1975 *14th & 15th June*
RTYC races for Level Rating classes
20th June
Morgan Cup Race
21st-22nd June
RTYC races for Solent classes
21st June
RTYC race for SPC
July
Transatlantic Race to Nab Tower
26th & 27th July
RTYC Bicentenary Regatta for Handicap,
Level Rating and Solent classes
28th July
Team racing versus Seawanhaka Corinthian YC
for English Speaking Union Trophy
3rd August
RTYC races in Cowes Week

May
Fitting Out Rally in Cowes
28th June
Rally to Yarmouth (cancelled - lack of entries)
September
Rally to Bucklers Hard

1976 *12th June*
RTYC race for SPC
12th & 13th June
RTYC races for Solent classes
19th & 20th June
RTYC races for 1 Ton Cup contenders
26th & 27th June
RTYC races for Level Rating classes
28th June-2nd July
BLRA National Championship
2nd July
Morgan Cup Race
25th July
RTYC Regatta
1st August
RTYC races in Cowes Week
14th-23rd August
$^{3}/_{4}$ Ton Cup at Plymouth

29th September
Rally at Bucklers Hard

Year	Date	Event

1977 *14th May*
RTYC race for SPC
15th May
RTYC races for Level Rating classes
28th May
RTYC races for Admiral's Cup contenders
5th June
Silver Jubilee races
27th June-1st July
BLRA National Championship at Lymington
2nd & 3rd July
RTYC races for Solent classes
24th July
RTYC Regatta
31st July
RTYC races in Cowes Week
2nd-12th September
Team racing versus Seawanhaka Corinthian YC
in USA for English Speaking Union Trophy

10th September
Rally at Lymington
1st & 2nd October
Rally at Warsash and on to Bucklers Hard

1978 *13th May*
RTYC race for SPC
14th May
RTYC races for Level Rating classes
18th-26th June
BLRA National Championship at Lymington
30th June
Morgan Cup Race
23rd July
RTYC Regatta
30th July
RTYC races in Cowes Week
9th-22nd August
$^1/_2$ Ton Cup at Poole

22nd July
Rally at Cowes
30th September
Rally on Beaulieu River

1979 *19th May*
RTYC race for SPC
20th May
RTYC races for Level Rating classes
16th-23rd June
BLRA National Championship at Harwich
22nd June
Morgan Cup Race
15th-28th July
2 Ton Cup at Poole
29th July
RTYC Regatta
5th August
RTYC races in Cowes Week

28th July
Rally at Cowes

1980 *10th May*
RTYC race for SPC
19th & 20th June
BLRA National Championship at Cowes
27th July
RTYC Regatta
3rd August
RTYC race in Cowes Week

26th July
Rally at Cowes
11th August
Rally at Dartmouth
22nd November
Rally at Cannes

1981 *9th May*
RTYC race for SPC
23rd-27th May
RTYC races for Admiral's Cup Contenders
19th June
Morgan Cup Race
26th July
RTYC Regatta
27th-31st July
BLRA National Championship at Lymington
2nd August
RTYC races in Cowes Week
5th-18th September
$^1/_2$ Ton Cup at Poole

13th June
Rally Osborne Bay
25th July
Rally at Cowes
17th & 18th August
Rally at Dartmouth
23rd-26th October
Rally at Cannes

1982 *22nd May*
RTYC race for SPC
23rd May
RTYC Invitation Match Racing
23rd-24th June
RTYC race for Level Rating classes
25th July
BLRA National Championship at Lymington
26th-30th July
RTYC races in Cowes Week
1st August
RTYC Invitation Match racing

26th June
Rally at Osborne Bay
24th July
Rally at Cowes
28th-29th August
Rally at Jersey

Year	Date	Event

1983 *20th February*
RTYC races for Admiral's Cup contenders
28th-30th May
Serpentine Regatta
16th-17th June
BLRA National Championship
23rd July
RTYC race for SPC
24th July
RTYC Regatta
31st July
RTYC races in Cowes Week
5th-8th September
Team racing versus New York YC
at American YC, Rye
17th-18th September
Multihull Regatta at Poole
12th November
Illusion Regatta on Serpentine

18th-19th June
Rally at Cowes
23rd July
Rally at Beaulieu River

1984 *12th February*
Serpentine Cup
21st-22nd June
BLRA National Championships
13th-16th July
Team racing versus NYYC at Lymington
28th July
RTYC races for SPC
29th July
RTYC Regatta
5th August
RTYC races in Cowes Week
1st-5th October
Team racing versus Royal Bermuda YC
in Bermuda for the General Sir Thomas
Ashley Cubitt Cup
18th November
Illusion Regatta on Serpentine
15th June
Rally at St Vaast
28th July
Rally at Cowes

1985 *2nd March*
Serpentine Cup (cancelled due to ice)
25th-27th May
RTYC races for Admiral's Cup contenders
11th-14th June
BLRA National Championship
9th-22nd July
1 Ton Cup at Poole
27th July
RTYC races for SPC
28th July
RTYC regatta
4th August
RTYC races in Cowes Week
17th November
Illusion Regatta on Serpentine

Year	Date	Event

1985 *15th-16th June*
Rally at Deauville
27th July
Rally at Cowes

1986 *8th February*
Serpentine Cup
20th-22nd June
BLRA National Championship
21st-24th July
Viyella Cup - RTYC boat helmed by RA Aisher
26th July
RTYC races for SPC
27th July
RTYC Regatta
3rd August
RTYC races in Cowes Week
11th-24th August
$^3/_4$ Ton Cup at Torbay with RORC
8th-13th September
Team racing versus NYYC in the USA
8th November
Illusion Regatta on Serpentine

7th-13th June
Rally in Majorca
5th-6th July
Rally in Guernsey
26th July
Rally at Cowes

1987 *7th February*
Serpentine Cup
9th-10th May
Team racing versus Seaview YC
23rd-25th May
RTYC races for Admirals Cup contenders
30th May
RTYC races for SPC
8th-10th June
RTYC entry (helm - I S Macdonald - Smith)
wins the Viyella Cup
26th July
RTYC Regatta
2nd August
RTYC races in Cowes Week
6th-10th September
Team racing versus Royal Bermuda YC in Solent
18th October
Team racing versus Sigma 33 Association
for Mums Bucket
15th November
Illusion Regatta on Serpentine

3rd-5th July
Rally to Dartmouth
22nd Sept-6th Oct
Rally in Turkey

Year	Date	Event

1988 *23rd January*
Serpentine Cup
2nd May
RTYC races for SPC
7th-8th May
Team racing versus Seaview YC
7th-9th June
RTYC races for Solent classes
18th-19th June
European and National Championships
for 6 metre class at Falmouth
3rd-17th July
RTYC races in Cowes Week
31st July
RTYC entry (helm-P Curtis) second
in Viyella Cup
13th-14th August
Team racing for Mums Bucket
5th-17th September
$^1/_2$ Ton Cup at Poole
8th-9th October
Sigma 38 National Championship
12th November
Optimist Regatta on Serpentine

8th-9th June
Rally at Alderney
12th-18th June
Cruise to Brittany
6th-10th October
Rally in Cannes

1989 *28th January*
Serpentine Cup
22nd & 23rd April
RTYC races for Admiral's Cup Contenders
6th May
Team racing versus Seaview YC
June
Viyella Cup RTYC entry helmed by R Walker
1st July
RTYC races for SPC
1st-2nd July
RTYC races for Solent classes
30th July
RTYC races in Cowes Week
12th-15th August
RYA National Match Racing Championship
in Christchurch Bay
19th-20th August
Team racing for Mums Bucket
27th-31st August
Team racing versus NYYC for George Nicholls
Trophy in Solent
23rd&24th September
Team racing versus Royal St George YC
in Ireland
16th&17th September
Sigma 38 National Championship
29th September
Etchells Class National Championship
25th November
'Optimist' regatta on Serpentine

1989 *22nd-27th June*
Rally to St Vaast
7th & 14th October
Rally in Majorca

1990 *3rd February*
Serpentine Cup
12th & 13th May
Team racing versus Seaview YC
30th June
RTYC races for SPC
30th June-1st July
RTYC races for Solent classes
24th-29th June
6 metre class National Championship at Poole
5th August
RTYC races in Cowes Week
18th-19th August
Team racing for Mums Bucket
22nd &23rd September
Team racing in IOD's versus Royal Northern
& Clyde YC
24th-29th September
Etchells Class European Championship
at Yarmouth
5th-8th October
Team racing versus Royal Bermuda YC
in Bermuda
24th November
Optimist Regatta on Serpentine

15th-19th June
Rally at Deauville
4th August
Rally at Cowes

1991 *23rd February*
Serpentine Cup (Cancelled due to ice)
27th & 28th April
Team racing versus Seaview YC
2nd June
Team racing for Mums Bucket
29th & 30th June
RTYC races for Solent Class
4th-6th July
Etchells Class National championships at Poole
20th July
RTYC race for SPC
4th August
RTYC races in Cowes Week
26th-30th August
RTYC races for Solent classes
7th-8th September
Team racing versus Royal St George
YC in Solent
September
6 metre class World Championship in Torbay
23rd November
Optimist Regatta on Serpentine

Year	Date	Event
1991	*February*	Rally to New Zealand, Bay of Islands
	4th-9th July	Rally to Dartmouth
	27th July	Rally to Lymington
	21st-28th September	Rally to Majorca
1992	*22nd February*	Serpentine Cup
	April	Team racing versus Seaview YC
	9th & 10th May	Team racing versus Royal Burnham YC
	23rd & 24th May	RTYC races for Solent classes
	3rd July	RTYC races for SPC
	3rd August	RTYC races in Cowes Week
	September	$^3/_4$ Ton cup at Torbay (cancelled due to lack of entries)
	23rd November	Optimist Regatta on Serpentine
	1st-6th July	Rally to Falmouth
	11th July	Rally at Cowes
	12th-19th September	Rally to Corsica
1993	*27th February*	Serpentine Cup
	24th & 25th April	Team racing versus Seaview YC
	1st & 2nd May	Team racing for Mums Bucket
	29th-31st May	J24 class Southern Area championship
	15th & 16th May	Team racing for Royal Burnham YC
	22nd & 23rd May	
	19th & 20th June	RTYC races for Solent classes
	3rd July	RTYC races for SPC
	4th July	RTYC Regatta
	17th-21st July	50' World Championship from Hayling Island
	2nd August	RTYC races in Cowes Week
	11th&12th September	Team racing versus Royal St George YC in Ireland
	1st-3rd October	Team racing versus Royal Hong Kong YC in Hong Kong
	6th November	Optimist Regatta on Serpentine

Year	Date	Event
1993	*3rd-8th June*	Rally to St Vaast
	9th-19th October	Rally to French Canals
1994	*19th February*	Serpentine Cup
	7th & 8th May	Team racing for Mums Bucket
	19th -15th May	Team racing versus Royal Burnham YC
	30th April-2nd May	
	21st & 22nd May	
	11th-12th June	RTYC races for Solent classes
	28th-30th May	RTYC races for Commodore's Cup contenders
	2nd July	RTYC race for SPC
	9th & 10th July	RTYC Regatta
	1st August	RTYC races in Cowes week
	23rd-30th July	New York YC Sequiscentennial racing
	8th-11th September	Sigma 38 National Championship
	12th November	Optimist Regatta on Serpentine
	12th-17th May	Rally to Dublin
	2nd-6th June	Rally to Dartmouth
1995	*18th February*	Serpentine Cup - extended to 8 clubs
	May	Sigma 33 Team Racing Championships
	29th-30th April	
	20th-21st May	
	3rd-4th June	RTYC races for Solent classes
	6th-7th May	Team racing for Mums Bucket
	1st July	RTYC Regatta
	2nd July	RTYC race for SPC
	15th-16th July	RTYC races for Contessa 32 class
	30th July	RTYC races in Cowes Week
	11th-15th August	Team racing versus New York YC at Lymington
	11th November	Optimist Regatta on Serpentine
	14th-15th June	Rally to St Vaast and Channel Islands
	7th-14th October	Rally to Greek Islands

Year	Date	Event
1996	*February*	
		Serpentine Cup
	11th & 12th May	
		Sigma 33 Team Racing Championship
	18th & 19th May	
		Team racing versus Royal Burnham YC
	1st & 2nd June	
	8th & 9th June	
		RTYC races for Solent classes
	5th-7th June	
		Solent Clubs Championships
	20th-21st July	
		RTYC Regatta
	4th August	
		RTYC races in Cowes Week
	21st&22nd September	
		Team racing for Mums Bucket
		Team racing versus Royal St George
	23rd November	
		Optimist Regatta on Serpentine
	12th June	
		Rally to St Vaast
	13th-27th October	
		Rally to St Lucia
1997	*15th March*	
		Serpentine Cup
	10th & 11th May	
		Sigma 33 Team Racing Championship
	17th & 18th May	
		Team Racing versus Royal Burnham YC
	17th & 18th May	
	7th & 8th June	
	12th & 13th July	
		RTYC races for Solent classes
	11th-14th June	
		Etchells Class National Championship in Christchurch Bay
	19th & 20th July	
		RTYC Regatta
	3rd August	
		RTYC races in Cowes Week
	20th September	
		Team racing for Mums Bucket
	22nd November	
		Optimist Regatta on Serpentine
	6th-14th June	
		Cruise on Irish Waterways
	16th-22nd August	
		Rally at St Malo

Year	Date	Event
1998	*21st February*	
		Serpentine Cup
	9th & 10th May	
		Sigma 33 Team racing Championship
	16th & 17th May	
		Team racing versus Royal Burnham YC
	16th & 17th May	
		RTYC Schools Cup at Poole
	16th & 17th May	
	6th & 7th June	
	11th & 12th July	
		RTYC races for Solent classes
	13th & 14th June	
		RTYC Regatta
	22nd-26th June	
		International 5.5 metre Scandinavian Gold Cup
	27th June	
		Morgan Cup Race
	4th & 5th July	
		RTYC Regatta for CHS classes
	2nd August	
		RTYC races in Cowes Week
	5th September	
		Team racing for Mums Bucket
	21st November	
		Optimist Regatta on Serpentine
	14th Feb-3rd March	
		Rally in New Zealand
	30th & 31st May	
		Rally in Chichester Harbour
	5th-7th June	
		Rally to St Vaast
	15th-22nd August	
		Rally to West Country
	9th-12th October	
		Rally in Cannes

Appendix 15

*Gentlemen, I have great pleasure in seconding the proposal that Mr Cecil King be elected Marine Artist of the Club.
I think, as he is a personal friend of mine, I might say a few words on the subject of his qualities. Mr Cecil King is not only an expert Marine Artist, and an expert in many other nautical matters, but he is also a jolly good fellow, and I think that ought to appeal to members of the Club, where the percentage of jolly good fellows is so very near the three figure mark. Mr Cecil King is one of the best Marine Artists in our country. I do not say the best because there may be other claimants to that title in the room among some of you, perchance, who have had experienced in painting the sea blue and the town red and so forth, but at all events he is one of the best Marine Artists in the country, and personally I prefer his marine paintings and etchings above any others. I possess a good many of them, and I have seen a great many more. He exhibits in the Academy and the Royal Institute of Water Colours, and in the Paris Salon, and so on. He is also an expert on many other nautical matters. For instance, he is a great authority, perhaps the greatest authority, on bunting - all matters relating to bunting, from the days of Noah to the present day; National Flags, House Flags, Burgees - all sorts of flags. In this capacity he was called in as the adviser to the Home Office on the flags which decorate the Cenotaph in Whitehall. He is also an expert on the designs and their decorations, and on the rigging of ships in all ages, and is this capacity he was the designer, and with a staff of assistants, also the actual maker of all those models of ships from the days of William the Conqueror up to the present day which were exhibited at Wembley, and which I daresay a good many of you have seen. He is also, I may say a great personal friend of mine. Possibly in the minds of some that may discredit him to some extent - some of you perhaps who have a vivid recollection of my extraordinary unconventional conception of the duties of Chairman of the Committee of this Club a few years ago. But it is in the hope that with the majority, my personal knowledge of him and my affection for him will turn the scales in his favour and that you will vote for him as our Marine Artist.*

Appendix 16

7.9.1843	Nicholas M. Condy
3.12.1851	Thomas Sewell Robins
28.1.1885	Barlow Moore
17.3.1897	R. T. Pritchett
29.3.1911	Louis Nevill
31.3.1920	Norman Wilkinson
29.3.1927	William L. Wylie
14.3.1932	Cecil King
27.3.1944	Lt Cdr Peter Scott
23.32.1952	Bernard Adams

Appendix 17

In her premature death the Mediterranean and the Solent have lost the most notable yachtswoman in the history of that great sport. There can be no question that for many years she had been in France the inspiring genius connected with small boat racing. She must have had built for her in France at least a dozen of these boats, many of them competing again and again in different waters for such cups as the Cumberland and the Coupe de France. She occasionally won, but though more often defeated was never discouraged. She was as sportsmanlike a loser as Sir Thomas Lipton and that is no faint praise.

She was the idol of the French Marine, and her services to yachting were so conspicuous and considered so valuable that a few years ago she received at the hands of the French President the much coveted decoration of the Legion d'Honneur. She owned at various times several big steam yachts, and a few years ago had a three masted schooner, *AILEE*, built for her at Southampton by Nicholson, in which she lived and cruised most of the year. She leaves a host of friends to mourn her - men and women who loved and admired her alike for the many noble qualities which were a part of her, the most conspicuous of which were her courage and patience and unrivalled bonhomie.

Appendix 18

What Royal support has done for yachting

The present high standing of the sport of yachting in British waters may be said to be due to Royal patronage through-out a long period of years. Since the war it is directly due to the active part the King has taken in it and the magnificent example set by his cutter BRITANNIA.

Had it not been for His Majesty restarting the sport with BRITANNIA in 1920 at a time when it had completely collapsed - goodness knows when it would have recovered.

It is almost forgotten now how disastrous the position of British yachting had become in 1919. Existing yachts had been broken up by the dozen, the lead from the keels of others had been removed during the war, while those that were credited with speed had been sold by their English owners to yachtsmen in Scandinavian countries. The price of building since 1914 had risen by 250 per cent and people wondered where the new yachts were to come from.

At the moment of crisis the King brought out the old

BRITANNIA. In 1920 she was more or less cruiser rigged, she had little resemblance to what she is now. She had a stumpy mast and high outworks and seemed a bit out-of-date.

Of course, all that has changed long ago. A few sporting owners came forward and made up a class to race against the King's yacht. It is a matter of history how BRITANNIA sailed far better that anyone expected, and her renovation followed.

I can remember when everybody was saying in 1892 that big class yachting was dead and would never be revived... then the Prince of Wales (King Edward VII) in 1893 ordered the BRITANNIA to be designed and built in Scotland and a class of vessels was built in Britain and America which eclipsed all the big cutter classes of previous history.

That was how BRITANNIA revived the sport in 1893 and history was repeated by her when she took the lead once again in 1920.

Index

For a free colour brochure of Fernhurst Books'
other titles phone, write, fax or email:

Fernhurst Books
Duke's Path
High Street
Arundel
BN18 9AJ

Tel: 01903 882277
Fax: 01903 882715
email: sales@fernhurstbooks.co.uk
website: www.fernhurstbooks.co.uk